World Economic and Financial Surveys

WORLD ECONOMIC OUTLOOK
April 2002

Recessions and Recoveries

International Monetary Fund

Production: IMF Graphics Section
Cover and Design: Luisa Menjivar-Macdonald
Figures: Lai Oy Louie
Typesetting: Choon Lee and Joseph A. Kumar

World economic outlook (International Monetary Fund)
World economic outlook: a survey by the staff of the International
Monetary Fund.—1980– —Washington, D.C.: The Fund, 1980–

v.; 28 cm.—(1981–84: Occasional paper/International Monetary
Fund ISSN 0251-6365)
Annual.
Has occasional updates, 1984–
ISSN 0258-7440 = World economic and financial surveys
ISSN 0256-6877 = World economic outlook (Washington)
1. Economic history—1971– —Periodicals. I. International
Monetary Fund. II. Series: Occasional paper (International
Monetary Fund)

HC10.W7979   84-640155

338.5'443'09048—dc19
AACR 2 MARC-S

Library of Congress   8507

Published biannually.
ISBN 1-58906-107-1

Price: US$42.00
(US$35.00 to full-time faculty members and
students at universities and colleges)

Please send orders to:
International Monetary Fund, Publication Services
700 19th Street, N.W., Washington, D.C. 20431, U.S.A.
Tel.: (202) 623-7430   Telefax: (202) 623-7201
E-mail: publications@imf.org
Internet: http://www.imf.org

recycled paper

CONTENTS

Boxes

Tables

Figures

CONTENTS

ASSUMPTIONS AND CONVENTIONS

A number of assumptions have been adopted for the projections presented in the *World Economic Outlook*. It has been assumed that real effective exchange rates will remain constant at their average levels during February 11–March 11, 2002, except for the currencies participating in the European exchange rate mechanism II (ERM II), which are assumed to remain constant in nominal terms relative to the euro; that established policies of national authorities will be maintained (for specific assumptions about fiscal and monetary policies in industrial countries, see Box A1); that the average price of oil will be $23.00 a barrel in 2002 and $22.00 a barrel in 2003, and remain unchanged in real terms over the medium term; that the six-month London interbank offered rate (LIBOR) on U.S. dollar deposits will average 2.8 percent in 2002 and 4.5 percent in 2003; that the three-month certificate of deposit rate in Japan will average 0.1 percent in 2002 and 2003; and that the three-month interbank deposit rate for the euro will average 3.7 percent in 2002 and 4.5 percent in 2003. These are, of course, working hypotheses rather than forecasts, and the uncertainties surrounding them add to the margin of error that would in any event be involved in the projections. The estimates and projections are based on statistical information available through early April 2002.

The following conventions have been used throughout the *World Economic Outlook*:

. . . to indicate that data are not available or not applicable;

— to indicate that the figure is zero or negligible;

– between years or months (for example, 1997–98 or January–June) to indicate the years or months covered, including the beginning and ending years or months;

/ between years or months (for example, 1997/98) to indicate a fiscal or financial year.

"Billion" means a thousand million; "trillion" means a thousand billion.

"Basis points" refer to hundredths of 1 percentage point (for example, 25 basis points are equivalent to ¼ of 1 percentage point).

In figures and tables, shaded areas indicate IMF staff projections.

Minor discrepancies between sums of constituent figures and totals shown are due to rounding.

As used in this report, the term "country" does not in all cases refer to a territorial entity that is a state as understood by international law and practice. As used here, the term also covers some territorial entities that are not states but for which statistical data are maintained on a separate and independent basis.

FURTHER INFORMATION AND DATA

This report on the *World Economic Outlook* is available in full on the IMF's Internet site, *www.imf.org*. Accompanying it on the website is a larger compilation of data from the WEO database than in the report itself, consisting of files containing the series most frequently requested by readers. These files may be downloaded for use in a variety of software packages.

Inquiries about the content of the *World Economic Outlook* and the WEO database should be sent by mail, electronic mail, or telefax (telephone inquiries cannot be accepted) to:

World Economic Studies Division
Research Department
International Monetary Fund
700 19th Street, N.W.
Washington, D.C. 20431, U.S.A.
E-mail: weo@imf.org   Telefax: (202) 623-6343

PREFACE

The analysis and projections contained in the *World Economic Outlook* are integral elements of the IMF's surveillance of economic developments and policies in its member countries, developments in international financial markets, and the global economic system. The survey of prospects and policies is the product of a comprehensive interdepartmental review of world economic developments, which draws primarily on information the IMF staff gathers through its consultations with member countries. These consultations are carried out in particular by the IMF's area departments together with the Policy Development and Review Department, International Capital Markets Department, the Monetary and Exchange Affairs Department, and the Fiscal Affairs Department.

The analysis in this report has been coordinated in the Research Department under the general direction of Kenneth Rogoff, Economic Counsellor and Director of Research. The project has been directed by David Robinson, Senior Advisor of the Research Department, together with Tamim Bayoumi, Division Chief, World Economic Studies Division.

Primary contributors to this report also include Luis Catão, Hali Edison, Thomas Helbling, Maitland MacFarlan, James Morsink, Silvia Sgherri, Torsten Sløk, Marco Terrones, Stephen Tokarick, and Cathy Wright. Emily Conover, Toh Kuan, and Bennett Sutton provided research assistance. Nicholas Dopuch, Mandy Hemmati, Yutong Li, Di Rao, and Anthony G. Turner managed the database and the computer systems. Sylvia Brescia, Viktória Kiss, and Laura Leon were responsible for word processing. Other contributors include Michael Bordo, Robin Brooks, Ximena Cheetham, Jean Le Dem, Atish R. Ghosh, Benjamin Hunt, Aasim Husain, Mads Kieler, Manmohan Kumar, Timothy Lane, Prakash Loungani, Guy Meredith, Ashoka Mody, Carmen Reinhart, Ron van Rooden, Nikola Spatafora, and Raju Jan Singh. Marina Primorac of the External Relations Department edited the manuscript and coordinated production of the publication.

The analysis has benefited from comments and suggestions by staff from other IMF departments, as well as by Executive Directors following their discussion of the report on March 27 and 29, 2002. However, both projections and policy considerations are those of the IMF staff and should not be attributed to Executive Directors or to their national authorities.

FOREWORD

When the *World Economic Outlook* is issued, there is a natural tendency for outside commentators to concentrate on the material contained in Chapter I, which provides a comprehensive review of recent global developments, forecasts and risks, and current policy recommendations. While the global outlook is and will remain the central focus of the *World Economic Outlook*, there is much more to the *WEO* than that. The remaining chapters are more than just a supplement; they are intended to provide an in-depth—and sometimes provocative—look at a number of topical policy issues, of interest to policymakers and analysts alike. Work on these typically begins six months in advance of publication, a lead time that is necessary given the rigorous nature of these studies, not least the substantial amount of original empirical work that is required.

Back in October 2001, late in the planning stage of the current issue, it was not hard to decide that we needed to provide an in-depth look at the economics of recessions. Was the deep and widespread global slowdown of 2001 as unusual as many analysts were claiming? Was it so exceptional in the degree of synchronization across the major regions? Was the type of fixed investment–led downturn really more typical of nineteenth century recessions than of modern recessions? These are not merely academic questions, but rather essential to our understanding of the appropriate policy responses to the current conjuncture. Thus, the main analytical chapter of this *WEO* (Chapter III) is devoted to placing the current global slowdown in context.

Most existing studies of business cycles concentrate on individual countries, but the number of recessions per country is sufficiently small that it is hard to draw out any reliable regularities. Chapter III ambitiously sets out to look at all the "level" recessions (negative GDP growth) in 21 industrial countries over the period 1973–2001, 93 recessions in all! We also review a narrower range of countries to look at the history of national recessions going back to 1881. The results are startling, certainly compared to conventional wisdom.

(1) *First and foremost, synchronization is the norm historically.* The staggered global downturn of the 1990s was the exception, not the rule. Idiosyncratic shocks in the early 1990s—including the asset price bubble in Japan and consequences of German reunification—masked the usual forces that tend to coordinate recessions across the G-3 and beyond. What are the main forces underlying synchronization? Certainly, global linkages in trade and asset markets are important, and these have been growing over time since World War II, after having been curtailed during the two World Wars and the Great Depression. But common shocks are probably the single most important factor, at least across industrial countries. In the recent downturn, the bursting of the tech bubble was an international phenomenon. Other common factors included high oil prices and the simultaneous tightening of monetary policy toward the end of the long expansion.

(2) *Second, a sharp drop in business fixed investment is a typical precursor to a recession.* Indeed, in recent decades, investment contractions have been even more synchronized across countries than have the recessions. The role of fixed investment in recessions has actually increased over time, with virtually all recessions in recent decades accompanied by contractions in fixed investment, compared with only about 60 percent of recessions in the late nineteenth century.

(3) *Recoveries do not have to wait for a turnaround in fixed investment.* Rather, they typically start with a pickup in consumption and inventories. Indeed, over time, inventories have been less of a factor in the swings associated with business cycles, perhaps owing to better inventory management techniques.

(4) *Stock prices typically peak about one year before output,* and a fall of 25 percent is typical of recent experience.

(5) *Finally, increases in short-term interest rates have regularly marked the onset of recessions, and the recent downturn was no different.* Admittedly, it is not easy to sort out cause from effect: tight monetary policy may be needed to stem inflationary pressures toward the end of an expansion that would ultimately die out on its own.

So, while every recession has its own unique features, the recent global slowdown had much in common with past downturns, far more so than is commonly recognized.

Chapter II contains three shorter analytical essays. The first looks at why many countries in Latin America have had a disproportionate number of debt crises. The essay emphasizes three broad features of Latin American economies that seem to have heightened their vulnerability. First, most of the economies are relatively closed to trade, magnifying the costs of servicing external debt. As a result, even though Latin American external debt levels have not been high relative to GDP, they have often still been high relative to exports. Second, the region is subject to a high degree of macroeconomic volatility, stemming not only from terms of trade shocks, but also from volatility due to procyclical fiscal policy. Third, historically, much of the region has suffered from financial underdevelopment and, partly associated with that, low domestic saving. As a consequence, government borrowing is disproportionately external, and disproportionately denominated in foreign currency. The resulting currency mismatch between government assets and liabilities has all too often left countries in the region quite exposed to the effects of a sharp sudden exchange rate depreciation.

These three characteristics—high external borrowing, low exports, and volatile fiscal policy—have a common starting point: problems with tax systems and expenditure controls. A weak internal tax system forces a government to rely more heavily on tariff revenue, reducing the incentive to export, and resulting in relatively closed economies. Similarly, revenue shortfalls and expenditure excesses underpin the history of hyperinflation in the region, as governments are periodically forced to resort to monetary financing of deficits, particularly during periods of economic crisis or political instability. Even during periods of relatively low inflation, the specter of a return to high inflation has undoubtedly slowed the development of domestic financial markets in some countries. A history of high inflation similarly makes it difficult for governments to borrow at reasonable rates without offering to repay in foreign currency. Finally, a weak tax system and poor spending controls make it difficult to adopt countercyclical fiscal policy. Absent any sort of cushion from accumulated surpluses, the government is typically forced to tighten up rather than expand into a recession. As a result, shocks to a country's terms of trade are all too often amplified rather than mitigated by fiscal policy. Of course, the problem is extremely complex, but it is clear that the vulnerability of Latin American economies over recent decades was an outgrowth of many institutional and political considerations, and not simply the result of mistakes in macroeconomic management. As the essay notes, many countries in the region have made substantial progress in recent years, including better fiscal systems and more flexible exchange rate systems, so going forward the situation promises to be quite improved. Nevertheless, the essay provides a cautionary tale.

The second essay looks at the impact of the huge run-up in household wealth in industrial countries in the 1990s on consumer spending. Based on original empirical work, which builds on the existing literature, the essay finds that the impact is larger in market-based financial systems (where financial markets play the dominant role, as in the United States, the United Kingdom, and Canada) than in bank-based systems (where banks play the dominant role, as in Japan, Germany, France, and Italy). In the former, the dramatic rise in stock market wealth over the 1990s reduced the savings rate by 6 percentage points as of 2000—and by 8 percentage points if housing wealth is taken into account. By contrast, in countries with bank-based financial systems, the saving rate was little affected by the rise in stock market wealth, and the increase in housing prices reduced the saving rate by about 1½ percentage points. Not only has household wealth increased sharply, but the analysis also finds that consumption has become increasingly sensitive to stock market and housing prices. To the extent that changes in wealth affect inflation and output, then it must be the case that stock market and housing prices have become more significant considerations for monetary policy over the past decade, though it does not imply that monetary policy should directly target asset prices.

The third essay looks at the challenges to monetary policy in a low inflation era. It was not so long ago that most industrialized countries experienced sustained double-digit inflation. The essay argues that success in restoring low inflation in these countries owed much to widespread changes in the conduct of monetary policy, including institutional changes toward a more focused attitude on inflation, and the associated beneficial shifts in private sector behavior. These changes only came after economists and policymakers began to realize that the key to maintaining low inflation lies not simply in setting appropriate rules for monetary policy, but in properly designing central banking institutions. Enhanced central bank independence, transparency, various forms of inflation targeting, and choosing highly competent central bankers with solid anti-inflation credentials have all played a role in systematically bringing down inflation in many parts of the world. Good policies and, more important, good institutions—that make these policies sustainable—matter.

In the new low-inflation environment, central banks' objectives need to become more symmetric, as concerns about higher inflation have to be counterbalanced by concerns about deflation. Downward nominal rigidities of prices and wages make adjustment to deflation painful. If, in addition, inflation expectations are sluggish, then deflation puts a floor on how low the central bank can push real interest rates (in the short run), given that nominal interest rates cannot go below zero. As Chapter III on recessions shows, deflation was a major factor in recessions prior to World War I and the interwar period, but has largely been unknown in industrialized countries since World War II. Problems resulting from the ongoing deflation in Japan highlight the dangers and risks of allowing inflation to drift into negative territory. Concerns about deflation suggest that central banks need to be more proactive in responding to sharp downward shocks to activity. How high an inflation rate should the central bank target to reduce the danger of sustained deflation? The essay argues that the danger of getting into a deflationary spiral increases as inflation targets are lowered below 2 percent. Nevertheless, a slightly lower rate should be acceptable in a region with sufficiently flexible markets, provided the authorities are alert to any temporary drift into negative inflation territory, should one ever occur.

Kenneth Rogoff
Economic Counsellor and Director, Research Department

CHAPTER I

ECONOMIC PROSPECTS AND POLICY ISSUES

Over recent months, there have been increasing signs that the global slowdown has bottomed out, most clearly in the United States and to a lesser extent in Europe and some countries in Asia. While serious concerns remain in a number of countries, notably Japan and—for different reasons—Argentina, most indicators suggest recovery is now under way, broadly along the lines described in the Interim World Economic Outlook *issued last December (Figure 1.1). With confidence stabilizing, uncertainties easing, and emerging market financing conditions improving more quickly than was then anticipated, the risks to the outlook have become more balanced, although the recent volatility in the oil market is a significant concern. While the stance of policies should remain relatively supportive for the time being, there is now—except in Japan—little case for additional easing, and in countries where the recovery is most advanced, attention will need to turn toward reversing earlier monetary policy easing. It will be important to take full advantage of the recovery to reduce remaining economic vulnerabilities, and to pursue a collaborative approach designed to promote an orderly resolution of global imbalances—which remain a serious risk to economic stability—over the medium term.*

There are now increasing signs that the global slowdown, which began in the middle of 2000, has bottomed out. As had been suggested in the October 2001 *World Economic Outlook*, the events of September 11 had a short-run impact on activity, but—in contrast to the fears that some expressed—have not prevented a recovery in the first half of 2002.[1] Leading indicators have turned up (Figure 1.2); consumer and business confidence have strengthened; and industrial production—including the information technology (IT) sector—is leveling off. This has been most apparent in the United States and, increasingly, the euro area; in Japan, while activity may now be bottoming out, the outlook remains very difficult with few signs of a sustained recovery in domestic demand. In emerging markets, there are signs of recovery in a number of Asian emerging markets—particularly Korea—aided by the nascent improvement in the IT sector, although not as yet in most Latin American countries.

Growing expectations of recovery have been particularly apparent in financial markets, which recovered strongly after the events of September 11 (Figure 1.3). Equity markets have picked up sharply across the globe, although flattening off in the first quarter of 2002; yield curves have steepened; and risk aversion and spreads—in both mature and emerging markets—have declined. Partly reflecting market expectations of the relative pace of recovery, the U.S. dollar has strengthened further, accompanied by a moderate weakening of the euro, while the yen has fallen to three-year lows. In emerging markets, contagion from the crisis in Argentina has to date been limited, reflecting the fact that the crisis was well anticipated, and that gross international capital flows were already at low levels (Figure 1.4), as well as a number of technical factors, including the relatively low leverage in the system.[2] Spreads for most emerging market debt have declined sharply since early November, and financing conditions for emerging market borrowers have improved more rapidly than

[1]See Box 1.1, *World Economic Outlook*, October 2001.
[2]See "Contagion and Its Causes," Chapter I, Appendix I, *World Economic Outlook*, December 2001.

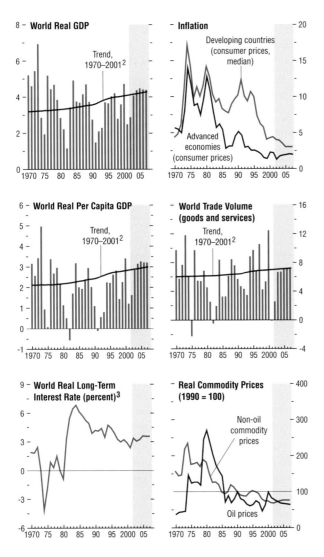

Figure 1.1. Global Indicators[1]
(Annual percent change unless otherwise noted)

While global growth is expected to increase moderately in 2002, this disguises a sharper pickup in activity during the year (see text). Inflation remains subdued.

[1]Shaded areas indicate IMF staff projections. Aggregates are computed on the basis of purchasing-power-parity weights unless otherwise indicated.
[2]Average growth rates for individual countries, aggregated using purchasing-power-parity weights; these shift over time in favor of faster growing countries, giving the line an upward trend.
[3]GDP-weighted average of the 10-year (or nearest maturity) government bond yields less inflation rates for the United States, Japan, Germany, France, Italy, the United Kingdom, and Canada. Excluding Italy prior to 1972.

earlier anticipated, with high-quality borrowers reaccessing markets toward the end of 2001, followed increasingly thereafter by non-investment-grade issuers.

The recovery is being underpinned by a number of factors. First, and most important, macroeconomic policies in advanced countries have been substantially eased over the past year, notably in the United States, and—particularly since interest rate cuts were anticipated by markets, and therefore built into asset prices in advance—should now be providing increasing support to demand. Policies in a number of emerging market countries, especially in Asia, have also been eased, although in most others the scope has been relatively limited. Second, the completion of ongoing inventory cycles, which appears most advanced in the United States but is also under way in Europe, will support economic activity. Finally, activity has also been supported by the decline in oil prices since late 2000. Since late February, however, oil prices have risen significantly, reflecting concerns about possible military intervention in the Middle East, the deteriorating security situation in Israel and the West Bank and Gaza, as well as the strengthening global recovery. At the time the *World Economic Outlook* went to press, oil prices had returned to broadly their mid-2001 level, still well below their fall 2000 peak, and prices in futures markets were only moderately higher than the oil price assumption on which the forecasts in this *World Economic Outlook* are based (Table 1.1). Nonetheless, the past fall in oil prices will provide less support to recovery than earlier expected, while the potential for further volatility has become a significant risk to the outlook.

Inflationary pressures have continued to ease, reflecting weaker global activity. In advanced countries, inflation is projected to fall to 1.3 percent in 2002, the lowest level on record, and—while important wage negotiations in the euro area are still in train—wage increases have in general been moderate. Indeed, if sustained, inflation this low could be a concern, since it could limit the ability of central banks to engineer negative real interest rates when necessary.[3] Deflation remains a central issue in Japan, where prices appear set to fall for the fourth successive year. Elsewhere, however, the forces restraining prices are likely to ease as recovery gets under way, as excess capacity declines and commodity prices—especially oil—pickup (see Appendix 1.1). In emerging and developing countries, inflation is also projected to fall, although it remains of concern in the Commonwealth of Independent States—especially the less advanced reformers—some European Union (EU) accession countries, and a few countries in Latin America and Africa.

Assuming that the recovery is sustained, this global slowdown—while seriously affecting many countries and regions—will have proved to be more moderate than most previous downturns, and would probably not qualify as a full-fledged global recession (Box 1.1). Global GDP growth and global per capita GDP growth (the best measure of the impact on global welfare) would remain above the troughs experienced in the three major global recessions of the past 30 years (although below the level experienced during the Asian crisis in 1997–98). This partly reflects long-run structural trends, including the tendency toward milder recessions in industrial countries (see Chapter III), and the growing role of China and India, which—being relatively closed—are less affected by global downturns (although these factors are at least partly offset by countervailing forces, including increasing financial and corporate sector linkages). However, it clearly also reflects the generally prompt and aggressive response of policymakers to the slowdown, and—linked to that—the progress that has been made in reducing vulnerabilities and strengthening economic fundamentals in advanced and developing countries.[4] As experience during the past year has shown, managing the downturn has been considerably easier in countries with the scope for policy flexibility,

[3]See Box 2.2, "Can Inflation Be Too Low?"
[4]See "Statement of the Managing Director on the Situation of the World Economy and the Fund Response," IMF News Brief No. 01/98, October 5, 2001.

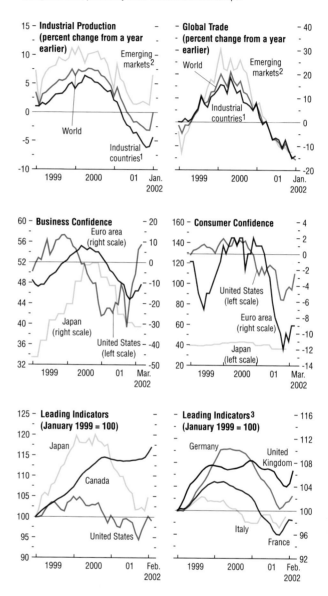

Figure 1.2. Emerging Signs of Recovery

Signs of recovery are suggested by recent improvements in confidence and other leading indicators, particularly in the United States and Europe.

Sources: Haver Analytic. Business confidence for the United States, the National Association of Purchasing Managers; for the euro area, the European Commission; and for Japan, Bank of Japan. Consumer confidence for the United States, the Conference Board; for the euro area, the European Commission; and for Japan, the Economic Planning Agency. Leading indicator for the United States, the Economic Cycle Research Institute; for Japan, the Cabinet Office; for Canada, Statistics Canada; and for Germany, France, Italy, and United Kingdom, OECD Main Economic Indicators.
[1] Australia, Canada, Denmark, Euro area, Japan, New Zealand, Norway, Sweden, Switzerland, United Kingdom, and United States.
[2] Argentina, Brazil, Chile, China, Colombia, Czech Republic, Hong Kong SAR, Hungary, India, Indonesia, Israel, Korea, Malaysia, Mexico, Peru, Philippines, Poland, Russia, Singapore, South Africa, Taiwan Province of China, Thailand, Turkey, and Venezuela.
[3] Seasonally adjusted.

Figure 1.3. Financial Market Optimism

As expectations of a recovery have increased, financial markets have strengthened in almost all countries, accompanied by steepening yield curves and declining risk premiums and spreads.

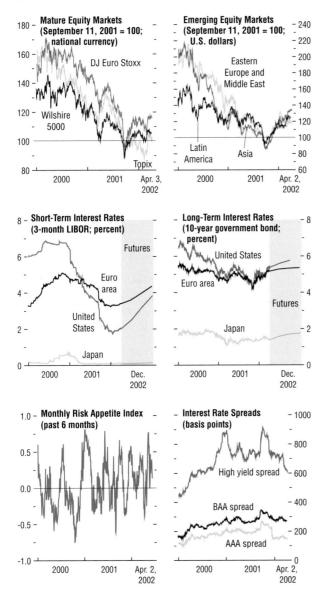

Sources: Bloomberg Financial Markets, LP; State Street Bank; and IMF staff estimates.

while others have been forced to follow more procyclical policies, deepening the downturn and likely also slowing the ensuing recovery.

The main elements of the IMF's global forecast published in the Interim *World Economic Outlook* last December—which projected an upturn in the first half of 2002—have remained broadly unchanged. Global growth in 2002 is projected at 2.8 percent, somewhat higher than expected in December (Table 1.1). Growth in the United States—and countries with close economic links—has been revised significantly upward, as the pace of recovery has exceeded expectations. Elsewhere, adjustments to the forecast are more modest—with the exception of the Western Hemisphere, mainly due to the crisis in Argentina; the Middle East, due to lower than expected growth in oil exporters; and the Commonwealth of Independent States, reflecting the improved outlook for Russia. It is important to recognize that, while global GDP growth for 2002 is projected to be only slightly higher than in 2001, this disguises a substantial pickup during the year. As can be seen from Figure 1.5, global growth is projected to rise from 1½ percent in the last quarter of 2001 to nearly 4 percent by the end of 2002. As the full impact of this is felt, global growth is expected to rise to 4.0 percent in 2003, significantly above the long-run trend.

The global downturn has been more synchronized than the one in the early 1990s (although, as discussed in Chapter III, the degree of synchronicity has been broadly typical from a longer-term historical perspective). This has primarily been due to the commonality of shocks—notably, the bursting of the IT bubble, the run-up in oil prices in 2000, and the tightening of monetary policy from mid-1999 to end-2000—but has also reflected the increasing linkages across countries, particularly in the corporate and financial sphere. This naturally gives rise to the question whether the upturn in activity will be as synchronized. The IMF staff's projections suggest that the recovery in most regions will begin in the first half of 2002, with the United States in the lead, but the nature and pace will vary depending on the depth of the preceding downturn, the openness of the economy, and the extent of policy stimulus in the pipeline, as well as country-specific factors and constraints.

- Among the *industrialized countries*, the upturn is expected to be strongest in the United States, driven initially by the completion of the inventory cycle, and a moderate pickup in final domestic demand (typical of the experience in past mild recessions), underpinned by the substantial macroeconomic stimulus in the pipeline as well as the effect of the previous fall in oil prices (Table 1.2). The pattern and drivers of the recovery in the *euro area* are likely to be broadly similar, but the pace slightly slower, reflecting the more moderate nature of the preceding slowdown, and the more limited policy easing in place. In contrast to the United States, there is less risk from domestic imbalances and corporate profitability remains strong, but weaker than expected external demand or rigidities in labor markets could dampen the pace of the rebound in the short and medium term. In contrast, the outlook for domestic demand in Japan remains very weak, and, while GDP growth (compared with the same period in the previous year) is expected to return to positive levels by the fourth quarter of 2002, this will primarily depend on an improvement in the external environment.

- Among the *major emerging markets*, the outlook varies widely. In Latin America, the recovery is likely to be strongest in Mexico and Central America, which are closely linked to the United States, as well as some Andean countries. In other countries, while they will benefit from improved conditions in financial markets, the pace of recovery will be more subdued; in *Argentina*, the situation remains extremely difficult and a substantial decline in output appears unavoidable. In emerging Asia, growth in China and to a lesser extent India is expected to remain relatively resilient. The highly open economies in the rest of the region will benefit from the pickup in external demand—supported in a number of cases by domestic policy stimulus—although much will depend on the pace of recovery in the IT sector, which ac-

Figure 1.4. Emerging Market Financing Conditions

Emerging market financing conditions have improved markedly, while contagion from the crisis in Argentina has been limited.

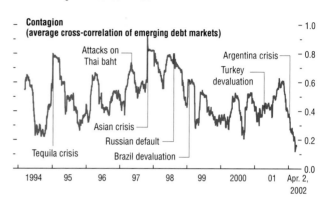

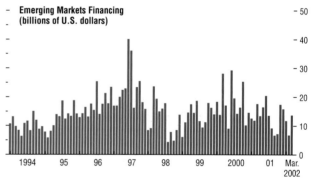

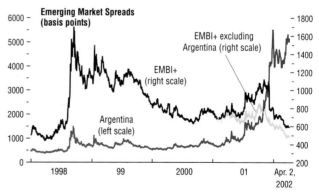

Sources: Bloomberg Financial Markets, LP; and IMF, *Emerging Market Financing.*

Table 1.1. Overview of the *World Economic Outlook* Projections

(Annual percent change unless otherwise noted)

	2000	2001	Current Projections 2002	Current Projections 2003	Difference from December 2001 Projections[1] 2001	Difference from December 2001 Projections[1] 2002
World output	**4.7**	**2.5**	**2.8**	**4.0**	**0.1**	**0.4**
Advanced economies	3.9	1.2	1.7	3.0	0.1	0.8
Major advanced economies	3.5	1.1	1.5	2.8	0.1	0.9
United States	4.1	1.2	2.3	3.4	0.2	1.6
Japan	2.2	−0.4	−1.0	0.8	—	—
Germany	3.0	0.6	0.9	2.7	0.1	0.2
France	3.6	2.0	1.4	3.0	−0.1	0.1
Italy	2.9	1.8	1.4	2.9	—	0.2
United Kingdom	3.0	2.2	2.0	2.8	−0.1	0.2
Canada	4.4	1.5	2.5	3.6	0.1	1.7
Other advanced economies	5.3	1.6	2.5	3.7	0.1	0.6
Memorandum						
European Union	3.4	1.7	1.5	2.9	—	0.2
Euro area	3.4	1.5	1.4	2.9	—	0.2
Newly industrialized Asian economies	8.5	0.8	3.6	5.1	0.4	1.6
Developing countries	5.7	4.0	4.3	5.5	−0.1	−0.2
Africa	3.0	3.7	3.4	4.2	0.1	−0.2
Developing Asia	6.7	5.6	5.9	6.4	—	0.2
China	8.0	7.3	7.0	7.4	—	0.2
India	5.4	4.3	5.5	5.8	−0.1	0.3
ASEAN-4[2]	5.1	2.6	3.3	4.1	0.2	0.4
Middle East and Turkey[3]	5.8	2.1	3.3	4.5	−0.1	−0.7
Western Hemisphere	4.0	0.7	0.7	3.7	−0.3	−1.0
Brazil	4.4	1.5	2.5	3.5	−0.3	0.5
Countries in transition	6.6	5.0	3.9	4.4	—	0.2
Central and eastern Europe	3.8	3.1	3.0	4.0	0.1	−0.2
Commonwealth of Independent States and Mongolia	8.3	6.2	4.5	4.6	0.1	0.6
Russia	9.0	5.0	4.4	4.9	−0.8	0.8
Excluding Russia	7.0	8.8	4.7	4.1	1.9	—
Memorandum						
World growth based on market exchange rates	4.0	1.4	1.8	3.2	—	0.6
World trade volume (goods and services)	**12.4**	**−0.2**	**2.5**	**6.6**	**−1.2**	**0.3**
Imports						
Advanced economies	11.6	−1.5	2.1	6.6	−1.2	0.7
Developing countries	16.0	2.9	6.4	7.7	−2.0	−0.1
Countries in transition	13.2	10.8	8.0	7.7	−0.5	0.2
Exports						
Advanced economies	11.7	−1.3	0.9	6.3	−1.0	0.3
Developing countries	15.0	3.0	4.8	7.0	−0.5	0.2
Countries in transition	14.6	6.3	5.2	6.1	−1.5	−1.4
Commodity prices (U.S. dollars)						
Oil[4]	57.0	−14.0	−5.3	−4.4	—	18.4
Nonfuel (average based on world commodity export weights)	1.8	−5.5	−0.1	7.2	—	−1.8
Consumer prices						
Advanced economies	2.3	2.2	1.3	1.8	−0.1	—
Developing countries	6.1	5.7	5.8	5.1	−0.3	0.5
Countries in transition	20.2	15.9	10.8	8.7	−0.3	−0.3
Six-month London interbank offered rate (LIBOR, percent)						
On U.S. dollar deposits	6.6	3.7	2.8	4.5	−0.1	0.1
On Japanese yen deposits	0.3	0.2	0.1	0.1	—	—
On euro deposits	4.6	4.1	3.7	4.5	—	0.8

Note: Real effective exchange rates are assumed to remain constant at the levels prevailing during February 11–March 11, 2002.
[1]Using updated purchasing-power-parity (PPP) weights, summarized in the Statistical Appendix, Table A.
[2]Includes Indonesia, Malaysia, the Philippines, and Thailand.
[3]Includes Malta.
[4]Simple average of spot prices of U.K. Brent, Dubai, and West Texas Intermediate crude oil. The average price of oil in U.S. dollars a barrel was $24.28 in 2001; the assumed price is $23.00 in 2002, and $22.00 in 2003.

counts for a substantial share of output and exports. In the Middle East, growth has been adversely affected by lower oil prices—although the recent rebound will help—as well as the deterioration in the security situation. Turkey is gradually recovering from the severe recession of 2001, but the economy remains vulnerable to adverse shocks. In contrast, growth in the Commonwealth of Independent States has been relatively unaffected by the slowdown, buoyed by solid growth in Russia and Ukraine. Activity in central and eastern European economies—except Poland—has also held up well, aided by robust domestic demand and foreign direct investment.

- While the *poorest* countries have clearly been adversely affected by the slowdown, primarily through lower commodity prices and falling external demand, growth has in general been surprisingly well sustained, especially in those countries with the strongest domestic policies. This has been aided by the ending of a number of conflicts in Africa, as well as the resources released under the Heavily Indebted Poor Countries Initiative (HIPC). Growth in the HIPC countries is projected to pick up further in 2003 and beyond, although it is important to recognize that in the past the IMF's forecasts for African countries have proved consistently optimistic.[5]

As noted above, the risks to the forecast have become more balanced over the past months. There are good reasons to expect a pickup in activity in the period ahead; indeed it is possible that the pace of recovery could exceed expectations, as has generally been the case in the past (Box 1.2). Nonetheless, there are also significant risks to the sustainability and durability of the upturn, in the United States and elsewhere, which will pose important challenges for policymakers in the period ahead.

- *First, the late 1990s saw the cumulative development of a number of imbalances in the U.S. and the*

[5]In part reflecting the impact of natural disasters and conflicts. See Box 3.1, Interim *World Economic Outlook*, December 2001.

Figure 1.5. Global Recovery
(Percent change from four quarters earlier)

Real GDP in most regions is expected to have bottomed out in late 2001, with a recovery beginning in the first half of 2002.

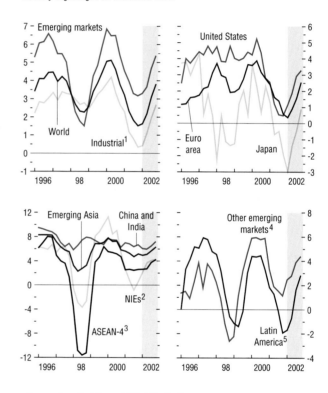

Sources: Haver Analytics; and IMF staff estimates.
[1]Australia, Canada, Denmark, euro area, Japan, New Zealand, Norway, Sweden, Switzerland, the United Kingdom, and the United States.
[2]Hong Kong SAR, Korea, Singapore, and Taiwan Province of China.
[3]Indonesia, Malaysia, Philippines, and Thailand.
[4]Czech Republic, Hungary, Israel, Poland, Russia, South Africa, and Turkey.
[5]Argentina, Brazil, Chile, Colombia, Mexico, Peru, and Venezuela.

Table 1.2. Advanced Economies: Real GDP, Consumer Prices, and Unemployment
(Annual percent change and percent of labor force)

	Real GDP				Consumer Prices				Unemployment			
	2000	2001	2002	2003	2000	2001	2002	2003	2000	2001	2002	2003
Advanced economies	**3.9**	**1.2**	**1.7**	**3.0**	**2.3**	**2.2**	**1.3**	**1.8**	**5.9**	**6.0**	**6.4**	**6.2**
Major advanced economies	3.5	1.1	1.5	2.8	2.3	2.1	1.1	1.7	5.8	6.0	6.5	6.3
United States	4.1	1.2	2.3	3.4	3.4	2.8	1.4	2.4	4.0	4.8	5.5	5.3
Japan	2.2	−0.4	−1.0	0.8	−0.8	−0.7	−1.1	−0.5	4.7	5.0	5.8	5.7
Germany	3.0	0.6	0.9	2.7	2.1	2.4	1.5	1.2	7.9	7.9	8.2	8.1
France	3.6	2.0	1.4	3.0	1.8	1.8	1.5	1.4	9.5	9.0	9.2	8.7
Italy	2.9	1.8	1.4	2.9	2.6	2.7	2.2	1.6	10.6	9.5	9.3	8.9
United Kingdom[1]	3.0	2.2	2.0	2.8	2.1	2.1	2.4	2.5	5.6	5.1	5.4	5.4
Canada	4.4	1.5	2.5	3.6	2.7	2.5	0.9	1.8	6.8	7.2	7.1	6.7
Other advanced economies	5.3	1.6	2.5	3.7	2.4	2.9	2.0	2.1	6.2	6.1	6.3	5.8
Spain	4.1	2.8	2.3	3.2	3.5	3.2	2.3	2.3	14.1	13.0	13.0	12.4
Netherlands	3.5	1.1	1.4	2.7	2.3	5.1	3.4	2.3	2.6	2.0	2.5	2.7
Belgium	4.0	1.1	0.9	3.2	2.7	2.4	1.1	1.2	6.9	6.6	7.3	7.0
Sweden	3.6	1.2	1.6	2.7	1.0	2.6	2.3	2.2	4.7	4.0	4.4	4.3
Austria	3.0	1.0	1.3	2.9	2.0	2.3	1.8	1.6	3.7	3.8	4.1	3.8
Denmark	3.0	0.9	1.3	2.4	2.9	2.1	2.3	2.2	5.2	5.0	5.2	5.2
Finland	5.7	0.7	1.4	3.1	3.0	2.6	1.5	1.6	9.8	9.2	9.8	9.7
Greece	4.3	4.1	3.4	2.9	2.9	3.7	3.3	2.7	11.4	10.9	10.9	10.7
Portugal	3.2	1.6	0.8	2.0	2.8	4.4	2.9	2.2	4.0	4.1	4.2	4.3
Ireland	11.5	6.0	3.2	6.2	5.3	4.0	4.4	3.0	4.3	4.0	4.7	4.7
Luxembourg	7.5	5.1	3.0	6.0	3.2	2.7	1.9	1.8	2.6	2.5	2.9	2.7
Switzerland	3.0	1.3	0.8	2.6	1.6	1.0	1.0	1.0	2.0	1.9	2.6	2.3
Norway	2.3	1.4	2.3	2.2	3.1	3.0	1.5	2.5	3.4	3.6	3.8	3.7
Israel	6.4	−0.6	1.3	3.8	1.1	1.1	3.1	2.1	8.8	9.3	10.5	9.4
Iceland	5.0	2.1	−0.9	1.9	5.0	6.7	6.4	3.5	1.3	1.7	2.3	2.6
Cyprus	5.1	4.0	3.0	4.2	4.1	2.0	1.8	2.2	3.4	3.6	3.8	4.0
Korea	9.3	3.0	5.0	5.5	2.3	4.1	2.7	2.6	4.1	3.7	3.5	3.5
Australia[2]	3.2	2.4	3.9	4.0	4.5	4.4	2.3	2.3	6.3	6.7	6.7	6.5
Taiwan Province of China	5.9	−1.9	2.3	4.8	1.3	—	0.4	1.6	3.0	5.1	5.0	4.9
Hong Kong SAR	10.5	0.1	1.5	3.6	−3.7	−1.6	−2.5	—	4.9	5.0	5.6	5.4
Singapore	10.3	−2.1	3.2	5.1	1.1	1.0	1.1	1.6	3.1	4.7	4.4	3.7
New Zealand[2]	3.9	2.4	2.6	3.0	2.7	2.7	1.8	1.5	6.0	5.3	5.5	5.6
Memorandum												
European Union	3.4	1.7	1.5	2.9	2.3	2.6	2.0	1.8	8.2	7.7	7.9	7.7
Euro area	3.4	1.5	1.4	2.9	2.4	2.6	1.9	1.6	8.8	8.3	8.5	8.2

[1]Consumer prices are based on the retail price index excluding mortgage interest.
[2]Consumer prices excluding interest rate components; for Australia, also excluding other volatile items.

global economy—notably, the large U.S. current account deficit and surpluses elsewhere (Table 1.3), the low U.S. personal savings rate, the apparent overvaluation of the U.S. dollar and undervaluation of the euro, and relatively high levels of corporate and household indebtedness in a number of countries. As has been discussed extensively in previous issues of the *World Economic Outlook*, these imbalances have been driven in large part by the relatively rapid growth in the United States relative to other countries. This, in turn, partly reflected cyclical factors, but also resulted from the improvement in U.S. productivity

growth relative to other countries. Partly because the downturn has been so synchronized and the recession in the United States has been mild, there has been only a moderate correction in these imbalances during the downturn, and the process by which this correction eventually occurs will importantly affect the outlook. For example, given the substantial stimulus in the pipeline, it is possible U.S. growth could rebound more quickly than expected, which would lead to a further widening of these imbalances. While this would likely be manageable in the short term, especially if underlying U.S. productivity growth remained

Table 1.3. Selected Economies: Current Account Positions

(Percent of GDP)

	2000	2001	2002	2003
Advanced economies	**−1.0**	**−0.8**	**−0.8**	**−0.7**
Major advanced economies	−1.6	−1.4	−1.4	−1.4
United States	−4.5	−4.1	−4.1	−4.0
Japan	2.5	2.1	2.9	3.4
Germany	−1.0	0.5	0.5	0.6
France	1.8	2.5	2.5	2.2
Italy	−0.5	0.4	0.7	1.0
United Kingdom	−1.8	−1.8	−2.1	−2.3
Canada	2.5	2.7	1.8	1.6
Other advanced economies	1.8	2.5	2.4	2.3
Spain	−3.1	−2.0	−1.7	−1.6
Netherlands	3.0	3.1	3.7	3.3
Belgium-Luxembourg	4.8	4.9	4.9	4.7
Sweden	2.6	3.3	3.0	3.0
Austria	−2.8	−2.4	−1.6	−1.4
Denmark	1.6	2.9	2.5	3.2
Finland	7.4	5.4	4.8	4.9
Greece	−6.8	−6.2	−6.1	−6.0
Portugal	−10.4	−9.7	−9.3	−8.9
Ireland	−0.6	−0.6	−1.4	−1.6
Switzerland	12.9	10.2	10.8	11.3
Norway	14.3	14.8	13.9	13.1
Israel	−1.2	−1.5	−1.7	−2.1
Iceland	−10.3	−6.9	−5.2	−3.9
Cyprus	−5.2	−4.3	−3.9	−3.7
Korea	2.7	2.0	1.5	0.6
Australia	−4.0	−2.6	−3.2	−2.7
Taiwan Province of China	2.9	6.7	6.6	6.6
Hong Kong SAR	5.5	7.4	7.7	7.7
Singapore	17.0	23.3	21.4	21.4
New Zealand	−5.6	−3.2	−4.5	−4.2
Memorandum				
European Union	−0.4	0.4	0.4	0.4
Euro area[1]	−0.2	0.7	0.8	0.8

[1]Calculated as the sum of the balances of individual euro area countries.

strong, it could adversely affect the sustainability of recovery later on, particularly if growth in other countries did not pick up, and increase the possibility of an eventual disorderly adjustment.[6] It is also possible, however, that the recovery in the United States could be weaker than expected, partly because of the imbalances—for instance, if private investment is held back by weak profitability or excess capacity proves more widespread than presently believed, or if U.S. households and businesses seek to strengthen savings and balance sheets earlier. In that case, the imbalances would likely correct sooner, but at the cost of a more subdued recovery in both the United States and the rest of the world.

- *Second, as also stressed in the IMF's* Global Financial Stability Report, *financial markets may still embody relatively optimistic expectations for corporate profitability and the pace of recovery.* Were these expectations to be disappointed, there would likely be a downward adjustment in asset prices, which could adversely affect both consumer and business confidence and demand more generally. These risks may be heightened by the weaknesses in the accounting and auditing framework highlighted following the recent collapse of Enron, which has raised concerns that the financial positions of other firms could also prove weaker than expected. Beyond this, while the international financial infrastructure has generally held up well in the face of the shocks experienced in 2001, a decline in asset prices or delayed recovery could put pressure on financial institutions in countries where the pace of consolidation and restructuring has lagged, as well as the performance of certain financial markets, notably for credit derivatives.

- *Third, the situation in Japan, which is presently undergoing its worst recession in the postwar period, remains a source of serious concern.* Given the limited macroeconomic policy options, weak activity in Japan is proving increasingly difficult to offset through policy actions—with negative consequences, particularly for the rest of the region. The financial position of the banking system has become increasingly strained as loan-loss announcements have increased, and this is undermining confidence. Further, growing concerns about debt sustainability and additional downgrades by rating agencies make the government bond market vulnerable to a sharp swing in investor sentiment and a spike in yields.

---

[6]See also "Alternative Scenarios: How Might Medium-Term Productivity Growth Affect the Short-Term Outlook?" Chapter I, Appendix II, *World Economic Outlook*, October 2001, for a detailed discussion.

Box 1.1. Was It a Global Recession?

Perhaps the most conventional rule of thumb for defining a national recession is two straight quarters of negative GDP growth (see Chapter III on recessions). Unfortunately, this simple rule does not translate well to the global context. First, quarterly real GDP data are weak; for a number of major emerging market countries, quarterly output data do not exist before the mid-1990s, and there are still many countries that do not report GDP on a quarterly basis. Even among those that do, national methods for seasonally adjusting output data differ to such an extent that meaningful aggregation is difficult. Second, while we cannot measure it exactly, it is likely that quarterly global growth does not turn negative nearly as often as does GDP within the typical country. Indeed, annual global growth has never been negative for any year in recent history (see the first figure, which shows global GDP growth using the IMF's purchasing-power-parity (PPP) weights to aggregate country income.)

The principal reason that global growth is rarely negative is that world output is more di-versified than national output. For example, the United States, Europe, and Japan do not always experience downturns at the same time. Data on annual real GDP indicate that this slowdown has a similar level of synchronization as earlier episodes in the mid-1970s and early 1980s, even though growth in China (in particular) has re-mained relatively robust over this slowdown. The lower level of synchronization in the early 1990s was an exception—largely reflecting spe-cific regional events, including the asset price bubble in Japan and the consequences of German unification activity in continental Europe. It is also the case that trend growth for the world is higher than for most advanced economies because developing countries grow faster on average, so it takes a steeper dip to hit negative territory.

The main authors are Kenneth Rogoff, David Robinson, and Tamim Bayoumi, in consultation with other members of a committee that included Carmen Reinhart, Manmohan Kumar, and Aasim Husain.

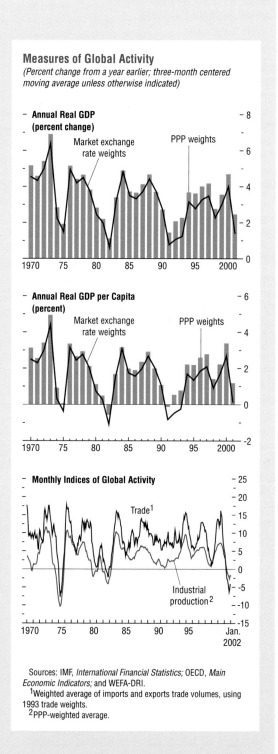

Measures of Global Activity
(Percent change from a year earlier; three-month centered moving average unless otherwise indicated)

Sources: IMF, *International Financial Statistics;* OECD, *Main Economic Indicators;* and WEFA-DRI.
[1]Weighted average of imports and exports trade volumes, using 1993 trade weights.
[2]PPP-weighted average.

While global output may rarely decline, it is useful to have a simple benchmark for identify-

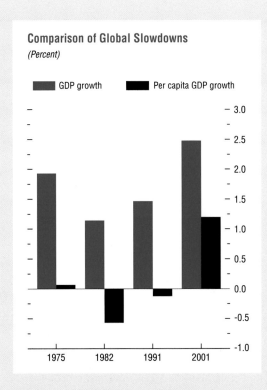

Comparison of Global Slowdowns
(Percent)

GDP growth   Per capita GDP growth

ing slowdowns that could be labeled as global recessions. One reasonable solution to this conundrum is to adjust world output growth for growth in world population, and declare that a sufficient (although not necessary) condition for a global recession is any year in which world per capita growth (on a PPP basis) is negative. In the second figure, the first bars show unadjusted world GDP growth during the major recent slowdowns, 1975, 1982, 1991, and 2001. In no case did world growth dip below 1 percent, much less turn negative. In 1975, GDP growth of 1.9 percent was almost exactly offset by world population growth, so that per capita GDP growth was about zero. However, per capita GDP growth actually turned negative in 1982 and, to a lesser extent, in 1991. By contrast, per capita GDP growth in 2001 was over 1 percent, well above zero. Compared with the earlier episodes, unadjusted growth was stronger at 2.5 percent, instead of dipping below 2 percent as in the previous episodes. Also, world population growth is lower today (1.3 percent) than it was a

decade earlier. Thus, the current slowdown has not come close to meeting the hurdle of negative per capita annual GDP growth, which would automatically qualify it as a recession. This partly reflects the relatively high weight of China, which has continued to grow strongly, in the IMF PPP weights. Nonetheless, even going to the extreme of using market exchange rate-based weights (which substantially reduce China's weight), per capita GDP growth would still remain slightly positive in 2001.

Can we declare that the world is not in recession simply because annual global per capita growth is positive? No, not necessarily. While negative per capita GDP growth (using IMF PPP weights) is a sufficient condition to identify a global recession, by itself it would probably be unduly conservative. As in the case of individual recessions, one can not rely absolutely on any mechanical rule, but instead some element of judgment is required. That is how recessions are identified in the United States by the National Bureau of Economic Research (NBER), for example. The NBER defines a recession as a significant decline in activity spread across the economy and lasting more than a few months, and focuses on economy-wide monthly series (especially nonfarm employment and real personal income less transfers). It also looks at data from manufacturing (real manufacturing and trade sales and industrial production), although—as the NBER notes—this is a relatively small part of the U.S. economy whose movements often differ from those of other sectors. The rule of thumb of two quarters of negative growth often referred to by commentators is simply a useful way of approximating this system. Indeed, in the recent downturn, the NBER committee chose to identify the U.S. slowdown as a recession even though, based on current information, GDP growth was only negative in the third quarter.

How might one apply these principles to identifying global recessions even when per capita GDP growth is positive? Given the data inadequacies, there is no simple extension of the NBER's methodology to the global economy. We have al-

Box 1.1 *(concluded)*

ready noted the difficulties in getting satisfactory quarterly global GDP, and certainly global versions of the main monthly indicators used by the NBER for the United States will not be available for the foreseeable future. However, there are monthly data on global industrial production and merchandise trade volumes, although—as in the United States—these focus on the manufacturing sector, which comprises less than one quarter of global GDP.[1] The first figure shows the change in industrial production and trade volumes at a global level since 1970. Both series clearly identify the global slowdowns after the two oil crises that are also clear in the real GDP data. Subsequently, however, the correspondence is less close. For example, growth in both monthly series remained positive in the recession of the early 1990s. Moreover, for the Asian crisis, both series suggest a more severe slowdown than does real GDP (partly reflecting the large manufacturing sectors in many Asian economies). The most recent data show a sharp fall in production and trade—corresponding to the synchronized and disruptive decline in manufacturing production, partly related to the information technology (IT) sector—but again the picture from these series appears more severe than that from

data on real GDP. Cyclical movements in manufacturing and trade tend to be larger than in overall activity. In addition, the manufacturing and trade series have been disproportionately impacted by the rapid fall in global IT.

Aside from the global aggregates, it is important to also look at the extent to which the slowdown is spread across the globe and the speed of the decline. If, for example, the United States experienced a sufficiently severe recession, global average numbers could be quite poor even if there were positive GDP growth elsewhere. This scenario would not, in our definition, qualify as a global recession. On the other hand, a particularly rapid and generalized fall from a high level to a much lower level should be an element of one's assessment. To ascertain the global nature of the slowdown, we considered, among other factors, quarterly GDP where available. These data indicate negative growth for the third quarter in some regions of the world, including the United States, Germany, Japan, and several emerging markets. While weakness remained in Germany and Japan in the fourth quarter, the United States rebounded. Growth in China and India has remained robust throughout.

Overall, therefore, our reading of the data indicates that the recent slowdown falls somewhat short of a global recession, certainly in comparison with earlier episodes that we would have labeled as global recessions. That said, it was a close call.

[1]Manufacturing currently makes up slightly under 20 percent of GDP in industrial countries (down from almost 30 percent in 1970), and a relatively stable 23 percent in developing countries.

- *Finally, there are a number of specific risks to the outlook.* Most recently, the volatility in the oil market has become a significant potential risk to the recovery, especially if the security situation in the Middle East were to deteriorate further.[7] Were oil prices to rise substantially further, there could be a significant impact on the global recovery (see Table 1.12 in Appendix 1.1, which shows the impact of higher oil prices on global growth). While oil

exporting countries would clearly benefit, there would be adverse effects on most industrial and many emerging market economies, notably in Asia, and many of the heavily indebted poor countries and several CIS countries could be quite seriously affected. Beyond this, the war against terrorism has so far gone better than expected but setbacks could adversely affect confidence; and, although contagion from developments in Argentina has so

[7]See IMF (2000) for a detailed discussion of the impact of oil price changes on the global economy.

Box 1.2. On the Accuracy of Forecasts of Recovery

The consensus among economic forecasters is that the U.S. recession that started in March 2001 will be over during the course of this year. For example, the mean forecast for U.S. growth in 2002 reported by the March survey of *Consensus Forecasts* is 2.1 percent, which would imply a robust recovery in the second half of the year. Given economic forecasters' poor performance in predicting recessions,[1] it is natural to ask whether they are any better at predicting recoveries. It is difficult to answer this question using data for a single country as the number of recoveries for which consistent growth forecasts are readily available would be too small to make reliable inferences. Therefore, this box reviews the experience from a large sample of industrial countries to assess how well forecasters have done.

Cross-Country Evidence on Predicting Recoveries

The publication *Consensus Forecasts* has provided macroeconomic forecasts for 26 industrialized countries on a monthly basis since October 1989. Each issue of the publication surveys a number of prominent financial and economic analysts, and reports their individual forecasts as well as the mean forecast (the consensus). Every month, *Consensus Forecasts* contains a new forecast of average annual GDP growth in the current and forthcoming year. Thus, for example, between January 1990 and December 1991 there are 24 separate forecasts of real GDP growth in 1991.[2]

The behavior of forecasts during the U.S. recession and recovery of 1991–92 provides a good example of the behavior of forecasts around turning points (see the figure). In January 1990, the forecast for U.S. growth during 1991 was about 2.5 percent. Following Iraq's

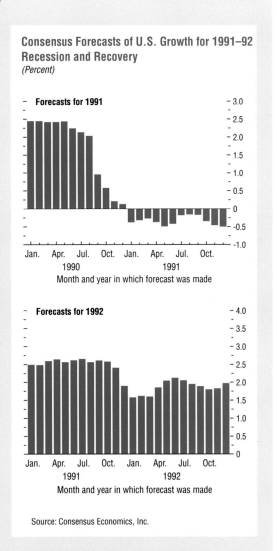

Consensus Forecasts of U.S. Growth for 1991–92 Recession and Recovery
(Percent)

Source: Consensus Economics, Inc.

invasion of Kuwait in August 1990, forecasts for U.S. growth started to be marked down substantially. By the start of 1991, the forecast was for a modest recession that year (figure, top panel).

How did the recognition of the recession in 1991 affect the forecasts for 1992? Initially, not very much. The year-ahead forecasts for 1992 (the ones made during 1991) remained virtually unchanged at about 2.5 percent. The current-year forecasts for 1992 showed somewhat greater variation but clearly never came close to forecasting a continuation of the recession of the previous year (figure, bottom panel). The econ-

The main author is Prakash Loungani.
[1]See Box 1.1, *World Economic Outlook*, May 2001, and Loungani (2001).
[2]The first 12 forecasts—the ones made during 1990—are referred to as *year-ahead* forecasts; the 12 forecasts made during 1991 are called *current-year* forecasts.

Box 1.2 *(concluded)*

omy did indeed recover and the forecast error
was small.

The pattern displayed in the figure is quite
typical of forecasts around turning points for
the 25 other episodes of recessions and potential recoveries (in the subsequent year) since
October 1989.[3] Recessions typically arrive before
they are forecast. The recognition that the country is in a recession does not generally lead to
drastic markdowns of the forecast for the post-
recession year. That is, forecasters act as though
the recession is not going to lead to a second
year of negative growth.

How well does this strategy work in delivering
accurate forecasts? The simple answer is:
"Reasonably well." In three-fourths of cases over
the 1990s, the recession did not result in a second year of negative growth.[4] Hence, even
though large forecast errors are made in the
case of multiyear recessions, forecasting a recovery in the year following a recession turns out to
be a reasonably good bet on average. Using the
April survey of *Consensus Forecasts*, the mean absolute error of current-year forecasts for the 26
episodes of potential recoveries is 1.29 percentage points. This is only about half as large as the
mean absolute error from a naive forecasting
strategy of predicting a continuation of the recession. While the accuracy of the forecasts is
quite good, there is a tendency for forecasts
made at the start of the year of the recovery to
underpredict it. This property was noted in the

case of forecasts of U.S. recoveries over the period 1972 to 1984 by Zarnowitz (1986). The U.S.
recovery of 1992 and recoveries in the cross-
country sample studied in this box also tended
to be underpredicted—by about ½ to ¾ of a
percentage point—in forecasts made near the
start of the year.

Comparison with WEO

On average, there is a high degree of similar-
ity between forecasts made by the April
Consensus survey and those reported in the
IMF's May *World Economic Outlook* during the
years of potential recoveries: the mean absolute
error of the May WEO forecasts is 1.24 percentage points, virtually identical to that of *Consensus
Forecasts*. The forecast errors are also highly correlated at other forecasting horizons as well,
such as comparing the October *Consensus* with
the fall WEO current-year forecasts or comparing year-ahead forecasts; hence, the mean absolute errors for the two sources of forecasts are
virtually the same at every forecasting horizon.

Conclusion

Conventional wisdom among forecasters is
that the U.S. economy will start to grow again
this year. What these forecasts have going for
them is the fact that multiyear recessions are
somewhat rarer than those that end in about a
year. Over the 1990s, for the set of industrialized
countries studied here, forecasting a recovery in
the year following a recession has therefore
turned out to be a reasonably good bet. So even
though forecasters are caught flat-footed when
recessions turn out to be multiyear, the message,
broadly speaking, is, most recessions catch forecasters by surprise; most recoveries do not.

[3]See Loungani (2002) for evidence from other industrialized countries.
[4]Over a longer period, as noted in Chapter III, 60
percent of recessions in industrial countries since 1973
lasted just one year.

far been contained, risks remain, particularly
for the other countries in the region.

In setting the stance of policies, policymakers
will need to consider not just the baseline projections, but also the balance of these various risks
and the costs associated with each. In making this
assessment, a number of considerations are rele-

vant. First, given the past fall in commodity prices
and substantial excess capacity in most industrial
countries, and increasing evidence that the improvement in central bank credibility in recent
years is helping to anchor inflationary expectations (Chapter II), long-term inflationary risks remain limited at this stage. Second, if growth in

some industrial countries were to disappoint, there could be a significant impact on the rest of the world, particularly in emerging market and developing countries. Third, while wider global imbalances would clearly be of concern, these should be addressed primarily through appropriate medium-term policies in the United States and better growth policies elsewhere. Overall, there appear to be three main policy priorities.

- *Macroeconomic policies in most industrial countries should remain broadly supportive of activity, although in countries where the recovery is most advanced, attention will need to turn toward reversing earlier monetary policy easing; in Japan, aggressive action to address deflation is required.* The Federal Reserve appropriately left U.S. interest rates on hold in March, while noting that the risks to price stability and growth had become broadly balanced. As the recovery progresses, some withdrawal of stimulus is likely to be required, while the focus of fiscal policy should shift to medium-term consolidation. In the *euro area*, with growing signs of recovery, the present stance of monetary policy is broadly appropriate, while the automatic stabilizers should be allowed to operate to support activity within the constraints of the Stability and Growth Pact. In Japan, macroeconomic policies should be as supportive as possible, including through more aggressive monetary easing to address deflation, even if this results in some further depreciation of the yen, and through an additional supplementary budget to maintain a broadly neutral fiscal stance in 2002 and 2003 (Table 1.4).

- *The medium-term policy framework needs to be geared toward supporting sustainable growth and an orderly reduction in the global imbalances.* As has been argued in many previous issues of the *World Economic Outlook*, the global imbalances reflect not just not the past strong growth in the United States—and the excesses that were associated with it—but also relatively weak growth in other parts of the world. Consequently, decisive action to reinvigorate activity in Japan, continued structural reforms to encourage growth in the euro area, building on the progress

made at the Barcelona summit, and continued corporate and financial sector reform in some Asian emerging markets with large current account surpluses, are a priority from both national and international perspectives. In the United States, in turn, it will be important to avoid exacerbating external imbalances by ensuring that fiscal balance (excluding social security) is restored over the medium term (see Appendix 1.2 for a detailed discussion).

- *As experience during the downturn has shown, it remains essential to press ahead with efforts to reduce vulnerabilities and maximize the scope for policy flexibility in response to external shocks.* In industrial countries, this requires accelerated efforts to address the looming problems resulting from aging populations, where progress in many countries falls short of what is required; a sustained effort to use the recovery to achieve broadly balanced budgets in the euro area within a reasonable time frame, as called for under the Stability and Growth Pact; and the design and publication of a credible medium-term fiscal consolidation plan in Japan. In emerging markets, corporate and financial reforms remain a central priority, particularly in Asia; in Latin America—and in some Asian countries, including India and China—medium-term efforts to strengthen fiscal positions are also critical (Chapter II).

For many developing countries, an overarching priority over the longer run remains an enduring reduction in poverty, which in turn will require a sustained improvement in growth. From this perspective, it is encouraging that GDP growth in China, India, and sub-Saharan Africa, where the bulk of the poorest live, has been relatively well sustained during the downturn, and is expected to pick up in 2002–03. In both China and India, poverty has been on a steady downward trend, although in India GDP growth may still fall short of the level consistent with further sustained progress, underscoring the need for fiscal and structural reforms (see below). The most entrenched problems remain in sub-Saharan Africa, where GDP growth is well below the level needed to make substantial inroads in poverty.

Table 1.4. Major Advanced Economies: General Government Fiscal Balances and Debt[1]
(Percent of GDP)

	1986–95	1996	1997	1998	1999	2000	2001	2002	2003	2007
Major advanced economies										
Actual balance	−3.9	−3.6	−2.0	−1.6	−1.2	−0.3	−1.7	−2.6	−2.1	−0.6
Output gap[2]	−0.6	−1.9	−1.3	−1.1	−0.7	0.3	−1.0	−1.7	−1.4	—
Structural balance	−3.5	−2.7	−1.4	−1.0	−0.9	−1.0	−1.5	−2.0	−1.7	−0.6
United States										
Actual balance	−4.5	−2.4	−1.3	−0.1	0.6	1.5	0.1	−1.4	−1.2	−0.5
Output gap[2]	−1.4	−2.8	−1.6	−0.5	0.4	1.4	−0.4	−0.8	−0.5	—
Structural balance	−4.0	−1.5	−0.7	0.1	0.5	1.0	0.1	−1.2	−1.0	−0.5
Net debt	53.2	59.2	57.0	53.4	48.9	43.7	42.2	42.0	40.9	34.6
Gross debt	67.3	72.8	70.3	66.6	63.4	57.4	55.4	54.7	53.0	44.3
Japan										
Actual balance	−0.4	−4.9	−3.7	−5.6	−7.6	−8.5	−8.5	−8.7	−7.6	−2.3
Excluding social security	−3.2	−7.0	−5.8	−7.2	−9.0	−9.2	−8.8	−8.7	−7.4	−2.9
Output gap[2]	0.7	0.8	1.0	−1.6	−2.2	−1.3	−2.7	−4.6	−4.8	—
Structural balance	−0.6	−5.2	−4.1	−5.0	−6.9	−8.3	−7.8	−7.3	−6.1	−2.1
Excluding social security	−3.5	−7.2	−6.0	−6.8	−8.6	−9.2	−8.6	−8.1	−6.8	−2.8
Net debt	13.8	21.6	27.9	38.0	44.4	52.7	62.2	72.4	80.2	85.3
Gross debt	71.8	91.7	97.4	108.4	120.6	130.8	143.4	157.0	166.4	166.5
Euro area										
Actual balance	−4.5	−4.2	−2.5	−2.2	−1.3	0.2	−1.4	−1.6	−1.1	0.2
Output gap[2]	−0.2	−2.1	−2.0	−1.4	−1.1	−0.1	−0.9	−1.9	−1.4	−0.2
Structural balance	. . .	−3.0	−1.4	−1.4	−0.8	−1.1	−1.1	−0.8	−0.5	0.2
Net debt	46.2	62.6	62.9	61.4	60.5	58.3	57.6	57.4	56.4	51.4
Gross debt	61.0	76.1	75.4	73.7	72.6	70.2	69.1	68.9	67.5	58.4
Germany[3]										
Actual balance[4]	−2.2	−3.4	−2.7	−2.2	−1.6	1.2	−2.7	−2.7	−2.0	0.2
Output gap[2]	0.1	−0.7	−1.2	−1.1	−1.1	—	−1.2	−2.1	−1.4	—
Structural balance	−1.8	−2.7	−1.6	−1.3	−0.8	−1.3	−2.0	−1.4	−1.1	0.2
Net debt	27.6	51.1	52.3	52.2	52.6	51.6	51.1	52.5	52.7	47.9
Gross debt	45.1	59.8	61.0	60.9	61.3	60.3	59.8	61.2	61.4	56.6
France										
Actual balance[4]	−3.5	−4.1	−3.0	−2.7	−1.8	−1.4	−1.4	−2.1	−1.9	—
Output gap[2]	−0.5	−3.3	−3.1	−1.8	−1.2	−0.2	−0.5	−1.5	−0.9	—
Structural balance	−3.0	−1.9	−1.0	−1.6	−1.0	−1.2	−1.3	−1.4	−1.3	—
Net debt	30.6	48.1	49.6	49.8	48.9	47.8	48.8	48.3	48.0	51.6
Gross debt	39.3	57.1	59.3	59.5	58.5	57.5	57.1	58.0	57.7	51.6
Italy										
Actual balance[4,5]	−10.4	−7.1	−2.7	−2.8	−1.8	−0.5	−1.4	−1.2	−0.2	−0.3
Output gap[2]	−0.1	−2.0	−2.3	−2.4	−2.7	−1.9	−2.0	−2.5	−1.6	—
Structural balance	−10.4	−6.2	−1.7	−1.7	−0.6	−2.1	−1.2	−0.7	−0.1	−0.3
Net debt	97.8	116.1	113.8	110.1	108.4	104.6	103.5	101.9	99.2	86.2
Gross debt	103.7	122.7	120.2	116.4	114.5	110.6	109.4	107.7	104.8	91.1
United Kingdom										
Actual balance[4]	−3.4	−4.1	−1.5	0.3	1.5	4.4	0.4	−0.9	−1.2	−1.0
Output gap[2]	0.5	−1.3	−0.5	0.2	−0.5	0.1	−0.1	−0.8	−0.7	—
Structural balance	−3.0	−3.3	−0.9	0.5	1.6	2.1	0.3	−0.7	−0.8	−1.0
Net debt	25.7	46.2	44.6	41.9	39.0	34.5	30.9	28.9	28.6	28.6
Gross debt	43.4	51.8	49.6	46.5	43.9	40.9	37.9	35.7	34.6	33.9
Canada										
Actual balance	−6.5	−2.8	0.2	0.5	1.6	3.2	2.4	1.7	1.7	1.5
Output gap[2]	−2.5	−6.5	−5.1	−3.7	−1.4	0.3	−0.9	−1.0	−0.2	—
Structural balance	−5.1	—	2.1	2.4	2.4	3.1	2.9	2.3	1.9	1.5
Net debt	69.9	87.8	84.1	81.2	74.9	66.3	61.8	58.7	53.9	38.8
Gross debt	101.6	120.3	117.6	115.7	112.3	102.6	97.8	93.9	87.3	66.6

Note: The methodology and specific assumptions for each country are discussed in Box A1.
[1]Debt data refer to end of year; for the United Kingdom they refer to end of March.
[2]Percent of potential.
[3]Data before 1990 refer to west Germany. For net debt, the first column refers to 1988–94. Beginning in 1995, the debt and debt-service obligations of the Treuhandanstalt (and of various other agencies) were taken over by general government. This debt is equivalent to 8 percent of GDP, and the associated debt service to ½ to 1 percent of GDP.
[4]Includes one-off receipts from the sale of mobile telephone licenses equivalent to 2.5 percent of GDP in 2000 for Germany, 0.1 percent of GDP in 2001 and 2002 for France, 1.2 percent of GDP in 2000 for Italy, and 2.4 percent of GDP in 2000 for the United Kingdom.
[5]Includes asset sales equivalent to 0.6 percent of GDP in 2001 and 2002, 0.5 percent in 2003, and 0.1 percent in 2004.

The main responsibility, of course, continues to lie with national governments, which must create conditions favorable to domestic savings mobilization and private sector investment and ensure the effective use of both domestic and external public resources—for which good governance is clearly key. The New Partnership for Africa's Development embodies a concerted and welcome approach to these issues. However, as the Managing Director has stressed,[8] these efforts must be matched by "stronger, faster, and more comprehensive" support from the international community. Substantial assistance has now been provided under the Heavily Indebted Poor Countries Initiative (HIPC), and the progress made at the Monterrey Conference—including the pledges of higher aid by the European Union and the United States—is encouraging, but much more needs to be done to increase aid flows, which are less than one-third of the U.N. target of 0.7 percent of GNP.

The most important issue, however, remains to further open up industrial country markets and phase out trade-distorting subsidies—particularly in agriculture—which seriously limit the ability of poorer countries to compete in areas where they would otherwise have a comparative advantage. This would directly support growth and reform efforts in the poorest countries, and would ultimately also be to the benefit of the richer countries themselves. More generally, the recent decision by the United States to raise tariffs on steel products is regrettable, and has already led to the prospect of retaliation from other countries. It will be essential for all countries to make renewed efforts to resist protectionist pressures, and to ensure that substantive progress is made with multilateral trade negotiations under the Doha round.

North America: A Strengthening Recovery

In the *United States,* activity remained weak during the second half of 2001, but there are increasingly strong indications that recovery is under way, as the negative effects of the September 11 events have proved more moderate than earlier feared. Manufacturing output has begun to turn up, including in the high-tech sector; the housing market has remained strong; retail sales have remained surprisingly robust, although aided by auto incentives; and initial jobless claims have fallen back, while the unemployment rate, which would generally still be increasing at this stage of the cycle, remains below its December 2001 peak. Forward-looking indicators, including business and consumer confidence, have picked up significantly, equity markets have rebounded after September 11, and the yield curve has steepened. At the same time, aided by the earlier decline in oil prices and substantial excess capacity, inflationary pressures remain moderate.

With activity expected to accelerate significantly in the first half of 2002, the recent recession is likely to be the mildest on record. While the decline in fixed investment and inventories has been similar to previous downturns (Figure 1.6), private consumption has remained surprisingly strong. This has been supported by the substantial reductions in interest rates, and tax cuts over the past year; strong wage growth; widespread auto incentives, which—after netting off the inventory draw down—boosted GDP growth by an estimated ¾ percentage point (annualized) in the fourth quarter; the strength of house prices (which appears to have offset a significant portion of the impact on consumption from lower equity prices—see Chapter II); and lower oil prices.

Given signs of a sharp turnaround in inventory adjustment in early 2002, as well as the substantial stimulus that is already in the pipeline, the staff's projections envisage a strong recovery in activity in the first half of the year, falling back somewhat thereafter as the effects of these two factors begin to dissipate. The risks to the projection appear broadly balanced, and are importantly linked to the process by which the various

---

[8]See "Working for a Better Globalization," address by the Managing Director to the Conference on Humanizing the Global Economy, January 28, 2002 (www.imf.org/external/np/speeches/2002/012802.htm).

Figure 1.6. United States: Recessions and Recoveries
(Percent unless otherwise indicated)

The U.S. recession has been remarkably mild compared with previous experience, and the pace of recovery is correspondingly projected to be somewhat more moderate. The low level of private saving and the high corporate financing requirement remain potential brakes on activity.

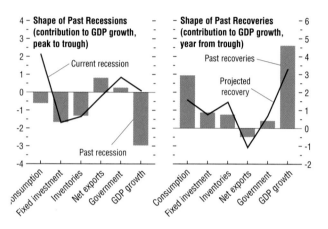

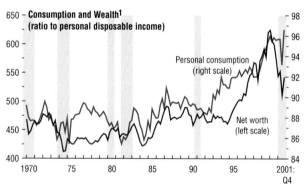

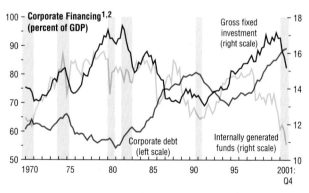

Sources: Haver Analytics; and IMF staff estimates.
[1] Shading indicates business cycle from peak to trough.
[2] All data for nonfinancial corporate business sector.

imbalances in the economy—notably the high current account deficit, low personal savings rate, and relatively large financing requirement in the corporate sector (Figure 1.6)—are resolved. On the one hand, it is certainly possible—given the size of the stimulus in the pipeline—that activity will recover more strongly than projected. While this would be welcome in a number of respects, it could—as discussed above—exacerbate these imbalances, especially if growth in other countries disappoints. On the other hand, there remain questions about the sustainability of a pickup in final domestic demand. In particular, private sector investment could be constrained by excess capacity and weak profitability (although the improvement in the fourth quarter of 2001 is welcome); and private consumption growth could be dampened if consumers seek to increase savings and rebuild balance sheets, Both of these could be exacerbated by a correction in equity markets, which still appear richly valued. This would likely result in an earlier correction in imbalances, but at the cost of a more subdued U.S. and global recovery. Finally, much continues to depend on external developments, including the speed of recovery in the rest of the world, oil prices, and geopolitical developments.

In assessing the appropriate stance of policies, policymakers need to take account of the risks and costs related to the uncertainties on both sides of the forecast, within a longer-term policy framework that is consistent with a gradual reduction in the imbalances in the economy over time. With clear evidence that recovery is under way, the Federal Reserve noted in March that the risks to economic growth and price stability had become more evenly balanced. Provided signs of economic strength continue, attention will soon need to shift to withdrawing the substantial stimulus provided last year. On the fiscal side, the combination of the June 2001 tax cuts and the emergency spending measures passed in the aftermath of the terrorist attacks, along with the operation of the automatic stabilizers, has provided substantial support to the economy. This has come, however, at the cost of a significant deterioration in the fiscal position; the administration's recent budget—adjusted to take account of the latest stimulus package as well as the faster than expected recovery—provides additional stimulus in 2002 and would result in budget deficits (excluding the social security surplus) persisting into the medium term. Moreover, with the budget based on relatively optimistic assumptions with regard to the containment of non-defense expenditures, even this may prove difficult to achieve. With economic activity improving, efforts will now need to focus on returning the budget to broad balance (excluding social security) over the medium term, and to address the longer-term financial problems in the social security system. This would help manage the pressures associated with the aging population, as well as being supportive of adjustment in the current account deficit.

Given the strong trade and financial linkages, *Canada* was strongly affected by the faster than expected slowdown in the United States, and experienced a mild downturn in the second half of 2001. As activity slowed, and with core inflation at the lower end of the 1–3 percent target band, the authorities eased monetary policy substantially during 2001; at the same time, the exchange rate depreciated to near historically low levels in real effective terms, which is helping to cushion the impact of the external slowdown and weak commodity prices. Fiscal policy has also provided support through the operation of the automatic stabilizers, previous expenditure and tax measures, and a moderate discretionary stimulus in the 2001/02 budget. Aided by the pickup in the United States, growth rebounded in the fourth quarter of 2001, and economic indicators suggest that a strong recovery is now under way. With the economy expected to reach its potential output sometime during the next year, the process of withdrawing monetary stimulus also will likely need to begin in the near term.

Japan: Significant Challenges Remain

Japan is experiencing its third—and most severe—recession of the past decade. While the proximate causes of the current downturn in ac-

tivity include a variety of domestic and external factors, including falling consumer confidence and the global slowdown, the inability to achieve sustained growth over the past decade reflects the failure to deal decisively with deep structural impediments (a pattern also seen in other countries, as discussed in Chapter III). This is most urgent in the case of the banking system, whose difficulties go back to the bursting of the asset price bubble in the early 1990s.

Short-term prospects are a source of considerable concern. Output is expected to fall by 1 percent in 2002 after a decline of ½ percent in 2001, as the pronounced weakness in private demand seen in 2001 continues through the first half of 2002 even as external demand revives, a path consistent with the results of the March *Tankan* survey and the depressed levels of equity prices even after a recent rebound. To date, the fall in activity has been driven by both external and domestic developments. Exports declined in the face of the global slowdown and rapid fall in demand for IT goods. Consumption slumped since early 2001 as the unemployment rate has set new records, overtime hours have fallen, and real earnings have stagnated. Business investment showed some resilience over much of 2001, but weakened dramatically late in the year. The government announced a package to combat deflation late in February, including a restatement of its intention to proceed with the disposal of nonperforming loans (NPLs) and an explicit commitment to take any necessary measures to ensure the stability of the financial system. The package also sets out new measures such as strengthened regulation of short selling of equities. While growth in 2002 could be more rapid than projected—most notably if recovery comes more speedily in the rest of the world and the IT cycle rebounds more rapidly than currently anticipated—downside risks predominate given the difficult domestic environment.

Weak growth over the 1990s reflects a failure to deal decisively with structural weaknesses, especially in the banking system. Since the mid-1990s, bank equity prices have been falling relative to the rest of the market (which has also

Figure 1.7. Japanese Policy Dilemmas

Japan's financial problems are reflected in the falling relative equity price of the banking sector and in the decline in bank lending. Meanwhile, deflation is intensifying and real interest rates are rising. Current fiscal plans involve a significant withdrawal of stimulus later this year, while debt ratios continue to climb.

Banking System

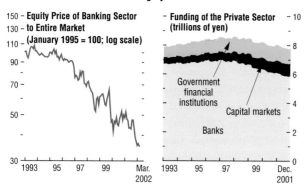

Monetary Policy

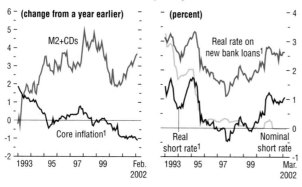

Fiscal Policy
(ratio to potential GDP unless otherwise indicated)

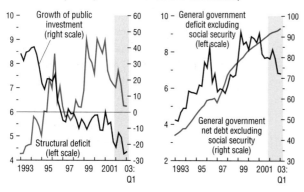

Sources: CEIC Data Company Limited; Nikkei Telecom; Nomura Security; and IMF staff estimates.
[1]Adjusted for changes in indirect taxes in 1997.

been on a downward trend, eroding bank capital held in the form of equities), and loans to the private sector have been declining (Figure 1.7, top panels). Despite past deregulation of the financial system—most notably the "big bang" completed in 2000—and its accomplishments so far, the level of direct financing from capital markets remains limited (Bank of Japan, 2001). These bleak trends have in many respects worsened since mid-2001, with NPLs remaining at high levels despite large write-offs, the relative equity prices of banks falling further (partly as a result of recent regulatory actions imposing greater market discipline on banks), increasing real interest rates on bank loans, and, more recently, a significant increase in bank borrowing costs for debentures and certificates of deposit, especially for weaker banks.

The banking sector will be a significant impediment to sustained recovery unless decisive action is taken. Progress has been made in tackling banking sector reform and the allied issue of corporate restructuring. In particular, the Financial Services Agency (FSA) has tightened NPL classifications for banks and strengthened the role of market forces through initiatives such as mark-to-market accounting. However, the FSA should further its efforts to encourage banking sector restructuring through more accurate classification of problem loans (where the FSA's special audits will be critical), rapid disposal of a wide range of such loans (which will also help with corporate restructuring), encouraging banks to raise further private capital, and, if appropriate, targeted injections of public money. The basis for effective corporate restructuring has been laid through a number of welcome initiatives, including the introduction of consolidated corporate taxation and reform of the commercial code, but rapid disposal of problem loans and a more aggressive industrial deregulation policy are needed to push this process forward.

On the macroeconomic front, policymakers currently face the difficult task of supporting the implementation of structural reforms in the face of very limited room for monetary and fiscal maneuver. Monetary policy should be used aggressively to address deflation, thereby lowering real interest rates and supporting activity, while the fiscal stance should remain broadly unchanged and be flexible to changing economic conditions. This policy advice partly reflects the following assessment of two key policy questions.

- *How effectively can monetary policy support activity?* Despite zero nominal short-term interest rates, deflation means that short-term real rates are positive and, if anything, rising (Figure 1.7, middle panel). Monetary policy should be clearly focused on reviving activity by ending deflation; evidence from the U.S. Great Depression indicates that aggressive quantitative easing can be effective in this regard, especially if financial sector issues are also tackled. To this end, the Bank of Japan has recently raised its target for excess bank reserves from over ¥6 trillion to ¥10–15 trillion, as well as raising its purchases of government bonds somewhat. Reserves will need to be kept at or above the ¥15 trillion upper range to engineer a continued rapid expansion of the monetary base. Quantitative easing and official pronouncements have recently been associated with a weakening of the yen, which will help revive external demand. However, further easing will be required if deflationary forces do not abate soon, including a commitment to end deflation within a relatively short time period.

- *Is high and rising government debt reducing the effectiveness of fiscal policy?* The initial budget for FY2002/03 implies a ½ percentage point of GDP withdrawal of stimulus, concentrated in the second half of 2002 when spending increases earlier in the year associated with the second supplementary budget of 2001/02 are expected to be rapidly reversed (Figure 1.7, lower panels). A timely supplementary budget should be considered to mitigate fiscal contraction in the latter part of 2002 to avoid the outcome in 1997, when aggressive consolidation plans helped to propel the economy into a recession. At the same time, it should be recognized that experience in a number of European countries suggests that policies to curb high and rising debt levels can have confidence effects that reduce the impact of fiscal contraction on activity. The evidence to date on Japan is more ambiguous, although potential further downgrades of Japanese government debt by credit rating agencies appear to reflect concerns over debt sustainability. This underlines the need to set any further provision of stimulus within a concrete medium-term plan for fiscal consolidation to boost confidence and make current policy commitments more credible, including ending the earmarking of tax revenues, and reform of public enterprises and of the health care system.

The Japanese recession, and the possibility that an easing of monetary policy would result in a further weakening of the yen, has raised concerns about the consequences for the rest of the region. The Japanese economy and exchange rate have significant regional impacts (see Box 1.4 of the October 2001 *World Economic Outlook*). Even so, given the increased exchange rate flexibility and strengthened macroeconomic cushions in the region since the Asian crisis, a depreciation of the yen would appear generally manageable (although the impact could be greater in those countries with fixed exchange rate systems). This could be particularly the case if yen weakness was a byproduct of a comprehensive package of structural and macroeconomic measures to restore sustained growth in Japan, which would clearly provide significant medium-term benefits to the region and the rest of the world.

How Will the Recovery in Europe Compare with That in the United States?

In Europe, GDP growth began to slow from mid-2000, and—after a temporary rebound in late 2000 and early 2001—continued to weaken in the remainder of the year. The speed and extent of the slowdown, as well as the degree of synchronization with the United States, has taken most forecasters and policymakers by surprise. To a considerable extent, it has been due to the commonality of shocks, including the rise in oil prices during 2000, the bursting of the technology bubble, and the repricing of global

Figure 1.8. European Slowdown
(Percent)

The slowdown in Europe has been more moderate than that in the United States. However, there are substantial differences across countries, which mainly reflect consumer behavior.

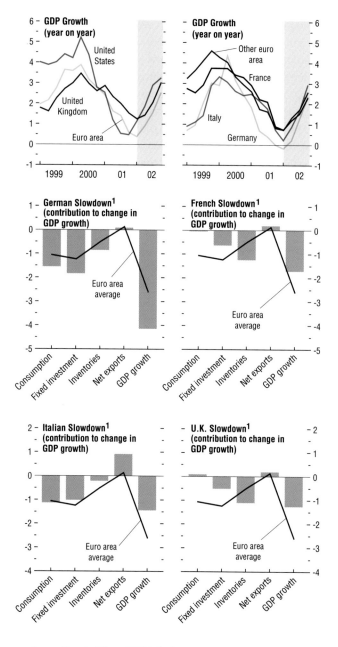

Sources: Haver Analytics; and IMF staff estimates.
[1]Defined as the difference between average annualized GDP growth rate during 2000:Q2 to 2001:Q4, and the year to 2000:Q2. The remaining variables show the contributions of consumption, fixed investment, inventories, and net exports to the change in GDP growth.

equity markets, but also increased corporate and financial linkages with the rest of the world. Europe-specific factors—notably animal diseases—have also played a role, as has the strength of cross-country linkages, particularly among the euro area countries.

Partly as a result, the nature of the slowdown has become increasingly similar to—although less steep than—that in the United States. Since mid-2000, the major countries have all experienced a weakening in fixed investment and inventories (Figure 1.8), and falling export growth (although this has been offset by lower import growth, resulting in some strengthening in net exports). The extent of the slowdown has differed considerably across countries, being particularly marked in *Germany*—which has experienced a technical recession (i.e., two quarters of negative growth)—*Belgium, the Netherlands,* and, particularly since the second quarter of 2001, *Italy.* In contrast, growth in *France* and the *United Kingdom* has in general been better sustained; and growth in *Spain*, while slowing, has also remained above the euro area average. The differences in the depth of the slowdown appear to reflect domestic, rather than external, factors. In particular, consumption behavior has differed markedly across countries, weakening significantly in Germany and Italy, but remaining surprisingly strong in the United Kingdom and France, buoyed by relatively strong real wage growth, stronger labor market conditions, and, in the United Kingdom, rising house prices.

In the euro area, although activity and demand remain weak, signs of recovery have begun to emerge. Business confidence—and to a lesser degree consumer confidence—have improved: the German IFO business climate index has risen for five successive months; indices of purchasing managers' sentiment have strengthened; and industrial production has begun to rise. Overall, GDP growth is expected to turn up in the first half of 2002, slightly behind the pickup in the United States, spurred by a turnaround in the inventory cycle, recent monetary policy easing, the strengthening external environment, and the past decline in oil prices. While there is relatively little policy stimulus in the pipeline compared with the United States, there are also fewer macroeconomic imbalances to constrain recovery (although equity markets in some countries appear highly valued); and corporate profitability remains strong, which should help support a rebound in fixed investment. The main risks to the outlook include a weaker-than-expected upturn in Germany, given its size and close links with other euro area countries; structural weaknesses, particularly in labor markets; and a further increase in oil prices. Among individual countries, the Argentine crisis has adversely affected some banks and corporations in Spain, although there do not appear to be systemic risks; the high current account deficit in *Portugal*—projected at 9 percent of GDP in 2002—and the rising debt burden associated with it, are also of concern.

As growth has slowed, inflationary pressures have eased. After a temporary pickup early in the year due largely to temporary factors, including a modest impact from the changeover to the euro, area-wide CPI inflation has since moderated. Headline inflation is expected to fall below 2 percent in the coming months, underlying inflation remains moderate, and wage growth is reasonably subdued (although much will depend on ongoing wage negotiations, especially in Germany, as well as oil price developments). Since mid-2001, the European Central Bank (ECB) has reduced interest rates by 125 basis points; with growing signs of recovery, the monetary policy stance appears broadly appropriate. On the fiscal side, most countries have appropriately allowed the automatic stabilizers to operate, resulting in a widening of the area-wide deficit in 2001 and 2002. In Germany, the fiscal deficit in 2002 is projected to be close to the 3 percent deficit limit specified in the Stability and Growth Pact (SGP). While measures to meet SGP commitments may need to be taken in Germany if further budgetary shortfalls emerge, at present the risks do not appear to warrant immediate action—action that would seem, however, to be called for in the case of Portugal, par-

ticularly if the authorities' planned deficit review indicated that the deficit would breach the 3 percent limit. Once the recovery takes hold, it will be important for those countries with significant structural deficits to achieve an enduring strengthening in fiscal positions, an opportunity that was missed in the late 1990s; this in turn will require, inter alia, that countries stick to the expenditure targets set out in their Stability Plans even if revenues exceed expectations. This will ensure that fiscal policy is able to play an adequately supportive role during subsequent downturns, as well as help address increasing fiscal pressures from aging populations.

The introduction of euro notes and coins is an historic step, and has been accomplished remarkably smoothly (Box 1.3). By increasing price transparency and reducing transactions costs, it will be a powerful force promoting greater economic integration. To maximize the benefits from the introduction of the euro, it will be important to move forward with structural reforms, both in the financial sector and in other areas. Despite important initiatives in a number of countries, the pace of reform has not in general accelerated since the Lisbon European Council in mid-2000, which set out an ambitious agenda for economic and social renewal. At the Barcelona Summit in March, further progress was made in liberalization of energy markets, and EU leaders reaffirmed their intention to accelerate the reform process, including through swift implementation of the Financial Services Action Plan. Reforms in all areas are clearly closely interlinked, but two—labor markets and pension reform—appear to be of particular importance. While progress has been made in reducing taxation of labor and in encouraging part-time work, notably in France and some of the smaller European economies, labor markets remain relatively inflexible and there remains a need to increase wage differentiation (Germany and Italy) and to strengthen incentives for the unemployed to find work (Germany and France). On pensions, the adoption of a privately funded pension pillar in Germany is an important step forward, but

Box 1.3. The Introduction of Euro Notes and Coins

On January 1, 2002, nearly 10 years after the signing of the Treaty on European Union and 3 years after the launch of EMU, cash euros entered circulation in 12 European countries with more than 300 million inhabitants.[1] Despite the unprecedented scale of the operation, the changeover went remarkably smoothly. In short order, the euro—which had been available as an electronic means of payment and was used in financial markets since 1999—had replaced the former national currencies in virtually all cash transactions.

The immediate macro implications of the changeover appear to have been modest, yet the shift to euro pricing is expected to produce long-term benefits in the form of increased price transparency, competition, and integration across the area. While the lack of historical precedent makes it difficult to judge the associated gains in economic efficiency and living standards, many proponents believe that they may be substantial. However, wide-ranging supporting measures are still needed to maximize the gains from market integration.

One-Off Effects

The changeover appears to have had only modest short-term macroeconomic effects. Competitive forces and a relatively weak cyclical position helped to ensure that cases in which retailers took advantage of the redenomination to raise prices (including a bias toward rounding up when setting new "attractive prices") were broadly offset by price-cutting elsewhere, particularly among large retailers seeking to win market share by promising to round prices down. The small changeover-induced increase in the CPI (estimated to be at most 0.2 percent in January, although some increase may have occurred already in 2001) plausibly reflects a tendency to bring forward planned price changes rather than a sustained increase in margins.

Beyond the short term, increased cross-border price transparency and arbitrage are expected to act as a force for lower prices (see below).

The total circulation of banknotes in the legacy currencies declined by one-fourth during 2001 (corresponding to about 1½ percent of GDP) as cash held for store-of-value purposes was either deposited with banks, spent (and then deposited by the receiver), or exchanged for foreign currency. Some of this cash had been held in the informal economy, and some abroad. Most of the currency held abroad (roughly ½ percent of euro area GDP in 2000) was returned before January 1, 2002, after being deposited or exchanged at foreign banks.

Anecdotal evidence of a pickup in sales of luxury items and cars in late 2001 may have been related to spending of hoarded cash—although the increase in retail sales in November also represented a bounce-back from very weak conditions after September 11 and should be seen in the context of a budding revival in confidence.[2] Spending of hoarded cash may further affect the timing of purchases in early 2002. In addition, shifts in the relative holdings of cash and deposits (affecting the money supply via the money multiplier) have rendered the interpretation of money aggregates for policy purposes more delicate than usual. Finally, despite fluctuations in the euro exchange rate around the time of the changeover, the transition does not appear to have had lasting consequences for the currency.

Longer-Term Benefits of Cash Euro: Price Transparency and Increased Integration

The more durable and important implications of the changeover stem from the facilitation of price comparisons across the area when all countries use the same unit of account. Regulatory obstacles to market integration will also seem more glaring and pressure to remove them is likely to intensify.

The main author is Mads Kieler.

[1]The euro area comprises Austria, Belgium, Finland, France, Germany, Greece, Ireland, Italy, Luxembourg, the Netherlands, Portugal, and Spain.

[2]There have also been reports of greater demand for property in parts of the euro area.

Currency unions, price convergence, and trade integration

Although price levels will continue to vary across the euro area as they do across other currency areas—owing among other things to differences in indirect taxes and nontradables prices—the transparency induced by the euro is likely to strengthen price convergence. In conjunction with enabling factors such as better communications, convergence pressures will intensify at both the wholesale and retail levels as well as for nontradables (at least in border regions). Parsley and Wei (2001) show that institutional currency stabilization—in the form of currency boards or currency unions—promotes price convergence far beyond an incremental stabilization of the exchange rate. Between them, currency unions are more effective than currency boards.

By the same token, the institutional commitment to far-reaching integration that is part and parcel of adopting a common currency may promote trade integration far beyond exchange rate stabilization. Although hotly contested, several recent studies suggest that countries trade much more when they share a common currency than when they do not, and that euro-area countries stand to reap substantial welfare gains from the single currency (e.g., Rose, 2000, and Rose and van Wincoop, 2001; for a critique, see Persson, 2001). Perhaps the most important channel through which currency union can have large trade effects is by acting as a catalyst for the removal of a wide range of administrative, legal, and regulatory impediments to integration.

Financial market integration

In financial markets, the euro has already acted as a compelling force for integration—although by doing so it has exposed a web of remaining barriers to cross-border operations

stemming from both private and public policy practices. The arrival of cash euros may only have a small direct effect on retail financial services, but it could well strengthen the constituency for removing such obstacles. Recently, political agreement was reached on a directive to bring the costs of cross-border retail payments in line with national payments, and EU institutions are working on a Financial Services Action Plan (consisting of more than 40 individual measures) that aims to integrate financial markets by 2005.

Reaping the Gains from Integration

The example of financial markets illustrates the need for accompanying measures to allow European Monetary Union (EMU) countries to reap the full benefits of the common currency. The single market still needs to be completed— for example, through the liberalization of energy, gas, and other network industries, and by making progress on common standards. The European Commission's proposal to end exclusive car dealerships (which led to blatant price discrimination across markets) is a good example that the euro cannot achieve price convergence on its own but may be a catalyst for removing other hindrances to integration.

If the euro is successful in furthering the integration of product, capital, and labor markets, the adjustment to a more optimal allocation of resources may accelerate structural change and increase regional specialization. In the absence of sufficiently flexible product and labor markets, the potential of EMU would not be realized to the full, and countries could even find themselves worse off in the new regime. Consequently, the need for structural reforms that facilitate EMU members' ability to adjust to shocks and cope with secular change is more pertinent than ever.

more adjustments in the parameters of the system are likely to be needed; in Italy, it will be important to move forward rapidly with the consultative approach to pension reform that the

authorities propose. In France, reforms have remained on hold and should be a high priority for the new government following the upcoming elections.

In the United Kingdom, growth in 2001 was the strongest among the G-7 economies. Underlying this strong performance, however, were significant disparities in the various sectors of the economy. While private consumption remained strong, external demand weakened, which—along with the continued strength of sterling and weakening confidence in the aftermath of September 11—contributed to a sharp decline in manufacturing output, although this now appears to be stabilizing. During 2002, output growth is expected to remain relatively resilient, underpinned by the substantial interest rate cuts last year, the projected fiscal stimulus in the 2002/03 budget, and the global recovery. Against this background, the Bank of England has appropriately left interest rates on hold for the time being, although if consumption remains strong and the external recovery unfolds as expected, a policy tightening may have to be considered soon—especially given the potential imbalances in the economy, notably the high levels of household and corporate debt. The cyclically adjusted fiscal deficit should not rise above the path projected in the November pre-budget report, and—given the already sharp increase in public spending—caution will need to be exercised on introducing new expenditure measures.

In the countries of Northern Europe, the pace of recovery is expected to be somewhat faster than elsewhere on the continent, as domestic demand remains relatively solid and—given their open economies—they benefit commensurately more from the global recovery. In late March, *Sweden* (along with New Zealand) became the first major country to raise interest rates following the recent downturn. Among individual countries, activity is expected to be supported by tax cuts (*Norway* and Sweden), an improvement in the IT sector, a highly competitive currency (Sweden), and by generally strong labor market conditions. In *Switzerland*, GDP growth is expected to be more moderate, and—in part reflecting the continued strength of the franc—interest rates were recently lowered by 25 basis points.

Latin America: Resisting Spillovers from the Crisis in Argentina

Recent economic attention on Latin America has been focused on the crisis in *Argentina* and its implications for the rest of the region. The outlook for Argentina and the extremely difficult adjustment this country now faces are discussed in more detail below. With the possible exception of Uruguay, economic and financial spillovers from the Argentine crisis appear to have been generally limited to date—as indicated, for example, by the muted reactions of bond spreads in most other regional economies and their declining correlation with those of Argentina, together with other favorable trends in financial market access and the general stability of exchange rates over recent months (Figure 1.9). Substantial risks and uncertainties remain, however. For example, more severe spillover effects from the Argentine crisis may still lie ahead, especially if there is no rapid turnaround in policies, if confidence deteriorates further, and if the magnitude of losses for investors and bondholders ends up being greater than estimated so far. Regional economies may also adjust less smoothly than assumed in the current outlook to a sharp improvement in international competitiveness in Argentina. Beyond these concerns, conditions and prospects for individual countries will continue to be shaped by their external trade and financial links—especially with the advanced economies; by developments in commodity markets and other key sectors; by conditions in the world oil market; and by the stance of domestic macroeconomic policies and a range of country-specific factors.

Argentina's short-term economic prospects remain highly uncertain, but a significant contraction in output and acceleration of inflation during 2002 appear unavoidable. Domestic demand is likely to fall substantially this year, given the impact of rising unemployment, lower confidence, the freeze on bank deposits, and other downward pressures on incomes and spending. Exports are likely to pick up in response to the depreciation of the exchange rate and projected strengthening in regional and global economic conditions, although in the short run much will depend on a strengthening of trade financing. Correspondingly, with imports slumping and external financing largely cut off, the trade surplus is expected to strengthen further and the current account to move into surplus this year. The depth and duration of the downturn in Argentina will hinge primarily on the new government's economic program and on how effectively it is implemented. While many details of this program have yet to be announced, the broad outline of what is required to restore economic stability and growth is reasonably well defined. Of key importance will be reining in the fiscal deficit—despite a sharp fall in tax revenues—to a level that can be covered with available, noninflationary sources of finance; avoiding, in this regard, reliance on the printing of money to fund public spending; ensuring a functioning, solvent banking system; and promoting an open external trade regime.

Prospects for Latin America as a whole will be strongly influenced by economic developments in the advanced economies—both through trade links, which vary quite widely across the region in strength and direction (Figure 1.10), and through the financial flows that are needed to meet the region's high external funding requirements (Table 1.5). Such flows appear closely related to investor sentiment in the major financial centers and, as they become dominated by equity-based flows, may well be procyclical.[9] *Mexico* and other countries in *Central America* were hit hard in 2001 by the U.S. slowdown, and the *Caribbean nations* suffered from a downturn in tourism after September 11. With both of these influences turning around in 2002, growth among these countries should pick up strength during the year and return to robust rates in 2003 (Table 1.6). In addition to the recent rise in oil prices, strong policy credibility should help Mexico's prospects for a sound recovery: firm monetary and fiscal policies have been maintained during the economic downturn, including through a range of revenue-enhancing meas-

[9]See Chapter II of the October 2001 *World Economic Outlook*.

Figure 1.9. Western Hemisphere: EMBI Plus Spreads and Exchange Rate
(September 11, 2001 = 100, unless otherwise indicated)

Most Latin American financial markets have strengthened since the September 11 shock and shown little reaction to the crisis in Argentina.

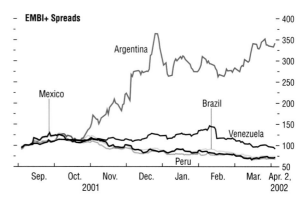

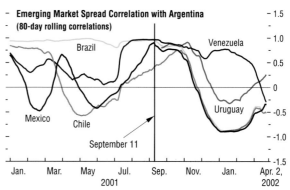

Sources: Bloomberg Financial Markets, LP; Haver Analytics; and IMF staff estimates.

Figure 1.10. Selected Latin American Countries: Export Shares, 2001
(Percent of GDP)

Exports account for a relatively low share of GDP in most Latin American countries and are diversified across advanced and emerging economies—apart from Mexico, which has close trade links with the United States.

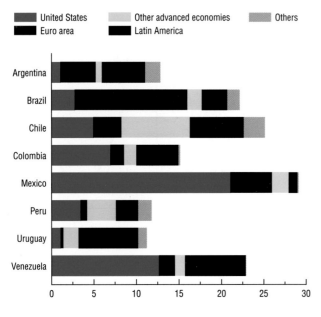

Source: IMF, *Direction of Trade Statistics.*

ures approved in the 2002 budget (although not the more comprehensive tax reforms originally envisaged). Reflecting this, financial market sentiment has remained favorable, with the peso appreciating against the dollar since September, inflation below its target level, and further upgrades to investment-grade status for foreign currency–denominated sovereign bonds. A continuation of these trends should provide some scope for a further lowering of borrowing costs, thus helping Mexico's public finances.

With recent indicators suggesting that trade performance is improving and domestic demand recovering, growth in *Brazil* is also expected to gain strength this year and next—helped by recoveries in the United States and Europe, further easing of the power crisis that hurt activity in 2001, and improving domestic confidence. Vulnerabilities remain, especially in view of Brazil's large (though declining) external financing requirement, although recent developments in this regard appear promising: improvements in market access are indicated by the successful placement in the first quarter of three government bond issues, more than covering the government's 2002 external amortization burden, and by strong foreign direct investment inflows. Monetary policy has eased modestly in recent months, but needs to remain vigilant so as to ensure the achievement of the inflation target, while fiscal policy remains on track. *Uruguay's* recent difficulties—including a widening bond spread, exchange rate pressures, and a downgrade of sovereign bonds from investment-grade status—have been exacerbated by its relatively high trade exposure to Argentina. But a core problem is Uruguay's vulnerability to exchange rate movements, given that public and private debt is mainly denominated in U.S. dollars—highlighting the need for measures to strengthen the fiscal position, ensure debt sustainability, and support the new more flexible exchange rate regime.

Countries in the *Andean region* have been affected both by the overall slowdown in global trade and, more specifically, by the weakening in certain commodity markets in 2001—notably those for oil (of particular importance for

Table 1.5. Emerging Market Economies: Net Capital Flows[1]

(Billions of U.S. dollars)

	1994	1995	1996	1997	1998	1999	2000	2001	2002	2003
Total[2]										
Private capital flows, net[3]	150.9	212.0	234.2	111.9	65.4	69.4	7.7	31.3	58.0	76.8
Private direct investment, net	80.8	100.1	117.0	142.7	154.7	163.8	153.4	175.5	157.1	165.7
Private portfolio investment, net	113.0	41.2	86.9	46.3	−4.6	33.9	−4.3	−30.2	14.6	15.8
Other private capital flows, net	−42.9	70.7	30.3	−77.2	−84.7	−128.2	−141.4	−114.0	−113.7	−104.7
Official flows, net	3.5	26.9	−1.5	64.9	60.5	13.7	5.7	37.2	32.7	15.2
Change in reserves[4]	−69.1	−116.7	−108.8	−59.8	−45.0	−85.8	−114.3	−134.3	−87.6	−60.6
Memorandum										
Current account[5]	−72.2	−92.4	−96.8	−69.0	−52.6	32.9	128.3	89.4	16.9	−16.7
Africa										
Private capital flows, net[3]	13.4	11.9	16.8	8.2	11.9	10.6	3.9	7.9	7.3	8.4
Private direct investment, net	3.2	2.1	3.8	8.0	6.5	8.9	7.3	22.2	10.8	11.8
Private portfolio investment, net	3.6	3.1	2.8	7.0	3.7	8.7	−2.4	−8.8	3.4	3.5
Other private capital flows, net	6.6	6.8	10.1	−6.8	1.6	−7.0	−1.0	−5.5	−6.9	−6.9
Official flows, net	3.3	4.1	−1.9	1.9	3.1	1.9	1.4	1.1	1.0	1.1
Change in reserves[4]	−5.5	−1.4	−8.9	−11.0	1.5	−3.4	−13.7	−10.5	−0.5	−5.5
Memorandum										
Current account[5]	−11.6	−17.3	−6.0	−7.2	−20.0	−15.3	3.1	−2.1	−10.8	−9.9
Developing Asia[6]										
Crisis countries[7]										
Private capital flows, net[3]	35.4	56.8	74.3	−5.6	−31.6	−13.9	−15.7	−16.2	−6.4	−3.9
Private direct investment, net	6.5	10.3	11.7	10.2	11.5	14.6	14.3	8.3	10.3	10.6
Private portfolio investment, net	13.3	18.6	26.9	8.9	−9.0	11.8	7.0	3.2	5.1	1.5
Other private capital flows, net	15.6	27.9	35.7	−24.7	−34.1	−40.4	−36.9	−27.7	−21.9	−16.0
Official flows, net	0.7	8.8	−4.7	13.7	17.0	−2.2	6.6	0.6	1.4	3.3
Change in reserves[4]	−6.5	−17.5	−4.8	40.6	−46.9	−38.2	−22.4	−11.7	−11.3	−12.1
Memorandum										
Current account[5]	−23.2	−39.8	−53.1	−25.5	69.7	62.7	47.1	32.6	23.1	17.9
Other Asian emerging markets										
Private capital flows, net[3]	34.9	40.7	46.0	19.6	−15.4	15.2	0.2	35.4	15.9	9.5
Private direct investment, net	38.2	44.1	43.9	47.3	48.3	47.3	40.1	45.2	49.2	50.1
Private portfolio investment, net	7.5	2.1	3.3	−2.1	−9.2	2.4	−2.6	−17.6	−4.3	−5.9
Other private capital flows, net	−10.8	−5.4	−1.2	−25.6	−54.4	−34.6	−37.3	7.8	−29.1	−34.7
Official flows, net	2.5	−3.3	−7.3	−6.6	3.1	3.8	−2.1	−2.0	4.0	4.8
Change in reserves[4]	−51.4	−25.4	−41.7	−46.8	−16.6	−38.6	−26.2	−80.7	−42.8	−34.4
Memorandum										
Current account[5]	18.3	8.5	14.7	51.4	41.0	32.7	35.8	54.7	42.1	36.9
Memorandum										
Hong Kong SAR										
Private capital flows, net[3]	−7.3	−7.2	−9.4	11.7	−8.5	1.0	4.2	−5.1	−9.9	−10.4

Venezuela and to a lesser extent *Colombia* and *Ecuador*), copper and other metals (*Chile, Peru*), and coffee (Colombia). In particular, Venezuela is facing severe political and economic pressures, which have affected domestic and foreign investor confidence. Notwithstanding the recent rally in oil prices, a substantial increase in government spending last year combined with lower oil output (under production cuts agreed with OPEC) has led to fiscal pressures, a weakening of the external current account, and a sizable loss of international reserves in the period through mid-February 2002. Subsequently, the authorities replaced the exchange band system by a floating exchange rate regime and announced a significant reduction in government expenditure relative to the 2002 budget level. Although these measures constitute a step in the right direction, the overall economic situation remains worrisome, particularly because the degree of fiscal restraint is not yet clear. Firmer policies are needed to strengthen the fiscal position and help reduce interest rates, improve the management of oil revenue, reduce the role of the state in the economy, and foster business confidence to stimulate private investment.

Table 1.5 *(concluded)*

	1994	1995	1996	1997	1998	1999	2000	2001	2002	2003
Middle East and Turkey[8]										
Private capital flows, net[3]	15.7	9.9	7.2	15.1	9.5	0.6	−24.0	−27.1	−10.2	−0.7
Private direct investment, net	4.8	6.4	4.7	5.2	6.3	5.4	7.3	8.5	8.5	9.7
Private portfolio investment, net	7.6	2.0	1.8	−0.9	−13.2	−3.2	−13.7	−10.2	−7.1	−4.6
Other private capital flows, net	3.4	1.4	0.7	10.8	16.3	−1.7	−17.6	−25.5	−11.6	−5.9
Official flows, net	3.5	4.5	6.6	9.3	2.9	2.4	−0.1	7.1	11.0	3.5
Change in reserves[4]	−4.7	−11.6	−22.2	−19.4	9.7	−6.5	−27.6	−14.3	−7.5	4.0
Memorandum										
Current account[5]	−5.7	−4.9	5.0	3.3	−23.3	11.7	63.1	42.9	10.5	−5.8
Western Hemisphere										
Private capital flows, net[3]	47.1	44.0	66.4	70.6	71.3	43.2	42.5	27.1	37.7	45.4
Private direct investment, net	22.8	24.2	40.3	56.2	60.6	64.1	61.6	67.2	46.3	53.1
Private portfolio investment, net	65.0	0.8	38.8	25.9	18.7	11.1	4.6	0.9	13.6	17.0
Other private capital flows, net	−40.7	19.0	−12.7	−11.5	−8.0	−32.0	−23.8	−41.0	−22.2	−24.7
Official flows, net	4.7	18.6	3.4	13.7	16.1	7.4	−0.5	29.1	11.8	2.2
Change in reserves[4]	4.0	−23.3	−29.0	−13.8	8.7	7.8	−2.8	1.7	−5.5	0.2
Memorandum										
Current account[5]	−52.2	−36.5	−40.5	−67.1	−90.7	−56.7	−47.9	−54.3	−50.2	−49.6
Countries in transition										
Private capital flows, net[3]	4.4	48.6	23.5	3.9	19.8	13.9	0.8	4.2	13.8	18.1
Private direct investment, net	5.3	13.1	12.5	15.8	21.4	23.4	22.8	24.0	31.9	30.3
Private portfolio investment, net	16.1	14.6	13.3	7.5	4.5	3.1	2.8	2.4	3.8	4.3
Other private capital flows, net	−17.0	20.9	−2.4	−19.4	−6.1	−12.6	−24.8	−22.2	−22.0	−16.5
Official flows, net	−11.2	−5.8	2.3	32.9	18.2	0.4	0.4	1.4	3.5	0.3
Change in reserves[4]	−5.1	−37.5	−2.3	−9.4	−1.4	−7.0	−21.5	−18.8	−19.9	−12.8
Memorandum										
Current account[5]	2.2	−2.4	−16.9	−24.0	−29.4	−2.2	27.1	15.6	2.2	−6.1
Memorandum										
Fuel exporters										
Private capital flows, net[3]	18.6	23.4	0.6	−16.6	−1.4	−24.2	−58.3	−38.8	−38.0	−23.2
Nonfuel exporters										
Private capital flows, net[3]	132.4	188.6	233.7	128.5	66.8	93.6	66.0	70.1	97.8	100.4

[1]Net capital flows comprise net direct investment, net portfolio investment, and other long- and short-term net investment flows, including official and private borrowing. Emerging markets include developing countries, countries in transition, Korea, Singapore, Taiwan Province of China, and Israel.

[2]Excludes Hong Kong SAR.

[3]Because of data limitations, "other private capital flows, net" may include some official flows.

[4]A minus sign indicates an increase.

[5]The sum of the current account balance, net private capital flows, net official flows, and the change in reserves equals, with the opposite sign, the sum of the capital account and errors and omissions.

[6]Includes Korea, Singapore, and Taiwan Province of China.

[7]Includes Indonesia, Korea, Malaysia, the Philippines, and Thailand.

[8]Includes Israel and Malta.

Among other Andean nations, activity may remain subdued in most cases at least through the first half of 2002; but then, with non-oil commodity prices—including those for metals and coffee—expected to pick up as global demand firms (see Appendix 1.1), growth is generally projected to strengthen later in the year and in 2003. A strong recovery is expected in Chile, for example, helped by sound institutions. Low inflation has enabled the central bank to lower interest rates in early 2002, and other financial market indicators have also been positive. The pickup in Colombia may be more subdued, with the outlook clouded by uncertainties stemming from the breakdown of peace negotiations, forthcoming elections, and possible spillovers from economic difficulties in Venezuela. Progress with disinflation and fiscal consolidation, including pension reform, remains important in order to strengthen market sentiment and the base for sustained growth.

Table 1.6. Selected Western Hemisphere Countries: Real GDP, Consumer Prices, and Current Account Balance
(Annual percent change unless otherwise noted)

	Real GDP				Consumer Prices[1]				Current Account Balance[2]			
	2000	2001	2002	2003	2000	2001	2002	2003	2000	2001	2002	2003
Western Hemisphere	**4.0**	**0.7**	**0.7**	**3.7**	**8.1**	**6.4**	**8.2**	**7.4**	**−2.4**	**−2.9**	**−2.4**	**−2.5**
Mercosur[3]	**2.9**	**0.2**	**−0.9**	**3.0**	**5.0**	**4.9**	**10.5**	**9.7**	**−3.8**	**−3.7**	**−2.0**	**−2.1**
Argentina[4]	−0.8	−3.7	−10--−15	0–3	−0.9	−1.1	25–30	30–35	−3.1	−2.1	4.2	5.5
Brazil	4.4	1.5	2.5	3.5	7.0	6.8	6.1	3.9	−4.1	−4.6	−3.7	−4.1
Uruguay	−1.3	−3.1	−1.7	3.0	4.8	4.4	7.1	9.4	−2.7	−2.6	−1.7	−1.9
Andean region	**3.3**	**2.2**	**2.1**	**4.0**	**13.0**	**8.8**	**8.7**	**7.6**	**3.3**	**−0.1**	**−1.1**	**−1.3**
Chile	4.4	2.8	3.0	6.0	3.8	3.6	2.3	3.0	−1.3	−1.4	−1.8	−2.4
Colombia	2.8	1.5	2.5	3.3	9.2	8.0	7.1	5.3	0.4	−2.6	−3.2	−3.7
Ecuador	2.3	5.2	3.1	6.0	96.2	37.0	15.5	8.0	5.3	−4.6	−6.1	−3.1
Peru	3.1	0.2	3.7	5.0	3.8	2.0	1.8	2.3	−3.1	−2.0	−2.3	−2.7
Venezuela	3.2	2.7	−0.8	1.3	16.2	12.5	20.8	20.2	10.8	3.6	2.6	2.3
Central America and Caribbean	**6.0**	**0.2**	**1.9**	**4.6**	**8.8**	**6.6**	**4.5**	**4.0**	**−3.5**	**−3.2**	**−3.4**	**−3.3**
Dominican Republic	7.8	3.0	3.5	5.2	7.7	8.9	3.7	3.9	−5.1	−3.9	−4.8	−4.1
Guatemala	3.6	1.8	2.3	3.5	5.1	8.7	5.0	3.9	−5.5	−4.6	−4.5	−4.1
Mexico	6.6	−0.3	1.7	4.9	9.5	6.4	4.3	3.8	−3.1	−2.8	−3.0	−3.0

[1]In accordance with standard practice in the *World Economic Outlook*, movements in consumer prices are indicated as annual averages rather than as December/December changes during the year, as is the practice in some countries.
[2]Percent of GDP.
[3]Includes Argentina, Bolivia, Brazil, Paraguay, and Uruguay.
[4]Because of the high level of uncertainty regarding the economic outlook, projections for output and inflation in Argentina are presented as ranges. The regional aggregates are based on the midpoint of the range.

The Asia-Pacific Region: Turning the Corner

Most economies in the Asia-Pacific region have experienced a sharp fall-off in growth since 2000, but are now showing signs of a turnaround. The path has been largely driven by the external environment including the global electronics cycle, a sector that also contributed significantly to rapid recoveries following the financial crises of 1997–98 (see Figure 1.11). With most countries being oil importers, the oil price cycle has also affected activity, with high oil prices in late 2000 contributing to the subsequent weakening of incomes and demand in many countries, weaker oil prices in 2001 providing support for recovery, and recent increases in oil prices reducing this impetus. The opposite pattern is of course true for the region's oil producers. While Japan's prolonged economic difficulties have not prevented strong growth in other Asian economies over the past decade, Japan remains an important trading partner and source of capital for many of these countries.[10] These links, together with increased

concerns about the implications of the recent depreciation of the yen for other regional currencies (see below), suggest that the current contraction in Japan may be adding to weaknesses in the region more generally. Poorer external conditions during last year also spread into domestically exposed sectors, further lowering demand, confidence, and employment, with other economic and political uncertainties in some countries putting downward pressures on growth. Activity has remained relatively buoyant in China and to a lesser extent India, which are less dependent on external trade than other economies in the region, although they too have experienced a marked decline in exports, lower confidence, and some slowing in growth since 2000.

Recent economic indicators have generally provided encouraging signs about the prospects for recovery. Increases in semiconductor prices, orders, and shipments over recent months, together with the broader strengthening of activity now appearing in the United States and other

[10]See Box 1.4 of the October 2001 *World Economic Outlook*.

Figure 1.11. Asia: Slowdown In Electronics Exports

Across Asia, electronics exports as a share of GDP have fallen since 2000. Real exchange rates for most countries remain more depreciated than in the lead up to the financial crises of 1997–98.

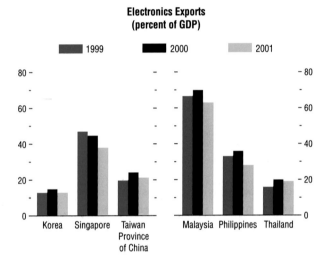

**Electronics Exports
(percent of GDP)**

**Real Effective Exchange Rate
(1995 Q1 = 100)**

Sources: CEIC Data Company Limited; and IMF, *Information Notice System.*

advanced economies, will support export performance and industrial production in Asia. Indeed, production has already picked up a number of countries (including *China, Korea, Malaysia,* and *Thailand*), as has consumer and/or business confidence, although increases in unemployment across the region may mute the pickup in household spending.

Financial sector indicators have also been generally positive. In particular, most equity markets have recovered from the September 11 shock and continued to rise in 2002, and bond spreads have declined to below their early September levels and shown little reaction to the turmoil in Argentina. Regional exchange rates have not moved substantially over recent months, although the depreciation of the yen has heightened concerns among policymakers in other Asian economies about their competitive positions, particularly China and Malaysia. While allowing more flexibility in the latter currencies would at some point be desirable to provide an additional buffer against external shocks, these and most other exchange rates in the region are still lower in real terms than before the Asian financial crisis of 1997 (Figure 1.11). Moreover, the external vulnerability of these countries has been lowered as a result of the buildup of reserves over recent years and reductions of short-term debt. These trends suggest that most Asian economies still have some capacity to absorb the effects of the weaker yen without this jeopardizing their international competitiveness or financial sector confidence.

Strong economic fundamentals have also allowed many regional economies to use macroeconomic policies in support of recovery. With inflation generally subdued, most countries have been able to ease monetary policy. Sizable fiscal packages have also boosted activity in several countries, although in some cases, notably *India, Indonesia,* and the *Philippines,* the scope for fiscal easing is constrained by already high levels of public deficits or debt.

Looking at the projections, activity in almost all countries is expected to pick up in 2002 and gain further strength in 2003 (Table 1.7).

Table 1.7. Selected Asian Countries: Real GDP, Consumer Prices, and Current Account Balance
(Annual percent change unless otherwise noted)

	Real GDP				Consumer Prices[1]				Current Account Balance[2]			
	2000	2001	2002	2003	2000	2001	2002	2003	2000	2001	2002	2003
Emerging Asia[3]	**6.9**	**5.0**	**5.6**	**6.2**	**1.8**	**2.5**	**2.3**	**2.8**	**2.8**	**3.1**	**2.2**	**1.8**
Newly industrialized Asian economies	**8.5**	**0.8**	**3.6**	**5.1**	**1.1**	**1.9**	**1.3**	**1.9**	**4.5**	**6.3**	**5.8**	**5.3**
Hong Kong SAR	10.5	0.1	1.5	3.6	−3.7	−1.6	−2.5	—	5.5	7.4	7.7	7.7
Korea	9.3	3.0	5.0	5.5	2.3	4.1	2.7	2.6	2.7	2.0	1.5	0.6
Singapore	10.3	−2.1	3.2	5.1	1.1	1.0	1.1	1.6	17.0	23.3	21.4	21.4
Taiwan Province of China	5.9	−1.9	2.3	4.8	1.3	—	0.4	1.6	2.9	6.7	6.6	6.6
ASEAN-4	**5.1**	**2.6**	**3.3**	**4.1**	**3.0**	**6.6**	**6.6**	**5.5**	**7.9**	**5.7**	**3.4**	**2.9**
Indonesia	4.8	3.3	3.5	4.0	3.8	11.5	12.4	8.2	5.3	4.5	1.8	1.4
Malaysia	8.3	0.4	3.0	5.5	1.6	1.4	1.8	2.5	9.4	8.2	5.8	5.3
Philippines	4.0	3.4	4.0	4.2	4.3	6.1	5.0	5.1	12.1	5.6	3.6	3.5
Thailand	4.6	1.8	2.7	3.5	1.6	1.7	0.6	2.7	7.6	5.4	4.0	3.1
South Asia[4]	**5.3**	**4.2**	**5.2**	**5.6**	**4.0**	**3.9**	**4.2**	**4.2**	**−1.2**	**−0.3**	**−0.7**	**−0.7**
Bangladesh	5.5	4.5	3.9	4.0	2.3	1.8	3.8	5.3	−1.6	−1.9	−1.8	−1.8
India	5.4	4.3	5.5	5.8	4.0	3.8	4.1	4.0	−0.9	—	−0.5	−0.5
Pakistan	3.9	3.4	4.2	5.1	4.4	3.8	3.7	4.0	−1.9	−1.2	−1.0	−1.4
Formerly centrally planned economies[5]	**7.9**	**7.2**	**6.9**	**7.4**	**0.4**	**0.7**	**0.4**	**1.6**	**1.9**	**1.7**	**1.0**	**0.4**
China	8.0	7.3	7.0	7.4	0.4	0.7	0.3	1.5	1.9	1.7	1.1	0.5
Vietnam	5.5	4.7	5.3	7.0	−1.7	0.1	4.9	3.7	2.1	1.7	−1.6	−2.9

[1]In accordance with standard practice in the *World Economic Outlook*, movements in consumer prices are indicated as annual averages rather than as December/December changes during the year, as is the practice in some countries.
[2]Percent of GDP.
[3]Includes developing Asia, newly industrialized Asian economies, and Mongolia.
[4]Includes Bangladesh, India, Maldives, Nepal, Pakistan, and Sri Lanka.
[5]Includes Cambodia, China, Lao People's Dem. Rep., Mongolia, and Vietnam.

Among the newly industrialized economies, the recovery in global activity and in the electronics sector should support modest growth in *Hong Kong SAR, Singapore,* and *Taiwan Province of China* in 2002 following sharp downturns in 2001, and firmer growth is expected in Korea, where the recovery appears to be more advanced. While activity should gain momentum during the year and into 2003, the rebound is not expected to be as strong as that seen in the late 1990s—especially as the rapid growth of investment and exports associated with the information technology sector in that earlier period appears unlikely to be repeated. Domestic sources of growth in these countries may become more important than in the past, therefore, as will ongoing efforts to broaden their manufacturing and export base. Steady pickups are projected for the Association of South East Asian Nations (ASEAN) over 2002 and 2003, also stemming in part from the stronger external environment. Especially in

Indonesia, the Philippines, and Thailand, however, the structural problems that muted their recoveries following the 1997–98 downturns continue to place a damper on current conditions and the outlook. Hence, the strength and robustness of growth in the period ahead will be contingent on progress with reforms needed to strengthen financial and corporate sectors, improve fiscal positions, and boost international and domestic confidence.

Growth in China is expected to be about 7 percent in 2002, supported by robust domestic demand. External demand, however, will continue to contribute negatively to growth, as China's recent entry to the World Trade Organization (WTO) will boost imports, especially of capital goods, more rapidly than the global recovery will increase exports. The recent easing of monetary policy is appropriate, especially as deflationary pressures have reemerged and real interest rates have been edging up. China's vulnerability to weaknesses in external demand and confidence appears to be limited, given its high reserves, favorable debt indicators, and rising FDI inflows; as noted above, a gradual move to a more flexible exchange rate regime would also be desirable. But ongoing progress with structural reforms and meeting associated fiscal challenges will be key in sustaining strong medium-term growth (Box 1.4). In this regard, the stronger competition that is likely to arise from WTO membership will increase pressures for reform in such sectors as agriculture, manufacturing, and banking. Reform priorities include the intertwined issues of restructuring the state-owned enterprises, reforming the banking sector—especially addressing the substantial non-performing loans problem in the state-owned commercial banks—and redesigning the pension system. The capacity of the new asset management companies to dispose of assets effectively also needs to be enhanced.

In India, a modest pickup of growth to 5½ percent is expected in 2002, with robust service sector activity and a projected record level of agricultural output helping to offset lingering weaknesses in external demand and industrial production. As in China, India faces a comfortable external position, given its low current account deficit—reflecting, in part, buoyant transfers from nonresident Indians—together with high reserves and strong capital inflows. The main concerns surrounding the medium-term outlook stem from the continued difficult fiscal position—the public sector deficit is again expected to be over 11 percent of GDP in 2001/02—and inadequate progress with structural reforms. These pressures need to be tackled by moving ahead with fiscal consolidation as envisaged in the fiscal responsibility bill, addressing fiscal pressures at the state level, and implementing the ambitious set of reforms proposed by the Prime Minister's Economic Advisory Council.

Growth in *Pakistan* weakened in 2001 under the impact of the global slowdown, increased regional uncertainty arising from the conflict in Afghanistan and heightened tensions with India, and a fall in cotton production. External bal-

ances have improved, however, contributing to an appreciation of the exchange rate and hence to lower inflation and interest rates. These trends, in the context of firmer global activity and improvements in the regional security situation, should support stronger growth in the period ahead. Also needed to sustain this improved outlook will be ongoing commitments to strengthen the fiscal position—particularly by ensuring adequate revenue performance—and to push ahead with structural reform, where there has been encouraging recent progress with privatization and financial sector reforms. With the conflict apparently winding down and political stability returning, *Afghanistan* should be able to begin laying the groundwork for economic and social recovery (see Box 1.5). Key measures, which will need major financial and technical backing from the international community, are to restore the institutions and infrastructure needed to underpin economic activity. These steps would involve the enactment and implementation of legal and regulatory reforms, the establishment of effective monetary and fiscal arrangements, and a liberal exchange and trade system, to ensure reconstruction under a stable macroeconomic environment.

Growth in *Australia* and *New Zealand* has held up relatively well during the global slowdown. The housing sector has performed strongly in both countries—supported by lower interest rates and, in Australia, by incentives for first-time home buyers and by a rebound following changes in the tax regime. Although exports weakened in the second half of 2001, strong earnings growth in the first half, helped by lower exchange rates, also underpinned robust domestic activity during the year and contributed to a large reduction in each country's current account deficit. Looking ahead, recent improvements in confidence and in employment levels should broaden the base of growth this year and next—with growth of about 4 percent expected in Australia in 2002 and 2003 and 2½ to 3 percent in New Zealand. In New Zealand, given favorable developments in the domestic economy and the stronger external environment, the Reserve Bank raised its official interest rate by ¼ percentage point in March. It is important that the fiscal positions of both countries remain sound, despite some recent easing and potential pressures that may arise in the year ahead—especially in New Zealand, which faces an election year and where the public sector's role in the economy has expanded somewhat in the recent past.

European Union Candidates: Resisting the Global Downturn

Economic performance among the EU accession countries in central and eastern Europe generally held up well compared with other regions during the global slowdown. Not surprisingly, exports—which are largely directed to the European Union—have weakened significantly over the past year as external demand slowed. But this has been largely offset by relatively robust domestic demand, generally underpinned by lower inflation and interest rates, strong investment spending, and fiscal stimulus in several countries (Figure 1.12). There are two important exceptions to this pattern. In *Poland*—by far the largest of the 10 transition countries currently negotiating for EU accession—domestic activity has been weak and growth has slipped sharply since 2000. And *Turkey*—also an EU candidate, although formal negotiations have not yet begun—suffered a severe contraction in 2001 under the impact of domestic and external shocks, although a moderate recovery is expected in 2002. Looking forward, the emerging recovery in western Europe can be expected to provide support to activity in all of these countries in the period ahead, although the possibility of further oil price volatility is for many—including Turkey—an important risk.

Most of the EU candidates in central and eastern Europe continue to run high current account deficits—a potential source of vulnerability should international investor sentiment toward the region or toward individual countries change for the worse (Figure 1.12). So far, though, external financing flows have been well sustained, even during recent periods of height-

Figure 1.12. Growth and External Balances in Central and Eastern Europe

The strength of domestic demand has helped offset external trade weakness among many EU accession candidates, while robust direct investment inflows have contributed to the financing of current account deficits.

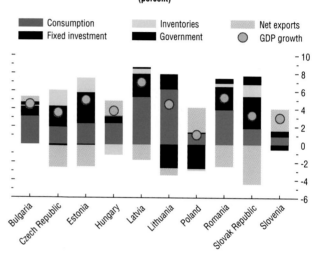

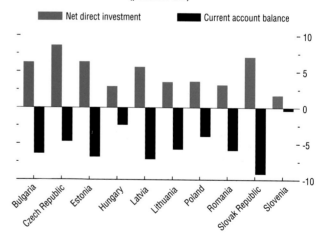

Box 1.4. China's Medium-Term Fiscal Challenges

Over the past two decades, China's progress in reforming its economy has resulted in sustained large increases in incomes and deep reduction in poverty. Despite these impressive achievements, a long reform agenda remains to be accomplished. While reforming the financial sector, restructuring the state-owned enterprises, and improving the social safety net are at the top of this agenda, intrinsically linked to these objectives is the need to assure the medium-term sustainability of China's fiscal situation.

At first glance, fiscal sustainability may not appear to be a pressing issue for China. The official debt stock is low and the state budget deficit modest. Official data show that the state budget deficit[1] has hovered at relatively low levels over the last 20 years (see the figure). While the budget deficit widened somewhat in the wake of the Asian crisis, it gradually narrowed over the past two years (to about $3\frac{1}{3}$ percent of GDP in 2001, from its recent peak of 4 percent of GDP in 1999).[2] Reflecting the low state budget deficits, the stock of explicit government debt stood at 23 percent of GDP at end-2000,[3] of which 18 percent of GDP was domestic.

Fiscal activity in China, however, extends well beyond the official state budget. For example, following the formal separation of state-owned

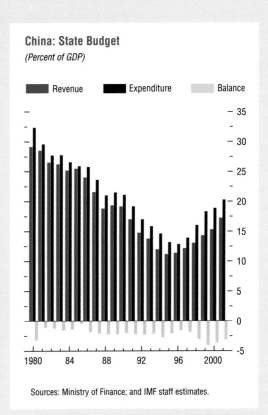

China: State Budget
(Percent of GDP)

Revenue ■ Expenditure ■ Balance

Sources: Ministry of Finance; and IMF staff estimates.

The main author is Raju Jan Singh.

[1]Including funds borrowed by the central government and on-lent to local governments and official external lending to government agencies, but excluding quasi-fiscal activities.

[2]From the early 1980s till the mid-1990s, both revenue and expenditure declined steadily. This was largely due to the separation of the financial accounts of state-owned enterprises from the budgetary accounts, which was undertaken to improve the state-owned enterprises' managerial and financial autonomy. The turnaround in revenue and spending since the mid-1990s reflects, in part, tax reforms that are still ongoing, and the fiscal stimulus packages introduced in response to the Asian crisis.

[3]Including bonds issued to recapitalize the four state-owned commercial banks in 1998, and bonds used for on-lending to local governments.

enterprise finances from the budget, the government extensively used the banking system to support state-owned enterprises, and a significant share of these loans have become nonperforming. The loan losses of the state-owned banks, although not legally a liability of the government, are likely to require additional state resources in the future.

If the government's quasi-fiscal liabilities from the banking system were included, the broader fiscal deficit and public debt-to-GDP ratio would be significantly larger. Although a precise estimation of these liabilities is constrained by data limitations, it is likely that the fiscal deficit including new nonrecoverable bank loans is currently on the order of 5–6 percent of GDP. The stock of nonrecoverable bank loans at end-2000 was estimated at between 50 to 75 percent of GDP (of which an amount equivalent to $15\frac{1}{2}$ percent of GDP has been transferred to asset management companies).[4] Hence, taking into account the stock of these loans would raise public debt to 75–100 percent of GDP (as of end-2000).

Furthermore, substantial pressures exist for additional public spending in the coming years.

- Over the next decade, China will need to increase its expenditure on health, education, poverty alleviation, infrastructure, and the environment to meet its stated development goals.
- Progress in state-owned enterprise reform will also entail costs, as the remaining social responsibilities (such as health, education, and pensions) carried out by these entities will have to be taken up at least partly by the government.
- The pension system will need to be reformed with potentially large fiscal costs. The current pay-as-you-go system (which covers mainly state sector employees) will require increasing government support in the long run as the ratio of contributors to beneficiaries declines. In addition, the government intends to move in time toward a new three-pillar nationwide pension system, with one pillar being a publicly funded minimum pension for all workers.[5]

[4]In 1999 and 2000, Y1.4 trillion of nonperforming loans from the state banks and one policy bank were transferred to four newly created asset management companies (AMCs). The AMCs have started disposing of these assets, including to foreigners, with the assistance of international investment banks. The losses of the AMCs will eventually have to be borne by the government.

[5]As currently envisaged, a nationwide three-pillar pension system would consist of a public pension, mandatory individual pension accounts, and voluntary supplementary individual accounts. A pilot provincial pension reform project was started in late 2001. The government also intends to use part of the proceeds from privatization (sales of state enterprise shares) to finance reforms.

- The current system of fiscal federalism, where each province is more or less fiscally independent, will have to be reexamined with a view toward ensuring that all provincial governments have sufficient resources to provide certain minimum standards of basic government services.

The fairly high level of total (explicit and contingent) debt, combined with the additional pressures described above, suggests that strong economic growth alone will not provide sufficient fiscal resources to meet the country's needs without an unsustainable buildup in public debt. Stabilizing the fiscal outlook will require

- dealing forcefully with the flow of new bad loans in the banking system, which is a key objective of the ongoing state-owned enterprise and banking reforms;
- reducing the state budget deficit further; given the expenditure needs foreseen, this will have to involve a continued strengthening of the revenue effort through improvements in tax administration and policy (sustaining the buoyancy of revenues), as well as further reorientation of spending to priority areas; and
- reforming the pension system through both parameter changes in existing pension arrangements (including raising the retirement age and increasing contributions) and careful design of new institutional arrangements.

Overall, China's fiscal position, while not calling for sharp and immediate corrective measures, will require a gradual but sustained adjustment effort over the medium term. With such an effort, including measures to reduce the budget deficit and to effect continued state-owned enterprise, financial sector, and pension reforms, the public sector debt burden could be contained and gradually reduced over the medium term.

ened uncertainty following the events of September 11 and the crisis in Argentina. Indeed, increasing optimism regarding these countries' prospects for EU accession in a few

years' time appears to be contributing to strong inflows of foreign direct investment (despite economic weakness in western Europe), which are also reflected in the robustness of domestic de-

Box 1.5. Rebuilding Afghanistan

Afghanistan is one of the poorest members of the Fund, following 20 years of conflict and a prolonged drought. The tasks ahead are daunting: much infrastructure is destroyed, key government institutions have been inoperative for the last six years. Transactions are cash-based, several currencies are circulating, and no banks are operative. Large parts of the population are displaced, and key social indicators are grim.

The Afghan Interim Administration (AIA) was established in December 2001 for six months, to be followed by a two-year transitional administration until a fully representative government can be elected. In January 2002, the donor community pledged over $4.5 billion for the next five years to assist the reconstruction efforts and finance current expenditure and reconstruction projects in the budget. Currently, however, actual foreign aid inflow is limited to humanitarian aid and payment of civil servant wages in Kabul, through an emergency United Nations Development (UNDP) Trust Fund.

Role of the IMF

The Fund's main task is to provide technical assistance and policy advice in its areas of expertise, to ensure a sound foundation for economic management, and to promote macroeconomic stability during the reconstruction period. This involves assisting in
- rehabilitation of basic institutions for the economy and for the government to conduct policy (such as Ministry of Finance and Central Bank); and
- development of a macroeconomic framework to guide decision making for a sustainable, noninflationary recovery.

Afghanistan may receive postconflict financial assistance under the Fund's Emergency Assistance Facility once there is sufficient capacity for planning and policy implementation. Once a medium-term economic strategy has been elaborated, the Policy Reform and Growth Facility (PRGF) could support reforms.

The main author is Ron van Rooden.

Although the central bank and key ministries survived, capacity for essential functions is weak. The IMF is providing technical assistance (TA) to the central bank for currency reform, basic payments system, and a minimum regulatory framework. On fiscal issues, TA is being extended to revive the treasury, prepare a budget, develop tax policy, strengthen revenue administration and expenditure management, and ensure accountability and transparency (of key concern to donors). TA is furthermore provided to rebuild the statistical base (no data has been collected in 6 years), while the IMF will also provide training.

In two key issues the IMF has been offering policy advice. First, currency reform: two domestic currencies now co-circulate (including one counterfeit), along with several foreign currencies. The authorities will at some point introduce a new Afghan currency, once sound financial policies and a well-developed institutional and legal framework are fully in place. IMF staff are advising the authorities on how to ensure a smooth transition from the present situation of co-circulating currencies to the introduction of the new currency. Second, the IMF and the World Bank assisted the authorities with the preparation of a budget for recurrent expenditures for the new fiscal year that started March 21, 2002. These expenditures are projected at about US$460 million and cover the payment of wages for about 220,000 civil servants and employees of state-owned enterprises and for the military, as well as essential operations and maintenance expenditures. Most of these expenditures will be financed by budget support from donors, although some $80 million is expected to be collected in revenues.

Regional Impact

Reconstruction should bring substantial benefits to neighboring countries. In the near term, some of the 3.5 million refugees are expected to return to Afghanistan, easing the burden on Pakistan and Iran. Imports for reconstruction are also expected to come largely from the neighbors; activity in Pakistan, such as the cement industry, has already been boosted. Over the longer term, a calmer regional political situation should improve plans for movement of natural resources, such as gas, across the region. Finally, establishing a strong customs and tax administration in Afghanistan should reduce smuggling across borders with neighbors.

Risks

Considerable risks remain. First, the security situation is still problematic. The AIA is in full control of Kabul, but not in the provinces, which prevents forward movement with country-wide economic reforms. Second, the interim government will be in office only until June 2002, and then will be followed by another transitional government; the possible lack of continuity among policymakers mitigates against taking difficult decisions. Third, while donors have pledged large amounts of financial assistance, delays in receiving actual cash resources may make it difficult to execute the budget.

mand and import growth. More generally, the EU accession process continues to provide a key anchor for the domestic policy agenda in these countries. This external discipline will be important, for example, in the context of current pressures for higher public spending that are being generated by economic or political tensions in several countries, and in ensuring that the region's generally sound macroeconomic performance can continue. Accession aspirations should also help these countries maintain the momentum of progress that is needed with fiscal reforms, privatization, other structural improvements, and environmental cleanups. Such macroeconomic and structural measures, in turn, will help ensure that the favorable climate for investment and growth is sustained.

Looking at developments and prospects for central Europe, activity remains particularly weak in Poland, reflected in falling employment and record-high unemployment. Given improvements in the current account, appreciation pressures on the zloty, and lower inflation—which ended 2001 well below the target range—the central bank has been able to lower interest rates significantly over the past year (including a reduction of 1½ percentage points in the intervention rate in late January). There should be scope for further monetary easing if weak economic conditions persist and inflation remains subdued. The combination of somewhat easier monetary conditions, improvements in domestic

confidence, and a stronger external environment is expected to lead to a steady pickup in growth this year and next (Table 1.8). Growth has been better sustained in the *Czech Republic*, *Hungary*, and the *Slovak Republic*, supported by relatively strong confidence and domestic demand, lower inflation and interest rates, and varying degrees of fiscal stimulus. A further increase in growth is expected in the period ahead—reaching about 4 percent in 2003—as exports pick up and domestic activity strengthens further. In this context, a winding back of fiscal support will be important—including in Hungary, where a large stimulus is currently expected in 2002—as such stimulus could make it more difficult to reach the key policy objectives of lower inflation, sustainable current account deficits, and medium-term fiscal consolidation. Strong domestic demand in the Slovak Republic has led to a particularly large increase in its current account deficit since 2000 and, while capital inflows have also been strong, this external vulnerability adds to pressures on the authorities to maintain a firm fiscal stance and to push ahead with privatization and other structural reforms.

Robust growth of about 4 to 5 percent is expected to continue in *Bulgaria* and *Romania*, accompanied by falling inflation and a gradual reduction in current account deficits. In Bulgaria, it will be important for the authorities to maintain a cautious fiscal stance to support the currency board and help ensure continued external

Table 1.8. European Union Candidates: Real GDP, Consumer Prices, and Current Account Balance
(Annual percent change unless otherwise noted)

	Real GDP				Consumer Prices[1]				Current Account Balance[2]			
	2000	2001	2002	2003	2000	2001	2002	2003	2000	2001	2002	2003
E.U. candidates	**4.9**	**0.4**	**3.1**	**4.2**	**24.7**	**21.1**	**17.7**	**11.5**	**−5.2**	**−2.9**	**−3.6**	**−3.6**
Turkey	7.4	−6.2	3.6	4.7	54.9	54.4	49.1	26.9	−4.9	1.4	−1.2	−1.2
Accession candidates	3.8	3.0	2.9	3.9	13.1	9.7	6.8	5.7	−5.3	−4.4	−4.5	−4.6
Baltics	**5.4**	**5.4**	**4.1**	**5.3**	**2.2**	**2.7**	**3.0**	**3.1**	**−6.3**	**−6.4**	**−6.4**	**−6.0**
Estonia	6.9	5.0	3.7	5.5	4.0	5.8	3.5	3.5	−6.4	−6.8	−6.8	−6.5
Latvia	6.6	7.0	4.5	6.0	2.6	2.5	3.0	3.0	−6.9	−7.1	−7.0	−6.4
Lithuania	3.9	4.5	4.0	4.8	1.0	1.3	2.8	3.0	−6.0	−5.8	−5.8	−5.5
Central Europe	**3.9**	**2.3**	**2.4**	**3.5**	**8.9**	**6.2**	**4.0**	**3.8**	**−5.3**	**−4.0**	**−4.1**	**−4.4**
Czech Republic	2.9	3.6	3.3	3.7	3.9	4.7	4.0	3.7	−5.6	−4.7	−4.8	−5.0
Hungary	5.2	3.8	3.5	4.0	9.8	9.2	5.4	4.0	−2.9	−2.4	−2.9	−3.5
Poland	4.1	1.1	1.4	3.2	10.1	5.4	3.2	3.2	−6.3	−4.0	−4.2	−4.5
Slovak Republic	2.2	3.3	3.7	3.9	12.0	7.3	4.3	7.0	−3.7	−9.2	−8.8	−7.9
Slovenia	4.6	3.0	2.6	3.6	8.9	8.4	6.5	5.5	−3.4	−0.4	−0.3	−0.4
Southern and south eastern Europe	**3.0**	**4.9**	**4.3**	**5.0**	**32.9**	**25.0**	**18.2**	**12.9**	**−5.0**	**−5.8**	**−5.2**	**−5.0**
Bulgaria	5.8	4.5	4.0	5.0	10.4	7.5	4.5	3.5	−5.8	−6.4	−5.9	−5.8
Cyprus	5.1	4.0	3.0	4.2	4.1	2.0	1.8	2.2	−5.2	−4.3	−3.9	−3.7
Malta	5.4	0.4	4.4	4.9	2.4	2.9	2.0	2.0	−14.8	−6.9	−5.7	−4.4
Romania	1.8	5.3	4.5	5.0	45.7	34.5	25.2	17.5	−3.7	−5.9	−5.3	−5.1

[1]In accordance with standard practice in the *World Economic Outlook*, movements in consumer prices are indicated as annual averages rather than as December/December changes during the year as is the practice in some countries.
[2]Percent of GDP.

and domestic confidence. Macroeconomic policies are broadly on track in Romania, with fiscal policy having been tightened in late 2001 and monetary policy striking an appropriate balance between achieving further disinflation and preventing an excessive appreciation of the currency. Further progress with structural reforms, including in the energy sector, remains important to help sustain the recent recovery in growth.

Turning to the Baltic countries, growth has slowed somewhat from the rapid pace of 2000–01. While domestic demand remains robust, export growth in *Estonia* and *Latvia* has declined—particularly as a result of the EU slowdown and, for Estonia, the additional effects of weaknesses in the information technology sector in Finland and Sweden. In contrast, exports from *Lithuania* have held up relatively well—possibly because Lithuania has greater trade exposure to other emerging markets in Europe—and this is expected to contribute to firm growth of about 4 percent this year. As in the other EU accession countries, however, high current account deficits remain of concern in the Baltic region.

While readily financed through foreign direct investment (FDI) and other inflows, such deficits require that macroeconomic policies remain well-disciplined—for example, in the face of fiscal pressures arising from prospective EU and NATO accession—and that the momentum of structural reforms be maintained, including privatization in Latvia and Lithuania. Sound fiscal and structural policies will also add support to these countries' hard currency pegs, which are at the center of their macroeconomic strategies; in this regard, Lithuania's move from a dollar to a euro peg in February 2002 went smoothly, without disruptions to financial markets or confidence, and should promote prospects for greater trade and financial integration with western Europe.

Turkey suffered its worst recession in over 50 years in 2001, with the events of September 11—particularly through their impact on trade, tourism, and financial market confidence—setting back the tentative signs of recovery that had been emerging following the economic and financial crisis at the start of the year. While recent real and financial have been mixed, GDP growth is expected to pick up to about 3½ percent in 2002, aided by low interest rates and rising confidence. There are significant risks in the outlook, however, in view of developments in the Middle East, Turkey's high public indebtedness, its record of persistent high inflation, and the need for bank and corporate debt restructuring. The projected recovery will therefore need to be underpinned by continued determined implementation of sound macroeconomic and structural adjustment policies. The IMF-supported program approved in February this year aims to maintain the reform momentum. On the macroeconomic side, this includes maintaining a firm monetary policy, which has already helped to reduce monthly inflation significantly, and a strong primary surplus to achieve a marked decline in government debt ratios. Restructuring efforts are designed to strengthen the banking sector, government operations, enterprise restructuring and privatization, and to encourage private sector development.

Commonwealth of Independent States (CIS): Continued Resilience

Growth in the CIS countries remained remarkably resilient to the global slowdown in 2001, falling only slightly to 6¼ percent, the highest growth rate among the major developing country regions. This was underpinned by continued solid growth in Russia, driven by strong domestic demand (Box 1.6, on pp. 46–47); activity also rebounded strongly in the region's second largest economy, Ukraine, aided by buoyant growth in the agricultural and industrial sectors. Given the strong trade and financial linkages, especially with Russia, this contributed importantly to the strength of activity in the rest of the region, helped in many cases by improved macroeconomic stability and policy implementation, as well as country-specific factors (including a rapidly emerging petroleum sector in Kazakhstan, strong revenues from the oil and gas sectors in Turkmenistan, and growth in cotton and aluminum production in Tajikistan). In general, asset markets (both stock markets and Eurobond

spreads) performed strongly in the CIS in 2001 compared with other regions.

In 2002, regional GDP growth is expected to slow to 4.5 percent (Table 1.9). Within this, GDP growth in Russia is expected to slow modestly to 4.4 percent, mainly due to lower oil exports and the lagged effect of the real appreciation of the ruble over the past year. Among the more *advanced reformers,* GDP growth is generally expected to fall back from the exceptional levels of 2001, partly as a result of slowing demand in Russia, but still to remain relatively resilient. In contrast, growth among the *less advanced reformers* is expected to fall to 2.0 percent, as the impact of the factors that boosted GDP growth in Tajikistan in 2001 fades, while the absence of structural reforms in Belarus and Uzbekistan continues to slow their growth.

Macroeconomic policy challenges vary significantly across the region. In *Russia,* the strength of the balance of payments—reflecting a combination of oil exports, a competitive exchange rate, and declining capital outflows—has continued to complicate economic management. During 2001, the expansionary impact of foreign exchange purchases by the central bank to prevent a nominal appreciation of the ruble was partially offset by a larger-than-expected fiscal surplus. Nonetheless, monetary aggregates grew rapidly and inflation exceeded the authorities' target. Even with the current account surplus expected to decline in 2002, the central bank will need to stand ready to sterilize excess liquidity as necessary to ensure the inflation target is achieved. In *Ukraine* and *Kazakhstan,* where the balance of payments has also been strong, price pressures eased. Fiscal adjustment played a key role in Kazakhstan, while for both countries the process of remonetization continued, allowing rapid monetary growth to be absorbed without an increase in inflation. However, the sharp increase in domestic credit accompanying this remonetization raises concerns with regard to both credit quality and risk, and needs to be carefully monitored.

Elsewhere in the region, inflation has fallen significantly during 2001, but remains a serious problem among a number of the less advanced

Table 1.9. Commonwealth of Independent States: Real GDP, Consumer Prices, and Current Account Balance

(Annual percent change unless otherwise noted)

	Real GDP				Consumer Prices[1]				Current Account Balance[2]			
	2000	2001	2002	2003	2000	2001	2002	2003	2000	2001	2002	2003
Commonwealth of Independent States	**8.3**	**6.2**	**4.5**	**4.6**	**25.0**	**19.8**	**13.4**	**10.5**	**13.3**	**8.4**	**4.9**	**3.3**
Russia	9.0	5.0	4.4	4.9	20.8	20.7	14.1	10.8	17.4	11.3	7.2	5.3
Excluding Russia	7.0	8.9	4.7	4.1	34.9	18.0	11.9	10.0	2.0	−0.6	−2.4	−3.0
More advanced reformers	**6.8**	**9.5**	**5.6**	**4.7**	**19.7**	**9.4**	**6.5**	**7.1**	**2.6**	**−0.8**	**−2.8**	**−3.6**
Armenia	6.0	7.5	6.0	6.0	−0.8	3.4	3.0	3.0	−14.5	−10.5	−9.6	−9.0
Azerbaijan	11.1	9.0	8.5	8.5	1.8	1.5	2.4	3.3	−2.4	−2.3	−23.4	−33.3
Georgia	1.9	4.5	3.5	4.0	4.0	4.7	4.6	5.0	−5.3	−5.6	−5.5	−5.8
Kazakhstan	9.8	13.2	7.0	5.1	13.3	8.3	6.4	5.1	5.0	−5.3	−3.9	−3.0
Kyrgyz Republic	5.0	5.0	4.5	4.5	18.7	7.0	6.1	5.5	−7.9	−6.2	−6.3	−6.5
Moldova	2.1	4.0	4.8	5.0	31.3	9.8	6.6	6.0	−8.4	−7.4	−8.1	−7.9
Ukraine	5.9	9.1	5.0	4.0	28.2	12.0	7.6	9.4	4.7	3.5	1.5	0.9
Less advanced reformers[3]	**5.1**	**4.6**	**2.0**	**2.7**	**89.4**	**45.1**	**27.6**	**17.8**	**−0.4**	**0.2**	**−1.0**	**−0.7**
Belarus	5.8	4.1	1.5	2.3	168.9	61.3	33.9	22.4	−1.8	1.7	−0.4	—
Tajikistan	8.3	10.0	6.0	5.0	32.9	38.6	10.5	7.6	−6.5	−7.4	−6.0	−5.2
Uzbekistan	3.8	4.5	2.2	3.0	25.0	27.2	22.2	13.5	1.3	−0.6	−1.0	−0.9
Memorandum												
Net energy exporters[4]	9.3	6.0	4.7	4.9	19.6	19.2	13.2	10.2	16.1	9.9	5.9	4.1
Net energy importers[5]	5.3	6.9	3.8	3.6	45.2	22.1	14.0	11.7	1.1	1.1	−0.3	−0.5
Highly indebted countries[6]	4.0	5.7	4.6	4.7	13.0	9.4	5.6	5.2	−8.4	−7.3	−7.0	−6.9

[1]In accordance with standard practice in the *World Economic Outlook*, movements in consumer prices are indicated as annual averages rather than as December/December changes during the year as is the practice in some countries.
[2]Percent of GDP.
[3]Updated data for Turkmenistan not available.
[4]Includes Azerbaijan, Kazakhstan, Russia, and Turkmenistan.
[5]Includes Armenia, Belarus, Georgia, Kyrgyz Republic, Moldova, Tajikistan, Ukraine, and Uzbekistan.
[6]Armenia, Georgia, Kyrgyz Republic, Moldova, and Tajikistan.

reformers—with the exception of *Tajikistan,* where a tightening of monetary policy led to a sharp fall in inflation through 2001—mainly as a result of excessive credit expansion to finance state-sponsored projects and to subsidize state enterprises. Beyond this, there are two major medium-term issues. First, the high level of external debt—averaging close to 200 percent of exports—among five of the poorest CIS countries (*Armenia, Georgia, Kyrgyz Republic, Moldova,* and Tajikistan) remains a serious concern. To address this, a number of these countries are implementing strengthened adjustment programs. Nonetheless, the outlook remains very difficult, particularly if external developments are worse than anticipated or GDP growth falls short of expectations, and additional external assistance may also be required. Second, with oil exporting countries accounting for about 80 percent of regional output, the region remains highly de-

pendent in developments in oil prices (Figure 1.13). To date, however, diversification has been limited—in Russia, for example, investment has been concentrated in the energy and transport sectors—in part reflecting the still difficult environment for private investment, including in some cases governance problems and the limited intermediation provided by underdeveloped financial systems.

The central challenge facing the region continues to be to accelerate progress in structural reforms—notably, institution building and governance, enterprise and financial sector restructuring, and transforming the role of the state—which with some exceptions has been relatively disappointing in recent years. In Russia, structural reforms have focused on strengthening the investment climate through a combination of tax reform, deregulation, strengthening property rights, and developing financial markets and institutions; and some progress is being made in other countries. In contrast, reforms in a number of countries have remained on hold, in part because progress is being blocked by vested interests that benefit from a situation of partial reforms. It is to be hoped that the acceleration of reforms in Russia will, given its central role in the region, also spur more rapid progress in other countries in the period ahead.

Africa: Solid Growth Despite a Weak External Environment

Despite the weak external environment, growth in Africa held up relatively well in 2001 compared with other parts of the world and, while slowing slightly, is still expected to be respectable in 2002 (Table 1.10). Although conditions and prospects vary widely across individual countries, the key influence on the outlook for much of the region continues to be the interaction between commodity market developments, the conduct of economic policies, and the extent of armed conflict and other sources of civil tension. Recent increases in oil prices are clearly supporting the outlook for Africa's oil producers, but are having a deleterious effect on the many other commodity exporters in the region, which include many of the poorest countries, despite some pickup in non-oil commodity prices. That said, both strong and weak performers can be found within each of these groups, with the quality of domestic policies and the extent of conflict having a key impact on whether countries have been able to resist the external downturn or not.

Growth among the oil exporting countries, including *Nigeria,* generally picked up in 2001 as a whole, supported by the carryover effects of higher oil prices in late 2000, and in the case of Algeria, an increase in public expenditures and a rebound in agriculture output following a severe drought in 2000. The pace of activity slowed among oil exporters during 2001, reflecting the combination of the subsequent decline in oil prices, lower OPEC production quotas, and the broader slowdown in the advanced economies, and is expected to slow further in 2002 despite

Figure 1.13. Commonwealth of Independent States: Managing Oil Price Volatility
(Percent of GDP)

Oil earnings have been correlated with current account balances and fiscal balances.

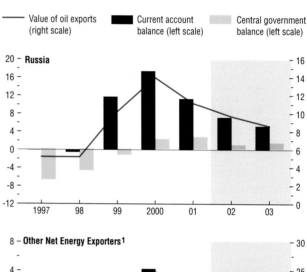
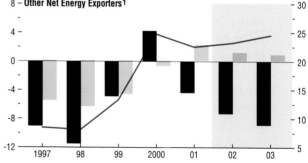

[1]Azerbaijan, Kazakhstan, and Turkmenistan.

Table 1.10. Selected African Countries: Real GDP, Consumer Prices, and Current Account Balance
(Annual percent change unless otherwise noted)

	Real GDP				Consumer Prices[1]				Current Account Balance[2]			
	2000	2001	2002	2003	2000	2001	2002	2003	2000	2001	2002	2003
Africa	**3.0**	**3.7**	**3.4**	**4.2**	**14.2**	**12.6**	**9.3**	**6.1**	**0.7**	**−0.5**	**−2.6**	**−2.3**
Maghreb	**2.8**	**4.7**	**3.1**	**4.2**	**1.3**	**2.5**	**3.8**	**3.3**	**7.1**	**5.8**	**1.8**	**1.8**
Algeria	2.4	3.5	2.3	3.4	0.3	4.1	5.6	4.4	16.8	11.3	4.9	4.6
Morocco	2.4	6.3	4.0	4.1	1.9	0.5	1.4	1.8	−1.7	3.0	0.7	1.0
Tunisia	4.7	5.0	3.8	6.4	3.0	1.9	3.4	3.0	−4.2	−4.2	−4.6	−3.8
Sub-Sahara[3]	**3.0**	**3.9**	**4.0**	**4.8**	**24.7**	**20.6**	**12.4**	**7.7**	**−2.0**	**−3.8**	**−6.4**	**−5.6**
Cameroon	4.2	5.3	4.6	4.9	0.8	2.8	2.9	2.5	−1.7	−2.3	−5.0	−5.0
Côte d'Ivoire	−2.3	−0.9	3.0	4.5	2.5	4.4	3.6	3.4	−2.8	−2.4	−1.7	−1.1
Ghana	3.7	4.0	4.5	5.0	25.2	33.0	15.9	10.2	−8.4	−4.0	−6.4	−5.1
Kenya	−0.2	1.1	1.4	2.4	6.2	0.8	3.2	3.9	−2.1	−2.5	−3.7	−4.3
Nigeria	3.8	4.0	−1.1	3.4	6.9	18.9	14.7	11.2	4.9	−0.2	−10.9	−5.5
Tanzania	5.1	5.1	5.5	6.0	6.2	5.2	4.4	3.9	−1.6	−1.6	−3.5	−3.4
Uganda	4.0	4.9	5.8	6.3	6.3	4.6	0.2	5.5	−9.0	−8.4	−9.1	−8.8
South Africa	**3.4**	**2.2**	**2.3**	**3.0**	**5.4**	**5.7**	**8.1**	**5.2**	**−0.3**	**−0.5**	**1.1**	**0.7**
Memorandum												
Oil importers	3.0	3.6	3.6	4.4	13.6	11.0	7.8	5.4	−2.8	−2.5	−3.3	−3.2
Oil exporters	3.1	4.1	2.7	3.5	16.3	18.0	14.6	8.3	10.6	5.0	−0.9	0.2

[1]In accordance with standard practice in the *World Economic Outlook*, movements in consumer prices are indicated as annual averages rather than as December/December changes during the year, as is the practice in some countries.
[2]Percent of GDP.
[3]Excludes South Africa.

recent rises in oil prices. This weakness is likely to be particularly severe in Nigeria, aggravated by fiscal policy and other domestic uncertainties (see below).

Despite signs of recovery in global output, many countries in Africa continue to face low prices for their non-oil commodities—including the very weak prices of coffee (a key export of *Kenya, Ethiopia,* and *Uganda*) and cotton (exported by *Benin, Burkina Faso, Cameroon, Chad, Côte d'Ivoire,* and *Mali*), and cyclical falls in most metals prices (affecting South Africa, *Ghana, Zambia,* and others). Relatively favorable growing conditions—especially the absence of the severe floods or drought that affected some countries in the late-1990s and 2000—are helping to support agricultural output across much of the region, although drought conditions continue in some parts of southern Africa, and severe food shortages are occurring in some areas. Countries with sizable tourism sectors—including *Morocco, Tunisia,* and *Kenya*—were hit by the sharp drop in travel and tourism following September 11, although this downturn does not appear to have been as sharp or prolonged as earlier feared.

Overall, the oil importing countries of Africa are expected to grow about 3½ percent on average in 2002, as in 2001. Most non-oil commodity prices are expected to pick up as global activity strengthens, supporting a further strengthening in growth among these countries in the period ahead.

Sound economic policies have also enabled a sizable number of African economies—including *Botswana,* Cameroon, *Senegal, Tanzania,* and Uganda—to offset the effects of export price weaknesses and the global slowdown, and instead to reach and sustain strong rates of growth over recent years (Figure 1.14). Progress is most apparent in the macroeconomic sphere, with a tight fiscal stance being maintained in many countries and inflation generally coming down (although remaining high in Ghana and Nigeria). However, uneven policy implementation has constrained growth in some countries (Kenya, *Malawi,* and *Seychelles*), while continued inappropriate economic policies and political turmoil have led to a marked contraction in economic activity and a surge in inflation in *Zimbabwe.* Structural reforms still lag behind in much of the region, and prospects for economic growth and diversification would be improved by better governance and public service delivery, including education, poverty alleviation, improving the security of property rights, and reducing corruption. Adding to these difficulties are poor infrastructure and insufficient liberalization. Conflict management also remains important, especially in sub-Saharan Africa; it is encouraging to note, however, that the number of countries involved in armed conflict has recently diminished, and this appears to be contributing to the sharp improvement in growth forecast for the group of countries affected by conflict over recent years.

Policies and initiatives at a multilateral level can also help to provide the basis for stronger growth in Africa. An important recent development within the region is the New Partnership for Africa's Development, which emphasizes African ownership, leadership, and accountability in improving the foundations for growth and eradicating poverty. In addition, 20 of the poorest countries have now become eligible for debt relief under the enhanced Initiative for Heavily Indebted Poor Countries (HIPC) and a number of others are expected to qualify in 2002. With this step, the countries concerned have been able to free up budgetary funds for public expenditure and investment—focused particularly on education, health, and other forms of human capital development—in accordance with commitments undertaken in their poverty reduction strategies. Further trade liberalization by the advanced economies—particularly opening their markets to agricultural goods and reducing their own production subsidies in this sector—would provide a major boost to the region's export performance and hence to prospects for sustained growth and poverty reduction. Ongoing international support is also needed to fight HIV/AIDS, which is taking a staggering toll on young and working age people in many southern African countries. Priorities include building up the medical infrastructure, better education, and making available advanced drug therapies to combat the pandemic.

Figure 1.14. Sub-Saharan Africa: Solid Growth in 2002 and 2003 [1]
(Per capita real GDP growth, percent)

After a strong pickup in 1995–96, per capita GDP growth has slowed markedly, mainly due to war and civil disturbances and commodity shocks. However, growth in countries with strong policies has been better sustained.

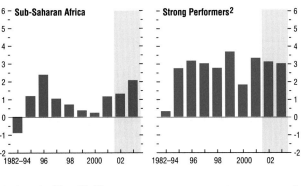

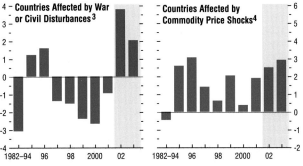

[1]Excluding South Africa.
[2]Countries with generally strong macroeconomics and structural policies; comprises Benin, Botswana, Burkina Faso, Cameroon, Mali, Mauritius, Mozambique, Tanzania, Senegal, and Uganda (24 percent of sub-Saharan African GDP).
[3]Countries experiencing war or significant civil disturbances during 1998–2000; comprises Angola, Burundi, Comoros, Congo, Dem Republic of, Congo, Republic of, Côte d'Ivoire, Ethiopia, Guinea-Bissau, Lesotho, and Sierra Leone (18 percent of sub-Saharan African GDP).
[4]Countries experiencing adverse commodity price shocks exceeding 10 percent in 2000 compared with the 1995–97 average; comprises Benin, Burundi, Burkina Faso, Central African Republic, Chad, Côte d'Ivoire, Ethiopia, Ghana, Madagascar, Mali, Mauritius, Rwanda, São Tomé and Príncipe, Tanzania, Togo, Zambia, and Uganda (31 percent of sub-Saharan African GDP).

Box 1.6. Russia's Rebound

Russia's economic performance since the 1998 crisis has far surpassed most observers' expectations. Growth rates have averaged 6 percent a year over the last three years, after almost a decade of output declines, while inflation has been gradually reduced to about 20 percent. Large precrisis fiscal deficits have turned into overall surpluses exceeding 2 percent of GDP; current account deficits have given way to surpluses exceeding 11 percent of GDP; and international reserves have risen to record levels (see the figure). Similarly, the authorities have not only formulated a wide-ranging structural reform program but, in marked contrast with earlier experience, have already secured approval of some of the crucial underlying legislation. Reflecting this, the Russian stock market has soared, yields spreads on sovereign debt have narrowed, and nonsovereign borrowers are regaining access to international capital markets, even as other emerging markets have faced sharp losses of confidence.

The sharp turnaround in Russia's macroeconomic performance stems from a combination of a large real depreciation, a major terms-of-trade improvement, and significant fiscal retrenchment. After the crisis, the *real effective exchange rate* depreciated by 40 percent, dramatically improving competitiveness, and it still stands about 15 percent below its precrisis level. In addition, Russia's *terms of trade* improved by about 45 percent between 1998 and 2000, as world prices for oil and gas, two key exports, strengthened considerably. This positive terms-of-trade shock (equivalent in magnitude to about 13 percent of Russia's GDP), combined with the real depreciation, led to a significant increase in industrial profitability and investment, and eventually to higher economy-wide real wages and consumption. The energy price increase directly accounted for more than half of the turnaround on the current account; it also strengthened fiscal balances, largely because of increased crude-oil export tariffs and gas excises.

Fiscal policy in general displayed considerable prudence after the crisis. Federal revenues rose as

The main author is Nikola Spatafora.

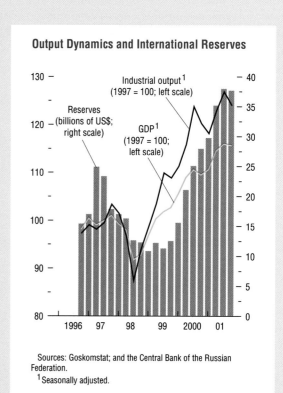

Output Dynamics and International Reserves

Sources: Goskomstat; and the Central Bank of the Russian Federation.
[1] Seasonally adjusted.

major efforts were launched to raise tax compliance, reduce tax arrears, increase the share of taxes paid in cash, and reverse the steady erosion of revenues in favor of the regions. Meanwhile, the authorities restrained noninterest expenditures, so that the federal government's primary balance strengthened by nearly 8 percent of GDP between 1997 and 2000. This fiscal effort both helped support a sustained reduction in inflation and contained the pressures for real appreciation and "Dutch disease," which would otherwise have arisen in the face of massive current account surpluses.

So far, Russia has weathered the slowdown in the world economy, reflecting the large share in its exports of oil and gas. However, some weakening of growth is expected in 2002. Further, the continued uncertainty about future developments in the external environment poses significant risks for the economic outlook. Staff estimates indicate that each $1 decline in Russian oil prices would lower GDP growth by 0.5 percentage points, export revenues by 0.6 percent of GDP, and government revenues by 0.4 percent of GDP. A significant worsening of the external environment and an economic slowdown could also undermine recently achieved gains in strengthening financial discipline, including the improved tax compliance and the reduced reliance on barter and non cash transactions.

At a more fundamental level, prospects for sustained growth depend critically on success in passing and, above all, implementing structural reforms. In the past two years, impressive progress has been made on a broad front. In particular, the investment climate has improved through a combination of tax reform, deregulation, strengthening property rights, and developing financial markets and institutions. *Tax reforms* simplified the tax system, broadened the tax base, and reduced the tax burden. Key elements included simplifying mineral-resource taxation, reducing turnover and payroll taxes, introducing a flat personal income tax with a marginally reduced effective rate, and lowering the statutory profit-tax rate while eliminating most exemptions. These reforms will significantly reduce distortions and—with continued improvements in tax compliance—ensure fiscal sustainability. *Deregulation and strengthening property rights* involved a significant reduction in the number of business activities requiring a license; a new Land Code, which allows ownership of urban land and significantly reduces the uncertainty associated with fixed investment; and a new Labor Code, which liberalizes hiring and firing procedures. New reform strategies for railways and the electricity sector aim to restructure, liberalize, and privatize potentially competitive segments. Some progress was also made with *financial sector reform*: the legal framework for banking supervision and restructuring was strengthened, a pilot scheme for adopting international accounting standards was initiated, and new anti-money-laundering legislation was enacted.

Nevertheless, after over a decade, much remains to be done to complete the transition process. For the immediate future, the authorities' agenda faces three challenges. First, continuing the financial sector reforms, and in particular strengthening finan-

cial regulation and supervision, as well as stimulating competition within the banking sector, including by clarifying the future role of the currently dominant state banks. Second, completing the negotiations on WTO accession. This will require agreement on tariff rates, passage of a new customs code, and measures aimed at broader business deregulation. Third, completing and implementing other reforms, including allowing trade in agricultural land; restructuring the gas sector; strengthening bankruptcy procedures to eliminate the current scope for asset-stripping; simplifying small-business taxation; increasing cost-recovery in public housing; and overhauling pensions and the judiciary.

Looking beyond Russia, its strong performance has supported economic recovery throughout the CIS, where growth averaged over 8 percent in 2000 and 6 percent in 2001. Russia's influence reflects both the relatively large size of its economy, accounting for about three-fourths of the region's GDP, and the generally close trade linkages within the region: the CIS forms a free-trade area, and typical export-to-GDP ratios are about 40–50 percent. Overall, Russia is the main export market for almost all CIS countries, absorbing on average over 25 percent of their total exports. Cross-border financial linkages with Russia are also significant; in the past, they mainly took the form of energy trade–related credits, but in recent years FDI flows have increased, as investment climates have improved. Looking ahead, staff estimates suggest that a slowdown in Russian growth of 2 percentage points would reduce average growth in other CIS countries by 0.5 percentage point. The largest impact would be in those countries with the closest trade links with Russia: growth in Belarus and Moldova could slow by 1 percentage point, with an even larger decline in Turkmenistan.

In sum, the rebound in Russia has been truly impressive. Prudent policies, aided by a large and positive terms-of-trade shock, have produced strong improvements in key macroeconomic indicators. The acceleration in structural reform and the commitment to strengthening the investment climate raise hopes that the rebound can be sustained and that Russia will continue to be an engine of growth for the region.

Looking at the region's largest economies, *South Africa*—which constitutes just under 40 percent of sub-Saharan African GDP—has experienced some slowing in growth as a result of lower commodity prices and the global slowdown. However, these influences are expected to turn around and contribute to a steady pickup later this year and in 2003. The rand continued to weaken in 2001, sharply so in the final quarter, but appears to have stabilized in early 2002—supported by an appropriate increase in interest rates by the central bank. The reasons for the sharp depreciation are not entirely understood, but seem to follow a pattern of similar exchange rate weakness in other countries, such as Australia, Canada, and New Zealand, where commodities comprise an important share of exports. In part, though, it may reflect growing regional uncertainties, including the turmoil in Zimbabwe, and delays in the implementation of the privatization program. Looking ahead, confidence in the currency should be supported by the expected closing in 2002 of the central bank's net open forward position, and by the maintenance of firm monetary policies to keep inflation under control and build credibility in the inflation-targeting regime. Also important—for the currency and for prospects more generally—will be ongoing fiscal restraint, progress with privatization, and structural reforms to improve the business climate, boost investment, and hence make inroads on extremely high levels of unemployment and poverty.

In *Algeria,* growth is expected to slip to under 2½ percent in 2002, owing partly to cuts in oil output. Activity continues to be sustained by an expansionary fiscal stance. Despite considerable economic and policy progress since the early 1990s, the Algerian economy still suffers from growth well below potential, high unemployment, and vulnerability to developments in energy markets.

The situation in Nigeria remains a source of concern despite recent increases in oil prices, as OPEC production cuts are taking their toll following a period of above-quota production. Fiscal policy has been too expansionary, particu-

larly in the context of oil market volatility; but monetary conditions have tightened considerably, with the central bank trying to offset the effects of fiscal expansion and to slow inflation. In addition, some parts of the banking sector appear to be in distress, and the system as a whole faces poor governance and supervision; and distortion in the foreign exchange market between official, interbank, and parallel market rates has increased. Domestic confidence has been further disrupted by recent disasters and incidents of conflict.

Middle East: Oil Price Volatility and Regional Security

Growth in the Middle East is projected to slow significantly in 2002, continuing the pattern of 2001, largely reflecting lower oil production and the regional security situation. For the developing countries in the region, growth is expected to slow in 2002, while in Israel, after a fall in activity in 2001 partly reflecting weakness in the IT sector, growth is expected to resume (Table 1.11). The curtailment of oil production associated with OPEC agreements to limit global supply has depressed activity in the oil exporting countries although recent increases in oil prices, if sustained, will help support growth. The security situation has also had a significant negative impact on activity, including tourism, in particular in the Mashreq countries and Israel.

For the oil exporting countries, growth is expected to slow from 5.0 percent in 2001 to 3.4 percent in 2002, largely reflecting lower oil production and the lagged impact of lower oil prices in late 2001. The slowdown in growth has generally been limited by the use of more prudent macroeconomic policies. In particular, the boom and bust cycle of the past associated with sharp increases and decreases in government spending as oil revenues rose and fell has been much more muted. As a result, current account and fiscal balances have broadly followed oil price developments (Figure 1.15). This pattern is particularly evident in the smaller Gulf states (*Kuwait, United Arab Emirates, Bahrain, Oman,* and

Table 1.11. Selected Middle Eastern Countries: Real GDP, Consumer Prices, and Current Account Balance
(Annual percent change unless otherwise noted)

	Real GDP				Consumer Prices[1]				Current Account Balance[2]			
	2000	2001	2002	2003	2000	2001	2002	2003	2000	2001	2002	2003
Middle East[3]	**5.3**	**4.5**	**3.1**	**4.4**	**9.8**	**8.0**	**9.5**	**8.3**	**12.1**	**6.9**	**2.5**	**−0.2**
Oil exporters[4]	**5.7**	**5.0**	**3.4**	**4.7**	**12.6**	**10.0**	**11.5**	**9.8**	**16.5**	**9.6**	**4.4**	**0.8**
Saudi Arabia	4.5	2.2	−0.5	3.2	−0.6	−1.4	—	1.1	9.0	4.9	−1.3	−6.5
Iran, Islamic Rep. of	4.9	5.1	5.3	5.1	12.6	11.7	15.0	12.0	12.5	5.4	4.6	1.7
Kuwait	1.7	2.7	−1.8	3.3	1.7	2.5	2.5	2.5	39.3	32.2	20.9	20.2
Mashreq[5]	**4.2**	**3.2**	**2.4**	**3.6**	**1.9**	**1.9**	**3.2**	**3.9**	**−2.2**	**−2.3**	**−3.8**	**−3.6**
Egypt	5.1	3.3	1.7	3.5	2.8	2.4	3.2	4.4	−1.2	—	−2.3	−1.5
Jordan	4.0	4.2	5.1	6.0	0.7	1.8	3.5	2.4	0.7	0.4	−0.3	−0.4
Memorandum												
Israel	6.4	−0.6	1.3	3.8	1.1	1.1	3.1	2.1	−1.2	−1.5	−1.7	−2.1

[1]In accordance with standard practice in the *World Economic Outlook*, movements in consumer prices are indicated as annual averages rather than as December/December changes during the year, as is the practice in some countries.
[2]Percent of GDP.
[3]Includes Bahrain, Egypt, Islamic Rep. of Iran, Iraq, Jordan, Kuwait, Lebanon, Libya, Oman, Qatar, Saudi Arabia, Syrian Arab Republic, United Arab Emirates, and Republic of Yemen.
[4]Includes Bahrain, Islamic Rep. of Iran, Iraq, Kuwait, Libya, Oman, Qatar, Saudi Arabia, and United Arab Emirates.
[5]Includes Egypt, Jordan, Lebanon, and Syrian Arab Republic.

Qatar). In *Saudi Arabia*, however, the slowdown in activity has been more pronounced, and growth is expected to be negative in 2002, partly reflecting the more difficult fiscal situation. In order to reduce inflation and avoid a sustained appreciation of their real exchange rates, oil exporting countries should maintain prudent macroeconomic policies.

The main policy priority, however, remains the need to diversify production into other sectors than energy, to make these economies less dependent on oil revenues. The benefits of past reforms can be seen in the increased availability of imported capital and intermediate goods in many countries. If these economies are to remain attractive to both foreign and domestic investors, however, a broadening and deepening of structural reform is required, including in the areas of trade and exchange rate reforms, price liberalization, financial sector deregulation, public enterprise restructuring and privatization, and labor market and social safety net reforms. Recently, progress in some of these areas has been made by the *Islamic Republic of Iran*, where expanding non-oil private sector activity is expected to provide significant support to activity, as a result of which growth in 2002 is projected at 5.3 percent, slightly higher than in 2001. The

Gulf Cooperation Council (GCC) countries, which already have liberal trade, exchange rate, price systems, and free movement of capital, have also taken some steps to promote private sector activity, resulting in a more gradual expansion in non-oil activity.

In the Mashreq, *Egypt* was adversely affected by the events of September 11, especially through lower tourism earnings. While there are indications that tourism is beginning to recover, the balance of payments is expected to show a sizable overall deficit in 2002. Growth is projected to slow to under 2 percent this year, down from 3.3 percent in 2001, before recovering in 2003. The depreciation of the Egyptian pound over the past 18 months will help strengthen Egypt's balance of payments performance, and continuing flexibility will also be important in the period ahead. On fiscal policy, the deficit has widened, partly reflecting the operation of automatic stabilizers, and a reduction in the deficit will be important as activity recovers. Steps to reinvigorate structural reform will be required to achieve the sustained strong employment growth needed to absorb Egypt's rapidly rising labor force and reduce unemployment. The situation in *Lebanon* remains extremely difficult, with a large fiscal deficit and government debt of over

Figure 1.15. Middle East: Responding to Oil Price Volatility
(Percent of GDP)

In most countries, the recent windfall increases in oil prices have been prudently used, and the projected decline in 2002–03 will be manageable.

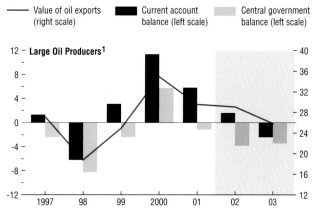
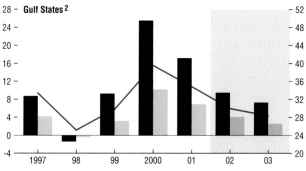

[1] Iran, Islamic Republic of, Libya, and Saudi Arabia.
[2] Bahrain, Kuwait, Oman, Qatar, and United Arab Emirates.

170 percent of GDP. The fiscal situation and the debt dynamics have led to a loss of international reserves of the central bank in the context of a fixed exchange rate regime, and a comprehensive policy package will be needed to achieve a sustainable macroeconomic framework. Owing to limited regional links, developments in Lebanon would be unlikely to significantly affect neighboring countries. In *Jordan,* growth in 2002 is projected to be 5.1 percent, boosted by strong performance in exports and additional fiscal stimulus under the authorities' Plan for Social and Economic Transformation. The government continues to build on its structural reform program.

After a fall in activity in 2001, largely reflecting weakness in exports as demand for IT goods decelerated rapidly and growth in the United States slowed, growth in *Israel* is expected to pick up modestly to 1.3 percent in 2002 as these effects reverse. This will depend, however, on an early and substantial improvement in the extremely difficult regional security situation, in the absence of which the growth rate will be considerably lower. The design and execution of fiscal policy have improved in recent years, but further progress with fiscal reform is needed as ratios of general government expenditures and of public debt to GDP remain high relative to those of many other advanced economies. The Bank of Israel's decision to raise interest rates by 0.6 percentage points in late February, partly reversing the 2 percentage point cut in December 2001, was aimed at confirming the Bank's commitment to medium-term price stability, against the background of potential inflation pressures stemming from the significant depreciation of the sheqel since the December easing. In the *West Bank and Gaza,* the security situation—in particular the border closure with Israel and internal blockades—has severely affected economic activity, which is estimated to have declined by over 30 percent in 2001. Economic conditions have worsened markedly in 2002 with the escalation of hostilities, which have inflicted widespread damage on physical infrastructure.

Appendix 1.1. Commodity Markets[11]

Recent Developments

Following the surge to $32 a barrel in the third quarter of 2000, crude oil prices weakened in reaction to the slowing world economy (Figure 1.16).[12] Despite a short-lived spike immediately following the September 11 terrorist attacks, prices tumbled to less than $19 a barrel by end-2001. In conjunction with lower crude prices, refining margins were compressed by weak product demand and mounting inventories. Heating oil consumption fell in response to unseasonably warm weather in North America, while jet fuel demand slumped amid cutbacks in travel activity.

The softening in world oil markets during 2001 occurred despite efforts by OPEC to maintain prices within the target range of $22–28. Production cuts of 3½ million barrels a day (4½ percent of global supply) were insufficient to offset falling demand, and prices fell well below the lower edge of the range. In December 2001, after negotiating commitments to cuts of close to half a million barrels a day with major non-OPEC producers, OPEC announced further cuts of 1½ million barrels a day to start in the beginning of 2002 for a period of six months. Against the background of these cuts, and with signs of unexpected strength in U.S. activity, oil market conditions firmed in early 2002 to close to $23 a barrel. These factors were reinforced in March and early April by fears of disruptions in supply due to possible military intervention in the Middle East and the deteriorating security situation in Israel and the West Bank and Gaza. As a result of these concerns, oil prices spiked up by early April to about $27 a barrel before falling subsequently as fears of significant disruptions of supply eroded. That said, the situation remains highly volatile, with oil prices depending as much on political as economic developments. To help assess future developments, Table 1.12 pro-

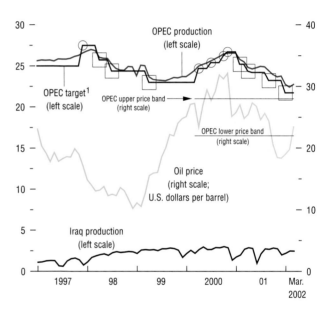

Figure 1.16. OPEC Target and Actual Production of Oil
(Millions of barrels per day unless otherwise indicated)

Source: Bloomberg Financial Markets, LP.
[1]Circles denote increases in OPEC target production and squares denote decreases in OPEC target production. In 2001, Iran announced it would move its April cuts to May.

---

[11]The main author is Guy Meredith.
[12]References to oil prices relate to the IMF's unweighted average of West Texas Intermediate (WTI), U.K. Brent, and Dubai crude oil prices.

vides some indicators of the impact of changes in oil prices on output and trade balances.

As regards demand, International Energy Agency projections show global oil demand growing by about 420,000 barrels a day in 2002, up about ½ percent over 2001. This would be similar to expectations of increased production by non-OPEC producers, including those not covered by production agreements. Hence, if OPEC's production cuts are maintained, but no further disruptions occur, this would result in a relatively stable balance between supply and demand in markets. The WEO baseline reflects such a scenario, with a weighted-average price of $23 a barrel in 2002 and $22 in 2003. As discussed above, the recent spike in oil prices appears to reflect market concerns over possible additional reductions in supply.

In undertaking production cuts, OPEC faces the issue of its declining share in global oil supply (Figure 1.17).[13] OPEC has traditionally produced almost 40 percent of world oil, and holds more than 77 percent of proven reserves. Its members include 11 of the top 20 world oil producers; OPEC also holds most of the world's excess capacity, as non-OPEC producers tend to produce close to their maximum output. This position has allowed OPEC to have a significant effect on the market at times when there are no major imbalances. Its share of the world market declined to about 36 percent in late 2001, however, following last year's production cuts, and could drop further to close to 35 percent this year if recent cuts are maintained. This decline could raise concerns in OPEC about a secular decline in their ability to influence the market, and an erosion of revenue in favor of alternative producers. The equilibrium in oil markets is thus likely to remain rather fragile as OPEC navigates the trade-off between losing market share and supporting prices.

Conditions in nonenergy commodity markets have remained basically unchanged in early

Table 1.12. Impact of a $5 a Barrel, Permanent Increase in Oil Prices After One Year
(Percentage points of GDP)

	Real GDP	Trade Balance
World GDP	**−0.3**	**—**
Industrial countries	**−0.3**	**−0.2**
United States	−0.4	−0.1
Euro area	−0.4	−0.1
Japan	−0.2	−0.2
Other	−0.2	0.2
Developing countries	**−0.2**	**0.2**
Of which:		
Latin America	−0.1	—
Asia	−0.4	−0.5
Emerging Europe and Africa	0.1	0.2

Source: IMF staff estimates based on IMF (2000).

2002, with global recovery prospects arresting the downward trend in prices through 2001. The staff's nonfuel price index rose by 2.9 percent in February over January, but remained 3.2 percent below the level a year ago. Metals prices, especially for copper and aluminum, have shown the clearest signs of recovery from recent lows, as they are perceived to be relatively sensitive to cyclical conditions. Gold prices also picked up early in the year, in response to falling equity prices and aggressive Japanese buying. But the fundamentals in metals markets have not changed significantly, and increasing stocks should dampen near-term price increases.

Market conditions for agriculture commodities have been mixed, as brighter global recovery prospects have been offset by rising supply. Wheat and sugar prices have been relatively weak in expectation of increasing exports from Argentina and Brazil, respectively. Cotton prices, in contrast, have shown some signs of strengthening from depressed levels; the outlook is clouded, however, by the risk that agricultural policies in industrial countries could further exacerbate problems of global oversupply.

The global market for semiconductors collapsed in 2001, with a decline in the value of

---

[13]OPEC's members are Algeria, Indonesia, Iran, Iraq, Kuwait, Libya, Nigeria, Qatar, Saudi Arabia, United Arab Emirates, and Venezuela. Although it remains a member of OPEC, Iraq is outside the quota system, with exports instead being currently governed by the U.N. food-for-oil agreement.

sales of about 30 percent, and in unit shipments of 20 percent. An important factor was a decline in global sales of personal computers—the first since 1986. The volatile market for memory chips was hit particularly hard, as prices plunged amid oversupply and rising inventories. Some signs of a turnaround in the market were evident toward the end of the year, however, as both prices and volumes firmed in response to a recovery in final demand for electronics products, and the closure of some production facilities as prices fell below production costs.

Assuming a general recovery in global activity, the semiconductor market is expected to regain momentum in 2002. In particular, the market for memory chips is showing signs of rebounding, helped by innovations such as double-data rate (DDR) technology and the erosion of inventories. The last major replacement purchases for computers took place in 1999 in anticipation of Y2K. With historical replacement cycles being in the range of 3–4 years, there will likely be significant demand for renewal of this equipment, although firms appear less willing to embrace new technology, as the operational boundaries of current hardware and software are not being pushed

Industrial reorganization is also affecting supply. Some traditional producers have suffered large losses during the recent slump, resulting in facilities' closures. There have also been merger talks among the largest producers of memory chips that would concentrate control of supply in the hands of fewer decision makers. Finally, China is becoming an increasingly important location for production.

Cyclical Movements in Nonfuel Commodity Prices

Commodity price movements appear to have closely tracked changes in the outlook for growth in major industrial countries recently. It is interesting to compare this correspondence with the typical historical relationship between commodity prices and activity. Looking ahead, most forecasters anticipate a pickup in global activity through 2002 and 2003: should this be expected to reverse the recent weakness in commodity

Figure 1.17. Share of World Oil Production of OPEC[1]
(Percent)

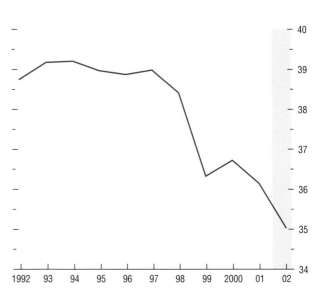

Sources: International Energy Agency; and IMF staff estimates.
[1]OPEC is defined here as not including Iraq, whose production amounts are affected by the Oil-for-Food program, and includes Natural Gas Liquids, which for our purposes are considered oil products.

Figure 1.18. Movements in Nonfuel Commodity Prices and G-7 Real GDP

(Annual log change multiplied by 100)

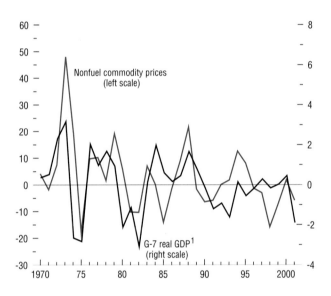

Sources: OECD; and IMF staff estimates.
[1]Adjusted by subtracting the mean of the log change from 1970 to 2001.

prices, or do current prices already reflect expectations of a future recovery in activity?

Conceptually, the relationship between commodity prices and activity in industrial countries will reflect both supply and demand factors. On the supply side, shocks in commodity markets that raise prices are likely to reduce output in importing countries; as industrial countries are, in aggregate, net importers of commodities, this would imply a negative correlation between prices and activity. On the demand side, higher activity in industrial countries will tend to raise world commodity consumption and thus prices.

Figure 1.18 shows the historical movements in nonfuel commodity prices and real GDP in G-7 countries from 1970 to 2001. A strong pattern of positive comovements between prices and activity is apparent, suggesting that demand shocks have dominated during the historical period; for the period as a whole, the correlation coefficient between the two series is 0.49. Commodity prices have been considerably more volatile than output, though, with typical annual movements about six times as large.

Against this background, the sharp declines in nonfuel commodity prices since the mid-1990s are somewhat anomalous, in that they have been associated with relative stability in G-7 GDP growth. Instead, they appear to have reflected, at least in part, the impact of the Asian financial crisis and external financing constraints on emerging market countries more generally, which put downward pressure on exchange rates of some commodity exporters and reduced demand outside of the industrial countries. Other supply factors, including improved technology and agricultural support policies in some developed economies, have also played a role. The further drop in prices in 2001 was, more typically, associated with the sharp slowdown in G-7 activity.

Looking ahead, an important question is whether the projected upturn in global activity in the period ahead will generate a rebound in nonfuel commodity prices. Taken at face value, the historical correlation suggests that it should, but the issue is potentially more complicated. In particular, one must address the question of whether current commodity prices already reflect expectations of global recovery. If they do, prices may not respond to the actual upturn when it occurs; if they do not, a rebound is more plausible. The answer depends on two factors—the relationship between spot and futures prices in commodity markets; and the extent to which futures prices already reflect recovery prospects. If futures prices are "efficient" in reflecting future growth prospects, and arbitrage is feasible between spot and futures markets, then current prices should embody future growth prospects. If these conditions fail, however, commodity prices could still pick up, even though the recovery in activity is generally expected.

The scope for arbitrage between spot and futures markets can be assessed by comparing prices in the two markets at a point in time. In general, in competitive markets, the futures price should exceed the spot price only by the financial and physical costs of storing commodities—otherwise, risk-free profits could be made by buying commodities in the spot market for future delivery. The financial storage cost is represented by the nominal interest rate, while the physical cost will vary from commodity to commodity. Figure 1.19 shows the relationship as of early February between the spot and futures prices for several non-fuel commodities. Gold is included as a reference price, because the low storage costs of gold and competitive markets make for efficient arbitrage. The pattern is mixed. For cotton and coffee, futures prices are well above spot prices, suggesting that storage opportunities are limited. The futures premium for wheat and copper, in contrast, is only moderately higher than that for gold. Finally, for sugar, the futures price is well below the spot price. This varied pattern among commodities raises questions about the general tightness of the link between spot and futures markets.

The second issue is whether futures prices accurately predict future spot prices. Futures prices will be the best available predictor if markets are efficient and investors are risk-neutral. Looking backward, these conditions could be assessed by comparing futures prices with those actually realized in spot markets to see whether the errors are systematic. A lack of long time-series data on futures and spot prices for identical commodities, though, makes this approach difficult to implement.

Rather than attempting to test separately for the predictive ability of futures prices and the scope for arbitrage between spot and futures markets for commodities, a more general approach is taken here to addressing the question of whether expected output movements are already reflected in existing commodity prices. This involves separating actual output growth into its expected and unexpected components. If futures markets are efficient and physical storage is costless, only the *unexpected* component of output growth should affect prices, after controlling for the impact of nominal interest rates on financial storage costs. If, in contrast, these conditions do not hold, *expected* growth should also play a role.

To distinguish between expected and unexpected output growth, the OECD's forecast for growth in aggregate real GDP of the G-7 countries was used as a proxy for expected growth (defined as the forecast published in December for the following year); the unexpected component was the difference between actual growth and this forecast. The 12-month change in commodity prices from December to December of the following year was then regressed on these two components of growth, as well as the December interest rate on 12-month U.S. treasury bills.[14] The results are as follows (*t*-statistics in parentheses):[15]

---

[14]The growth forecast is based on annual average data, while the commodity price change is December-to-December. This difference in definition should bias the results against finding a significant lagged effect from expected growth, because the December level of commodity prices would already embody part of the impact of the growth forecast. Hence, the lagged effect of expected growth is potentially stronger than the estimates indicate.

[15]The nominal change in the commodity price index was used as the dependent variable to be consistent with the use of the nominal interest rate as the financial cost of storing commodities. The slope parameters are very similar, and the overall fit somewhat higher, if the commodity price index is expressed in real terms by deflating by the U.S. CPI.

$$\Delta \ln PCOM = -0.10 + 6.1 \; growth\_expected$$
$$(1.0) \quad (3.3)$$
$$+ \; 3.2 \; growth\_unexpected - 0.7 \; tbill\_rate$$
$$(1.6) \qquad\qquad (0.6)$$

$$R^2 = 0.36 \qquad Sample \; period = 1970–2001$$

Interestingly, the coefficient on expected GDP growth is positive, significant, and large: an increase in expected growth of 1 percentage point is associated with a rise in the commodity price index of about 6 percentage points over the following 12 months. The coefficient on unexpected growth is only about one-half the size, and marginally significant at conventional levels. Finally, the (insignificant) negative coefficient on the interest rate is contrary to the value of +1 that would be expected if it captured the financial cost of storing commodities.

The strong role for expected growth is contrary to what one might expect if arbitrage were costless between futures and spot markets and markets were efficient. One implication, then, is that these conditions have not held over the historical period—consistent with the evidence for limited arbitrage provided above by the relationship between spot and futures prices. The relatively weak coefficient on unexpected growth is, at first sight, more difficult to explain. It can be rationalized, however, by considering the nature of the shocks underlying the correlation between commodity prices and unexpected growth. If these reflect a larger component of (unexpected) supply shocks in commodity markets, which in turn have a negative impact on activity in G-7 countries, the lack of a strong positive relationship between unexpected innovations in activity and commodity prices becomes more plausible.

Looking ahead, what would this relationship imply for nonfuel commodity prices? To answer this question, the expected component of growth was set to the WEO forecast for G-7 activity in 2002 and 2003, the U.S. interest rate was set to its WEO baseline value, and the unexpected component of growth was set to zero. Under these assumptions, the nonfuel price index is predicted to stay relatively flat in 2002,

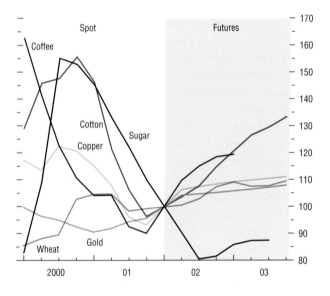

Figure 1.19. Spot and Futures Commodity Prices
(2002:Q1 = 100)

Source: Bloomberg Financial Markets, LP.

given the weak growth projection for G-7 output. Some recovery is then predicted in 2003 given the pickup in growth, but even then the rise is moderate, as the projected growth rate of G-7 output does not significantly exceed its average historical value. The implications of the regression, then, are that the strong historical relationship between expected output growth and commodity prices would not translate into a marked rise in prices over the next two years—growth would have to significantly exceed its historical average for this to occur.

Appendix 1.2. Weakness in Japan, Global Imbalances, and the Outlook[16]

This appendix explores how two underlying risks to the forecast—further weakness in Japan and global imbalances—could affect the outlook. The baseline contains a scenario in which recovery in the three main currency areas is relatively synchronized, as was the slowdown in activity in 2000 and 2001. In the United States and the euro area, recovery starts in early 2002 and gains momentum in the second half of the year, while in Japan there is a similar profile, albeit at lower rates of growth. As always, however, there is a high degree of uncertainty about the future path of output. This appendix explores some of the consequences coming from two of the more important risks and uncertainties to the outlook: the difficult situation in Japan, including the limited room for macroeconomic policy stimulus and continuing problems in the banking sector, which make the economy particularly vulnerable to unexpected negative shocks; and the limited progress made during the slowdown in reducing significant imbalances in the global economy, most notably the large current account deficit and low household saving rate in the United

States. This in turn reflects the synchronization of the slowdown in activity across most of the major regions of the global economy and, in particular, the inability of the euro area to maintain robust growth in the face of weakness in the United States. Combined with the mildness of the U.S. recession, this means there has been much less adjustment of the external imbalances across the major currency areas and of the U.S. household saving rate than had been anticipated in most "hard landing" scenarios (see, for example, Box 1.1 in the May 2000 *World Economic Outlook*). Consequently, many of the medium-term concerns over the late 1990s associated with the sustainability of the U.S. current account remain pertinent.

These observations are incorporated into an alternative scenario using the Fund's macroeconomic model, MULTIMOD, through the following assumptions:

- In *Japan*, a continuation of the deterioration in the financial system is assumed to increase the risk premium on all assets by 1 percentage point compared to baseline for the next 10 years. As a result, in early 2002 there is a 12 percent depreciation in the real exchange rate against the U.S. dollar and a somewhat larger fall in the equity market.

- Investors in the *euro area* and parts of the *other industrial countries* become increasingly unwilling to further extend their exposure to the United States and other industrial countries that have structural current account deficits (such as the United Kingdom).[17]

In the simulation, monetary policy is assumed to follow a Taylor-type rule in which interest rates respond to core inflation and to the output gap (unless constrained by the zero nominal interest rate bound, as happens in Japan). Fiscal policy is assumed to be passive, with the authori-

[16]The main author is Tamim Bayoumi.

[17]This shift in portfolio preferences is modeled by assuming that each percentage point increase in ratio of U.S. net foreign assets to GDP above a fixed target level leads to a 10 basis point increase in the risk premium on the U.S. dollar. To simulate a loss of confidence, the target level of net foreign assets to GDP is set 2½ percentage points below its level in 2001 (which is slightly over 20 percentage points of GDP). This causes the euro to appreciate by some 8 percent against the U.S. dollar while the other industrial countries as a group appreciate by some 4 percent—implying a reduction in capital flows to the United States of some $20 billion.

Figure 1.20. Alternative Scenario
(Derivative from baseline)

A faster recovery in the United States and weaker activity in Japan could delay recovery in the euro area.

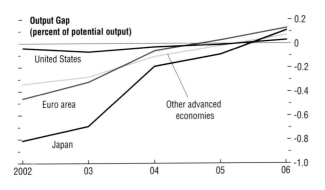

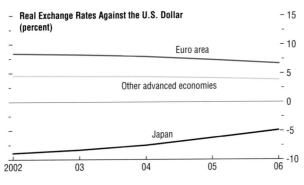

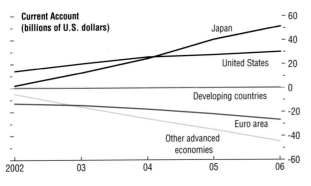

Source: IMF MULTIMOD simulations.

ties initiating no active policy changes but allowing automatic stabilizers to operate.

The result is a scenario in which Japanese activity remains weak through the medium term, recovery in the euro area is delayed, while the United States is little affected (see Figure 1.20 and Table 1.13). In Japan, the increase in the risk premium on assets leads to a significant fall in growth in 2002 because of falling asset prices exacerbated by constraints on countercyclical macroeconomic policies. The loss of market confidence in growth prospects translates into significant additional wealth destruction, resulting in a sharp fall in investment as equity prices dive and financial intermediation becomes less efficient. Consumption also falls significantly compared with the baseline, as wealth destruction and the loss of incomes reduce the desire and ability to spend and—while net exports provide some support for activity as a result of the depreciation of the yen—the impact is limited by the relatively closed nature of the economy. Most important, the macroeconomic policy response cannot provide stimulus because of the lack of policy maneuver. Monetary policy is unable to cushion activity because of the zero bound on interest rates—indeed, real interest rates rise as deflationary forces intensify—while fiscal policy is constrained by the high level of government debt. As a consequence, a modest shock to financial markets translates into a significant reduction in activity and increased deflationary pressures. Reflecting the depreciation in the yen and the weakness of activity, the current account improves some $25 billion by 2004.

Despite the fact that there are no direct effects on domestic activity, recovery in the euro area is delayed by developments in Japan and the appreciation of the euro. The downward pressure on growth in the short term comes through trade and wealth channels. Turning first to trade, the appreciation of the real multilateral exchange rate by 7 percent results in a fall in real net exports compared to baseline, an effect that accounts for about half of the reduction in activity in 2002, again compared with the baseline. In addition, significant wealth losses on holdings of foreign assets due to the appreciation in the exchange rate and the wealth destruction in Japan dampen real consumption and investment over the short term. Monetary policy provides some support to activity, but the limited pass-through of real exchange rate appreciation to core inflation—continuing a trend that has been seen in many industrial and emerging market countries over the last decade—constrains the vigor of the response. The current account deteriorates by over $15 billion by 2004 compared with the baseline. A similar set of considerations, although in a somewhat less virulent form, pertain to the other industrial countries as a group. Again, net exports tend to reduce activity while losses on overseas holdings of financial assets constrain domestic demand, and the current account deteriorates significantly.

In contrast, the impact on the United States is quite limited. Activity is barely affected as the loss of output from lower external demand is largely offset by stronger net exports. There is a modest improvement in the current account of $25 billion (0.2 percentage points of GDP) by 2004. Turning to developing countries, weakness in the industrial countries has a modest negative impact. Given the differences in behavior across the major currency regions, however, the impact varies significantly depending on where the country is located and its exchange rate regime. Continued weakness in Japan, including a depreciation of the yen, leads to generally weaker growth in the rest of east Asia, particularly those countries with links to the dollar. For Africa and the countries in transition, whose links are greatest with the euro area, the short-term impact is mixed, depending on whether the increase in demand created by euro depreciation outweighs the loss in demand from slower activity. Latin America is largely unaffected, reflecting its limited trade with the rest of the world (see the first essay in Chapter II) and links to the United States.

The results in this scenario underline some of the vulnerabilities attached to the baseline forecast. The first is how the recession and limited room for macroeconomic maneuver in Japan in-

creases vulnerability to unanticipated problems. The second is how exchange rate weakness of the yen and the U.S. dollar can hurt short-term prospects for the euro area (and some other countries).

Looking to the medium term, the simulation also illustrates some of the difficulties in resolv-

Table 1.13. Alternative Scenario: Japanese Weakness and Exchange Rate Adjustment
(Percent deviation from baseline unless otherwise specified)

	2002	2003	2004	2005	2006
World real GDP growth	−0.3	—	0.2	—	0.1
United States					
Real GDP growth	−0.1	—	—	—	—
Output gap	—	−0.1	—	—	—
Real domestic demand growth	−0.1	−0.1	−0.1	—	—
Real effective exchange rate	−1.1	−1.1	−1.2	−1.4	−1.5
Current account ($billion)	14.2	20.4	25.9	27.6	30.1
Core inflation (percentage points)	—	−0.1	−0.1	—	0.1
Short-term real interest rate (percentage points)	—	−0.1	—	—	0.1
Euro area					
Real GDP growth	−0.5	0.2	0.3	0.1	0.1
Output gap	−0.5	−0.3	−0.1	—	0.1
Real domestic demand growth	−0.2	0.2	0.3	0.1	0.2
Real effective exchange rate	6.9	6.7	6.3	5.6	5.0
Real U.S. dollar exchange rate	8.4	8.2	7.9	7.4	6.7
Current account ($billion)	−12.7	−14.2	−17.5	−21.7	−26.6
Core inflation (percentage points)	−0.1	−0.1	−0.2	−0.2	−0.1
Short-term real interest rate (percentage points)	−0.4	−0.4	−0.3	−0.2	−0.2
Japan					
Real GDP growth	−1.0	−0.1	0.4	−0.1	0.1
Output gap	−0.8	−0.7	−0.2	−0.1	0.1
Real domestic demand growth	−1.7	−0.3	0.3	−0.1	0.1
Real effective exchange rate	−11.7	−11.1	−10.2	−8.8	−7.3
Real U.S. dollar exchange rate	−8.9	−8.3	−7.5	−6.2	−4.9
Current account ($billion)	2.3	13.0	24.9	40.5	51.4
Core inflation (percentage points)	−0.2	—	−0.1	−0.2	−0.1
Short-term real interest rate (percentage points)	—	0.1	−0.4	−0.5	−0.4
Other industrial economies					
Real GDP growth	−0.4	0.1	0.3	0.1	0.2
Output gap	−0.3	−0.3	−0.1	—	0.1
Current account ($billion)	−4.9	−15.7	−25.6	−34.7	−44.6
Industrial countries					
Real GDP growth	−0.4	—	0.2	0.1	0.1
Output gap	−0.4	−0.3	−0.1	—	0.1
Current account ($billion)	−1.1	3.5	7.6	11.7	10.3
Developing countries					
Real GDP growth	−0.1	—	0.1	—	—
Current account ($billion)	1.1	−3.5	−7.6	−11.7	−10.3

ing the large imbalances across the globe even with an appreciation of the euro against the U.S. dollar, particularly in the face of weak activity in Japan. The necessary slowdown of activity in the United States, which was showing increasing evidence of being above its potential, has not led to a significant reduction in global imbalances. This reflects the continued resilience of U.S. consumption and the inability of the other major currency areas and emerging market regions to maintain robust growth in the face of weakness in the United States. It also implies that significant exchange rate movements may be needed to make notable progress on the imbalances.

How, under such circumstances, will an orderly adjustment of the U.S. current account deficit be achieved? Ideally, the counterpart to any significant reduction in the U.S. current account balance would be a more modest deterioration in the external position of a number of other regions, rather than a large adjustment in one, although weakness in Japan would complicate such an adjustment. As emphasized in previous *World Economic Outlooks*, adjustment in external imbalances would be facilitated by greater progress on structural reform in the euro area, Japan, and emerging markets regions such as emerging Asia. Such reforms would make these regions a more attractive location for investment, thereby reducing the flow of world saving to the United States, which reflects, at least in part, disappointing potential output growth and unattractive climates for investment elsewhere. For example, if productivity growth in the rest of the industrial countries were to increase relative to the United States by ½ percent a year, this could reduce the U.S. current account balance by almost $100 billion after 5 years.[18] In the United States, it will be important

to ensure that fiscal policy is conducted in a manner that does not reduce domestic saving over the medium term. In short, a generalized failure to make significant progress on structural reforms across a range of countries would exacerbate global vulnerabilities.

References

Bank of Japan, 2001, "Japan's Financial Structure in View of the Flow of Funds Accounts," *Bank of Japan Quarterly Bulletin* (February).

IMF, 2000, "The Impact of Higher Oil Prices on the Global Economy." Available on the Interest at *www.imf.org/external/pubs/ft/oil/2000/index.htm.*

Loungani, Prakash, 2001, "How Accurate Are Private Sector Forecasts? Cross-Country Evidence from *Consensus Forecasts* of Output Growth," *International Journal of Forecasting,* Vol. 17 (July–September), pp. 419–32.

———, 2002, "There Will Be Growth in the Spring: How Credible Are Forecasts of Recovery" *World Economics,* Vol. 3 (January–March), pp. 1–6.

Parsley, David, and Shang-Jin Wei, 2001, "Limiting Currency Volatility to Stimulate Goods Market Integration: A Price-Based Approach," IMF Working Paper 01/197 (Washington: International Monetary Fund).

Persson, Torsten, 2001, "Currency Unions and Trade: How Large Is the Treatment Effect?" *Economic Policy,* Vol 16, Issue 33 (October), pp. 433–48.

Rose, Andrew K., 2000, "One Money, One Market: The Effect of Common Currencies on Trade," *Economic Policy,* Vol. 15, Issue 30 (April), pp. 7–46.

———, and Eric van Wincoop, 2001, "National Money as a Barrier to International Trade: The Real Case for Currency Union," *American Economic Review, Papers and Proceedings,* Vol. 91 (May), pp. 386–90.

Zarnowitz, Victor, 1986, "The Record and Improvability of Economic Forecasting," NBER Working Paper No. 2099 (Cambridge, Massachusetts: National Bureau of Economic Reserrch).

---

[18]See Appendix II of the October 2001 *World Economic Outlook.* The actual simulation was of an increase in productivity growth in the United States, relative to other countries, rather than a fall in relative growth.

CHAPTER II

THREE ESSAYS ON HOW FINANCIAL MARKETS AFFECT REAL ACTIVITY

This chapter contains three essays on current policy issues associated with debt defaults, wealth effects, and monetary policy, which have a common theme of linking financial, monetary policy, and institutional developments to the real economy. The first essay, for example, discusses why public debt crises have been relatively frequent in Latin America, notwithstanding the fact that the region's total external debt has actually been lower than other regions and that government debt has *not* been particularly high as a fraction of national income. The essay notes that, while the region has made considerable progress in improving underlying macroeconomic conditions over the past decade, three key vulnerabilities remain—namely, relatively low integration with the world economy, the instability of macroeconomic policies, and shallow domestic financial markets. The various channels through which these factors undermine these countries' capacity to repay their external debt are examined, and policy implications drawn.

The second essay discusses how the tremendous wealth creation in industrial countries since the mid-1990s has affected consumption. It puts particular emphasis on the interaction between the wealth effect and financial markets, discussing how the wealth effect has risen over time as financial markets have deepened, been larger in countries whose financial systems are based on direct finance, and become increasingly correlated across countries as financial markets have become more globalized.

The third essay examines the policy challenges of an environment of low inflation. It discusses how better monetary policies since the 1970s—a larger response to inflationary shocks and more predictable policies—led to a more forward-looking wage-price process, creating a virtuous circle that lowered the volatility of both output and inflation. It concludes that, because of the existence of the zero interest bound, central banks' concerns about higher inflation have to be balanced by concerns about deflation. In particular, it notes that the danger of getting into a deflationary spiral increases markedly as inflation targets are lowered below 2 percent and that there are grounds for becoming more proactive with regard to sharp falls in output.

Debt Crises: What's Different About Latin America?[1]

Latin America has a long and turbulent history of external financing crises. Not only have sovereign defaults and reschedulings been far more frequent in Latin America than elsewhere over the past one-and-a-half centuries, but also their recurrence has remained high in recent decades (Figure 2.1). While policy reforms in the 1990s raised expectations of a clear break with this pattern, debt crises have continued to crop up in recent years, albeit at a more moderate rate, including Mexico (1994/95), Ecuador (1999), and Argentina (2001/02). Against this background, and with continuing high sovereign spreads for most of the region, external debt remains a central issue in Latin America.

The causes of sovereign debt crises are complex and multifaceted. They have economic and legal, as well as political roots, a full assessment of which is beyond the scope of this essay. Instead, the aim is to focus on three key factors that have exacerbated the external financing difficulties faced by Latin American emerging markets as a group—namely, the relatively weak trade links with the world economy, the instability of macroeconomic policies, and domestic financial underdevelopment and associated low

---

[1]The main author of this essay is Luis Catão; Bennet Sutton provided research assistance.

Figure 2.1. Sovereign Defaults and Reschedulings
(Number of events per country in region)

Sovereign defaults and reschedulings have been more frequent in Latin America than in other regions.

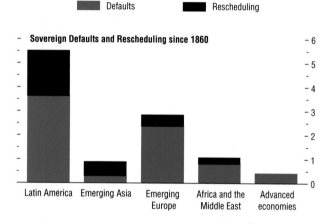

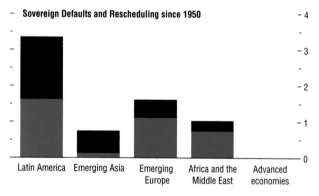

Sources: Lindert and Morton (1989); and Reinhart (2001).

saving rates. As argued below, these factors together help explain apparent paradoxes about Latin American debt crises, such as the fact that debt crises have been more frequent there even though average ratios of debt to GDP have been lower than in other regions and that the countries affected have displayed very distinct fiscal positions at the onset of debt crises.

That said, it should be acknowledged that there are very considerable differences in macroeconomic policies and economic fundamentals within Latin America. In a similar vein, notable progress on structural reforms has been made over recent years, although again with significant variation across countries. While a comprehensive discussion of particular cases is impossible within the confines of this relatively short essay, progress across a range of issues has been made by Brazil, Chile, and Mexico.

External Debt and Openness

Latin America's external borrowing exhibits three key distinctive features relative to other regions. First, total external debt (private plus public) is not overly high relative to GDP on average (Figure 2.2). Thus, contrary to what is sometimes suggested, these economies do not appear to overborrow relative to their income.

Second, most of Latin America's external debt is accounted for by the public sector. This is the case not only for low-income countries but also for virtually all emerging markets in the region—the group of countries on which the remainder of this essay will focus. As can be seen from the second panel of Figure 2.2, the share of public and public-guaranteed debt in Latin America has been higher than in Asia, including through the 1997/98 crisis when Asian governments took over a large part of these countries' private sector external debt. The flip side of this heavy participation of sovereigns in Latin America's external borrowing is that financial linkages through borrowing between the region's private sector and world capital markets have been thin. In this context, it is hardly surprising that external debt crises in the region have generally been triggered by governments' financing problems rather than by private sector default on external obligations.

A third but no less significant Latin American singularity is that while external debt is not so high relative to GDP, it is very high relative to exports (see bottom panel of Figure 2.2). This long-standing feature of most countries in the region stems largely from a combination of macroeconomic imbalances and protectionist policies started in the 1930s, which set off an inward-looking development pattern that only recently has begun to be reversed.[2] Although economic liberalization and associated policy reforms over the past decade have helped boost external trade, and export growth did accelerate in the 1990s relative to the 1980s, most Latin American economies still remain far more closed to foreign trade than their Asian counterparts. As Table 2.1 indicates, this is not only because the starting level of openness was low at the onset of the reforms, but also because export growth in many countries is yet to match the strong performance of several Asian emerging markets.

The resulting mismatch between capital account openness and trade openness, and the ensuing high ratio of foreign debt to exports—and in particular of foreign *public* debt to exports—increases a country's vulnerability to debt crises through several channels. First, external solvency requires the country to generate enough foreign exchange through trade surpluses to meet present and future payments on its foreign debt. To the extent that low exports make it more difficult to realize future trade surpluses through depreciations in the exchange rate, they raise concerns about the country's debt repayment capacity. These concerns can be especially troublesome when international liquidity is highly cyclical. Whenever international liquidity

[2]For a discussion of what triggered—as well as the description of those policies that led to—Latin America's gradual closure to foreign trade from the 1930s to the 1980s, see Diaz-Alejandro (1970), Thorp (1984), and Taylor (2000). Prior to the 1930s, even large countries such as Argentina and Brazil were far more open to foreign trade than they are today.

Figure 2.2. External Debt

Latin America's external debt has not been relatively high as a share of GDP but it has been high as a ratio to exports.

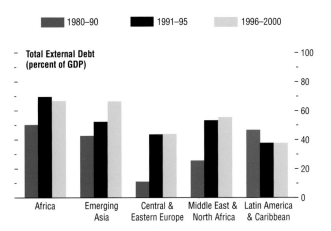

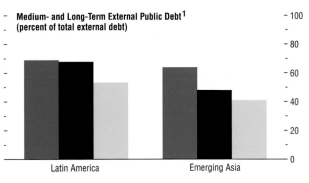

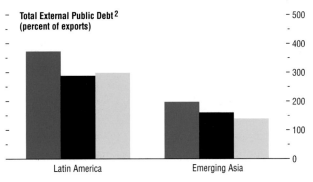

Sources: World Bank, *Global Development Finance;* and IMF staff estimates.
[1]Latin American countries include Argentina, Brazil, Chile, Colombia, Mexico, Peru, Uruguay, and Venezuela. Emerging Asian countries include Indonesia, Korea, Malaysia, the Philippines, and Thailand. Weighted averages using nominal GDP in U.S. dollars.
[2]Latin American countries include Argentina, Brazil, Chile, Colombia, Mexico, Peru, Uruguay, and Venezuela. Emerging Asian countries include India, Indonesia, Korea, Malaysia, the Philippines, Singapore, and Thailand. Weighted averages using nominal GDP in U.S. dollars.

Table 2.1. Export Performance in Latin America and Asia[1]

	Export Volume (annual percent change)		US$ Export Value (annual percent change)		Exports (percent of GDP)	
	1980–90	1990–2000	1980–90	1990–2000	1980–90	1991–2000
Argentina	5.04	6.38	2.84	7.52	8.96	9.05
Brazil	5.59	7.34	4.73	6.41	10.10	9.04
Chile	6.09	9.34	5.43	8.01	27.23	29.54
Colombia	7.37	3.68	5.03	6.08	15.07	17.00
Mexico	7.67	11.36	8.22	9.98	16.96	25.20
Peru	−7.74	8.05	−1.57	7.65	16.74	13.38
Venezuela	2.33	2.41	−0.72	6.28	27.49	27.75
Latin American average[2]	3.76	6.94	3.42	7.42	17.51	18.71
Hong Kong, SAR[3]	13.11	9.22	14.65	9.27	110.70	139.86
Indonesia	1.15	10.44	3.35	8.87	25.06	31.68
Korea	10.87	15.76	13.97	10.86	41.56	34.18
Malaysia	9.65	9.79	8.83	13.10	59.32	96.21
Philippines	3.57	9.25	5.03	13.72	24.17	40.96
Singapore[3]	9.44	10.65	10.77	9.42	179.55	170.17
Thailand	12.39	10.95	14.73	9.93	26.61	46.25
Emerging Asia average[2] excluding Hong Kong SAR	8.60	10.87	10.19	10.74	66.71	79.90
and Singapore	7.53	11.24	9.18	11.30	35.34	49.86

Source: IMF staff estimates.
[1]Exports of goods and non-factor services.
[2]Unweighted averages.
[3]Exports inclusive of re-exports.

becomes abundant (often following monetary loosening and low interest rates in advanced economies), lending booms to emerging markets usually follow, and these tend to be especially marked in Latin America.[3] If the ratio of foreign debt to exports is high to begin with, and rises further during the boom, it is likely that at a certain point foreign lenders will start wondering whether the country is externally insolvent. As discussed elsewhere, such concerns are typically exacerbated by terms-of-trade shocks, hikes in world interest rates, or crises in other emerging markets.[4] Against the background of a rising debt to export ratio, one or more of those adverse shocks can readily raise solvency concerns and trigger a capital outflow precisely at the moment when the international

provision of liquidity is most needed to ride out the shock. Debt-servicing problems typically arise at those junctions.

Low trade openness also has a negative bearing on foreign debt repayment through two other channels. First, incentives to debt repayment are lower the more closed the economy, since gains from trade and losses from commercial sanctions following debt repudiation amount to a smaller fraction of GDP.[5] Second, exchange rate devaluations can exacerbate fiscal problems when the economy is highly open on the capital account but relatively closed on the external trade side. This is because when the export to GDP ratio is low, and the bulk of government borrowing is foreign currency–denominated, a devaluation provides a limited boost to real

[3]For evidence that swings in the supply of external finance have been a main determinant of lending booms in emerging markets and Latin America in particular, see Calvo, Reinhart, and Leidermann (1996) and Arora and Cerisola (2001) on the 1990s, and Diaz-Alejandro (1983) and Fishlow (1989) for interesting parallels with the pre–World War II era.

[4]See Catão and Sutton (2002).

[5]The view that trade losses and commercial sanctions are a key deterrent to debt repudiation was first formalized by Bulow and Rogoff (1989). Rose (2002) provides evidence that this channel has been quite effective in practice. This point does not rule out, of course, the possibility that losses to defaulting countries may extend far beyond the foreign trade area.

activity and hence to government revenues, while the domestic currency value of the debt service will rise in tandem with the devaluation.[6] Thus, external debt crises are more likely to arise when this mismatch exists. This happened, for instance, in several Latin American countries during the 1980s, when export growth following devaluations failed to pull those economies out of recession and automatically generate tax revenues needed to meet external debt payments. Partly as a result, the ratio of external debt service to tariff revenues rose sharply and remained high for years (Figure 2.3). In contrast, the drop was not as dramatic (despite similarly sharp devaluations) and the rebound was much quicker in the more open economies in Asia following the 1997/98 crisis, as rapid export growth helped pull those economies out of recession and raise tax revenues.

In sum, while external debt is not overly high in Latin America as a share of GDP, it is quite high in relation to exports. This appears to be a distinctive source of macroeconomic vulnerability in Latin America, affecting in particular the region's main borrower—the public sector—and the more so when external liquidity and exchange rates are volatile. This point is further elaborated on below.

Macroeconomic Volatility

A key contributing factor for the higher incidence of debt crises in Latin America is macroeconomic volatility. As in the case of an individual with highly variable income and facing a given borrowing constraint, an economy with larger and less predictable macro fluctuations tends to experience liquidity shortfalls that can

[6]Recent experience indicates that this problem is particularly acute following the collapse of fixed exchange rate regimes, when devaluations tend to be dramatic and immediately preceded by a substantial buildup of external debt. The links between exchange rate regimes and financial crises have been extensively analyzed elsewhere and thus will not be dealt with here. See Mussa and others (2000) and the May 2001 *World Economic Outlook* for useful references.

Figure 2.3. Debt Service[1]
(Percent of general government revenues)

The ratio of external debt service to government revenues rises sharply following large devaluations.

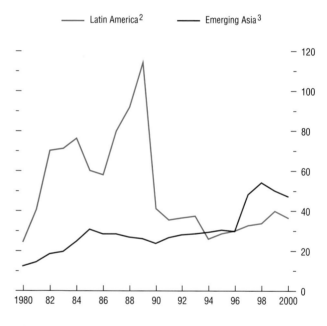

[1]Weighted averages using GDP at market exchange rates.
[2]Latin American countries include Argentina, Brazil, Chile, Colombia, Mexico, Peru, Venezuela, and Uruguay.
[3]Asian countries include India, Indonesia, Malaysia, the Philippines, and Thailand.

Table 2.2. Volatility and Sovereign Debt Defaults and Reschedulings[1]

Group	Number of Debt Events[2]	Standard Deviation					
		Real GDP growth	General government revenues (percent of GDP)[3]	General government expenditures (percent of revenue)	Terms of trade	Real effective exchange rates	Real interest rates
1971–80							
Latin America	0.44	3.79	3.18	13.41	33.63	6.61	8.65
Emerging Asia	0.25	2.91	1.75	8.52	14.16	5.26	5.45
Advanced economies	. . .	2.50	2.58	4.43	17.60	2.51	2.92
1981–90							
Latin America	0.89	4.89	2.81	16.47	27.36	39.24	15,797.41
Emerging Asia	0.13	2.85	1.96	10.28	7.65	24.83	3.32
Advanced economies	. . .	3.09	1.11	5.27	7.20	6.21	2.39
1991–2000							
Latin America	0.33	3.74	2.19	7.94	8.70	18.00	13.18
Emerging Asia	0.25	4.11	1.82	8.29	5.92	8.65	2.52
Advanced economies	. . .	2.09	1.02	7.23	3.73	5.90	2.07

Source: IMF staff estimates.

[1]Volatility of real GDP growth, government revenues, real effective exchange rate, real domestic interest rate, terms of trade, and government expenditures measured by standard deviation over period.

[2]Number defaults or reschedulings per country in group.

[3]General government.

readily lead to debt-servicing problems. While a country's decision to default at the end will depend on a complex weighing of costs and benefits—including the windfall gain from shedding the debt versus the potential cost of being cut off from credit markets, losing reputation and/or suffering commercial retaliation that may hamper future trade gains—higher macroeconomic volatility tends to exacerbate liquidity problems and thus increase default risk in a world of less-than-perfect credit markets.[7]

The higher volatility of real macroeconomic aggregates in Latin America has a long history, and has not gone away in recent years despite the region's impressive success in stabilizing inflation and carrying out important reforms.[8] This point is readily summarized by the (unconditional) standard deviations of variables that have an important bearing on a country's debt repayment capacity.[9] As shown in Table 2.2, macroeconomic aggregates in Latin America have generally been far more volatile than in advanced countries or emerging Asia despite substantial improvement during the 1990s. And as the decennial averages by country groups in Table 2.2 also indicate, the higher volatility of key variables such as real GDP, real exchange rates, and the ratio of government expenditure to revenue ratios has been closely associated with a higher incidence of defaults and debt reschedulings.

This raises the question of what drives macroeconomic volatility in Latin America. A key difficulty in this connection is to isolate the exogenous factors at play, not only because most of the variables listed in Table 2.2 respond to both external shocks and domestic policy actions, but

[7]A standard view in the literature is that a country will continue servicing its debt until the marginal benefit of defaulting is no higher than that of having open access to external markets and smoothing consumption through external borrowing. In this setting, if income variations are random and an unpredictable succession of bad shocks increases the relative marginal benefit of defaulting, then default risk will turn out to be positively related to volatility under a given credit ceiling. See Eaton and Gersovitz (1981).

[8]The volatility of distinct sets of macroeconomic and financial variables in Latin America has been documented in Gavin and others (1996), Caballero (2000), and Gourinchas, Valdes, and Landerretche (2001).

[9]See Catão and Sutton (2002) for econometric evidence on the relationship between those variables and default probabilities.

also because they feed back on each other. Yet, some causal connections can be discerned. One variable that can be taken as largely exogenous is the terms of trade, since Latin American countries are, generally, price takers in world markets. As shown in Table 2.2, terms of trade have been considerably more volatile in Latin America and typically deteriorate prior to debt crises.[10] Such terms-of-trade volatility partly reflects the heavy weight of a handful of primary commodities in these countries' exports—a long-standing structural feature of these economies with the exception of Brazil and Mexico, where manufactured goods have recently accounted for nearly 60 and 90 percent of total exports, respectively.

Another key "autonomous" source of macroeconomic instability in Latin America is fiscal policy. While the large fluctuations in the ratios of fiscal revenues, expenditures, and deficit to GDP in Latin America reflect the heavy exposure of public sectors to terms of trade and output shocks, these explain only part of the instability of fiscal balances. The proximate magnitude of *autonomous* fiscal policy instability can be gauged from the residual of a regression of primary fiscal balance on real GDP and terms-of-trade cycles and the preceding year's fiscal balance.[11] Staff estimates of the average residual for Latin American emerging markets indicate that such *autonomous* fiscal impulses often range between ±2 percent of GDP but sometimes reach even higher values, thus giving a nonnegligible contribution to macro instability. At the same time, government primary balances in Latin America typically display procyclical behavior— that is, moving into higher surpluses during downswings in economic activity, and rearing into deficits during cyclical upturns. This can be

Table 2.3. Sensitivity of Governments' Primary Deficits to the Business Cycle in Selected Emerging Markets[1]

	Mean	Standard Error	t-statistic
Argentina	0.07	0.16	0.47
Brazil*	0.36	0.21	1.74
Chile	0.13	0.10	1.28
Mexico***	0.47	0.16	2.95
Peru	0.06	0.09	0.63
Venezuela***	0.51	0.16	3.24
India	−0.02	0.10	−0.19
Indonesia	0.06	0.10	0.59
Korea**	−0.27	0.10	−2.65
Malaysia	−0.35	0.23	−1.52
Thailand**	−0.39	0.20	−1.96

Source: IMF staff estimates.
Note. One, two, and three asterisks represent statistical significance at 10, 5, and 1 percent, respectively.
[1]Based on an OLS regression of the central government primary deficit (as a ratio to GDP) on the real GDP cycle and the one-year lagged primary fiscal deficit. Annual data for 1970–2000, with the exception of Brazil, for which consistent pre-1985 data are unavailable. Report estimates refer to the coefficient on the real GDP cycle.

gauged from the estimated coefficients on real GDP cycles estimated from the regression methodology described above and reported in Table 2.3.[12] For Latin American emerging markets, these coefficients are positive (and statistically significant for some countries), in contrast with estimates for Asian emerging markets, which point to broadly countercyclical fiscal stances.

This procyclicality of fiscal policy in Latin America is partly due to certain structural features of these countries' tax systems. These include greater reliance on cyclically sensitive revenue sources (such as indirect taxes and transfers from state-owned natural resource industries as in Chile, Mexico, and Venezuela) as well as tax enforcement problems, which tend to become more severe during downswings when the opportunity cost of complying with tax obligations is

---

[10]Catão and Sutton (2002) show that this deterioration typically starts in the year preceding sovereign defaults and debt rescheduling events. Using a broader definition of crises (which includes balance of payments as well as banking crises), Kaminsky and Reinhart (1999) also find that terms of trade typically deteriorate in the run-up to crises although their power to "predict" them is weaker when compared to other variables.

[11]A similar method for measuring the *autonomous* component of fiscal policy has been proposed in Gavin and others (1996).

[12]Using other indicators of fiscal position, Gavin and Perotti (1997) and Talvi and Végh (2000) also find that fiscal policy in Latin America has been broadly procyclical. This contrasts with OECD economies, where fiscal policy has been broadly countercyclical, and thus helps mitigate aggregate income fluctuations.

heightened.[13] But such fiscal shocks also appear to emanate from frequent changes in tax rates, as well as from changes in the more "autonomous" components of government expenditure responding to electoral cycle (although the effects of the latter on public spending appear to have been tamed in some countries in recent years). At the root of this fiscal instability problem lies the difficulty of containing government spending and accumulating budget surpluses during cyclical upswings. Among other things, this limits the government's ability to run deficits during recessions without creating inflationary pressure or facing external financing constraints (or a combination of the two). So, during "bad times" governments in the region are often *forced* to adjust, both to shore up policy credibility and to cope with the drying up of external financing. As a result, automatic fiscal stabilizers are seldom allowed to work.

Policy-induced macroeconomic instability in Latin America has not been confined to fiscal policy. Monetary policy, in particular, is well known to have been historically very unstable, although largely reflecting the passive accommodation of fiscal imbalances and inflationary financing of fiscal deficits before the 1990s. But while there is some consensus among researchers that the contribution of "autonomous" monetary shocks to the Latin America business cycle is relatively small and that monetary policy is constrained by the "unpleasant monetarist arithmetic" of fiscal policy in the longer run, monetary policy has not been a perfect island of

stability in the 1990s.[14] One manifestation of this has been changes in interest rates and/or adjustments in the money supply to offset fiscal developments at times or to defend sometimes unsustainable exchange rate pegs. Partly as a result, domestic interest rates have fluctuated widely in the region despite the environment of lower inflation (see Table 2.2).

Two other areas in which economic policy in Latin America has been particularly unstable are trade and capital controls. The latter, in particular, has historically oscillated between liberalization and stringent foreign exchange controls, the amplitude of these policy shifts being far greater than in any other regions (Figure 2.4).[15] In light of the well-documented links between capital account liberalization and lending booms, and the fact that lending booms in Latin America have often been followed by financial crises and sharp recessions, such swings in capital account controls policies have undoubtedly contributed to overall macroeconomic instability.[16] Recent research suggests that it takes a few years before capital account liberalization starts paying off in terms of stabilizing asset prices, implying that these cycles are generally destabilizing.[17]

In sum, external terms of trade, fiscal shocks, and financial liberalization cycles have been key drivers of macroeconomic volatility in Latin America. The causal links between the two latter variables and those that have an important bearing on debt-servicing costs (notably the real exchange rate and interest rates) are sometimes unclear because of endogeneity problems, but

---

[13]See Gavin and Perotti (1997) for evidence that structural characteristics of the tax system in Latin America tend to exacerbate the cyclical sensitivity of fiscal revenues. Figures reported in Table 2.5 corroborate this point, showing that the tax revenue/GDP ratio has been more volatile in Latin America relative not only to OECD countries but also to Asian emerging markets.

[14]For evidence that "autonomous" monetary policy shocks account for a relatively small proportion of output fluctuations in the region, see Hoffmaister and Roldós (1997) and Kydland and Zarazaga (1997). Longer-term dependence of monetary stability on fiscal policies is examined in the May 2001 *World Economic Outlook* and in Catão and Terrones (2001).

[15]One way of rationalizing these cycles is through the differential impact that capital account openness has on the distinct social groups. In a closed economy, for instance, workers' income tends to be more protected from the risk of productivity shocks. See Alfaro and Kanczuk (2001) for a model of liberalization cycles along these lines.

[16]The links between financial liberalization, capital inflows, and credit booms and busts in Latin America are discussed in Diaz-Alejandro (1985), Velasco (1987), and Gourinchas, Valdes, and Landerretche (2001), among others.

[17]Kaminsky and Schmuckler (2001) find that financial markets become more volatile in the first years following liberalization but become more stable than the pre-liberalization period after a few years. So, if liberalization policies are reversed in the meantime, the benefit of subsequently lower volatility is lost.

seem, on the whole, to underpin the tight correlation between macroeconomic volatility and frequent debt crises. Frequent debt crises, in turn, are very costly: country risk and hence the debt interest burden have been especially high in Latin America (Table 2.4). By undermining fiscal sustainability, such a high interest burden makes it harder to stabilize fiscal and monetary policies, feeding back into overall policy instability and thus further contributing to higher default risk.

Domestic Debt and Financial Deepening

A third main source of external vulnerability in Latin America is the heavily skewed composition of sovereign debt toward foreign currency–denominated liabilities. While—as seen above—Latin America's total external debt is a low fraction of GDP compared with that in other regions, the ratio of external government debt has been high relative to both GDP and total external debt (Table 2.5). Moreover, if the stock of foreign currency–denominated *domestic* debt is taken into account, the share of foreign currency denominated in Latin American public debt is even higher. In Argentina, for example, foreign currency–denominated debt amounted to about 95 percent of general government debt in the year prior to the recent crisis.[18]

A high share of foreign currency–denominated liabilities in total public debt poses two problems, which have been already mentioned. First, it produces a currency mismatch between the two sides of the government balance sheet. Since most government revenues stem from taxes, which are domestic currency–denominated whereas debt payments will be mostly in dollars, the combination of this mismatch with high exchange rate volatility can suddenly lead to spikes in debt service payments relative to government income. It is therefore no surprise that debt crises in the region have been often associated with large swings in real exchange rates and in particular with

[18]See Figure 1.9, Chapter 1, of the October 2001 *World Economic Outlook* for the respective numbers in other Latin American countries.

Figure 2.4. Foreign Exchange Restriction Index[1]

Capital account and foreign exchange control policies have been especially volatile in Latin America.

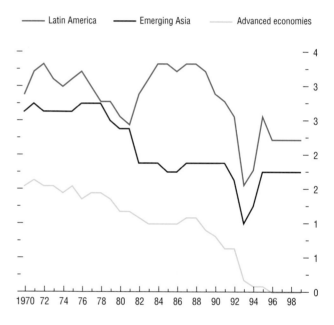

Source: IMF, *Annual Report on Exchange Arrangements and Exchange Restrictions.*
[1]Index comprises 4 types of capital controls: (1) separate exchange rates for some or all capital transactions; (2) restrictions on payments for current transactions; (3) restrictions on payments for capital transactions; and (4) surrender or repatriation requirements for export proceeds. Index for individual countries counts the number of controls in place for each year. Regional index is a simple average of country indices.

Table 2.4. General Government Interest Expenditure: Some International Comparisons

	Percent of GDP			Percent of Government Expenditure[1]			
	1982–90	1991–95	1996–2000	1982–90	1991–95	1996–2000	2001
Argentina	2.0	1.8	2.9	10.6	8.3	10.8	17.4
Brazil	5.0	4.1	8.0	20.1	13.1	20.5	21.5
Chile	1.8	1.4	0.5	6.6	6.3	2.1	. . .
Colombia	2.3	2.1	2.9	11.4	9.4	9.9	. . .
Mexico	14.1	3.8	3.7	37.0	16.0	16.5	. . .
Peru	3.4	3.8	2.1	19.1	17.0	9.1	. . .
Venezuela	2.1	4.7	3.3	16.7	24.7	17.1	. . .
Latin American average[2]	7.0	4.1	5.4	25.0	16.2	17.5	19.9
Indonesia	2.1	2.1	3.0	11.4	12.6	16.0	27.6
Korea	1.0	0.5	1.4	4.9	2.5	4.8	10.2
Malaysia	6.2	4.2	2.6	16.6	13.5	10.1	. . .
Philippines	3.7	5.1	3.7	21.8	26.0	17.9	. . .
Thailand	2.5	0.6	0.6	13.4	5.5	3.1	. . .
East Asian average[2]	2.1	1.5	1.8	9.9	7.8	8.2	15.4

Sources: IMF, *World Economic Outlook, International Financial Statistics,* and staff estimates.
[1]Brazilian and Mexican figures correspond to the ratio of real interest rate payments to real government expenditure.
[2]Weighted by U.S. dollar GDP of each country.

sharp depreciations that usually follow unsustainable pegs, as for instance in Mexico (1994/95) and, more recently, in Argentina. Second, the value of the debt becomes more sensitive to changes in international interest rates if the debt is contracted in floating rate terms, or if the country has to rely on international capital markets for debt rollover (which is bound to be the case if the share of short-term debt in total debt is high). In other words, greater reliance on foreign debt increases the vulnerability of public finances to hikes in external interest rates.

Why, then, do Latin American governments not adjust the composition of their debt toward domestic currency–denominated debt? This could be done, for instance, by issuing external debt denominated in national currency. However, for reasons that are not yet entirely clear to economists, historically only a handful of mature economies have been able to do so. Virtually all emerging market sovereign debt held by foreigners continues to be foreign currency–denominated, a phenomenon that is as striking today as it was a hundred years ago.[19]

There remains, however, the possibility of a larger share of government debt being issued domestically, and thus denominated in domestic currency. One possible reason why this has not been the case is related to the limited capacity of these countries' financial systems to absorb large issuances. One simple measure of the former is the ratio of total public sector debt to domestic credit. As shown in Figure 2.5, this ratio has been much higher in Latin American countries (although rapidly declining with the reactivation of domestic financial intermediation during the 1990s), only approaching that of Asian emerging markets in the immediate aftermath of the 1997/98 crisis. The relative shallowness of financial markets in several Latin American countries is also a factor contributing to the relatively low level of domestic private saving. As shown in Figure 2.6, notwithstanding a recovery from the lows of the early 1990s and some considerable cross-country differences, the average private saving ratio in Latin America remains well below those in emerging Asia.[20] This clearly limits the scope for domestic government borrowing without substantial crowding out of the private sector.

Another reason has to do with time inconsistency: unless the debt is fully indexed to actual inflation and indexation rules are unbreakable,

[19]See Bordo and Flandreau (2001).
[20]Capital flight may also contribute to low saving, as residents transfer their money abroad in a manner that is difficult to capture in official statistics.

Table 2.5. General Government Debt: Percentage Share of External Debt

| | External Debt/Total Debt | | |
	1982–90	1991–2000	End-2000
Argentina	89.7	69.2	58.4
Brazil	61.4	39.8	32.5
Chile	51.9	47.8	43.7
Colombia	85.1	74.0	64.8
Mexico	69.8	70.0	54.5
Peru	95.6	92.7	81.4
Venezuela	82.2	85.3	74.8
Latin American average[1]	76.5	68.4	58.6
India	27.9	29.9	22.0
Indonesia	97.1	87.8	51.3
Korea	49.6	15.1	13.5
Malaysia	41.7	37.1	43.9
Pakistan	60.1	55.2	57.7
Philippines	69.1	55.8	64.0
Thailand	51.8	74.6	66.4
Singapore	1.4	—	—
Asian average[1]	49.8	44.4	39.8
(excluding Singapore)	56.7	50.8	45.5

Sources: World Bank; IMF, *World Economic Outlook*, and IMF staff estimates.

[1]Arithmetic mean.

issuing domestic liabilities provides governments with an incentive to inflate the debt away. This incentive problem is no doubt exacerbated by the persistence of fiscal imbalances in several countries and a long history of inflationary financing in the region, which has been only partly mitigated by the current low inflation environment and sounder policies in recent years. Partly reflecting these credibility problems and shallower domestic financial markets, domestic debt also tends to have a much shorter maturity than does foreign debt. In this context, replacing longer-term foreign debt by shorter-term domestic debt would help solve the currency mismatch issue but at the expense of shortening the debt maturity. This is unsatisfactory in light of evidence that debt crises partly stem from temporary liquidity shortages.[21]

---

[21]Broad cross-country evidence that less liquid countries are more likely to default on their external debt is provided in Detragiache and Spilimbergo (2001) and the references cited therein. In their study, the definition of liquidity comprises international reserves and short-term debt, with allowance being made for the endogeneity of the latter with regard to alternative financing choices.

Figure 2.5. Total Public Debt
(Percent of domestic private credit)

Shallower financial markets in Latin America have constrained the share of public debt that can be financed domestically.

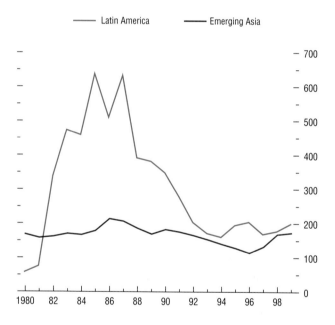

Source: IMF staff estimates.

Figure 2.6. Gross Private Saving
(Percent of GDP)

Lower domestic saving ratios in Latin America reduce the scope for domestic public sector borrowing.

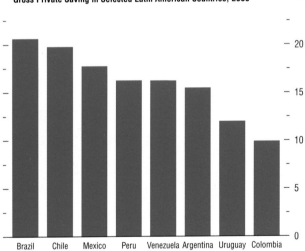

Sources: IMF, *International Financial Statistics;* and IMF staff estimates.

In sum, while a less skewed debt composition with lower foreign currency–denominated liabilities would be clearly preferable, the combination of domestic financial underdevelopment with the lack of a track record in macroeconomic policies has typically prevented Latin American governments from borrowing long term in domestic currency and skewed the debt composition toward foreign currency liabilities. In this regard, a comparison with Asian emerging markets is interesting in that several of these countries have been generally far more successful in tapping domestic markets for government debt—an important payoff for greater monetary stability and rarer occurrences of debt repudiation or confiscation of residents' assets by the government.

Policy Implications

The higher incidence of sovereign debt crises among Latin American emerging markets is a complex and multifaceted phenomenon, but three contributing factors stand out: (1) relatively low openness entailing higher ratios of foreign debt to exports; (2) high macroeconomic volatility, induced inter alia by domestic policy shocks; (3) heavy concentration of public debt on foreign currency–denominated liabilities and limited capacity to borrow long term in domestic financial markets. While there has been substantial progress on all these fronts in most of the region in the 1990s, it has been uneven, with some countries having moved considerably faster than others in key policy areas. For instance, progress has been made in some countries in limiting macroeconomic instability through the adoption of credible fiscal and monetary reforms (including inflation targeting), most notably in Brazil, Chile and Mexico. (See also Chapter IV of the May 2001 *World Economic Outlook* for a further discussion of monetary reforms.)

Overall, three issues seem worth singling out. First, to the extent that these emerging economies are more susceptible to large international liquidity shocks, the question arises as to why they do not insure themselves better during cyclical upswings against the high probability that "bad" times will lie ahead. Given the well-documented large costs of defaults—both economic and political—this seems a most sensible course of action. And yet, looking at the historical behavior of two basic macro insurance indicators—the ratios of international reserves to debt and of fiscal balances to GDP—one finds that not only are their levels typically low to begin with but they also drop rapidly in the years preceding debt crises (Figure 2.7). While one can think of possible justifications for this underinsurance, the bottom line is that sounder reserve management and less procyclical fiscal policies would be clearly desirable.

Second, policies that foster domestic financial deepening have an important role to play in allowing governments to resort more extensively to domestic financial markets and increase their share of domestic currency–denominated long-term debt. In this respect, several Latin American countries have made remarkable progress in recent years regarding key legal and microeconomic aspects of financial sector reform, and financial systems look far healthier relative to previous decades. For instance, bank capital adequacy ratios and disclosure of financial information have improved markedly in Brazil and Chile, as well as in Argentina before the recent crisis. The main challenge then appears to consist of keeping inflation low and enhancing monetary and fiscal policy credibility, so that these reforms can continue to pay off and bring further financial deepening.

Last but not least, debt to export ratios need to be lowered, preferably through a combination of lower fiscal deficits over the cycle and faster export growth in the longer term. Given the various channels through which trade openness positively affects external repayment capacity, it seems crucial that Latin America become more open to foreign trade. While countries such as Chile and Mexico have made remarkable progress on this front in recent years, heavy external borrowers in the region, such as Argentina and Brazil, continue to have relatively

Figure 2.7. Fiscal Balance and International Reserves in the Run-Up to Sovereign Debt Crises

Fiscal balances and foreign exchange reserves typically display a deterioration in the three year period preceding sovereign defaults.

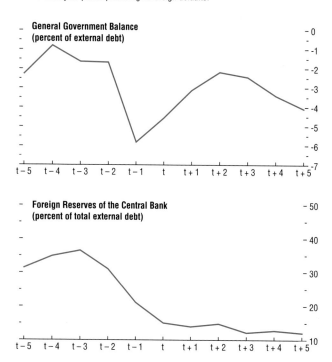

Sources: IMF, *International Financial Statistics;* and IMF staff estimates.

limited trade links with the rest of the world. Through its positive impact on policy discipline and by raising the macroeconomic costs of default as discussed above, further advances in this key area of globalization can be instrumental in reducing policy volatility and lowering external interest costs, thereby enhancing welfare. To this end, moving forward with broad regional trade agreements, avoiding unsustainable exchange rate pegs that hamper export growth, and eschewing resort to protectionism throughout the continent seem all the more essential.

Is Wealth Increasingly Driving Consumption?[22]

The 1990s saw an unprecedented increase in household net wealth in almost all G-7 countries, driven primarily by higher equity prices. This has been accompanied by a sharp decline in household saving rates, which are now almost all at or below their lowest levels during the past three decades (and which, in the United States, is at or close to zero, which has become an increasing policy concern). This has raised a series of important questions, including the following.
- To what extent has the decline in savings been caused by the rise in household wealth in the 1990s? How will savings be affected by the fall in equity markets since mid-2000? Could the effects be partly offset by increases in other forms of wealth, such as housing?
- Do different types of wealth have different effects on consumption? And do these effects vary across countries, for instance reflecting different types of financial systems?
- More generally, has the impact of wealth on household consumption been increasing over time, and will this trend continue? Looking forward, what are the implications for macroeconomic policymakers?

This essay seeks to provide some additional evidence on these issues, based on a cross-country study undertaken by IMF staff of the effect of changes in wealth on consumption in 16 advanced economies over the past 30 years. After describing recent trends in household wealth and savings, it outlines the channels through which asset price changes affect consumption, and presents the empirical results from the study. It concludes with a discussion of the implications of this analysis for the questions set out above.

Stylized Facts

While household wealth has historically tended to grow relatively slowly, most countries have experienced a rapid increase during the 1990s, largely driven by sharp increases in asset valuations (Figure 2.8). This has generally been associated with a decline in personal saving rates, reflecting both the increase in asset prices and lower inflation (which reduces the need to save to offset inflation-induced losses in real wealth). Among the G-7, there are two main exceptions to these trends. First, in Japan, wealth declined very sharply during the 1990s, reflecting the bursting of the land price bubble in the late 1980s and declining personal savings. Second, while wealth has continued to rise in France, personal savings has remained broadly constant in the latter half of the 1990s.

When reviewing trends in household wealth, it is useful to divide it into three main components: financial assets, which include equities, bonds, bank deposits, and indirect holdings in insurance companies and pension funds; nonfinancial assets, which comprise housing wealth—by far the largest component—other tangible assets, and consumer durables; and financial liabilities, which are dominated by mortgage borrowing. As can be seen from Table 2.6, the composition of household wealth, as a percent of disposable income, has changed very significantly over time. In the 1980s the bulk of G-7 wealth consisted of nonfinancial assets, but during the 1990s has shifted increasingly toward financial wealth, and equity holdings, in particu-

---

[22]The main author of this essay is Hali Edison; Bennet Sutton and Yutong Li provided research assistance.

lar.[23] The increase in equity wealth has also varied significantly, being lowest in the United Kingdom and Canada—countries that have market-based financial systems, and where stock wealth has historically been more important—and largest in France and Italy, countries with bank-based financial systems where households have historically had limited participation in the stock market.[24] Equity issuance traditionally has not been an important form of corporate finance in major continental European countries and as a result equity holdings and market capitalization have been small, but this has grown significantly with the rise of privatizations. The surge in the equity wealth was also quite large in the United States, owing to increases in equity prices and the substantial rise in the proportion of households holding equities.

Developments in Japan have been different. During the 1980s, Japan experienced a very rapid increase in net wealth, peaking at 800 percent of disposable income, substantially higher than any other G-7 country at that time. Following the bursting of the asset price bubble and the economic slowdown, the wealth-to-income ratio declined in the 1990s, but remains the highest among the G-7. It is striking that the distribution of Japanese wealth between financial and nonfinancial assets is roughly equal, whereas in the other countries—with the exception of Germany—financial wealth now exceeds nonfinancial wealth. In part, this is due to the relatively high value of land in Japan, but it also reflects the fact that—because Japan has a bank-based financial system—households have traditionally held their wealth in the form of bank deposits, while banks have held equity shares in

[23]The wealth data for Germany begin after 1990, owing to breaks in the series arising from the German unification.

[24]The OECD figures for equity wealth relative to disposable income include only directly held shares. For continental European G-7 countries, this will not make much of a difference as they do not have much in the way of thrift-type pensions, but it does for the United States and the United Kingdom and, to a lesser extent, Canada.

Figure 2.8. Ratio of Net Wealth to Disposable Income and Personal Saving Rate
(Percent of disposable income)

The 1990s saw an unprecedented increase in household net wealth and sharp decline in household saving rates.

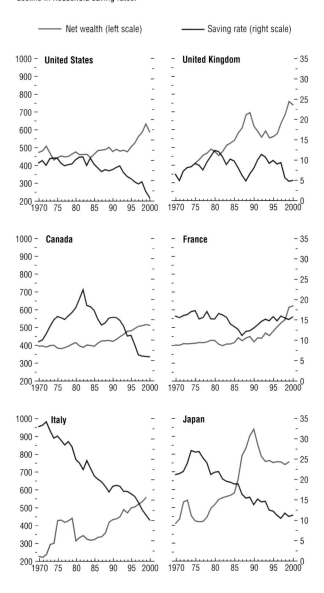

Sources: OECD, *Economic Outlook* and Analytical database.

Table 2.6. Household Wealth and Indebtedness
(Percent of disposable income)

	Canada	France	Germany[1]	Italy	Japan	United Kingdom	United States
Net wealth[2]							
1981–85	393	405	—	324	560	499	456
1986–90	419	433	—	373	823	636	485
1991–95	457	455	533	467	780	569	485
1996–2000	505	560	584	525	749	678	576
Nonfinancial assets							
1981–85	222	315	—	207	409	324	209
1986–90	234	298	—	201	592	413	222
1991–95	248	283	404	249	516	312	202
1996–2000	263	307	427	269	440	320	205
Financial assets							
1981–85	242	153	—	124	238	256	317
1986–90	271	216	—	189	342	333	347
1991–95	307	248	221	248	395	365	373
1996–2000	351	321	267	299	449	458	472
Equity holdings							
1981–85	49	28	—	8	25	27	37
1986–90	55	84	—	29	63	50	52
1991–95	64	102	36	49	40	68	81
1996–2000	91	134	63	104	38	99	146
Financial liabilities							
1981–85	72	63	—	8	86	80	71
1986–90	86	81	—	17	111	109	84
1991–95	98	76	91	30	131	109	90
1996–2000	109	67	110	37	133	111	100

Source: OECD.
[1]The wealth data for Germany are reported after 1990, owing to breaks in the series arising from German unification.
[2]Net wealth equals nonfinancial assets and financial assets minus financial liabilities.

companies. Consequently, the effect of the boom and bust in equity prices in Japan has been absorbed almost entirely by banks rather than households, contributing materially to the financial difficulties of the banks in recent years.

Households can increase their wealth in two ways: directly, through saving, or indirectly as the result of valuation changes in assets they already hold. During the 1990s, changes in wealth were dominated by equity price valuation changes, and—since equity prices were relatively strongly correlated across advanced countries— the increase in wealth was correspondingly synchronized (see Figure 2.9).[25] House price movements have historically been less correlated across countries, although there is some evidence that this has been changing over time (see Figure 2.10).[26] The increasing correlation of asset prices implies that wealth effects in consumption are also becoming more synchronous, and that consumption may therefore be becoming an increasingly important driver of the international business cycle (see Chapter III on

[25]Stock market valuations have become increasingly more correlated across advanced economies; for instance, the correlation between U.S. and European share prices increased from 0.4 in the mid-1990s to 0.8 in 2000 (see the May 2001 *World Economic Outlook*, pp. 10–11).

[26]For instance, the correlation between U.S. and European house prices increased from 0.4 in the 1980s to 0.6 in the 1990s (and to 0.85 in the latter half of the 1990s). One possible explanation for this increase is that the financial liberalization that occurred primarily in the late 1980s and early 1990s in several European countries has made housing markets more dynamic and more cyclically sensitive, so that with relatively synchronized business cycle across countries, the correlation across countries in housing price movements has increased.

the cross-country synchronization of the business cycle).

How Does Wealth Affect Consumption?

The effect of wealth on private consumption has traditionally been analyzed in the framework of the permanent income hypothesis or the life-cycle model (Friedman, 1957, and Ando and Modigliani, 1963).[27] In this framework, the level of consumption depends on households' current and expected future income stream, plus their stock of wealth. The latter is often separated into different categories, with stock and housing wealth being the most common. Wealth affects private consumption via two main channels. First, households can sell assets to finance consumption. Second, households may be able to borrow against their wealth, which in turn would allow households to raise their spending. Their ability to borrow, however, will depend importantly on the development of financial markets, with deeper markets allowing households greater access.[28]

The impact of wealth changes on consumption is likely to vary according to the type of wealth, for a number of reasons.

- *The liquidity of stock and housing market wealth differs significantly.* Until very recently it has been easier to directly realize equity gains than house price gains, since equities are divisible and traded in very liquid markets. However, it is increasingly easy to borrow against housing wealth through home equity loans. Moreover, rising housing prices may affect consumption not only through higher realized home values, but also by the household's ability to refinance a mortgage or take out (or expand) home equity loans based on higher property values. This may, in fact, bol-

[27]For a concise exposition of life cycle and permanent income models of consumption, see Deaton (1992).

[28]In a recent survey of the literature, Poterba (2000) calibrates a simple model of consumption responses to stock market wealth shocks. The calibrations suggest that a typical household can raise consumption outlays by 5 cents for each one-dollar increase in wealth, with variations in the range of 3 to 10 cents.

Figure 2.9. Ratio of Net Wealth to Disposable Income and Stock Price
(Net wealth in percent of disposable income; stock price 1990 = 100)

During the 1990s, changes in wealth were dominated by stock price changes.

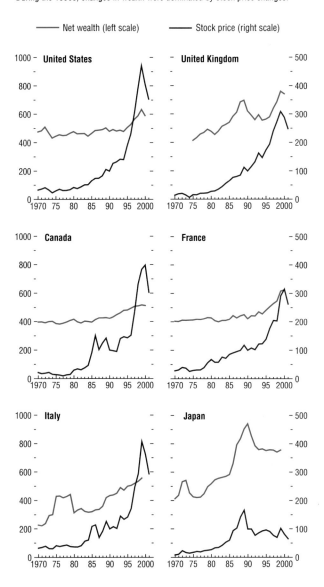

Sources: OECD, *Economic Outlook* and Analytical database; and Thomson Financial, Datastream.

Figure 2.10. Selected Advanced Economies: Housing Prices and Market Capitalization
(Housing price index 1995 = 100; market capitalization in percent of GDP)

Equity and house prices have become increasingly correlated across advanced economies.

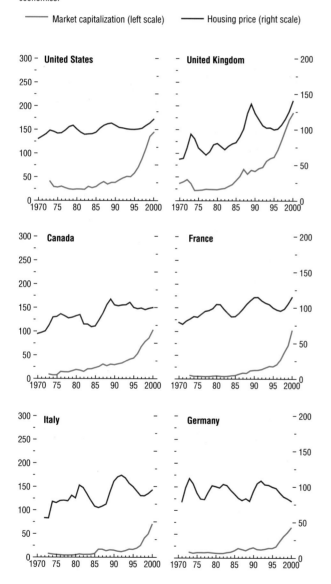

ster the sensitivity of consumption to housing price movements.[29]

- *Since equity prices are more volatile than house prices, households may find it more difficult to assess whether a change in stock wealth is permanent or temporary.* Therefore, they are likely to be more cautious borrowing against increases in stock wealth than housing wealth, suggesting a higher impact of increases in housing wealth on consumption.

- *House purchases are generally largely financed with borrowed money, while equity purchases are not.* Consequently, a rise in house prices is likely to confer a larger net return on investment to households than would a corresponding increase in equity prices, again implying that changes in housing wealth have a larger effect on consumption.[30]

The impact of the wealth effect may also vary according to the nature of the financial system in individual countries. Financial systems are generally divided between those that are based on bank loans (bank-based) and those where the role of the financial market is dominant (market-based).[31] There are two main differences between these systems.

- First, households in the market-based group tend to hold a greater share of their wealth in

[29]Another difference between housing wealth and stock wealth is that housing acts not only as a store of wealth but also provides a service—shelter. Housing services are included as part of consumption, so as house prices increase so will nominal consumption, but real consumption may not necessarily adjust. That is, an increase in house prices may or may not make the household sector better off because the positive effect for homeowners must be offset by the negative impact on renters.

[30]For instance, suppose a household invests $10,000 in a $100,000 house, financing the rest with a mortgage of $90,000. If house prices increase by 10 percent, the gain of $10,000 represents a 100 percent rate of return on the underlying investment. By contrast, suppose a household invests $10,000 in stocks and stock prices increased by the same 10 percent; the gain from this price increase would only be $1,000.

[31]Allen and Gale (2000) comprehensively review the vast literature on comparative financial systems. Empirical research on the comparative merits of bank-based and market-based financial systems has centered on Germany and Japan as bank-based systems and the United States and the United Kingdom as market-based systems.

financial assets, especially equities, relative to those households in the bank-based group (as noted above, for example, in the case of Japan). As a result, the distribution and ownership of equities and property tends to be wider in market-based economies.

- Second, it is generally easier for households to borrow against their assets in market-based economies since home equity loans—and the-infrastructure to support them, such as markets for mortgage-backed securities—are more readily available, owing in part to earlier and more widespread financial deregulation.

Therefore, it has been argued that housing wealth effects may be larger than stock market effects, especially in countries that have a more market-based financial system. It has also been suggested that the strength of stock wealth effects will be stronger in market-based systems, not only because household stock wealth is generally larger (relative to GDP), but also because consumers have access to deeper financial systems with more instruments that can provide greater access to their wealth.[32] A corollary of this argument is that the marginal propensity to consume out of wealth is likely to rise over time as financial systems become deeper, and that this effect may be particularly marked in bank-based financial systems, which have historically had relatively undeveloped financial markets.

Empirical Evidence

There is a large body of empirical work that suggests that changes in housing and equity prices have significant effects on private consumption in most advanced economies.[33]

[32]See, for example, Edison and Sløk (2001a, 2001b) and Ludwig and Sløk (2002).

[33]Nonetheless, controversies remain. Some researchers argue that the observed correlation between asset prices and consumption arise because they both react to some unidentified common economic factors (see, for example, Poterba and Samwick, 1995; Ludvigson and Steindel, 1999; and Kiley, 2000). However, the majority view is that it stems from real wealth effects, a view strongly supported by recent work using highly disaggregate data based on household-level data (Maki and Palumbo, 2001; and Dynan and Maki, 2001).

Figure 2.10 *(concluded)*

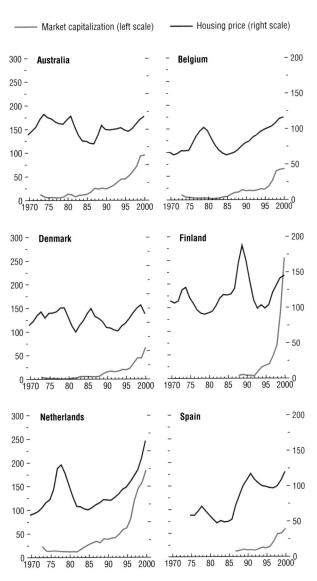

Sources: Bank for International Settlements; and Thomson Financial, Datastream.

Estimates of the magnitude of this effect vary considerably across countries, however, and are sometimes dependent on the type of asset in question.[34] Much of the existing literature focuses on the United States, where the effects of equity prices on consumption are in the range of 3–5 cents per dollar, with the effect taking one to three years to materialize. Spending out of housing wealth is somewhat higher, close to 4–6 cents per dollar, also taking one to three years to materialize.

The evidence for other advanced countries has been mixed. Many country-specific studies have focused specifically on the effects of equity prices on private consumption, finding significant wealth effects but somewhat smaller effects than those reported for the United States. For example, studies on the effect of equity prices on private consumption for Canada, Germany, Japan, the Netherlands, and the United Kingdom report estimates of the marginal propensities to consume out of wealth from about 1 cent up to about 3.5 cents.[35] This difference appears to reflect the small share of equity ownership relative to other financial assets in these countries as well as the more concentrated distribution of equity ownership across households in continental Europe when compared with the United States.

Other country-specific studies have focused on the impact of housing wealth, and these results have also varied between countries. For instance, in the United Kingdom a 10 percent increase in housing wealth would boost consumption between 0.2 and 0.8 percent within a year; in the Netherlands 0.7 percent over two years, and in Japan 0.6–1.0 percent. In contrast, there is little empirical evidence of a housing wealth effect in either France or Italy.[36]

A growing number of studies have examined the wealth effect using a panel of advanced economies rather than studying a specific country, and investigate the relative importance of the two wealth components—housing and stock market. Again, the results for these studies have been mixed. Several of these studies found the marginal propensity to consume out of stock wealth for the market-based economies to be roughly 4 cents per dollar, while they found a small stock wealth effect for the bank-based economies.[37] One study uncovered no stock wealth effect but a statistically significant and rather large effect of housing wealth upon household consumption with an elasticity of about 10 percent.[38]

To disentangle and clarify the effects of different types of wealth on consumption, the IMF staff undertook a new study focusing on a panel of 16 advanced economies over the period 1970–2000 using a conventional specification, with wealth split into stock wealth (proxied by stock market capitalization as a ratio to GDP) and house wealth (proxied by house prices since data on housing wealth were not generally available).[39] To examine differences in behavior over time and across financial systems, the equations were estimated over different time periods and the countries were split into two groups—market-based and bank-based economies—using a measure of stock market activity relative to bank

---

[34]For instance, Edison and Sløk (2001a) find significant differences between the effect of changes in the value of technology, media, and telecommunications (TMT) and non-TMT assets on consumption and investment in continental Europe (though not in the United States).

[35]See, for example, Boone, Giorno, and Richardson (1998) for recent evidence.

[36]For a review of recent evidence, see Girouard and Blöndal (2001).

[37]See, for example, Ludwig and Sløk (2002); Boone, Giorno, and Richardson (1998); Girouard and Blöndal (2001); and Boone, Girouard, and Wanner (2001).

[38]See Case, Quigley, and Shiller (2001).

[39]There is an important issue having to do with whether wealth effects are estimated in terms of cents per dollar change in wealth or percentage increase in wealth (that is, an elasticity). While the two approaches provide similar results when wealth is a relatively stable proportion of income, given the huge amount of wealth creation in equity markets in the 1990s, the elasticity approach implies an implausible fall in the impact of a dollar of wealth creation. Hence, at least for equities, the cents per dollar method is probably preferable.

Table 2.7. Equity and Housing Wealth Effects[1]

	Equity Effects (Cents per dollar)		House Effects (Elasticity × 100)		Speed of Adjustment (Average lag in years)	
	1970–2000	1984–2000	1970–2000	1984–2000	1970–2000	1984–2000
Marked-based	3.0	4.3	2.7	7.0	4.2	2.2
Bank-based	−0.2	0.9	4.5	4.3	9.1	6.3
Full sample	0.9	2.0	2.8	5.3	6.7	4.8

Source: IMF staff estimates.

[1]The relationship between consumption and wealth was estimated using a two-step procedure. The coefficients on equity wealth and house prices represent the long-run coefficients, whereas the speed of adjustment reflects the coefficient on the error correction term. See Box 2.1 for details.

activity.[40] Details of the approach are described in Box 2.1.

The results, reported in Table 2.7, can be summarized as follows.

- *The general impact of changes in wealth tends to be higher for the market-based group than the bank-based group, as expected.* For example, in a market-based economy a one-dollar increase in stock wealth would lead to a 4½ cent boost in consumption, whereas in a bank-based economy it would augment consumption by only 1 cent.

- *The speed of adjustment of consumption to the desired or targeted level of consumption is higher for the market-based group than the bank-based group.* The coefficients on the adjustment term indicate that when consumption deviates from its desired level, one-fourth to one-half of the adjustment will take place within the first year. Again, this conforms to prior expectations since it is likely to be easier to borrow against increases in wealth in market-based financial systems.

- *An increase in housing wealth has a bigger impact on consumption than a similar increase in stock wealth.* (See Box 2.2.) Using the sample estimates from 1984–2000 for the market-based group and focusing on the United States, the study finds that for every dollar increase in housing, wealth consumption increases by 7

cents, whereas a one-dollar increase in stock wealth would lead to a 4½ cent increase in consumption. For the bank-based group, the stock wealth effect is smaller; a dollar increase in wealth would lead to slightly less than a 1 cent increase in consumption, while housing wealth appears to have had a fairly consistent elasticity of about 4 percent.[41]

- *The impact of changes in wealth on consumption has increased over time in both groups of countries.* The coefficient estimates on the stock wealth and on the speed of adjustment rise over the later part of the sample for both groups, suggesting that the responsiveness of consumption to these changes has increased, possibly because financial markets have become deeper and more liquid. For example, as bank-based households increased their equity holdings they have increased their consumption out of this wealth and adjusted more quickly to these changes, although admittedly more slowly than the market-based group.

Conclusions

The second half of the 1990s has seen substantial increases in the wealth of households in advanced economies, primarily owing to devel-

[40]The method used to classify countries comes from Levine (2001). It is the ratio of the value of domestic equities traded on the domestic exchange divided by GDP divided by the value of deposit money bank credits to the private sector as a share of GDP. Larger values of this ratio imply a more market-based financial system. Market-based economies are Australia, Canada, Ireland, the Netherlands, Sweden, the United Kingdom, and the United States. Bank-based economies are Belgium, Denmark, Finland, France, Germany, Italy, Japan, Norway, and Spain.

[41]The results are not inconsistent with those in Ludwig and Sløk (2002), who find that the elasticity on stock wealth has a larger effect than the elasticity on housing wealth. The results reported above refer to the marginal propensity to consume and are in cents per dollar. Thus, for comparison to Ludwig and Sløk, these results would have to be scaled by the ratio of consumption to wealth.

Box 2.1 How Important Is the Wealth Effect on Consumption?

The background study uses a standard consumption model to estimate the wealth effect of the form:[1]

$$C_t = \alpha + \beta YP_t + \delta W_t + \varepsilon_t,$$

where C is real household consumer spending, YP is real disposable income, W is real household wealth, and ε is the error term. The derivations of such a relationship can be traced to the theory of consumer behavior as described by Friedman (1957) and Ando and Modigliani (1963).

The standard interpretation is that the coefficient δ is the marginal propensity to consume out of wealth—i.e., the increase in consumer spending associated with an increase in wealth. It is common practice to separate wealth into different categories, with equity market and housing wealth being the two most typical components. The coefficients on the two wealth components may differ because of liquidity, volatility, and leverage differences as well as differences in the distribution of ownership (see Box 2.2).

A general assumption, at least for the United States, is that the marginal propensity to consume is about 0.04 out of stock wealth and somewhat higher out of housing wealth.[2] These results suggest that four to seven cents of each dollar of an increase in wealth are spent after the dollar is earned. Given the large stock of wealth, such a propensity is large enough to have a significant bearing on the behavior of consumption over time.

In the background study the relationship between consumption and wealth was investigated for a sample of 16 OECD countries using panel data techniques.[3] In particular, the relationship was estimated using a two-step procedure. In the first stage, the long-run relationship between consumption and wealth was estimated. These results were then incorporated into a dynamic

specification as an "error correction mechanism." Consumption, disposable income, and equity wealth are all measured as a ratio of trend real GDP. As a result, the coefficient on wealth represents the marginal effects—that is, the cents per dollar (or cents per euro) impact of equity wealth—and can, therefore, capture the larger impact of the tremendous wealth creation of the late 1990s. Housing wealth was proxied by real house prices because of the lack of availability of comparable data on the stock of housing across all countries and, consequently, the estimated coefficient represents an elasticity.

The table shows that both types of wealth are statistically significant in the long run as well as in the short run. Building upon this general result, three aspects of the relationship between wealth and consumption were examined in more detail.

- *Does the wealth effect vary between countries with different domestic financial structures?* To examine this question the 16 countries were split into two groups—market-based and bank-based economies—and the model was estimated for each group separately.[4] Systematic differences in the results emerged, with the coefficient on equity wealth being consistently larger for the market-based group than the bank-based group.

- *Does the impact of wealth changes vary according to the type of wealth?* The estimated coefficients on equity wealth and housing wealth varied between the asset types. Comparisons are complicated by the fact that the equity coefficient is measured in cents to dollar while the coefficient on housing is an elasticity. However, comparing estimates for those countries that have data on the stock of housing wealth, as well as alternative specifications in which the

---

The main author is Hali J. Edison.

[1]See also Boone, Giorno, and Richardson (1998), Ludvigson and Steindel (1999), and Bertaut (2002).

[2]See, for example, Greenspan (1999, 2001).

[3]To determine the appropriate estimation procedure, tests for nonstationarity and cointegration were considered prior to estimating the error-correction model.

[4]Market-based economies are Australia, Canada, Ireland, the Netherlands, Sweden, the United Kingdom, and the United States. Bank-based economies are Belgium, Denmark, Finland, France, Germany, Italy, Japan, Norway, and Spain. This classification stems from ranking countries using indicators of financial structure based on relative size and activity as described in Levine (2001).

Consumption and Wealth Effects

	1970–2000			1984–2000		
	All[1]	Market-based[2]	Bank-based[3]	All[1]	Market-based[2]	Bank-based[3]
Long-run relationship						
Income	0.58*	0.57*	0.58*	0.52*	0.4*	0.58*
Equity wealth	0.009*	0.03*	−0.002	0.02*	0.043*	0.009
House wealth	0.042*	0.035*	0.046*	0.067*	0.096*	0.055*
House wealth x trend	−0.00009	−0.00026*	−0.00004	−0.00046*	−0.00083*	−0.00038*
Short-run relationship						
Change in income	0.52*	0.49*	0.53*	0.46*	0.3*	0.53*
Change in equity wealth	0.009*	0.011	0.009	0.006*	0.01	0.007
Change in housing wealth	0.06*	0.07*	0.04*	0.077*	0.01*	0.06*
Inflation	−0.04*	−0.05*	−0.02	−0.07*	−0.06	−0.06
Adjustment to long run	−0.15*	−0.24	−0.11*	−0.21*	−0.46*	−0.16*

Note: Regressions based on fixed-effects model. Asterisk indicates significance at the 5 percent level.
[1]The entire sample includes Australia, Belgium, Canada, Denmark, Finland, France, Germany, Ireland, Italy, Japan, the Netherlands, Norway, Spain, Sweden, the United Kingdom, and the United States.
[2]Market-based economies are Australia, Canada, Ireland, the Netherlands, Sweden, the United Kingdom, and the United States.
[3]Bank-based economies are Belgium, Denmark, Finland, France, Germany, Italy, Japan, Norway, and Spain.

coefficient on equity wealth was calculated as an elasticity, indicates that the marginal propensity to consume out of housing is larger than that out of equity wealth.

- *Has the wealth effect been rising over time?* The standard model for each financial market group was estimated over two different periods: 1970–2000 and 1984–2000. Comparison of the estimated coefficients indicates that the coefficients on wealth have been generally rising over time, particularly for the market-based financial systems.

opments in the stock market. As part of this change, the aggregate value of household sector equity holdings increased and financial markets deepened across all countries. These enormous swings in wealth have had major implications for household savings, because as households become wealthier they tend to spend more on goods and services. The impact can be illustrated by using the econometric results derived above to conduct two counterfactual experiments: first, what would have happened to private savings had equity wealth remained at its 1994 level (as a percentage of private disposable income); and, second, what would have happened if, in addition, housing prices had remained constant (relative to the consumer price index). For the countries with market-based financial systems, the rise in stock market wealth is estimated to have reduced the saving rate by over 6 percentage points by 2000 (Figure 2.11), and by 8 percentage points when higher house prices are taken into account. In contrast, in countries with bank-based financial systems, saving behavior is not affected much by changes in equity wealth.

However, in those countries where house prices increased, saving rates were reduced on average by 1.5 percentage points (third panel of Figure 2.11). Correspondingly, the fall in equity prices since March 2000 can be expected to raise the saving rate roughly ½–1½ percent in the G-7 countries. However, particularly in the United States and United Kingdom, the impact has so far been offset partly or wholly by higher housing prices, which rose by at least 15 percent over the corresponding period (Table 2.8).

The empirical results presented in this essay suggest that asset prices have become more im-

Figure 2.11. Saving Rate Behavior in Response to Asset Price Changes

The change in asset prices has had a substantial impact on market-based economies, but a modest impact on the bank-based economies.

——— Actual household saving rate
——— Household saving rate holding equity wealth constant at 1994 values
——— Household saving rate holding equity and housing wealth at 1994 values

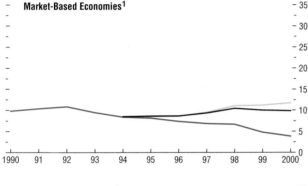

Market-Based Economies[1]

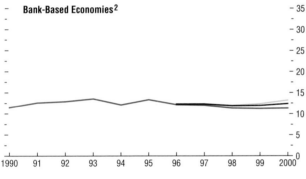

Bank-Based Economies[2]

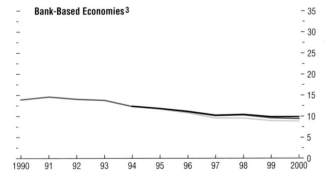

Bank-Based Economies[3]

Sources: OECD, *Economic Outlook* and Analytical database; and Thomson Financial, Datastream.
[1]Countries include Australia, Canada, Ireland, Netherlands, Sweden, the United Kingdom, and the United States.
[2]Countries include Belgium, Denmark, France, Finland, Norway, and Spain.
[3]Countries include Germany, Italy, and Japan.

Table 2.8. Estimated Impact of Change in Asset Value on Real Consumer Spending, 2000Q1–2001Q3
(Percentage terms of 2001Q3 consumer spending)

	United States	United Kingdom
Impact of equity wealth[1]	−1.9	−2.4
Impact of housing wealth[2]	1.6	4.5
Total impact of wealth effect[3]	−0.3	2.2
Actual change in real consumer spending	2.7	6.1

Source: IMF staff estimates.
[1]Estimate taken by applying the marginal propensity to consume from equity wealth to the fall in total stock market capitalization.
[2]Estimate taken by applying the house price elasticity, adjusted by the ratio of GDP to housing wealth, to the rise in household housing wealth.
[3]Estimate taken as sum of the two components.

portant over time as a determinant of consumer spending, a result that holds true for all countries regardless of their financial structure. Together with the increased correlation across countries, this suggests that asset prices have become increasingly more important in the transmission of domestic and global business cycles. Notwithstanding the correction in asset prices that is now under way, it appears likely that this trend will continue over the longer term. With bank-based systems—those countries where the role of banks dominates the financial system—continuing to evolve, households in these countries are likely both to hold an increasing part of their wealth as equities and to find it increasingly easy to borrow against wealth to finance consumption. The aging of populations across the industrialized world will also mean that consumption in an increasing proportion of households will be significantly dependent on asset holdings. Finally, the globalization of financial markets appears likely to continue, driven by deregulation and technological progress.

Looking forward, it seems clear that developments in asset prices are likely to become increasingly important for policymakers, both because of their direct impact on demand and—given their synchronization across countries—their role in the transmission mechanism of business cycle movements. While this does not mean that policymakers should target asset prices, it is clear that asset price developments both in an individual country and in the rest of the world will become an increasingly important input in the assessment of demand conditions, and therefore policy decisions.[42] Within this, as Federal Reserve Chairman Greenspan has pointed out, it is particularly important to focus on the differences within asset classes.[43] As noted in this essay, the impact of housing and stock wealth on consumption varies significantly, and this may also be true for their components.

Monetary Policy in a Low Inflation Era[44]

One of the most remarkable economic developments of recent decades has been the industrial countries' success in restoring low inflation. Following the great inflation of the 1970s, price increases have moderated and have been consistently below 3 percent since 1993 in the industrial countries as a whole and in the main industrial regions (North America, the European Union, and Japan), levels not experienced since the late 1950s (Figure 2.12). While this success was aided by a variety of factors—including more prudent fiscal policies, structural reforms, and declining oil and commodity prices—there is a widespread consensus that changes in the conduct of monetary policy have played a central role.[45]

Accordingly, this essay focuses on the role of monetary policy in achieving low and stable inflation, how this has affected the behavior of the private sector and the nature of the inflation process, and the new challenges that confront policymakers. Two key conclusions are that, because of the existence of the zero interest rate bound, the danger of getting into a deflationary

Figure 2.12. Inflation in Selected Advanced Economies
(Annual percent change)

From 1993 onward, inflation reached rates below 3 percent, levels not experienced since the late 1950s.

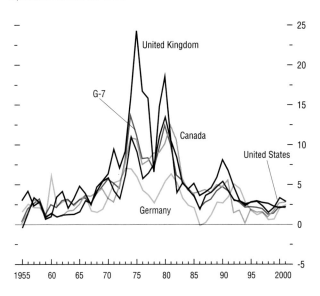

---

[42]See, for example, the May 2000 *World Economic Outlook* and Mishkin (2001).

[43]See Greenspan (1999 and 2001).

[44]The main authors of this essay are Marco Terrones and Silvia Sgherri; Bennet Sutton provided research assistance.

[45]See Chapter IV of the October 1999 *World Economic Outlook.* The improvement in fiscal policies is discussed in Chapter III of the May 2001 *World Economic Outlook.*

Box 2.2. A Household Perspective on the Wealth Effect

A growing literature explores the magnitude of the wealth effect from the stock market relative to other assets, notably housing. Some papers in this literature conclude that the stock market wealth effect, while significant at 3 to 5 cents out of every dollar, is smaller than the wealth effect from housing, which is estimated to be somewhat larger. A common explanation for this difference in magnitude is that house prices are less volatile than the stock market, so that gains in stock holdings are seen as less certain. This box offers an additional explanation based on recent work on the United States. Using recent household survey data, it finds that stock holdings are far more skewed toward the upper tail of the income distribution than is ownership of housing. Together with empirical evidence that the marginal propensity to consume may be declining in income, this is consistent with the view that, at the aggregate level, the wealth effect from housing is more important than the effect from the stock market.

The stock market boom during the 1990s has encouraged the view that corporate equity holdings are now the primary asset for a broad spectrum of households. Indeed, information from the flow of funds accounts indicate that, for the household sector in aggregate, equity wealth has been larger than housing wealth since 1996, and remains so even after the stock market decline in 2000 (upper panel of the figure). However, it remains true that ownership of housing is much more evenly spread across the income distribution than are holdings of corporate equities. The lower panel of the figure plots median equity holdings (direct and indirect) and housing wealth as ratios of income by decile of the income distribution, using data from the 1998 Survey of Consumer Finances;[1]

Residential and Equity Holdings in the United States

Sources: Federal Reserve Board, *Flow of Funds Accounts* and *1998 Survey of Consumer Finances;* and IMF staff estimates.

it shows that holdings of stocks are confined to the upper tiers of the income distribution and surpass housing in importance only in the upper decile.

The fact that equity holdings are so concentrated has been widely noted. Indeed, Maki and Palumbo (2001) show that the rise in consumer spending in the latter half of the 1990s can be explained largely by higher consumption among the richest households. The fact that equity holdings are more prevalent among the rich may, however, help explain why the

The main author is Robin Brooks.

[1]The Survey of Consumer Finances surveyed about 4,300 households in 1998 and oversampled relatively wealthy families to get an accurate picture of saving and portfolio behavior among this small segment of the population. The median estimates in the lower panel of the figure are weighted by the probability that a household is selected into the sample. For details on the survey, see Bertaut and Starr-McCluer (2002).

wealth effect from the stock market is estimated to be smaller than that from housing. Recent empirical evidence by Dynan and Maki (2001) suggests that the marginal propensity to consume falls as income rises.[2] Most likely, this reflects the fact that wealth-to-income ratios are much higher in the upper tail of the income distribution—rising from a weighted median of 53 percent in the lowest decile to 350 percent

[2]The marginal propensity to consume out of changes in stock market wealth is estimated at between 5 and 15 cents to the dollar for households with security holdings below $100,000, while for households with securities in excess of $100,000 it is estimated to lie between 1 and 5 cents.

in the highest.[3] As a result, the impact of changes in wealth on consumption is likely to be lower.

The fact that housing ownership is more evenly distributed across the income distribution, together with the fact that lower-income households have a larger propensity to consume, may therefore be an additional reason for the greater estimated magnitude of the wealth effect from housing.

[3]It could also reflect longer planning horizons among the rich, for example, because they are more likely to leave bequests. See also Bernheim, Shleifer, and Summers (1985).

spiral increases markedly as inflation targets are lowered below 2 percent and that there is a case for becoming more proactive with regard to sharp falls in activity. Much of the analysis focuses on the experience of four major countries with relatively independent monetary policy stance over the period since 1970—Canada, Germany, the United Kingdom, and the United States—but the lessons are equally valid for other industrial countries as well as many emerging market countries.[46]

How Was Inflation Brought Down, and What Were the Effects?

The main factor behind the achievement of low inflation in the 1990s was a widespread shift of central banks, including significant institutional changes, toward a more focused attitude

on inflation compared to the 1970s. Indeed, there has been an institutional sea change with the generalized adoption of independent central banks and the appointment of conservative central bankers, with low inflation as the first policy priority.[47] This largely reflected the recognition by the public and politicians that high inflation was associated with bad economic performance, as well as the recognition by central bankers that policies aimed at systematically exploiting the short-run output/inflation trade-off to increase output beyond potential were ineffective and self-defeating (Fischer, 1996, and Viñals, 2001).[48]

The shift in priorities can be illustrated by estimating monetary policy reaction functions that relate the short-term interest rates to inflation and the output gap.[49] Such functions provide a useful summary of central bank actions,

[46]The disinflation experience of emerging market countries, which reflects in part trends in the industrial countries, is discussed in Chapter IV of the May 2001 *World Economic Outlook*.

[47]For instance, independent central banks were created in the 1990s in France, Italy, Japan, New Zealand, the United Kingdom, and for the euro area.

[48]Barro and Gordon (1983) highlighted the possibility of higher inflation than desired as policymakers overstimulate the economy in an attempt to raise output above potential. This bias can be mitigated, however, by creating independent central banks with appropriate incentives and structure, including the appointment of conservative management (Rogoff, 1985; Walsh, 1995; and Svensson, 1997).

[49]See, for instance, Taylor (1993).

Figure 2.13. Inflation Has Become Less Volatile and More Predictable

As inflation has fallen, inflation volatility has declined and the spread of private sector forecasts has decreased.

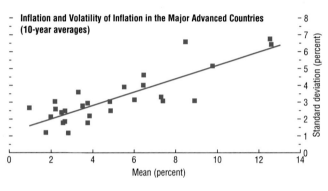

Inflation and Volatility of Inflation in the Major Advanced Countries (10-year averages)

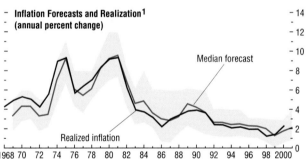

Inflation Forecasts and Realization[1] (annual percent change)

Sources: *Survey of Professional Forecasters*, Federal Reserve Bank of Philadelphia; and IMF staff estimates.
[1] Inflation density forecasts are represented by shaded region. The lower and upper bounds of the region represent the 5th and 95th percentile, respectively. The solid line represents the median forecast.

and are essential for some types of analysis, although it should be recognized that they reflect a stylized version of the policymaking process.[50] Empirical estimates of such functions for Canada, Germany, the United Kingdom, and the United States are reported in Appendix 2.1. They indicate that, compared with the 1970s, policy in the 1980s and 1990s became more responsive to changes in inflation and less responsive to output gaps and, in addition, central banks also changed interest rates in a smoother manner, thereby making policy more predictable.[51] These policy changes helped central banks build credibility with associated benefits for the private sector—in particular, a greater smoothing of target rates, known as gradualism, reduced policy uncertainty, and increased private sector confidence about the direction of policy.[52]

The return to low inflation has changed the nature of the inflationary process in three important ways.

- *Inflation has become less volatile.* The existence of a positive association between the average level of inflation and its volatility, both across countries and within each country, has long been recognized (Friedman, 1977, and Taylor, 1981). The correlation between mean and standard deviation of inflation for the G-7 countries has averaged 0.4 during the past 40 years (Figure 2.13, top panel). Consistent with this, as inflation has declined, its volatility has fallen by an average of one-third between the 1980s and the 1990s, with particularly striking

[50]In practice, central banks have access to a much wider range of information than estimates of the output gap and of expected inflation, and, given the importance of market responses in transmitting policy actions to the economy, central banking remains "as much an art as a science" (Blinder, 1997).

[51]As the output gap is an unobserved variable, it is measured with error. Indeed, systematic errors in estimating these gaps in the 1970s contributed to policy mistakes (Orphanides, 1998, and McCallum, 2001b).

[52]One consequence is that long-term interest rate movements often anticipate monetary policy actions, reducing the contemporaneous impact between short- and long-term interest rates.

reductions in France, Italy, and the United States.

- *Inflation has become more predictable.* As inflation volatility has fallen, it has—unsurprisingly—become easier to predict future inflation. For example, Diebold, Tay, and Wallis (1999), using information from the U.S. Survey of Professional Forecasters, found that the spread of private sector forecasts of inflation has decreased in the past decade in direct relation with the fall in inflation (Figure 2.13, bottom panel) and perhaps other factors such as more benign shocks to the economy. Similarly, the accuracy of econometric models of inflation has risen. For example, following the approach of Taylor (1981), staff estimates indicate that the standard errors of simple time-series models of inflation and conventional Phillips curves, which include past inflation and output gap, have generally fallen significantly since the 1970s for Canada, Germany, the United Kingdom, and the United States.

- *Inflation has become less persistent.* Simple tests indicate that inflation persistence has fallen as countries move from high to low inflation. For example, the time-series models referred to in the previous paragraph indicate that past inflation is becoming a less important factor in explaining its current level. One way of quantifying this change is to calculate how long it takes for a shock to inflation to dissipate. The half-life of a shock to inflation (i.e., the time it takes for half of a shock to inflation to be eroded) has been falling—in the United States it has been reduced by two-thirds since the 1970s. (On this issue, see also Cogley and Sargent, 2002, and the comments by Stock, 2002.)

Lower and less volatile inflation, by creating a more stable environment, is generally expected to result in better economic performance (Fischer, 1996). For example, it reduces the uncertainty of relative price signals, thereby making economic decisions more transparent. As a result, a reduction in inflation volatility should be associated with a reduction in output fluctuations.[53] As can be seen in Figure 2.14, this does indeed appear to be the case for the G-7 countries, with the correlation being particularly marked in the United Kingdom and the United States (Lucas, 1973; and Cecchetti, Flores-Lagunes, and Krause, 2001, document this effect across a wider range of countries).[54] Furthermore, recent research indicates that inflation volatility is one of the most important causes of output volatility, suggesting that the dampening of economic fluctuations during the 1980s and 1990s owes much to the fall in inflation volatility associated with reduction in the level of inflation, not simply a more benign underlying environment (Blanchard and Simon, 2001).

How Has Low Inflation Affected Private Sector Behavior?

The decline in inflation has had significant effects on private sector behavior. As inflation becomes low and more predictable, workers are more willing to increase the length of their labor contracts, as they are less concerned that their wages will be eroded by unexpectedly high inflation. Indeed, studies for the United States and other advanced economies have found that the average duration for wage contracts and the frequency of wage adjustment are inversely related to the level of inflation (Taylor, 1999). Second,

[53]A fall in inflation should also have a positive effect on economic growth. Empirical work confirms a negative association between inflation and output growth (see, for instance, Fischer, 1993; Barro, 1997; and Judson and Orphanides, 1996). The situation is more complex at low inflation rates. For instance, Khan and Senhadji (2001) found no relationship between inflation and output growth at low levels of inflation (0–3 percent in the case of industrial countries) but a robust negative association beyond this threshold.

[54]In Germany during the late 1980s, inflation volatility rose with no visible effect on output volatility; this suggests that the uncertainties surrounding the process of the German unification had an effect on prices, perhaps reflecting the private sector uncertainty about the future course of monetary policy.

Figure 2.14. Volatility in Output and Inflation
(Rolling 5-year standard deviation of quarterly growth rates)

Output volatility and inflation volatility are highly correlated, particularly in the United Kingdom and the United States.

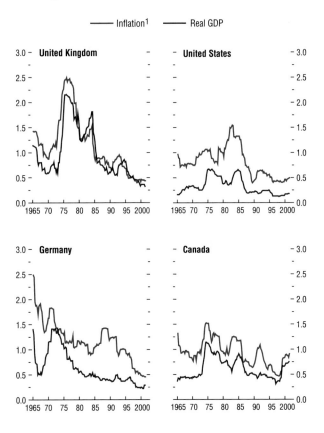

Sources: IMF, *International Financial Statistics;* and IMF staff estimates.
[1] GDP deflator.

private agents are willing to engage in longer-term financial contracts and hold longer-term financial assets, as the risks of unexpected wealth redistribution between debtors and creditors on fixed-rate contracts falls. Third, firms' pricing power has declined. In a low inflation environment firms are less able to pass through changes in their costs—including those linked to exchange rate fluctuations—to prices (McCarthy, 2000). One consequence of longer contracts is that the inflationary response to monetary policies might become more elongated. The decline in inflation has also helped mitigate the distortionary effects resulting from nominal rigidities in the tax system.

In addition, as central banks have become more credible and more predictable, private sector behavior seems to have become more forward looking in both labor and product markets. For example, despite the lengthening of contracts, several trends suggest that compensation schemes have become more flexible, sophisticated, and forward looking, particularly in relatively deregulated economies such as the United States, where the size of unionized labor has been in decline for several years. Labor contracts have also become more homogenous over time, both across firms and industries, and often include compensation provisions, such as annual bonuses paid at the end of the year. Finally, the number of companies that include forward-looking compensation schemes has grown large.

One way of measuring this change in behavior is to look at shifts in the weight given to inflationary expectations in an expectation-augmented Phillips curve—which is vertical in the long run—where current inflation depends on past and expected inflation (with weights that sum to unity) as well as the output gap.[55] Results reported in Appendix 2.1 indicate that price setting has indeed become more forward looking over time across a range of countries. Other

---

[55]Such a model is widely used and can be derived from particular forms of staggered wage/price contracts, particularly in the context of the slow diffusion of information (Mankiw and Reis, 2001).

studies suggest that the reduced weight on past inflation is linked to greater central bank credibility (Laxton and N'Diaye, 2002). More forward-looking private sector behavior, in turn, increases the effectiveness of monetary policy. This is because workers and firms become more responsive to anticipated changes in policy, which magnify the impact of current adjustments in the policy stance—an effect often described as the expectations channel of monetary policy. In sum, a virtuous circle was created in which as central banks became more concerned about inflation and, therefore, more predictable and credible, this led to more forward-looking behavior by the private sector, which in turn made monetary policy effects through the expectations channel faster and more effective.

This virtuous circle can be illustrated by looking at the results from a small macroeconomic model of the type often used in analysis of monetary policy.[56] Appendix 2.1 describes a three-equation model estimated by the IMF staff for Canada, Germany, the United Kingdom, and the United States. In addition to the monetary policy reaction function and expectation-augmented Phillips curve already discussed, the model comprises an aggregate demand curve, which relates the output gap to the real interest rate (a relationship that appears to have been broadly stable since 1970). While the relatively simple structure of such models does not take explicit account of many real-life transmission mechanisms—such as asset prices, balance sheet effects, fiscal policy, the role of the exchange rate, and external demand—their flexibility, sophisticated forward-looking dynamics, and transparency make them useful analytic tools.[57] In particular, the structure highlights the importance of two of the main monetary transmission channels: a conventional real interest rate channel, through which central banks affect the spending decisions of the private sector; and an expectation channel, through which central banks influence the private sector's inflationary expectations by conveying information about the future course of monetary policy.

The results from the model illustrate the benefits from the positive feedback between changes in the monetary policy rule and private sector behavior. Figure 2.14 reports the impact of changing the value of some of the key parameters of the model on inflation and output volatility, calculated using stochastic simulations in which the model is subjected to "typical" underlying shocks. The top left panel, for example, traces out the impact of changing the degree of forward-looking behavior in the Phillips curve on the volatility of inflation (assuming the other coefficients in the model remain at their estimated U.S. values since 1982),[58] while the top right panel reports the same relationship for output volatility. The lower panels repeat the exercise using the three parameters in the monetary reaction function, the coefficient on inflation, the coefficient on the output gap, and the smoothing parameter, respectively. To give a sense of the impact of changes in behavior over time, estimated parameter values for the 1970s and 1982 onward for the United States are identified. The results suggest that the large reductions in the variability of inflation and output since the 1970s were achieved through the increased responsiveness of the monetary authorities to inflation and the resulting increase in the forward-looking behavior of the private sector, as can be seen in the top half of Figure 2.15. The bottom two panels also indicate that interest rate smoothing has also

---

[56]See, for instance, Clarida, Galí, and Gertler (1999); Rudebusch and Svensson (1999); and King (2000).

[57]Ball (1999) and Svensson (2000a) both argue that even in small open economies these monetary policy rules are effective, as the exchange rate response increases the effect of changes in the interest rates. In a similar vein, Mishkin (2001) argues that although monetary policy works through a series of channels, including real estate prices, equity prices, and exchange rates, these assets are inappropriate targets for policies (see also Chapter III of the May 2000 *World Economic Outlook*).

[58]The impact on inflation volatility is generally much larger if several parameters are returned to their 1970s values at the same time, reflecting the relative instability of the monetary rule from that period.

Figure 2.15. Improving Monetary Policy Effectiveness[1]

Ceteris paribus, as private agents become more forward looking, and monetary policy becomes more responsive to inflation and more gradualist, both inflation and output volatility can be reduced.

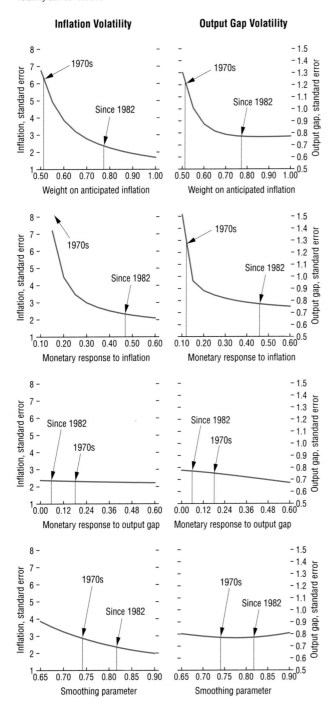

Source: IMF staff estimates.
[1]Each panel of this figure is drawn under the assumption that the other coefficients in the model remain at their 1982–2000 values.

played a role, particularly in the reduction in inflation volatility.

The results also suggest, however, that the benefits from movements in these three parameters are becoming more limited over time. Further increasing the monetary response to inflationary disturbances, the smoothing parameter, or the forward-looking coefficient in the Phillips curve appears likely to produce smaller results than in the past, particularly with regard to output volatility.

The Road Ahead

What are the new policy challenges for central banks now that monetary policymakers have succeeded in attaining relatively low and stable inflation across the industrialized world? The most obvious change is that central banks' objectives are becoming more symmetric, as concerns about higher inflation in the future have begun to be counterbalanced by concerns about deflation and the zero nominal interest floor. Deflation blunts the effectiveness of monetary policy and can lead to a downward spiral of activity in part through balance sheet effects on the financial system, as the example of Japan vividly indicates (DeLong, 2000). As a result, central banks can no longer be primarily focused on concerns about increases in inflation. Indeed, analysis suggests that the danger of getting into a deflationary spiral increases markedly as inflation targets are lowered below 2 percent (Box 2.3).

Concerns about deflation also suggest that central banks need to be more proactive in responding to sharp downward shocks to activity. In the 1980s and 1990s, monetary policy improved its efficiency through greater smoothing of interest rate changes—often referred to as gradualism—and credibility. These changes provided substantial benefits, most notably in reducing economic fluctuations (Sack and Wieland, 1999). However, with inflation low, gradualism may not be the best policy to follow in the face of sharp downward fluctuations in activity. A drawn out policy response runs the risk that inflation will continue to fall and may even turn

Box 2.3. Can Inflation Be Too Low?

One consequence of the achievement of low inflation in the 1990s has been a debate about whether inflation can be too low given the existence of a zero floor on interest rates.[1] In particular, it has been argued that the scope for adjusting the stance of monetary policy could become severely constrained if central bankers pursued a very low inflation target because such a choice would result in a low average level of nominal interest rates, significantly reducing the monetary authority's scope for reducing real interest rates when its output and inflation stabilization objectives were threatened by adverse deflationary shocks to the economy. The performance of the Japanese economy over the past decade has illustrated just how important this problem can be. This box summarizes some results from a recent study on Japan that uses the IMF's macroeconomic model MULTIMOD to assess how the zero-interest-rate floor (ZIF) can reduce the effectiveness of monetary policy.[2]

In the face of a negative demand shock similar in magnitude to that experienced by Japan in the late 1990s, the figure shows how the ZIF and the choice of target inflation can limit the effectiveness of monetary policy. The monetary authority is assumed to adjust the short-term interest rate according to a "Taylor-type" policy rule with a response coefficient on the inflation gap of 1.0 and a response coefficient on the output gap of 0.5.[3] The impact of the ZIF under the zero percent inflation target on the monetary authority's control over real interest rates is striking. Under the zero inflation target, the ZIF means there is less room to lower the nominal interest rate, constraining the initial decline in real interest rates.

Consequently, output recovers more slowly, causing inflation to decline more, which in turn

The main author is Benjamin Hunt.
[1]See Summers (1991).
[2]For more details of the analysis, see Hunt and Laxton (2001) and for a detailed description of MULTIMOD, see Laxton and others (1998).
[3]These coefficient magnitudes are within the range of empirically estimated coefficients using U.S. data.

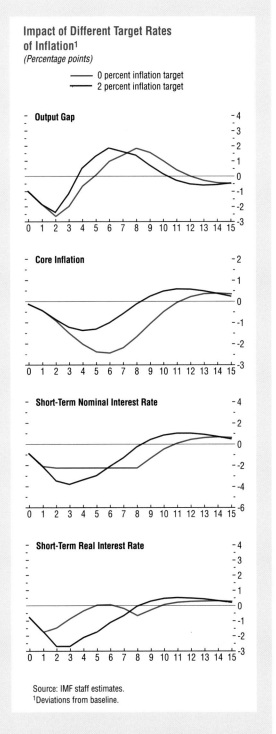

Impact of Different Target Rates of Inflation[1]
(Percentage points)

— 0 percent inflation target
— 2 percent inflation target

Source: IMF staff estimates.
[1]Deviations from baseline.

drives real interest rates upward, further depressing aggregate demand and leading to more

Box 2.3 *(concluded)*

Impact of Average Inflation Target Rate on Interest Rates and Output
(Percent)

	3.0	2.5	2.0	1.5	1.0	0.5	0
Probability that interest rates become zero	2.0	3.0	4.0	8.0	13.0	23.0	31.0
Probability of a deflationary spiral	0.0	0.0	0.0	2.0	3.0	8.0	11.0
Variance of real output	1.8	1.8	1.8	1.81	1.85	1.96	2.16

downward pressure on inflation. If the shocks hitting the economy are large enough, this dynamic interaction can lead to a deflationary spiral that cannot be reversed by adjustment of the short-term nominal interest rate alone, as a result of which the model cannot be solved without assuming additional actions by the fiscal or monetary authorities.

Given the potential difficulties presented by the ZIF, how can the monetary policy framework, as summarized by the policymaker's price stability objective and the rule governing the systematic adjustment of the short-term interest rate, be designed to minimize the possibility of the ZIF becoming a binding constraint? Further analysis suggests two modifications that can be effective. One is responding more aggressively to negative deviations of output from potential output and inflation from its target rate. In response to negative shocks, adjusting the short-term nominal interest rate aggressively reduces the probability and severity of periods of deflation.[4]

In model simulations another effective modification was found to be generalizing the monetary authority's reaction function to include an explicit price-level component. Incorporating an explicit price-level component gives monetary policy more influence on real interest rates once nominal interest rates become constrained at zero. To achieve the price-level target, inflation must exceed its underlying target rate following periods during which inflation has been below target, a factor that

affects inflation expectations and real interest rates.[5] This result relies on the price level target being credible. However, this credibility may be difficult to achieve in practice. Private agents may doubt the policymaker's ability to generate future inflation if the nominal interest rate is at or near the ZIF and, even more important, question the policymaker's commitment to achieve the future inflation once deflationary pressures have dissipated. This suggests that monetary authorities may need to rely on other mechanisms, besides the adjustment of short-term interest rates, to enhance the credibility of their announced objectives. Direct purchases of assets such as long-term bonds and foreign currency have been suggested as possibilities.[6]

Even under the best possible policy rule, where the commitment to generate future inflation when required is perfectly credible, the probability of getting into a deflationary spiral increases markedly as the target rate for inflation is lowered below 2 percent. The table reports results derived from stochastic simulations on MULTIMOD, in which the model is subjected to "typical" shocks. Output variability increases as the average inflation target declines below 2 percent and there is an increasing probability that the economy can be tipped into a deflationary spiral of prices and output that cannot be solved by adjusting the short-term nominal interest rate (hence preventing the model from computing a solu-

---

[4]Other researchers using models of the U.S. economy have also reached this conclusion. See Orphanides and Wieland (1998) and Reifschneider and Williams (1999).

[5]This is a channel through which several commentators have suggested Japanese monetary policy must now operate. For example, see Svensson (2000b) and Krugman (1998).

[6]See Clouse and others (2000).

tion).[7] While this work was done on the Japanese sector in MULTIMOD, preliminary work with the models for the United States and the euro area suggest that, if anything, the ZIF issue could be more compelling in these regions owing to the greater inertia in the inflation process. These conclusions are also consistent with other work examining the optimal level of

inflation using a variety of monetary policy models, which generally conclude that it is best if inflation does not fall below 1–1½ percent, implying target inflation rates above that level.[8] The fundamental point that emerges is that the easiest and best way to solve the issue of the ZIF is to target a sufficiently high rate of inflation.

[7]There are many other factors—such as alternative channels for monetary policy, uncertainty about the structure of the economy, distortionary effects of inflation, and biases in price indices—that influence the optimal level of inflation in the face of the ZIF that this MULTIMOD analysis does not incorporate.

[8]See Fischer (1996) for a general survey; Akerlof, Dickens, and Perry (2000), Orphanides and Wieland (1998), and McCallum (2001a) on the United States; and Wyplosz (2001) and Viñals (2001) on the euro area. By contrast, Reifschneider and Williams (2001) conclude that the inflation target can be as low as ¾ percent if appropriate policies are followed.

into deflation, while the effectiveness of monetary policy may be constrained either as interest rates hit the zero bound or if they are anticipated to do so in the future (Meyer, 2001). In these circumstances, it may be more appropriate to respond somewhat more aggressively to significant negative shocks to activity. Indeed, the relatively robust response of a number of central banks to the current downturn in activity appears consistent with this analysis.

Appendix 2.1. A Stylized Model of Monetary Policy[59]

There is an extensive and growing literature evaluating the performance of monetary policy in advanced economies. One popular method of analyzing the design of monetary policy rules is to use small macroeconomic models comprising a few key relationships and rational expectations, following the original work by Taylor (1979). See, for example, Clarida, Galí, and Gertler (2000); Rudebusch and Svensson (1999); Svensson (2000); and King (2000).

While such small models do not include many important economic mechanisms—such as asset prices and balance sheet effects—their analytical tractability and forward-looking dynamics make them a useful tool for the discussion of monetary policy and private sector responses.[60]

This appendix presents a closed-economy three-equation monetary model for the United States embedding rational expectations estimated by the staff. The system includes a reduced-form interest rate rule, an expectation-augmented Phillips curve, and an IS curve—or aggregate demand equation—which are characterized respectively as follows.

$$i_t = \alpha_0 + \alpha_1 \pi_{t+1}^e + \alpha_2 (y_t - \bar{y}_t) + \rho i_{t-1}; \qquad (1)$$

$$\pi_t = \beta \pi_{t+1}^e + (1 - \beta) \pi_{t-1} + \gamma (y_t - \bar{y}_t); \qquad (2)$$

$$(y_t - \bar{y}_t) = \delta_0 + \delta_1 (i_t - \pi_{t+1}^e) + \delta_2 (y_{t-1} - \bar{y}_{t-1}). \qquad (3)$$

Equation (1) relates the monetary authority's choice of short-term interest rate, i_t, to the next period's expected inflation, π_{t+1}^e, the output gap, $(y_t - \bar{y}_t)$, and the lagged interest rate i_{t-1}. According to this policy rule, the monetary authority

[59]The main author is Silvia Sgherri.

[60]Large macroeconomic models are also used to analyze monetary policy, as summarized in Reifschneider, Stockton, and Wilcox (1997) for the United States; Blake (1996) for the United Kingdom; Armour, Fung, and Mclean (2002) for Canada; and Drew and Hunt (2000) for New Zealand.

controls the path of the nominal interest rate to correct for deviations of expected inflation and real output (the feedback variables) from the inflation target and the potential level of output (the policy goals). The policy choices for the policymaker are the parameters α_1, α_2, and ρ. Higher values of α_1 (α_2) imply a more aggressive policy response for a given deviation of the inflation forecast (real output) from its target (potential). The coefficient ρ indicates the degree of instrument smoothing, which, in turn, dictates the speed at which the feedback variables are brought back to target, following inflationary disturbances. The constant α_0 embeds both the target level of inflation and the economy's underlying real rate of interest.

Equation (2) defines the model's supply side using an augmented Phillips curve, which relates current inflation, π_t, to expected inflation, π_{t+1}^e, to lagged inflation, π_{t-1}, and to the output gap, $(y_t - \bar{y}_t)$. The responsiveness of π_t to π_{t+1}^e, as measured by β, can be regarded as the proportion of informed agents who forecast future inflation by correctly understanding the underlying structure of the economy. On the other hand, $(1 - \beta)$ represents the proportion of uninformed agents, who use the past inflation rate to forecast future inflation.[61] Other things being equal, larger values of β imply a higher degree of nominal flexibility. The parameter γ governs how current inflation responds to deviations of output from potential: the larger the value of γ, the greater the effect of output on inflation, and the higher the real flexibility of underlying wages and prices.

Equation (3) makes the real output gap $(y_t - \bar{y}_t)$ depend on the (expected) real interest rate $(i_t - \pi_{t+1}^e)$ and on its own lagged value $(y_{t-1} - \bar{y}_{t-1})$. The parameter δ_1 determines the semi-elasticity of aggregate spending to real interest rate: the larger its absolute value, the larger the decline in demand following a given rise in the short-term real interest rate. Implicit in this IS equation is the conventional specification of the Fisher equation: the short-term

Table 2.9. Estimated Parameters of the Stylized Model for the U.S. Economy

	High Inflation	Low Inflation
Monetary reaction function		
Expected inflation	0.118**	0.461**
Output gap	0.181**	0.046*
Smoothing parameter	0.744**	0.816**
Memorandum		
Long-run elasticities		
Expected inflation	0.462**	2.51**
Output gap	0.705**	0.249*
Phillips curve		
Relative weight on expected inflation	0.511**	0.774**
Output gap	0.015**	0.044**
Aggregate demand function[1]		
Real interest rate	–0.157*	–0.157*
Lagged output gap	0.789**	0.789**
Memorandum		
Long-run elasticities		
Real interest rate	–0.745*	–0.745*

Note: Estimates of the intercepts are not reported in the table. One and two asterisks indicate that the coefficient is significantly different from zero at the 5 and 1 percent level, respectively.
[1]No significant structural break was identified over the two subsamples.

real interest rate equals the difference between the short-term nominal rate and the rate of inflation that is expected to prevail in the next period. The coefficient δ_2 on the lagged term in output measures the degree of persistence in output fluctuations, reflecting potential adjustment costs in private agents' spending decisions.

The structure of the model highlights the importance of two monetary transmission channels: a conventional real interest rate channel, through which monetary policy affects the spending decisions of the private sector and—thereby—inflation; and an expectation channel, through which central banks drive markets' expectations by conveying information about the future course of monetary policy. The relative importance of these two channels proves critical in understanding what makes monetary policy effective. In circumstances where the Phillips curve is predominantly myopic, policy is mainly effective through the standard interest rate

---

[61]For a micro founded model based on information frictions see Mankiw and Reis (2001).

Table 2.10. Estimated Parameters of the Stylized Model for Other Advanced Economies

	Germany[1,2]		United Kingdom[1,2]		Canada[2]	
	High inflation	Low inflation	High inflation	Low inflation	High inflation	Low inflation
Monetary reaction function[3]						
Expected inflation	−0.192**	0.212**	0.019	0.098**	0.268**	0.376**
Output gap	0.140**	−0.013**	0.002	0.023**	0.030**	0.040**
Smoothing parameter	0.696**	0.867**	0.788**	0.828**	0.894**	0.804**
Memorandum						
Long-run elasticities						
Expected inflation	−0.631*	1.59**	0.090	0.570**	2.55**	1.91**
Output gap	0.462**	−0.095	0.010	0.132*	0.286**	0.202*
Phillips curve						
Relative weight on expected inflation	0.563**	0.750**	0.584**	0.558**	0.429**	0.499**
Output gap	0.007**	0.005	−0.040**	0.037**	−0.004	0.015**
Aggregate demand function[3]						
Real interest rate	−0.194*	−0.194*	−0.254*	−0.254*	−0.143*	−0.143*
Lagged output gap	0.883**	0.883**	0.638**	0.638**	0.891**	0.891**
Memorandum						
Long-run elasticities						
Real interest rate	−1.67	−1.67	−0.800**	−0.800**	−1.31	−1.31

Note: Estimates of the intercepts are not reported in the table. One and two asterisks indicate that the coefficient is significantly different from zero at the 5 and 1 percent level, respectively.

[1]Additional dummy variables have been included in the German model, to account for the stress of unification on the economy in 1990Q4 and 1991Q1, and in the U.K. model, to account for disinflationary policies carried out in 1979Q2 and 1979Q3.

[2]For these open economies, additional indicators were found to be significant in explaining changes in the policy rate. However, for the sake of comparison, corresponding estimated parameters have not been reported here.

[3]No significant structural break was identified over the two subsamples.

channel, although with a lag. Indeed, the monetary authority can succeed in temporarily increasing activity with little impact on inflation. As the weight on forward-looking expectations in the Phillips curve grows, however, the consequences of such unstable policies become more evident, because of the expectation channel. As a result, the ability of monetary policy to stabilize current inflation hinges crucially on the belief that the monetary authority will maintain future inflation at its target level.

Table 2.9 reports the parameter estimates for this model for the U.S. economy, both for the high inflation period (1970Q1–1982Q1, hereafter the 1970s) and the subsequent move to the low inflation (1982Q2 onward) period. As can be seen from Table 2.10, generally similar results are obtained for other industrial countries with independent monetary policies in-

cluded in the sample (Canada, Germany, and the United Kingdom), so that while the discussion that follows below is based on the estimated parameters for the United States, the conclusions remain largely valid with respect to a range of other countries.[62] In the presence of unobservable expected variables, asymptotically efficient estimates of the parameters are obtained by using Hansen's (1982) Generalized Method of Moments estimation technique, with lagged endogenous variables as instruments. The significance of structural breaks between the high- and low-inflation period has been tested in each equation with the aid of step dummies, taking the value of one in the 1970s and zero otherwise. Significant breaks in the early 1980s were found in the monetary reaction function and the Phillips curve. No evidence of a significant break was found in the IS

[62]However, in the case of the open economies included in the sample, the model also allows for an interest parity condition. In addition, the real exchange rate (along with other indicators) has been found statistically significant in explaining changes in the nominal interest rate.

curve, so the full period estimates are used in both subperiods.[63]

The parameter estimates indicate that—since 1982—policymakers have become significantly more aggressive on inflation, less responsive to the output gap, and more gradualist in adjusting their policy instruments. Indeed, the parameter estimates for the 1970s indicate that monetary policy was close to being unstable, which may help explain the corresponding price instability (on this point, see Taylor, 1999; and Clarida, Galí, and Gertler, 2000). While the point estimate of the feedback coefficient on inflation in the 1990s is about four times as large as it was during the 1970s—rising from 0.12 to 0.46—the coefficient on output over the same period is approximately one-fourth its value in the era of great inflation—falling from 0.18 to 0.05. At the same time, the degree of instrument smoothing has increased, implying that policy has become more gradual and predictable (see also Sack and Wieland, 1999; and Batini and Haldane, 1999). Net, the long-run monetary policy response to inflation has increased fivefold, while the steady-state response to deviations of output from potential has more than halved. These shifts have also resulted in changes in private sector price-wage behavior. In particular, the coefficient on forward-looking inflation in the Phillips curve has risen significantly. This increases the effectiveness of monetary policy, as the private sector responds more rapidly to current and anticipated future actions by the monetary authority. This change in the private sector appears to be closely linked to the greater focus on (formal and informal) inflation targeting in policymaking, thereby providing an anchor to private agents' inflation expectations (see Amano, Coletti, and Macklem, 1999; Isard, Laxton, and Eliasson, 2001; and Laxton and N'Diaye, 2002). In addition, inflation—since 1982—appears to be significantly more responsive to deviations of output from potential, as revealed by estimates of the parameter γ in the Phillips curves (Tables 2.9 and 2.10). Hence, the traditional interest rate channel also appears to have become more effective over time.

References

Akerlof, George, William Dickens, and George Perry, 2000, "Near-Rational Wage and Price Setting and the Long-Run Phillips Curve," *Brookings Papers on Economic Activity: 1*, pp. 1–60.

Alfaro, Laura, and Fabio Kanczuk, 2001, "Capital Controls, Risk, and Liberalization Cycles" (unpublished; Cambridge, Massachusetts: Harvard Business School).

Allen, Franklin, and Douglas Gale, 2000, *Comparing Financial Systems* (Cambridge, Massachusetts: MIT Press).

Amano, Robert, Don Coletti, and Tiff Macklem, 1999, "Monetary Rules When Economic Behaviour Changes," in *Monetary Policy Under Uncertainty: Workshop Held at the Reserve Bank of New Zealand, 29–30 June, 1998*, ed. by Benjamin Hunt and Adrian Orr (Wellington, New Zealand), pp. 157–200.

Ando, Albert, and Franco Modigliani, 1963, "The 'Life Cycle' Hypothesis of Saving: Aggregate Implications and Tests," *American Economic Review*, Vol. 103, pp. 55–84.

Armour, Jamie, Ben Fung, and Dinah Maclean, 2002, "Taylor Rules in the Quarterly Projection Model," Bank of Canada Working Paper 2002–1 (Ottawa). Available on the Internet at *http://www.bank-banque-canada.ca/en/res/wp02–1.htm*.

Arora, Vivek, and Martin Cerisola, 2001, "How Does U.S. Monetary Policy Influence Sovereign Spreads in Emerging Markets?" *IMF Staff Papers*, Vol. 48, No. 3, pp. 474–98.

Ball, Laurence, 1999, "Policy Rules for Open Economies," in *Monetary Policy Rules*, ed. by John B. Taylor (Chicago, Illinois: University of Chicago Press), pp. 127–44.

Barro, Robert, 1997, *Determinants of Economic Growth: A Cross-Country Empirical Study* (Cambridge, Massachusetts: MIT Press).

———, and David Gordon, 1983, "Rules, Discretion, and Reputation in a Model of Monetary Policy," *Journal of Monetary Economics*, Vol. 12 (July), pp. 101–21

---

[63]Estimates of the coefficients α_1, α_2, ρ, β, and γ over the 1990s were significantly different from their corresponding estimates in the 1970s, at the usual 5 percent level.

Batini, Nicoletta, and Andrew Haldane, 1999, "Forward-Looking Rules for Monetary Policy," in *Monetary Policy Rules*, ed. by John B. Taylor (Chicago, Illinois: University of Chicago Press), pp. 157–92.

Bernheim, B. Douglas, Andrei Shleifer, and Lawrence Summers, 1985, "The Strategic Bequest Motive," *Journal of Political Economy*, Vol. 93 (December), pp. 1045–76.

Bertaut, Carol, 2002, "Equity Prices, Household Wealth, and Consumption Growth in Foreign Industrial Countries: Wealth Effects in the 1990s," forthcoming International Finance Discussion Paper (Washington: Board of Governors of the Federal Reserve System).

———, and Martha Starr McCluer, 2002, "Household Portfolios in the United States," in *Household Portfolios*, ed. by Luigi Guiso, Michael Haliassos, and Tullio Jappelli (Cambridge, Massachusetts: MIT Press).

Blake, Andrew, 1996, "Forecast Error Bounds by Stochastic Simulation," *National Institute Economic Review*, Vol. 156 (May), pp. 72–79.

Blanchard, Olivier, and John Simon, 2001, "The Long and Large Decline in U.S. Output Volatility," *Brookings Papers on Economic Activity: 1*, pp. 135–64.

Blinder, Alan, 1997, "What Central Bankers Could Learn from Academics and Vice-Versa," *Journal of Economic Perspectives*, Vol. 11 (Spring), pp. 3–19.

Boone, Laurence, Claude Giorno, and Pete Richardson, 1998, "Stock Market Fluctuations and Consumption Behavior: Some Recent Evidence," OECD Economics Department Working Paper No. 208 (Paris: Organization of Economic Cooperation and Development).

Boone, Laurence, Nathalie Girouard, and Isabelle Wanner, 2001, "Financial Market Liberalisation, Wealth and Consumption," OECD Economics Department Working Paper No. 308 (Paris: Organization of Economic Cooperation and Development).

Bordo, Michael, and Marc Flandreau, 2001, "Core, Periphery, Exchange Rate Regimes, and Globalization" (unpublished; New Brunswick, New Jersey: Rutgers University).

Bulow, Jeremy, and Kenneth Rogoff, 1989, "Sovereign Debt: Is to Forgive to Forget?" *American Economic Review*, Vol. 79 (March), pp. 43–50.

Caballero, Ricardo J., 2000, "Macroeconomic Volatility in Latin America: A Conceptual Framework and Three Case Studies," *Estudios de Economía*, Vol. 28, No. 1 (June), pp. 5–52.

Calvo, Guillermo, Carmen Reinhart, and Leonardo Leidermann, 1996, "Inflows of Capital to Developing Countries in the 1990s," *Journal of Economic Perspectives*, Vol. 10 (Spring), pp. 123–40.

Case, Karl, John Quigley, and Robert Shiller, 2001, "Comparing Wealth Effects: The Stock Market Versus the Housing Market," NBER Working Paper No. 8606 (Cambridge, Massachusetts: National Bureau of Economic Research).

Catão, Luis, and Ben Sutton, 2002, "Sovereign Debt: What's Different About Latin America?" (unpublished; Washington: International Monetary Fund).

Catão, Luis, and Marco Terrones, 2001, "Fiscal Deficits and Inflation: A New Look at the Emerging Market Evidence," IMF Working Paper 01/74 (Washington: International Monetary Fund).

Cecchetti, Stephen, A. Flores-Lagunes, and S. Krause, 2001, "Has Monetary Policy Become More Efficient? A Cross-Country Analysis" (unpublished; Columbus, Ohio: Ohio State University).

Clarida, Richard, Jordi Galí, and Mark Gertler, 1998, "Monetary Policy Rules in Practice: Some International Evidence," *European Economic Review*, Vol. 42 (June), pp. 1033–67.

———, 1999, "The Science of Monetary Policy: A New Keynesian Perspective," *Journal of Economic Literature*, Vol. 37 (December), pp. 1661–707.

———, 2000, "Monetary Policy Rules and Macroeconomic Stability: Evidence and Some Theory," *Quarterly Journal of Economics*, Vol. 115 (February), pp. 147–80.

Clouse, James, Dale Henderson, Athanasios Orphanides, David Small, and Peter Tinsley, 2000, "Monetary Policy When the Nominal Short-Term Interest Rate Is Zero," Finance and Economic Discussion Series, No. 2000–51 (Washington: Board of Governors of the Federal Reserve System).

Cogley, Timothy, and Thomas Sargent, 2002, "Evolving Post-World War II U.S. Inflation Dynamics," forthcoming in *NBER Macroeconomics Annual 2001*, ed. by Ben Bernanke and Kenneth Rogoff (Cambridge, Massachusetts: MIT Press).

Deaton, Angus, 1992, *Understanding Consumption* (Oxford: Clarendon Press).

DeLong, J. Bradford, 2000, "America's Historical Experience with Low Inflation," *Journal of Money, Credit and Banking*, Vol. 32 (November), pp. 979–93.

Detragiache, Enrica, and Antonio Spilimbergo, 2001, "Crises and Liquidity: Evidence and Interpretation," IMF Working Paper 01/02 (Washington: International Monetary Fund).

Deutsche Bank, 2001, "Disaggregating the Wealth Effect," *U.S. Economics Weekly*, pp. 4–6.

Diaz-Alejandro, Carlos F., 1970, *Essays on the Economic History of the Argentine Republic* (New Haven, Connecticut: Yale University Press).

———, 1983. "Stories of the 1930s for the 1980s," in *Financial Policies and the World Capital Market: The Problem of Latin American Countries*, ed. by Pedro Aspe Armella, Rudiger Dornbusch, and Maurice Obstfeld (Cambridge, Massachusetts: National Bureau of Economic Research), pp. 5–35.

———, 1985, "Goodbye Financial Repression, Hello Financial Crash," *Journal of Development Economics*, Vol. 19 (September–October), pp. 1–24

Diebold, Francis, Anthony S. Tay, and Kenneth Wallis, 1999, "Evaluating Density Forecasts of Inflation: The Survey of Professional Forecasters," Chapter 3 in *Cointegration, Causality, and Forecasting: A Festschrift in Honour of Clive W.J. Granger*, ed. by Robert F. Engle and Halbert White (Oxford: Oxford University Press).

Drew, Aaron, and Benjamin Hunt, 2000, "Efficient Simple Policy Rules and the Implications of Potential Output Uncertainty," *Journal of Economics and Business*, Vol. 52 (January–April), pp. 143–60.

Dynan, Karen, and Dean Maki, 2001, "Does Stock Market Wealth Matter for Consumption?" Finance and Economics Discussion Series, No. 2001–23 (Washington: Board of Governors of the Federal Reserve System).

Eaton, Jonathan, and Mark Gersovitz, 1981, "Debt With Potential Repudiation: Theoretical and Empirical Analysis," *Review of Economic Studies*, Vol. 48 (April), pp. 284–309.

Edison, Hali, and Torsten Sløk, 2001a, "Wealth Effects and the New Economy," IMF Working Paper 01/77 (Washington: International Monetary Fund).

———, 2001b, "New Economy Stock Valuations and Investment in the 1990s," IMF Working Paper 01/78 (Washington: International Monetary Fund).

Fischer, Stanley, 1993, "The Role of Macroeconomic Factors in Growth," *Journal of Monetary Economics*, Vol. 32 (December), pp. 482–512.

———, 1996, "Why Are Central Banks Pursuing Long-Run Price Stability?" in *Achieving Price Stability: A Symposium*, sponsored by the Federal Reserve Bank of Kansas City, Jackson Hole, Wyoming, August 29–31 (Kansas City, Missouri: Federal Reserve Bank of Kansas City), pp. 7–34.

Fishlow, Albert, 1989, "Lessons of the 1890s for the 1980s," in *Debt, Stabilization and Development: Essays in Memory of Carlos Díaz-Alejandro*, ed. by Guillermo Calvo and others (Oxford: Basil Blackwell for the World Institute for Development Economics Research), pp. 19–47.

Friedman, Milton, 1957, *A Theory of the Consumption Function* (Princeton, New Jersey: Princeton University Press).

———, 1977, "Nobel Lecture: Inflation and Unemployment," *Journal of Political Economy*, Vol. 85 (June), pp. 451–72.

Gavin, Michael, Ricardo Hausmann, Roberto Perotti, and Ernesto Talvi, 1996, "Managing Fiscal Policy in Latin America and the Caribbean: Volatility, Pro-cyclicality, and Limited Creditworthiness," Office of the Chief Economist, IDB Research Department Working Paper No. 326 (Washington: Inter-American Development Bank).

Gavin, Michael, and Roberto Perotti, 1997, "Fiscal Policy in Latin America," *NBER Macroeconomics Annual 1997*, ed. by Ben Bernanke and Kenneth Rogoff (Cambridge, Massachusetts: MIT Press), pp. 11–61.

Girouard, Nathalie, and Sveinbjörn Blöndal, 2001, "House Prices and Economic Activity," OECD Economics Department Working Paper No. 279 (Paris: Organization of Economic Cooperation and Development).

Gourinchas, Pierre-Olivier, Rodrigo Valdés, and Oscar Landerretche, 2001, "Lending Booms: Latin America and the World," *Estudios de Economía*, Vol. 1, No. 2, pp. 47–99.

Greenspan, Alan, 1999, "Mortgage Markets and Economic Activity," remarks at a conference sponsored by America's Community Bankers in Washington, D.C., November 2. Available on the Internet at *www.federalreserve.gov/boarddocs/speeches/1999/19911102.htm*.

———, 2001, Opening remarks at a symposium sponsored by the Federal Reserve Bank of Kansas City, Jackson Hole, Wyoming, August 31. Available on the Internet at *www.federalreserve.gov/boarddocs/speeches/2001/20010831/default.htm*.

Hansen, Lars, 1982, "Large Sample Properties of Generalized Method of Moments Estimators," *Econometrica*, Vol. 50 (July), pp. 1029–54.

Hoffmaister, Alexander, and Jorge E. Roldós, 1997, "Are Business Cycles Different in Asia and Latin America?" IMF Working Paper 97/9 (Washington: International Monetary Fund).

Hunt, Benjamin, and Douglas Laxton, 2001, "The Zero Interest Rate Floor (ZIF) and Its Implications for Monetary Policy in Japan," IMF Working Paper 01/186 (Washington: International Monetary Fund).

IMF, 2001, *International Capital Markets: Developments, Prospects, and Key Policy Issues,* Chapter 2 (Washington: International Monetary Fund).

Isard, Peter, Douglas Laxton, and Ann-Charlotte Eliasson, 2001, "Inflation Targeting with NAIRU Uncertainty and Endogenous Policy Credibility," *Journal of Economic Dynamics and Control,* Vol. 21 (January), pp. 115–48.

Judson, Ruth, and Athanasios Orphanides, 1996, "Inflation, Volatility, and Growth," Finance and Economics Discussion Series, No. 1996–19 (Washington: Board of Governors of the Federal Reserve System).

Kaminsky, Graciela L., and Carmen M. Reinhart, 1999, "The Twin Crises: The Causes of Banking and Balance-of-Payments Problems," *American Economic Review,* Vol. 89 (June), pp. 473–500.

Kaminsky, Graciela L., and Sergio Schmuckler, 2001, "On Boom and Crashes: Stock Market Cycles and Financial Liberalization" (unpublished; Washington: Georgetown University and World Bank).

Khan, Mohsin, and Abdelhak Senhadji, 2001, "Threshold Effects in the Relationship Between Inflation and Growth," *IMF Staff Papers,* Vol. 48, No. 1, pp. 1–21.

Kiley, Michael, 2000, "Identifying the Effect of Stock Market Wealth on Consumption: Pitfalls and New Evidence" (unpublished; Washington: Board of Governors of the Federal Reserve System).

King, Robert, 2000, "The New IS-LM Model: Language, Logic, and Limits," *Economic Quarterly,* Federal Reserve Bank of Richmond, Vol. 86 (Summer), pp. 45–103.

Krugman, Paul R., 1998, "Further Notes on Japan's Liquidity Trap." Available on the Internet at *http://web.mit.edu/krugman/www/liquid.html.*

Kydland, Finn E., and Carlos E.J.M. Zarazaga, 1997, "Is the Business Cycle of Argentina 'Different'?" *Economic Review,* Federal Reserve Bank of Dallas, Fourth Quarter, pp. 21–36.

Lange, Joe, Brian Sack, and William Whitesell, 2001, "Anticipations of Monetary Policy in Financial Markets," Finance and Economics Discussion Series, No. 2001–24 (Washington: Board of Governors of the Federal Reserve System).

Laxton, Douglas, Peter Isard, Hamid Faruqee, Eswar Prasad, and Bart Turtleboom, 1998, "MULTIMOD Mark III: The Core Dynamic and Steady-State Models," IMF Occasional Paper No. 164 (Washington: International Monetary Fund).

Laxton, Douglas, and Papa N'Diaye, 2002, "Monetary Policy Credibility and the Unemployment-Inflation Tradeoff: Some Evidence from Seventeen OECD Countries," forthcoming IMF Working Paper (Washington: International Monetary Fund).

Levine, Ross, 2001, "Bank-Based or Market-Based Financial Systems: Which Is Better?" (unpublished; Minneapolis, Minnesota: Carlson School of Management, University of Minnesota).

Lindert, Peter H., and Peter J. Morton, 1989, "How Sovereign Debt Has Worked," in *Developing Country Debt and Economic Performance,* Vol. I, ed. by Jeffrey Sachs (Chicago, Illinois: University of Chicago Press).

Lucas, Robert E., 1973, "Some International Evidence on Output-Inflation Tradeoffs," *American Economic Review,* Vol. 63 (June), pp. 326–34.

Ludvigson, Sydney, and Charles Steindel, 1999, "How Important Is the Stock Market Effect on Consumption?" *Economic Policy Review,* Federal Reserve Bank of New York, Vol. 5 (July), pp. 29–51.

Ludwig, Alexander, and Torsten Sløk, 2002, "The Impact of Changes in Stock Prices and House Prices on Consumption in OECD Countries," IMF Working Paper 02/01 (Washington: International Monetary Fund).

Maki, Dean, and Michael Palumbo, 2001, "Disentangling the Wealth Effect: A Cohort Analysis of Household Saving in the 1990s," Finance and Economics Discussion Series, No. 2001–21 (Washington: Board of Governors of the Federal Reserve System).

Mankiw, N. Gregory, and Ricardo Reis, 2001, "Sticky Information: A Model of Monetary Nonneutrality and Structural Slumps" (unpublished; Cambridge, Massachusetts: Harvard University).

McCallum, Bennett, 2001a, "Inflation Targeting and the Liquidity Trap," NBER Working Paper No. 8225 (Cambridge, Massachusetts: National Bureau of Economic Research).

———, 2001b, "Should Monetary Policy Respond Strongly to Output Gaps?" NBER Working Paper 8226 (Cambridge, Massachusetts, National Bureau of Economic Research).

McCarthy, Jonathan, 2000, "Pass-Through of Exchange Rates and Import Prices to Domestic Inflation in Some Industrialized Economies" (unpublished; New York: Federal Reserve Bank of New York).

Meyer, Laurence, 2001, "Before and After," remarks before the National Association of Business Economics, St. Louis, Missouri, November 27. Available on the Internet at *www.federalreserve.gov/boarddocs/speeches/2001/default.htm.*

Mishkin, Frederic, 2001, "The Transmission Mechanism and the Role of Asset Prices in Monetary Policy," NBER Working Paper 8617 (Cambridge, Massachusetts: National Bureau of Economic Research).

Mussa, Michael, and others, 2000, *Exchange Rate Regimes in an Increasingly Integrated World Economy,* IMF Occasional Paper No. 193 (Washington: International Monetary Fund).

Orphanides, Athanasios, 1998, "Monetary Policy Evaluation with Noisy Information," Finance and Economics Discussion Series, No. 1998-50 (Washington: Board of Governors of the Federal Reserve System).

———, and Volker Wieland, 1998, "Price Stability and Monetary Policy Effectiveness When Nominal Interest Rates Are Bounded by Zero," Finance and Economic Discussion Series, No. 1998-35 (Washington: Board of Governors of the Federal Reserve System).

Poterba, James, 2000, "Stock Market Wealth and Consumption," *Journal of Economic Perspectives,* Vol. 14 (Spring), pp. 99–119.

———, and Andrew Samwick, 1995, "Stock Ownership Patterns, Stock Market Fluctuations, and Consumption," *Brookings Papers on Economic Activity: 2,* Brookings Institution, pp. 295–357.

Reifschneider, David, David Stockton, and David Wilcox, 1997, "Econometric Models and the Monetary Policy Process," *Carnegie-Rochester Conference Series on Public Policy,* Vol. 47 (December), pp. 1–37.

Reifschneider, David, and John C. Williams, 1999, "Three Lessons for Monetary Policy in a Low Inflation Era," Finance and Economic Discussion Series, No. 1999–44 (Washington: Board of Governors of the Federal Reserve System).

———, 2001, "Three Lessons for Monetary Policy in a Low-Inflation Era," *Journal of Money, Credit and Banking,* Vol. 32 (November), pp. 936–66.

Reinhart, Carmen M., 2001, "Default, Currency Crises, and Sovereign Credit Ratings" (unpublished; Washington: International Monetary Fund).

Rogoff, Kenneth, 1985, "The Optimal Degree of Commitment to an Intermediate Target," *Quarterly Journal of Economics,* Vol. 100 (November), pp. 1169–89.

Rose, Andrew K., 2002, "One Reason Countries Pay Their Debts: Renegotiation and International Trade," CEPR Discussion Paper 3157 (London: Centre For Economic Policy Research).

Rotemberg, Julio, and Michael Woodford, 1997, "An Optimization-Based Econometric Framework for the Evaluation of Monetary Policy," in *NBER Macroeconomics Annual 1997,* ed. by Ben Bernanke and Julio Rotemberg (Cambridge, Massachusetts: MIT Press), pp. 297–346.

Rudebusch, Glenn, and Lars E.O. Svensson, 1999, "Policy Rules for Inflation Targeting," in *Monetary Policy Rules,* ed. by John B. Taylor (Chicago, Illinois: University of Chicago Press), pp. 203–46.

Sack, Brian, and Volker Wieland, 1999, "Interest Rate Smoothing and Optimal Monetary Policy: A Review of Recent Empirical Evidence," Finance and Economic Discussion Series, No. 1999-39 (Washington: Board of Governors of the Federal Reserve System).

Stock, James, 2002, "Comment," forthcoming in *NBER Macroeconomics Annual 2001,* ed. by Ben Bernanke and Kenneth Rogoff (Cambridge, Massachusetts: MIT Press).

Summers, Lawrence H., 1991, "How Should Long-Term Monetary Policy Be Determined?" *Journal of Money, Credit and Banking,* Vol. 23, No. 3, pp. 625–31.

Svensson, Lars, 1997, "Inflation Forecast Targeting: Implementing and Monitoring Inflation Targets," *European Economic Review,* Vol. 41 (June), pp. 1111–46.

———, 2000a, "Open Economy Inflation Targeting," *Journal of International Economics,* Vol. 50 (February), pp. 155–83.

———, 2000b, "The Zero Bound in an Open Economy: A Foolproof Way of Escaping From a Liquidity Trap," *Monetary and Economic Studies,* Vol. 19 (February), pp. 277–312. Available on the Internet at *http://www.princeton.edu/nsvensson.*

Talvi, Ernesto, and Carlos Végh, 2000, "Tax Base Variability and Pro-cyclical Fiscal Policy," NBER Working Paper No. 7499 (Cambridge, Massachusetts: National Bureau of Economic Research).

Taylor, Alan M., 2000, "Latin America and Foreign Capital in the Twentieth Century: Economics, Politics, and Institutional Change," NBER Working Paper No. 7394 (Cambridge, Massachusetts: National Bureau of Economic Research).

Taylor, John B., 1979, "Estimation and Control of a Macroeconomic Model with Rational Expectations," *Econometrica,* Vol. 47 (September), pp. 1267–86.

————, 1981, "On the Relation Between the Variability of Inflation and the Average Inflation Rate," *Carnegie-Rochester Conference Series on Public Policy*, Vol. 15 (Autumn), pp. 57–86.

————, 1993, "Discretion Versus Policy Rules in Practice," *Carnegie-Rochester Conference on Public Policy*, Vol. 39 (December), pp. 195–214.

————, 1999, "Staggered Price and Wage Setting in Macroeconomics," in *Handbook of Macroeconomics*, Vol. 15, ed. by John B. Taylor and Michael Woodford (New York: North-Holland), pp. 1009–50.

Thorp, Rosemary, ed., 1984, *Latin America in the 1930s. The Role of the Periphery in World Crisis* (New York: St. Martin's Press).

Velasco, Andrés, 1987, "Financial Crises and Balance of Payments Crises: A Simple Model of the Southern Cone Experience," *Journal of Development Economics*, Vol. 27 (October), pp. 263–83.

Viñals, José, 2001, "Monetary Policy Issues in a Low Inflation Environment," CEPR Working Paper No. 2945 (London: Centre for Economic Policy Research).

Walsh, Carl, 1995, "Optimal Contracts for Central Bankers," *American Economic Review*, Vol. 85 (March), pp. 150–67.

Wyplosz, Charles, 2001, "Do We Know How Low Inflation Should Be?" CEPR Discussion Paper No. 2722 (London: Centre for Economic Policy Research).

The world economy has experienced its most significant slowdown since the early 1990s (Box 1.1 and Figure 3.1). Much public discussion has focused on how the current downturn differs from other recessions in recent history, and some have argued that the current downturn is much more akin to those in the late nineteenth century. Specifically:

- The synchronization of the current slowdowns appears to be greater than that in the early 1990s. How common are synchronized recessions and what are the implications for the synchronization of the recoveries?

- The global collapse of high-tech investment has prompted comparisons with recessions in the late nineteenth century. If investment remains weak for a long time, will the recovery of output be anemic?

- Following the long and strong bull market of the 1990s, stock prices have fallen sharply in all major countries. Do these large contractions imply that the recessions will be especially deep? How soon will stock prices recover?

- Monetary policy in all three major currency areas was tightened prior to the downturn, and has since been loosened. How does the behavior of monetary policy during this cycle compare to previous cycles?

Business cycles are persistent features of market-oriented economies. More than 50 years ago, Arthur Burns (1947) wrote: "For well over a century, business cycles have run an unceasing round. They have persisted through vast economic and social changes; they have withstood countless experiments in industry, agriculture, banking, industrial relations, and public policy; they have confounded forecasters without num-

The main authors of this chapter are James Morsink (lead), Thomas Helbling, and Stephen Tokarick. Emily Conover provided research assistance.

Figure 3.1. Real Output Growth
(Percent)

The world economy has experienced its most significant slowdown since the early 1990s. The global business cycle is driven mainly by fluctuations in industrial countries.

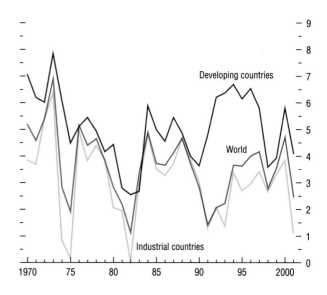

ber, belied repeated prophecies of a 'new era of prosperity' and outlived repeated forebodings of 'chronic depression.'" The same observations could be made today.

While every business cycle is different, business cycles share common elements that make them interesting for analysis. This chapter puts the current business cycles in industrial countries into perspective by describing the key features of previous recessions and recoveries. The focus of the chapter is on industrial countries, as global fluctuations in recent decades have been most closely associated with the business cycle in these countries. This is clear both from the coincidence of peaks and troughs in activity between the global economy and industrial countries and from formal work on synchronization.

Business cycles are defined here as recurrent sequences of expansions and contractions in the level of economic activity (Box 3.1). An alternative definition is that of cyclical fluctuations in economic activity around a trend—the growth cycle, which is more useful if underlying growth rates are high and level recessions relatively rare. However, the primary focus of this chapter is on business cycles in industrial countries after 1973, when growth rates were generally lower and level recessions were not uncommon. Also, growth cycles depend on an arbitrary distinction between trend and cycle, and key cyclical characteristics depend crucially on which detrending method is used. Another possibility is to consider level cycles using output per capita, which is a better measure of welfare and explicitly recognizes that high growth rates of output sometimes reflect rapid population growth. In practice, output per capita recessions in industrial countries after 1973 were similar to output recessions, as population growth rates were generally low.

The chapter contributes to the study of business cycles by describing the main empirical regularities of recessions and recoveries across industrial countries and across time, though it does not directly address their fundamental causes. This analysis complements the vast country-specific literature on business cycles, with the work on the United States alone being huge. The few studies of the international and historical evidence generally do not treat recessions and recoveries as events, but rather focus on the average properties of macroeconomic series over time. The very few studies that do identify expansions and contractions mostly look at growth cycles.

The key features of business cycles in industrial countries from the late nineteenth century to the present are discussed first. To anticipate some of the results: recessions are getting milder and expansions are getting longer; synchronized recessions are a common feature of the international and historical experience; and investment is playing a larger role in recessions now than in the late nineteenth century. The deeper examination of business cycles since 1973 that follows confirms these results. In addition, this analysis indicates that investment contractions and stock price declines are more synchronized than recessions; that investment contractions make important contributions to recessions but upturns in consumption tend to drive recoveries; and that cycles in interest rates and output in G-7 countries are closely related.

Were Business Cycles in the Late Nineteenth Century Different from Modern Cycles?

Business cycles have run an "unceasing round" since at least the late nineteenth century. This section compares and contrasts the amplitude, duration, and other key characteristics of recessions and recoveries across historical periods using annual data for 1881–2000 for 16 industrial countries (Appendix 3.1).[1] The choice of countries is determined mainly by the availability of data; the quality of the available historical data—especially for the earlier periods—is distinctly mixed. The sample is split into four

[1]The countries are Australia, Canada, Denmark, Finland, France, Germany, Italy, Japan, Norway, the Netherlands, Portugal, Spain, Sweden, Switzerland, United Kingdom, and the United States.

Box 3.1. Measuring Business Cycles

How should business cycles be defined? The classic definition of the business cycle is attributable to Burns and Mitchell (1946), who—along with other researchers at the National Bureau of Economic Research (NBER) in the United States—pioneered concepts and methodology in business cycle analysis: "A cycle consists of expansions occurring at about the same time in many economic activities, followed by similar general recessions, contractions, and revivals which merge into the expansion phase of the next cycle; this sequence of changes is recurrent but not periodic; in duration, business cycles vary from more than one year to ten or twelve years." In other words, a recession is a significant decline in the level of aggregate economic activity that lasts for more than a few months and an expansion is a sustained increase in the level of activity.[1] The NBER determines peaks and troughs in aggregate economic activity on the basis of turning points in a number of indicators, including aggregate employment, industrial production, and the volume of sales. An NBER business cycle dating committee identifies the turning points in the individual series, reconciles the conflicting dates among individual series, and, on this basis, determines peaks and troughs in aggregate economic activity.

For meaningful cross-country comparisons of business cycles in industrial countries since 1973, chronologies based on a consistent definition are needed. Such chronologies exist for some, but not all, industrial countries.[2]

Chapter III proposes business cycle turning points based on the behavior of real gross domestic product, which is the best available measure of aggregate economic activity.[3] (See Appendix 3.1.) This advantage is especially relevant for modern cycles in industrial countries, where manufacturing accounts for a small share of output. Recent studies have shown that NBER peaks and troughs can be closely approximated by applying a well-known business cycle dating algorithm to real GDP.[4] The algorithm looks for peaks and troughs in overlapping five-quarter periods and then picks those pairs that result in cycles that are at least five quarters long and phases that are at least two quarters long.

An alternative concept of business cycle fluctuations is that of growth cycles—fluctuations in economic activity around a long-run trend (Moore, 1983, and Zarnowitz, 1992). The growth cycle concept has some advantages, but also disadvantages, relative to the conventional business cycle concept (Stock and Watson, 1999).[5]

- Growth cycles are better suited for business cycle analysis in countries with high trend growth rates, including many emerging market economies, which tend to experience sharp contractions and expansions in rates of growth

The main author is Thomas Helbling.

[1]While the essence of this definition has remained unchanged, it has been revised slightly over time. For the latest definition, see the recent announcements by the NBER Business Cycle Dating Committee (available on the Internet at *http://cycles-www.nber.org/cycles/november2001/recessnov.html*).

[2]The Organization for Economic Cooperation and Development (OECD) and the Economic Cycle Research Institute (ECRI) in New York provide chronologies for only some industrial countries. Their chronologies are available on the Internet at *http://www.oecd.org/oecd/pages/home/displaygeneral/0,3380,EN-countrylist-509-15-no-no-287-509,FF.html* and *http://www.businesscycle.com/research/intlcycledates.asp*.

[3]Stock and Watson (1999) say that GDP is "the core of the business cycle."

[4]Harding and Pagan (2001 and forthcoming). See also King and Plosser (1994) on business cycle dating algorithms. The algorithms detect peaks and troughs on the basis of maxima and minima in the series that have been subjected to censoring rules to ensure that standard conditions for the minimal duration of cycles and phases are met.

[5]Another advantage of growth cycles is that standard statistical methods can be applied, since these cycles are less asymmetric in duration or amplitude of fluctuations during phases than classical cycles. Analyzing the latter often requires the application of cumbersome nonlinear statistical methods (e.g., Diebold and Rudebusch, 1999). However, recent advances in econometrics and information technology have greatly facilitated the use of nonlinear models in empirical economic research.

rather than in levels. However, level recessions are more relevant for industrial countries, which have generally experienced low average growth rates since 1973.

- Growth cycles are often more helpful in understanding the relationships between output, inflation, and unemployment.[6] However, growth cycles depend on an arbitrary distinction between trend and cycle, on which there is no professional consensus.[7] Moreover, key growth cycle characteristics vary considerably depending on the detrending method used (Canova, 1998).

- Growth recessions are sometimes minor in size, while level recessions are usually associated with major adverse macroeconomic events, which usually makes them more relevant from a policy perspective.[8]

Another possibility is to consider level cycles using real GDP divided by working age population ("per capita"), which is a better measure of welfare. In practice, in industrial countries after 1973, cycles based on output per capita closely matched those based on output. The total number of cycles was similar on the two measures, as a slightly higher number of shallow per capita recessions (compared to level recessions) was offset by the merging of a few double-dip level recessions into single, longer per capita recessions. Per capita recessions lasted on average

[6]See, for example, Boone and others (2002).

[7]In some macroeconomic models, the same shock may affect both long-run growth and business cycle fluctuations. See King and others (1991), among others.

[8]Classical recessions typically overlap with growth recessions, while the converse is not true.

Level Versus Per Capita Recessions

	Level	Per Capita[1]
	Quarters	
Average duration of recessions	3.8	4.4
	Percent of peak GDP	
Average depth of recessions	−2.7	−3.2
1970s	−3.8	−3.7
1980s	−2.1	−3.5
1990s	−2.2	−2.4
	Percent	
Share in total		
Length		
2 quarters	32.0	24.0
3–4 quarters	42.0	39.0
5–6 quarters	14.0	13.0
More than 7 quarters	12.0	24.0
Contractions of		
0–2 percent	48.0	40.0
2–4 percent	37.0	35.0
More than 4 percent	15.0	25.0

Source: IMF staff calculations.
[1]Working age population.

about one-half of a quarter longer than level recessions, and were about ½ percent of GDP deeper (see the table). Across decades, the most striking difference in depths was during the early 1980s, when working age population growth rates accelerated in many countries, thus increasing the severity of per capita recessions.[9] As per capita cycles are similar to level cycles, this chapter focuses on the latter because they match more closely existing business cycle chronologies, including the NBER's.

[9]Looking forward, as the working age population in many industrial countries starts to decline, level recessions will no longer be so severe in per capita terms.

time periods, divided by major world events: the prewar period before World War I (1881–1913); the interwar period between the World Wars (1919–38); the Bretton Woods period between World War II and the productivity slowdown, the oil shocks, and the move to generalized floating of exchange rates in the early 1970s (1950–

1972); and the post–Bretton Woods period (1973–2000).

For the analysis, a recession is defined as one or more consecutive years of negative real GDP growth, while an expansion consists of a year or more of positive growth. The resulting business cycle turning points broadly match the dates in

Table 3.1. Recessions and Expansions: 1881–2000

	Prewar 1881–1913	Interwar 1919–1938	Bretton Woods 1950–1972	Post–Bretton Woods 1973–2000
Recessions				
Decline in output				
Average decline in output (percent)	–4.3	–8.1	–2.1	–2.5
Proportion with a decline in output of:				
0–2 percent	29.4	23.5	50.0	57.5
2–4 percent	33.3	17.6	44.4	30.0
> 4 percent	37.3	58.8	5.6	12.5
Length of recessions				
Average length of recessions (years)	1.3	1.8	1.1	1.5
Proportion that were:				
One year in length	79.4	60.8	94.4	60.0
Two years in length	16.7	15.7	5.6	32.5
Three years or more in length	3.9	23.5	0.0	7.5
Proportion of years in recession	24.7	29.4	5.2	13.4
Proportion associated with a decline in investment	58.9	77.4	63.6	96.2
Expansions				
Increase in output				
Average increase in output (percent)	19.8	34.6	102.9	26.9
Length of expansions				
Average length of expansions (years)	3.6	3.7	10.3	6.9
Proportion of years in expansion	75.3	70.6	94.8	86.6
Average number of years until previous peak is reached	2.0	2.7	1.1	1.7
Memorandum				
Average growth rate (percent)	2.8	3.8	5.3	2.6

Source: IMF staff calculations.

the National Bureau of Economic Research (NBER) chronologies for the United States, the United Kingdom, France, and Germany (available in Glasner, 1997). The differences reflect the use by the NBER of higher frequency (monthly) data and a broader variety of indicators, such as employment, bank clearings, and department store sales. Also, since the analysis in this section uses annual data, differences might arise regarding the dating of business cycles, compared to the following section, which uses quarterly data.

Recessions Are Becoming Milder and Less Frequent

Recessions have become less severe and less frequent over time (Table 3.1). During the prewar period, the average decline in real GDP from peak to trough was 4.3 percent, and reces-

sions in the United States were on average deeper than in the United Kingdom, owing in part to greater financial instability in the United States, which did not have a central bank. Recessions were exceptionally deep (–8.1 percent on average) during the interwar period, mainly reflecting the Great Depression (Box 3.2). The severity of recessions moderated significantly after World War II, with the proportion of recessions in which output declined by just 0–2 percent almost doubling. Recessions were somewhat milder in the Bretton Woods period compared to the post–Bretton Woods period, partly reflecting the oil price shocks of the later period.[2] It is striking that recessions were considerably more severe in the prewar period compared to the post–Bretton Woods period, even though average growth rates were similar.

While recessions were shallower in the post–Bretton Woods period compared to the

[2]Hamilton (1983, 1996) has demonstrated a close relationship between oil price shocks and recessions in the United States.

prewar period, they were not shorter.[3] The proportion of recessions that lasted just one year fell from four-fifths in the earlier period to three-fifths in the later period. The interwar period was—once again—unusual, with recessions lasting longer than in any other period. The Bretton Woods period was characterized by short recessions, with about 95 percent lasting just one year. The increase in recession duration from the Bretton Woods period to the post–Bretton Woods period may partly reflect the fall in the underlying growth rate as well as the decline in labor-market flexibility in many countries, which would tend to slow the recovery of output following an adverse shock.[4]

Unlike recessions, expansions clearly became longer after World War II. During the Bretton Woods period, expansions were especially long, lasting about 10 years on average. Some expansions lasted 20 years, and several countries did not experience a year of negative output growth at all. The long expansions reflected in part the technological catch-up in many countries following World War II. One consequence of longer expansions was that countries spent less time in recession.[5] The Bretton Woods period had the lowest share of recession years, just 5 percent, compared to 30 percent in the interwar period. It is interesting that, even though average growth rates were similar in the prewar and post–Bretton

Woods periods, recession years were less common in the later period, because expansions were on average almost twice as long.[6]

The findings that expansions have become longer and recessions shallower in the post–World War II period are consistent with much of the literature on U.S. business cycles.[7] Using the NBER chronology of U.S. business cycles, Zarnowitz (1992) shows that expansions were 1½ times as long as recessions between the mid-nineteenth and mid-twentieth centuries, and 4 times as long since then. Zarnowitz also shows that, on several measures, output variability in the United States was highest during the interwar period, intermediate during the prewar period, and lowest during the post–World War II period.

The mainstream view of the post–World War II cyclical dampening in the United States has been challenged, mainly on grounds of data reliability. Romer (1989) created a new GDP series for the pre–World War II period, rather than using the series developed by Kuznets (1961), and showed that the volatility of real GDP was similar in the pre–World War II and post–World War II periods.[8] In response, Balke and Gordon (1989) challenged Romer's findings and demonstrated that output was about twice as volatile in the earlier period, in line with the original results.[9] Several studies, including

[3]The duration of a recession is defined as the number of consecutive years of negative output growth. The duration of an expansion is defined analogously.

[4]Blanchard and Wolfers (2000) present evidence that the interaction of shocks and labor market institutions does a good job of explaining the evolution of unemployment in Europe since 1960.

[5]The share of recession years is simply the number of country-years of negative output growth divided by the total number of country-years in each of the four sample periods.

[6]Since countries were expanding when they were not in recession, the share of expansion years is simply one minus the share of recession years. Thus, the share of expansion years was higher after World War II than before.

[7]Our findings support the view—held by Mitchell (1927) and Keynes (1936), among others—that contractions and expansions are asymmetric in their duration. Other business cycle asymmetries in the United States are the differences in the statistical properties of output growth across business cycle phases (Hamilton, 1989) and between the early and late stages of expansion (Sichel, 1994). DeLong and Summers (1986) have challenged this view, arguing that business cycles were symmetric, if detrended data were used. Using detrended data for many countries over a long time period, Bergmann, Bordo, and Jonung (1998) have found evidence that generally favors asymmetry.

[8]Romer found that the new series was 27 percent less volatile than the traditional Kuznets series. A related argument, posited by Romer (1994), Watson (1994), and Diebold and Rudebusch (1992), was that the NBER business cycle dates for the prewar period were based on inferior measurement techniques and fewer and weaker data sources. When the dates were corrected by these authors, the duration of recessions became more similar in the prewar and postwar periods.

[9]Separately, Zarnowitz (1992) has criticized Romer for ignoring structural changes.

Box 3.2. The Great Depression

The Great Depression of the early 1930s is the most severe recession on record (see the table). Most countries entered recession in 1929–30 and began their recoveries in 1932–33; in France, the contraction occurred somewhat later (1932–35). Output losses in the United States, Germany, France, Italy, Japan, Canada, Sweden, and Australia exceeded 10 percent of GNP, and were also sizable in many other countries. As the U.S. economy was at the time by far the largest, and experienced just about the deepest contraction, the Great Depression in the United States accounted for much of the decline in global output.

Most economic historians concur that the Great Depression—at least the first stage—was caused primarily by monetary policy in the United States, propagated mostly by a series of banking panics, and then spread to the rest of the world via the international gold exchange standard.[1] The U.S. Federal Reserve tightened monetary policy in early 1928, in response to the stock market boom that began in 1926 and the belief that banks should confine their lending strictly to commercial bills and not finance stock market speculation (the "real bills doctrine"). The contractions in central bank credit and the monetary base, along with a rise in the discount rate, precipitated a downturn in the U.S. economy starting in August 1929 (before the stock market crash of October 1929).

A series of banking panics beginning in October 1930 turned an otherwise serious recession into a depression. These panics, which resulted in the suspension of 9,000 banks (more than one-third of the total), exacerbated the economic contraction because they reduced broad money (Friedman and Schwartz, 1963). The U.S. Federal Reserve was insufficiently aggressive in trying to counter the collapse in broad money, for example via open market pur-

The main author is Michael Bordo.
[1]Many other causes of the Great Depression have been proposed, from more restrictive trade policy (Meltzer, 1976) to the stock market crash of 1929 (Galbraith, 1961).

The Great Depression

Country	Share of World Output, 1931 (percent)	Economic Activity		Output Loss (percent)[1]
		Peak	Trough	
United States	42.4	1929	1933	−29.4
United Kingdom	13.1	1930	1931	−0.5
Germany	9.5	1928	1932	−26.3
France	7.9	1932	1935	−10.4
Italy	5.4	1928	1933	−13.7
Japan	5.1	1930	1933	−14.9
Spain	4.2	1929	1931	−6.3
Canada	2.5	1929	1933	−29.7
Netherlands	2.1	1930	1934	−14.2
Switzerland	2.0	1930	1932	−6.5
Sweden	1.6	1930	1933	−12.1
Australia	1.4	1926	1931	−24.9
Denmark	1.1	1930	1932	−4.4
Norway	0.9	1930	1931	−8.0
Finland	0.5	1928	1931	−7.2
Portugal	0.4	1935	1936	−0.7

[1]Cumulative loss in output from peak to trough (based on annual data). The peak is defined as the year before real growth turned negative. The trough is defined as the year before real growth turned positive.

chases.[2] The collapse of broad money reduced output through several channels: (1) lower aggregate demand, which—in the face of nominal wage rigidity—decreased real output (Bernanke and Carey, 1996; Bordo, Erceg, and Evans, 2000); (2) disruption of financial intermediation from the bank failures (Bernanke, 1983); (3) asset price deflation, whereby declining asset prices reduced the value of collateral for bank loans, inducing weakened banks to engage in a fire sale

[2]The reason for this policy failure is still being debated. Friedman and Schwartz (1963) attributed it to a breakdown in governance at the U.S. Federal Reserve, following the death in 1928 of Benjamin Strong, Governor of the Federal Reserve Bank of New York, who they argued would have acted correctly to offset the banking panics, based on his record in the 1920s. Alternatively, Wheelock (1991) and Meltzer (forthcoming) argued that the policy failure stemmed from the adherence to two beliefs: (1) the "real bills doctrine," which posited that the low interest rates observed in the early 1930s were a sign of expansionary monetary policy and that even looser monetary policy would rekindle speculation; and (2) the liquidationist view, which posited that recessions were a necessary purge to the excesses of the previous booms.

of their loans and securities, leading to further asset price deflation (Bernanke and Gertler, 1989); and (4) debt deflation, in which falling goods prices led to rising debt burdens in an environment where contracts were not fully indexed (Fisher, 1933) and rising ex ante real interest rates (Cecchetti, 1992).

The fall in broad money in the United States raised interest rates, leading to a capital inflow from the rest of the world, and reduced output, lowering U.S. demand for the rest of the world's output. The United States ran persistent balance of payments surpluses with its main trading partners during 1929–31. In the rest of the world, the combination of the gold outflow and the fall in exports to the United States caused aggregate demand to decline. This was exacerbated by a loss of confidence in the currencies of the reserve countries, leading central banks to convert their holdings of foreign exchange into gold, which caused a contraction in the world money supply. Countries that did not adhere to the gold exchange standard, such as Spain, experienced milder contractions (Choudhri and Kochin, 1980).

The gold exchange standard also exacerbated the contractions in other countries by preventing central banks from responding aggressively to the banking panics prompted by weakened bank balance sheets. Central banks were reluctant to extend liquidity support to banks, fearing a speculative attack that would force them off the gold standard—they were confined by "golden fetters" (Bernanke and James, 1991; Eichengreen, 1992). At the same time, foreign depositors' fears of either devaluation or the imposition of exchange controls (or both) fueled the spread of banking crises from Austria in May 1931 to Germany and other central European countries, and then to France and Belgium. Finally, the banking crises on the continent led to a speculative attack on the Bank of England's gold reserves, leading the United Kingdom to suspend gold convertibility in September 1931. The contagion even reached the United States, leading the central bank to raise its discount rate in order to protect its gold reserves—thereby aggravating the banking crisis already under way.

The Great Depression generally ended once countries left the gold exchange standard and adopted policies that restored confidence in the financial system and stimulated aggregate demand, including expansionary fiscal and monetary policies. The United Kingdom and other countries in the sterling bloc, including Australia, Denmark, Finland, Norway, and Sweden, left gold in 1931 and started to recover. The United States ended its link to gold in 1933 and effectively devalued by raising the price of gold, which in turn revalued the monetary gold stock and expanded the monetary base. The principal remaining gold standard adherents were France, Belgium, the Netherlands, and Switzerland (the "gold bloc" countries), which had returned to gold in the late 1920s.[3] After the United Kingdom, the United States, and much of the rest of the world devalued, France and the gold bloc countries were placed at an ever deteriorating competitive disadvantage. To preserve their gold reserves, they followed increasingly contractionary macroeconomic policies, which served to exacerbate the Depression. In the end, Belgium left gold in 1935 and France in 1936, followed by the Netherlands and Switzerland.

The pace of recovery from the Great Depression varied widely across countries, depending in part on macroeconomic and structural policies. In the United Kingdom, which left gold early, it took only a year for output to exceed its peak level before the recession began. In the United States, recovery began in 1933 but was sluggish compared with the strength of the monetary expansion under way, and it took about three years for output to return to its previous peak level. Recent research suggests that the weak recovery and the following second stage of the Depression partly reflected New Deal policies that enhanced the monopoly power of firms and labor unions, which strongly reduced aggregate supply, especially in manufacturing (Bordo, Erceg, and Evans, 2000; Cole and Ohanian, 1999).

[3]In France, the monetary authorities were reluctant to abandon gold, because of the intense political struggle that had preceded stabilization of high inflation in the 1920s and the return to the gold standard in 1928.

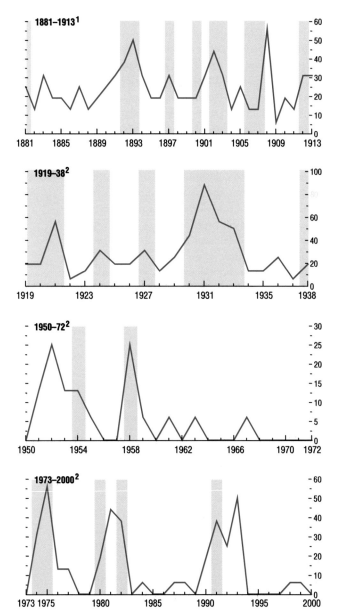

Figure 3.2. Synchronization of Recessions, 1881–2000
(Percent of countries in recession at the same time, 16 countries = 100)

Recessions have always been synchronized and, if anything, have become more so over time. Recessions in the largest economy have either led or coincided with the peaks.

Source: IMF staff estimates.
[1] The shaded areas indicate the years when the United Kingdom was in recession.
[2] The shaded areas indicate the years when the United States was in recession.

Backus and Kehoe (1992) and Bergman, Bordo, and Jonung (1998), examined output volatility in other countries and generally found a decrease in volatility after World War II, corroborating the mainstream view.

The lower amplitude of business cycles in the United States after World War II reflects several factors, including structural changes and more active stabilization policy. In a survey of the evidence, Zarnowitz (1992) attributes the decline in amplitude to the structural shifts from the volatile agricultural sector and the cyclically sensitive manufacturing sector toward the less cyclical service and government sectors; the advent of automatic fiscal stabilizers; and greater financial stability fostered by both the development of financial markets and the institution of effective lender-of-last-resort policies and deposit insurance—though recent international evidence does not suggest that financial crises are becoming less frequent or less severe (Box 3.3).

Synchronization, Investment, and Deflation

Contrary to the impression one gets from much of the public discussion, the tendency of recessions in one country to occur at the same time as recessions in other countries—synchronization—has been a persistent feature of the historical record (Figure 3.2).[10] Since the late nineteenth century, most recessions have been synchronized: before World War I, there were the global downturns in the early 1890s, the early 1900s, and 1907–08; in the interwar period, there was the worldwide recession of 1920–21 and the Great Depression of 1929–33; and in recent decades, there were the widespread slowdowns of the mid-1970s, the early 1980s, and the early 1990s. Even in the Bretton Woods period, the few recessions that occurred were highly synchronized.[11] The "background" (or ongoing)

[10]The measure of synchronization is the number of countries in recession at the same time.

[11]Zarnowitz (1992) shows that growth cycles in major industrial countries were highly synchronized throughout 1948–80.

Box 3.3. Historical Evidence on Financial Crises

Financial crises can exacerbate recessions for several reasons, as recognized in the early business cycle literature, including Mitchell (1941), Cagan (1965), and Zarnowitz (1992). A banking panic, like those that prevailed in industrial countries before World War II, reduces output by forcing a contraction in the money supply and thus aggregate demand, and by disrupting financial intermediation. Although classic banking panics are now rare, major banking insolvencies still occur and still disrupt financial intermediation (Honohan and Klingebiel, 2000). Currency crises exacerbate recessions because substantial depreciations are typically associated with sharp current account reversals, requiring the economy to quickly adjust the balance between domestic saving and investment (Milesi-Ferretti and Razin, 1998), and worsen financial distress, as many firms have net foreign exchange exposures. Twin crises—the simultaneous occurrence of a banking and a currency crisis—combine the negative effects of both types of crises (Kaminsky and Reinhart, 1998).

Does the association of severe recessions with financial crises still hold? A recent paper by Bordo and others (2001) looks at the experience of 21 industrial and emerging countries with both banking and currency crises over the

The main author is Michael Bordo.

four historical episodes described in the main text (the prewar period, the interwar period, the Bretton Woods period, and the post–Bretton Woods period).[1] The frequency of financial crises has changed significantly over time (see the table). Banking crises—defined as either a banking panic or major banking insolvencies—were especially prevalent during the interwar period and completely absent during the Bretton Woods period. Their declining frequency after World War II reflects in part the adoption in many countries of deposit insurance and effective lenders of last resort, which effectively eliminated classic banking panics (but not major banking insolvencies). Currency crises—defined as a successful speculative attack on a pegged exchange rate arrangement—were least frequent during the prewar period, reflecting the stability of the gold standard, and most frequent during the Bretton Woods period of fixed but adjustable exchange rates. Interestingly, the increase in the number of currency crises between the prewar and post–Bretton Woods periods (the two periods of relatively greater globalization) accounts for the higher incidence of

[1]The 21 countries are Argentina, Australia, Belgium, Brazil, Canada, Chile, Denmark, Finland, France, Germany, Greece, Italy, Japan, the Netherlands, Norway, Portugal, Spain, Sweden, Switzerland, the United Kingdom, and the United States.

Financial Crises and Recessions

	Prewar	Interwar	Bretton Woods	Post–Bretton Woods
Frequency of financial crises (percent a year)[1]	4.9	13.2	7.0	9.7
Banking crises	2.3	4.8	0.0	2.0
Currency crises	1.2	4.3	6.9	5.2
Twin crises	1.4	4.0	0.2	2.5
Severity of recessions (percent of GDP)[2]				
Without financial crises	10.7	8.5	6.7	14.3
Industrial economies	9.7	8.5	8.1	14.1
Emerging economies	11.0	8.5	4.2	15.1
With financial crises	19.6	29.3	14.6	19.9
Industrial economies	7.8	25.0	12.3	18.1
Emerging economies	24.5	39.0	18.1	27.8

Note: This table is based on Bordo and others (2001). For details, please consult that paper.
[1]Frequency is defined as the number of crises divided by the number of country-years.
[2]Severity is defined as the cumulative difference between actual growth and previous trend growth.

Box 3.3 *(concluded)*

financial crises in the later period. Like banking crises, twin crises were most frequent during the interwar period.

While it is difficult to disentangle the effects of financial crises on recessions from other factors, there is evidence that crises make recessions worse.[2] Bordo and others (2001) examine this relationship after controlling for other characteristics (such as a preceding credit boom and whether a country is industrial or emerging) and after taking account of possible simultane-

ity. The implication of these empirical tests is that the relationship between financial crises and recessions is probably causal (i.e., crises make recessions worse) rather than associative (i.e., other factors account for both crises and severe recessions). The general result is that financial crises—in both industrial and emerging market countries and across historical periods—make recessions more severe than they would be otherwise.[3]

---

[2]Mulder and Rocha (2001) show that the measurement of output losses is also difficult.

[3]Using a different approach, Gupta, Mishra, and Sahay (2002) examine the factors that affect the impact of currency crises on output in developing countries.

---

level of recessions fell sharply after World War II, so that the peaks in synchronization account for virtually all recessions since then—suggesting that, if anything, synchronization has in fact increased over time. Finally, recessions in the largest economy (the United Kingdom before World War I and the United States thereafter) tended to either lead or coincide with the peaks in synchronization.

The results are consistent with the international and historical evidence. Thorp (1926) describes the coincidence of business cycles across countries in the prewar period. Moore and Zarnowitz (1986) show a substantial degree of conformity across the business cycles between 1880 and 1920 in France, Germany, and the United Kingdom. More recently, Backus and Kehoe (1992) and Bergmann, Bordo, and Jonung (1998) find that output movements across countries were least synchronized during the prewar period, most synchronized during

the interwar period, and fairly synchronized after World War II.[12]

The role of investment in recessions has, if anything, increased over time, contrary to the view that the current investment-driven downturn represents a return to the recessions of the late nineteenth century.[13] Virtually all recessions in the post–Bretton Woods period were accompanied by investment contractions, compared with only about 60 percent of recessions in the prewar period, when the share of investment in output was much smaller.[14] However, it should be noted that our sample does not cover the railroad investment booms and busts of the mid-nineteenth century. While recognizing the data limitations, these results do not suggest that investment played a bigger role in recessions in the prewar period compared to recent decades.

About 40 percent of recessions before World War II were accompanied by deflation, but only one—Japan in the late 1990s—since then. The

---

[12]Backus and Kehoe (1992) attribute the higher correlation in the post–World War II period compared to the prewar period to greater measurement error in the earlier period.

[13]The important role of investment in recessions is consistent with most theories of the business cycle, including Austrian, Keynesian, and neoclassical views.

[14]Data on real investment are available for 10 countries: Australia, Denmark, Finland, Germany, Italy, Japan, Norway, Sweden, United Kingdom, and the United States. A recession was deemed to be associated with a decline in real investment if real investment fell in the year prior to, or in the year of the trough of, a recession. The average investment share in output in Denmark, Norway, Italy, Sweden, and the United Kingdom increased from 13 percent in the prewar period to 21 percent in the post–Bretton Woods period.

more common association of deflation with recessions prior to World War II reflected in part less activist monetary policy under the gold standard. Not all episodes of deflation were associated with recessions—in fact, France from 1929 to 1931, Germany from 1884 to 1886 and again from 1892 to 1896, and the United Kingdom from 1884 to 1887 were characterized by rapid growth—underlining that some deflations were driven by rapid productivity growth and others by declines in aggregate demand. That said, the combination of deflation and recession is a serious concern, not only because deflation increases the real burden of debt, but also because deflation makes it impossible for the central bank to engineer negative real interest rates.

Fluctuations in interest rates have long been recognized as an integral aspect of business cycles. Other things being equal, interest rates might be expected to fall during recessions and rise during expansions, reflecting either changes in the demand for credit or countercyclical monetary policy (or both). Indeed, there is a large literature that argues that, at least in the United States, the central bank has played a significant role in causing many of the recessions of the past century, partly reflecting its objective (before World War II) of maintaining gold convertibility or (after World War II) long-run price stability (Friedman and Schwartz, 1963, and Romer and Romer, 1989). Others have pointed to the role of monetary policy as one of the factors behind the diminution in the amplitude of business cycles after World War II. However, real short-term interest rates were not found to be related to the phase of the business cycle in the sample under consideration.[15] Clearly, a more rigorous analysis of this issue is needed.

Overall, the historical record suggests four broad lessons.

- Recessions have become less severe and less frequent.
- Synchronization has been a common feature of recessions throughout history.
- The role of investment in recessions has if anything increased over time.
- Since World War II, deflation has rarely been a feature of recessions.

Modern Business Cycles in Industrial Countries—A Tale of 93 Cycles

Building on the previous historical analysis, this section takes a closer look at the key empirical regularities of business cycles in recent decades. For the purpose of this section, the modern period begins in 1973, when three important developments occurred. First, the exchange rates between the major currencies began to float, marking a significant change in the international monetary regime. Second, long-term average growth rates in industrial countries decreased, reflecting a slowdown in productivity growth. Third, for the first time since World War II, a wave of level recessions started, reflecting in part the first oil shock.

The analysis focuses on business cycles in 21 industrial countries over the period 1973–2000.[16] During this period, 93 cycles were identified on the basis of turning points in the level of aggregate economic activity in each country (Appendix 3.1). The turning points define the two main phases of each cycle, recession and expansion: a recession is the period between a peak and a trough in activity, and an expansion is the period between a trough and a peak. The entire period from peak to peak determines the length of the cycle. Using quarterly real GDP as a proxy measure for aggregate economic activity, consistent dates for business cycle peaks and troughs in the 21 industrial countries during the

[15]Data on real short-term interest rates are available for seven countries: France, Germany, Japan, Netherlands, Switzerland, the United Kingdom, and the United States.

[16]The countries included in the sample are Australia, Austria, Belgium, Canada, Denmark, Finland, France, Germany, Greece, Ireland, Italy, Japan, the Netherlands, New Zealand, Norway, Portugal, Spain, Sweden, Switzerland, the United Kingdom, and the United States.

sample period were computed with a business cycle dating algorithm that closely matches the NBER chronology for the United States.

What Do Modern Cycles Look Like?

The typical or average cycle lasts about six years (Figure 3.3). It begins with a recession of about one year, during which output falls by slightly less than 3 percent (the depth of a recession), followed by a five-year expansion, during which output grows by a little more than 3 percent a year.[17] Hence, despite the initial recession, the level of output at the end of a cycle is about 14 percent higher than at the beginning. Strikingly, almost three-fourths of recessions were of mild to moderate depth and short to medium duration, while less than 10 percent of recessions were long and severe or worse (Figure 3.4). Short and medium-length recessions were more likely to be of mild to moderate depth. Although the relationship between depth and duration was generally less clear-cut for severe recessions, the most severe recessions were typically long or even protracted.

In line with the broad historical trends, business cycles have become longer and recessions shallower since 1973. The average length of business cycles increased from about four years during the 1970s to about six years during the 1980s and 1990s, reflecting mainly longer expansions (Figure 3.5).[18] Recessions became milder in the 1980s and 1990s, even though average growth rates were lower than in the 1970s. These results are in line with recent empirical work on declining output volatility in industrial countries (McConnell and Perez-Quiros, 2000; Blanchard and Simon, 2001; and Dalsgaard, Elmeskov, and

Figure 3.3. Recession Depth and Cyclical Path of Output[1]
(Initial peak = 100; x-axis in quarters)

Business cycles usually last about six years, during which cumulative output growth is about 14 percent. Mild recessions tend to be short as well.

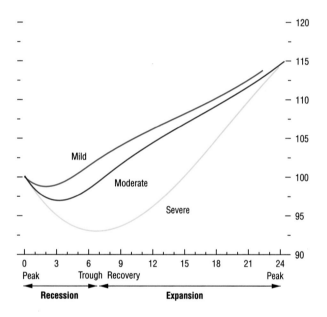

Source: IMF staff estimates.
[1]Stylistic representation of business cycles, based on averages associated with mild, moderate, and severe recessions in the sample.

[17]This result—that the durations of level recessions and expansions in industrial countries in recent decades are asymmetric—was noted by Artis, Kontolemis, and Osborn (1997).
[18]Roughly 40 percent of all cycles during the 1980s and 1990s lasted more than eight years, suggesting that the usual range of business cycle frequencies of 6–32 quarters may need to be revisited. Among other things, this frequency range is used in the estimation of the so-called cyclical components of economic time series.

Park, 2002). By contrast, the magnitude of output fluctuations in developing countries has not declined (Box 3.4).

The duration of recoveries—the time it takes for output to return to its previous peak—is not significantly related to either recession depth or duration, except for severe recessions. In other words, output does not on average recover significantly more quickly after a short and mild recession than after a medium-length and moderate recession. Recoveries lasted on average about 30 percent longer than recessions, indicating that output fell faster in recessions than it grew during the initial phase of the expansion. This result is consistent with that of Artis, Kontolemis, and Osborn (1997), who show that industrial production declined more quickly during recessions than it rose during expansions.

Sequences of short cycles could be related to structural rigidities that impede adjustment to adverse shocks. While most countries recorded three to five cycles after 1973, a few countries—Austria, Denmark, Greece, New Zealand, Norway, and Switzerland—registered more cycles. The higher number of cycles does not reflect generally shorter cycles throughout the sample period, but rather clusters of short cycles during a 5–10 year period. For example, four of Switzerland's seven recessions occurred during the early to the mid-1990s. The clusters of short cycles generally occurred in the context of relatively high labor and product market rigidity.[19] Against this background, it is not surprising that Japan—with its structural rigidities—is now in its third recession since 1993.

Most severe and long recessions could reflect the combination of structural problems and adverse shocks. The systemic banking crises in Finland and Sweden in the early 1990s showed how financial sector problems can amplify the output effects of adverse external shocks. Similarly, the combination of terms of trade shocks and structural rigidities led to large out-

---

[19]For cross-country comparisons of structural policies, see Nicoletti, Scarpetta, and Boylaud (1999) and Edwards and Schanz (2001).

Figure 3.4. Recession Depth and Duration
(Share of total number of recessions)

Almost three-fourths of recessions were of mild to moderate depth and short to medium duration, while less than 10 percent were long and severe or worse.

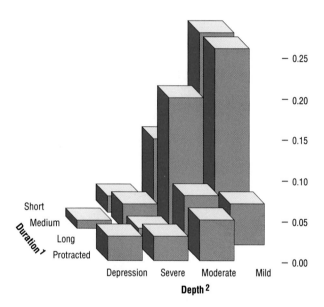

Source: IMF staff estimates.
[1] Time from peak to trough.
[2] Output contraction from peak to trough.

Figure 3.5. Key Business Cycle Characteristics
(Number of observations, 93 total)

Business cycles have become longer and recessions shallower since 1973.

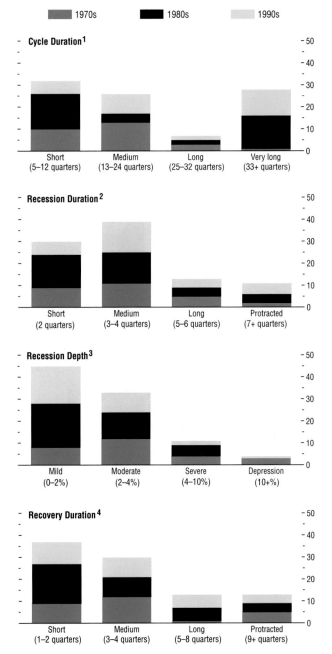

Source: IMF staff estimates.
[1]Cycle duration measured from peak to peak.
[2]Number of quarters from peak to trough (excluding peak quarter).
[3]Output contraction from peak to trough in percent of peak GDP.
[4]Number of quarters from trough for output to reach previous peak level.

put losses in New Zealand in the 1970s. Other deep recessions reflected the combination of oil shocks and especially aggressive disinflationary policy, as in Switzerland during 1974–75 and the United Kingdom during 1979–81.

Synchronization

Recessions tend to be synchronized, as manifested in their clustering in four periods during 1973–2000 (Figure 3.6). The first wave of recessions came in the mid-1970s, shortly after the first oil shock; the next two waves hit in the early 1980s, at the time of the second oil shock and the tightening of monetary policy in most countries; and the last wave occurred in the early 1990s. In the early 1990s, recessions clustered around two peaks rather than one, reflecting asymmetric shocks across the major currency areas.[20] As a result, business cycle peaks occurred at different times across countries, so that aggregate industrial country output did not go through a recession.

About half of all recessions in the modern period were synchronized, defining a recession in any one country as synchronized if at least one-half of the other countries (appropriately weighted) are in recession also.[21] Using this criterion, synchronized recessions were deeper but not longer than unsynchronized recessions. In particular, recessions that were concurrent with those in the G-7 countries were significantly deeper.

The results from our event-based analysis are consistent with those based on methods that effectively ignore the business cycle (i.e., the distinction between recession and expansion). Empirical studies of pairwise correlations, including Backus, Kehoe, and Kydland (1995) and Baxter (1995), document the high degree of comovement in output across industrial countries

[20]See Chapter II of the October 2001 *World Economic Outlook* and Helbling and Bayoumi (2002) for details.

[21]If the threshold is lowered to one-third, which then includes many recessions in Europe during 1992–93, then about three-fourths of all recessions were synchronized.

in recent decades. Among studies of the common components in macroeconomic fluctuations across countries, Lumsdaine and Prasad (1999) find that fluctuations were strongly and positively correlated with an estimated common component, and that these correlations increased in the post–Bretton Woods period. Kose, Otrok, and Whiteman (2001) also find a significant world component in output fluctuations, which accounted for a substantial fraction of fluctuations in advanced economies but a smaller fraction in developing countries. Helbling and Bayoumi (2002) indicate that, among G-7 countries, the U.S. component led the world factor.

What Happens to Components of Aggregate Demand?

Virtually all recessions in the modern period were accompanied by contractions in private fixed investment, based on an analysis of turning points in the components of aggregate demand.[22] In these recessions, investment peaked on average almost two quarters earlier than output and rebounded one quarter later, implying that the average duration of an investment contraction exceeded that of GDP (Figure 3.7). The average percentage contraction in private fixed investment was about six times larger than that of real GDP, while cumulative investment growth during the first four quarters after the trough was only about twice as large as that of real GDP. Not surprisingly, the depth of investment contraction and GDP contraction are positively correlated. Compared with aggregate economic activity, there are more cycles in private fixed investment, as minor investment contractions also occur during expansions. The most striking feature about private fixed investment contractions is their strong synchronization across countries, even for minor contractions (Figure 3.8). In periods with synchronized recessions, the number of countries experiencing investment

[22]In turn, virtually all recessions with no investment contractions were mild.

Figure 3.6. Synchronization of Recessions
(Share of countries in recession, percent)

Recessions tend to be synchronized, as manifested by their clustering in a few peaks.

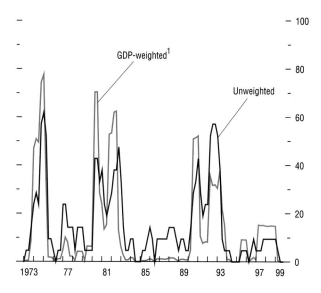

Source: IMF staff estimates.
[1]Countries are weighted by GDP at purchasing-power-parity exchange rates.

119

Figure 3.7. Cyclical Paths of Output and Investment[1]
(Initial peak = 100; x-axis in quarters)

Contractions in private fixed investment begin earlier, last longer, and are deeper than output contractions.

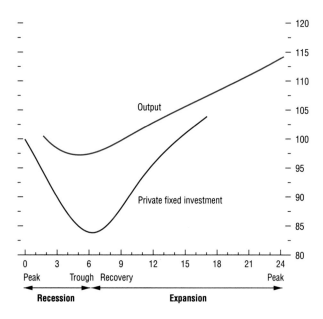

Source: IMF staff estimates.
[1]Stylistic representation of a business and an investment cycle, based on averages in the sample. The figure shows the average of investment cycles that coincide with output cycles. See text for details.

contractions exceeds that of those going through a recession, suggesting that global investment busts may be stronger than other linkages during downturns.

Cyclical peaks in private consumption, as well as the average duration and average depth of contractions, coincided more closely with those in output. However, consumption contracted in only about half of all recessions, mostly during moderate and more severe recessions. As a result, consumption contractions were less synchronized across countries than either fixed investment or output. This difference in the degree of synchronization between consumption and fixed investment matches the results of Kose, Otrok, and Whiteman (2001), who find that country-specific and idiosyncratic factors played a more important role in explaining consumption fluctuations, consistent with imperfect consumption risk-sharing across countries.

Shifting from the turning points in the components of aggregate demand to their contributions to growth, we find that—during a typical recession—declines in inventory changes and private fixed investment more than fully accounted for the contraction in output (Figure 3.9).[23] Private consumption contracted somewhat, while government spending and net exports were countercyclical. Short and mild recessions were mostly inventory-driven, with private consumption playing an even smaller role (Table 3.2). In unsynchronized recessions, which usually occurred in small, open economies, net exports tended to be procyclical, reflecting the greater vulnerability of such economies to adverse external shocks. Procyclical net exports were also an important factor in the severe recessions in emerging market countries associated with capital account crises (Box 3.5).

Over time, inventories have been contributing less to recessions, while fixed investment and

---

[23]In countries where GDP data are chain-weighted, contributions to growth are based on the cumulative sums of quarterly contributions that are corrected for changes in relative prices.

consumption have contributed more. The decline in the contribution of inventory changes from the 1970s and 1980s to the 1990s is consistent with the idea that improved inventory management, partly reflecting the increased use of information technology, has reduced the variability of inventories.[24] The increase in the contribution of fixed investment reflects the exceptionally large investment contractions after banking crises (Finland, Sweden) and the impact of sharp asset price falls (Japan, United Kingdom) in the 1990s.[25] The increase in the contribution of private consumption is consistent with the combination in the 1990s of especially large falls in asset prices and larger wealth effects (as discussed in Chapter II).

During a typical recovery, private consumption was the single largest contributor to the growth in output (Table 3.3).[26] Private consumption was the most important contributor to growth during the recovery, even if it did not contract during the recession. The smaller contribution of fixed investment to the recovery is consistent with the longer duration of investment contractions discussed above. As in the case of recessions, inventories contributed less to recoveries in the 1990s than in the 1970s, while private fixed investment contributed more.

While the contributions to growth of consumption and fixed investment are asymmetric between recessions and recoveries, the *changes* in their contributions to growth during the *transition* from recessions to recoveries are more symmetric. For fixed investment, a large rate of decline during the recession switches to a small

[24]See Box 3.4 in Chapter 3 of the October 2001 *World Economic Outlook.* The declining role of inventories may also reflect the increasing share of services in the economy, which reduces the ratio of inventories to output.

[25]Contractions in private fixed investment actually became somewhat milder in the 1990s, but by less than the corresponding moderation of output contractions.

[26]Surprisingly, net exports also contribute more than 10 percent to the recovery, although this appears to reflect the relatively large number of recoveries in smaller industrial economies after nonsynchronized recessions in the sample. If demand contributions are weighted by country size, the average contribution of net exports is zero.

Figure 3.8. Synchronization of Contractions in Output, Investment, and Consumption
(Share of countries experiencing contractions, percent)[1]

Contractions in investment are more synchronized than those in output or private consumption.

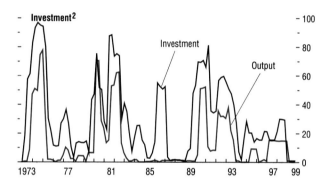

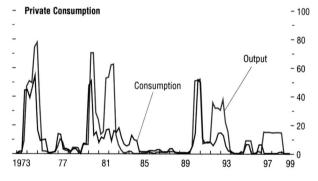

Source: IMF staff estimates.
[1]Countries are weighted by GDP at purchasing-power-parity exchange rates.
[2]Private gross fixed capital formation.

Figure 3.9. Contributions to Growth
(Ratio of change in component to change in output)[1]

Declines in inventories and private fixed investment largely account for output declines during recessions, while increases in private consumption are the most important driving force during recoveries.

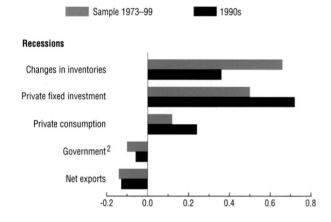

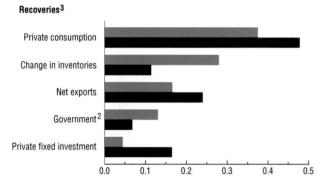

Source: IMF staff estimates.
[1]Unweighted average.
[2]Includes government fixed capital formation and government final consumption.
[3]Cumulative change during first four quarters after the trough.

growth rate during the recovery. For private consumption, a small rate of decline changes to a substantial rate of growth. The differences in the (weighted) rates of change for the two components are rather similar, indicating that both of them are important for the turnaround in output growth from recession to recovery. Similarly, the changes in the contributions of consumption and fixed investment to growth during the transition from expansion to recession are symmetric. The growth of fixed investment changes from slightly positive to strongly negative, while the growth of consumption changes from strongly positive to slightly negative.

The results from our event-based analysis are consistent with those in the broader literature. There is widespread agreement that investment spending is more volatile than output and highly procyclical.[27] Backus and Kehoe (1992), using more than a century of data on 10 industrial countries, show that investment was consistently two to four times as variable as output, while consumption was about as variable. They also show that both investment and consumption were strongly procyclical, while the trade balance was generally countercyclical, exhibiting larger deficits during booms than recessions.[28] Similar results are obtained by Basu and Taylor (1999) on the basis of a somewhat broader sample of countries and longer time period. They also find that investment was more highly correlated with output than consumption during the post–Bretton Woods period, but not in earlier eras.

---

[27]Using the bandpass filter to remove the high- and low-frequency components of U.S. macroeconomic time series and focusing on business cycle frequencies only, Stock and Watson (1999) have found that consumption, inventory investment, fixed investment, and imports have significant, positive contemporaneous correlations with output (i.e. they are strongly procyclical). As exports do not vary strongly with output, the trade balance is countercyclical. For other studies, see Gordon (1986), Fuhrer and Schuh (1998), or Diebold and Rudebusch (1999).

[28]Similarly, Prasad and Gable (1998) find little evidence that variations in the trade balance have contributed significantly to cyclical recoveries in industrial countries since the 1970s.

Table 3.2. Relative Contributions to Recessions

	Full Sample	Decade			Type of Recession			G-7 Countries
		1970s	1980s	1990s	Mild	Severe	Short	
	Ratio of peak-to-trough change in component to peak-to-trough change in GDP; percent							
Change in inventories	66	78	77	36	122	56	107	52
Private investment	50	47	36	72	41	47	−4	67
Private consumption	12	2	14	24	−14	16	8	22
Net exports	−21	−16	−21	−30	−29	−5	−4	−27
Government[1]	−10	−13	−9	−6	−22	−17	−12	−5
	Peak-to-trough change; percent of peak							
Memorandum								
GDP	−2.7	−3.8	−2.1	−2.2	−1.0	−7.1	−1.8	−2.4

Source: IMF staff calculations.
[1]Includes government final consumption and fixed investment.

Table 3.3. Relative Contributions to Recoveries

	Full Sample	Decade			Type of Previous Recession			G-7 Countries
		1970s	1980s	1990s	Mild	Severe	Short	
	Ratio of change in component to change in GDP during first four quarters after trough							
Change in inventories	25	38	25	−6	20	50	30	21
Private investment	5	6	9	—	—	—	10	18
Private consumption	45	44	38	63	50	30	40	52
Net exports	6	−2	11	18	30	10	10	−1
Government[1]	19	14	17	32	10	10	10	10
	Change during first four quarters after trough; percent of trough							
Memorandum								
GDP	3.5	5.6	3.0	2.2	2.7	6.2	4.0	3.4

Source: IMF staff calculations.
[1]Includes government final consumption and fixed investment.

Cycles in Asset Prices and Monetary Policy

The behavior of asset prices is closely related to that of aggregate economic activity.[29] Expectations of future changes in macroeconomic conditions can have important effects on current asset prices, so changes in asset prices usually lead economic activity. To examine the behavior of stock prices over the business cycle, we identified turning points in real stock price indices using the same methodology as for aggregate economic activity.[30]

Virtually all recessions were preceded by sharp contractions in stock prices.[31] On average between 1973 and 2000, stock price contractions were about 40 percent deep and lasted about nine quarters, much longer than the average re-

[29]For a review of the transmission mechanisms through which asset price and monetary policy shocks affect output, and vice versa, see Chapter III, "Asset Prices and the Business Cycle," in the May 2000 *World Economic Outlook*.

[30]Consistent data going back to 1970 were available for 15 countries. These countries account for 65 of the 93 recessions in the full sample.

[31]Typically, cycles in real stock price have been shorter, so that there were periods of prolonged stock price contractions during expansions in output. As noted by Samuelson (1966): "The stock market has predicted nine out of the last five recessions." To focus on stock price behavior during recessions and recoveries, turning points in real stock prices that were close enough to those in aggregate economic activity to be considered related were selected. To be considered "close," periods of contractions in real stock prices and aggregate economic activity had to be at least adjacent, that is, the trough quarter in stock prices had to be the same as the peak quarter in activity. If contractions in real stock prices with troughs up to 4 quarters prior to the peak in activity were considered, 58 out of the 65 recessions would have been accompanied by contractions and recoveries in real stock prices.

Table 3.4. Real Stock Price Contractions and Recoveries in Industrial Countries[1]
(Percent)

	Sample	1970s	1980s	1990s
Contractions				
Average	−39.2	−56.1	−35.5	−25.4
Standard deviation	20.9	17.5	20.0	11.6
Median	−34.1	−54.0	−31.7	−27.1
Recoveries[2]				
Average	28.6	22.8	31.7	31.2
Standard deviation	21.0	23.5	21.9	16.8
Median	25.1	19.7	27.4	31.9
Memorandum				
Contractions in G-7 countries				
Average	−36.4	−59.6	−30.2	−25.0
Standard deviation	20.1	14.0	14.3	15.2
Median	−37.7	−59.7	−31.7	−18.7
Recoveries in G-7 countries[2]				
Average	26.5	33.3	28.5	31.6
Standard deviation	22.0	33.6	17.1	18.6
Median	30.5	23.2	34.4	32.1

Source: Morgan Stanley Capital International (MSCI); IMF, *International Financial Statistics*; and IMF staff calculations.
[1]Real stock price indices were computed using MSCI indices and consumer prices for Australia, Austria, Belgium, Canada, Denmark, France, Germany, Italy, Japan, Netherlands, Spain, Sweden, Switzerland, the United Kingdom, and the United States. For details on selection of peaks and troughs in real stock prices, see text.
[2]Cumulative growth in real stock prices in the first four quarters after trough.

Figure 3.10. Synchronization of Contractions in Output and Stock Prices
(Share of countries experiencing contractions, percent)[1]

Stock price contractions are highly synchronized, reflecting global asset market linkages.

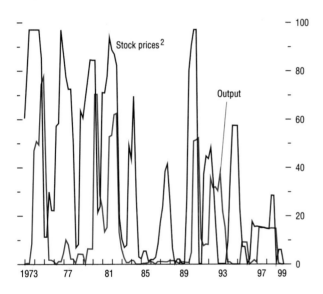

Source: IMF staff estimates.
[1]Countries are weighted by GDP at purchasing-power-parity exchange rates.
[2]Stock prices deflated by consumer prices.

cession (Table 3.4). The magnitudes of the stock price contractions were related to the depths of the associated recessions. Since stock prices peaked about five quarters before economic activity, the trough in stock prices usually coincided with the trough in activity.[32] Stock prices did not recover to their previous peaks within two years after the trough. However, in the 1990s, stock price contractions were shallower and stock prices regained their previous peaks within four quarters. Stock price contractions were highly synchronized across countries, as was the case with fixed investment (Figure 3.10). During periods of synchronized recessions, the number of countries experiencing stock price contractions exceeded the number of countries going through a recession, underlining the strength of global asset market linkages.

---

[32]Stock and Watson (1999) have found that in the case of the United States, stock prices are moderately procyclical and lead output.

Box 3.4. Economic Fluctuations in Developing Countries

Economic fluctuations in developing countries are more severe and have more serious consequences than those in industrial countries. As shown in the figure, the volatility of real GDP growth in developing countries is higher than that in industrial countries, and the volatility of consumption growth is much higher. Consumption in developing countries fluctuates much more than output, while consumption in industrial countries fluctuates about the same as output, indicating that households in industrial countries can maintain consumption levels even in bad times by running down assets accumulated in good times.[1] The harmful effects of output volatility on growth are well documented (Ramey and Ramey, 1995). A recent study finds that the welfare cost of consumption volatility in a typical developing country is much higher than that in the United States (Pallage and Robe, 2001).

Several factors account for the higher volatility in developing countries. First, emerging market countries are more vulnerable to commodity price shocks, both because many of them remain highly specialized in commodity exports and because many are more dependent on commodity imports, especially oil. As a result, the fluctuations in the terms of trade (the ratio of export prices to import prices) are larger in emerging market countries than in industrial countries and have remained high (Cashin and McDermott, 2002). In part, this reflects the high degree of competition among suppliers of commodities, who respond aggressively to changes in prices, thus generating large fluctuations.

Second, financial systems in emerging market countries are generally less developed than those in industrial countries. Financial systems can help smooth economic fluctuations by facilitating diversification and by making it easier to lend and borrow. However, sometimes financial

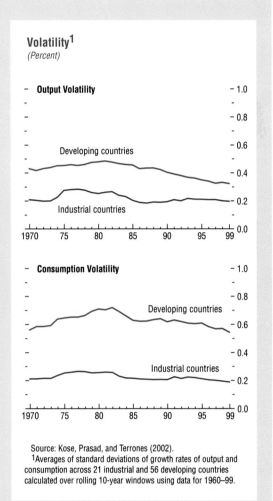

Volatility[1]
(Percent)

Source: Kose, Prasad, and Terrones (2002).
[1]Averages of standard deviations of growth rates of output and consumption across 21 industrial and 56 developing countries calculated over rolling 10-year windows using data for 1960–99.

The main author is Ashoka Mody.
[1]Blanchard and Simon (2001) show that in industrial countries except Japan volatility has declined steadily, but De Ferranti and others (2000) find that the experience in developing countries is more mixed.

---

systems are large because they are engaged in unproductive activities, resulting in so-called "lending booms," which tend to increase volatility (Eichengreen and Mody, 2000). Others have argued that volatile external capital flows can amplify the fragility of domestic financial systems (Caballero, 2000). Greater transparency and opportunities for diversification are therefore key to achieving the financial system's stabilizing function.

Third, developing countries face higher asset price fluctuations (Du and Wei, 2002) and their consequences are more severe. In industrial countries, exchange rates remain highly variable, though their effects do not appear to feed into

Box 3.4 *(concluded)*

consumption volatility (Rogoff, 2001). While stock price volatility feeds into consumption volatility through wealth effects, households in industrial countries have a wider scope for financial diversification than those in emerging market countries. For example, in the United States, an increasing share of equity market volatility is due to movements in the stock prices of individual companies, implying that—for the most part—individuals can diversify across relatively uncorrelated risks (Campbell and others, 2001). By contrast, in many emerging market countries, a very large fraction of stock market movement reflects overall market risk rather than individual company risk (Morck, Yeung, and Yu, 2000), implying less opportunity to diversify.

Finally, macroeconomic policies in emerging market countries may also help to explain some of the higher volatility of macroeconomic outcomes. In industrial countries, central banks have helped to create a more predictable macro-

economic environment and reduce output volatility by bringing inflation under control (see the essay on low inflation in Chapter II). By contrast, macroeconomic policies in many developing countries are often procyclical—that is, they tend to amplify macroeconomic disturbances (see the essay on Latin America in Chapter II). While this difference is important, it should be recognized that the policymaking environment in developing countries is typically more volatile than that in industrial countries, partly reflecting larger external shocks, such as commodity price shocks. Moreover, policymaking in developing countries occurs in an environment of weak institutions of conflict management, which are a source of volatility and which limit the ability to deal with the adverse consequences of macroeconomic fluctuations (Rodrik, 1999). As such, stronger institutions are necessary not just for growth, but also for dampening fluctuations.

Deliberate monetary tightening in major industrial countries is widely regarded as among the factors behind the recessions.[33] In the modern period, monetary tightening generally followed the acceleration in inflation that began in the late 1960s and was exacerbated by the collapse of the Bretton Woods system of pegged exchange rates and the oil price shocks. Attempts to fight inflation began in the early 1970s but weakened during the course of the 1973–75 recessions. Sustained efforts to implement disinflationary monetary policies in most countries began only in 1979 and continued through the early to mid-1980s. Another episode of widespread monetary tightening began in 1988–89, when major central banks started to reverse the large liquidity injections that followed the 1987 stock market crash.

While a rigorous assessment of the relationship between monetary policy and output is beyond the scope of this chapter, the focus here is on whether turning points in monetary policy were consistent with the idea that monetary policy had an impact on output.[34] In general, mon-

---

[33]A forceful expression of the role of monetary policy is due to Dornbusch (1997): "None of the U.S. expansions of the past 40 years died in bed of old age; every one was murdered by the Federal Reserve." Other important factors include oil and technology shocks; there is much less of a consensus on the role of fiscal policy in precipitating or mitigating the severity of recessions. Cochrane (1994) has concluded: "None of the popular candidates for observable shocks robustly accounts for the bulk of business-cycle fluctuations in output."

[34]The magnitude of the impact of monetary policy on output remains subject to considerable debate, as the results vary with the specification and identification of monetary policy shocks, as well as the estimation techniques used to remove the biases arising from the simultaneity between monetary policy and output. Romer and Romer (1989) argue that, in the United States, output fell substantially in every episode in which the Federal Reserve deliberately attempted to induce a recession to reduce inflation. By contrast, in a survey of the empirical literature, Christiano, Eichenbaum, and Evans (1999) argue that unanticipated changes in monetary policy in general have smaller output effects and account for only about 20 percent of the variation in output.

etary policy might be expected to tighten during the late stage of an expansion, and to loosen during a recession, reflecting the central bank's objectives of stabilizing inflation and output. As a result, turning points in the monetary policy stance might be expected to either lead or be coincident with those in output. The relationship between cycles in monetary policy and output were examined using nominal and real short-term interest rates as indicators of the monetary policy stance.[35]

The expected pattern of turning points in interest rates and output was more evident in larger than in smaller economies, and in synchronized than in unsynchronized recessions. In the full sample, interest rates peaked just before recessions about one-third of the time and during recessions about another one-third of the time, while in G-7 countries interest rates peaked prior to or during all recessions.[36] The weaker results for smaller countries could reflect the greater prominence of exchange rate considerations in these countries. In other words, interest rate changes may have been constrained by explicit or implicit exchange rate targets, which on occasion may have called for procyclical interest rates before and during recessions.

The cyclical behavior of monetary policy was also more evident in synchronized recessions than in unsynchronized ones, suggesting that many central banks pursued disinflationary policies at the same time. This also indicates that factors other than monetary policy cycles are more important in unsynchronized recessions (mostly in smaller countries), consistent with the earlier finding that these recessions were often accompanied by contractions in net exports. In these cases, accelerating inflation may either be absent, so that there would be no reason for a monetary policy tightening prior to a recession, or may be among the reasons for exchange rate

Table 3.5. Changes in Short-Term Interest Rates[1]
(Percentage points)

	Sample	1970s	1980s	1990s
All countries				
Increases during 4 quarters to peak				
Nominal interest rates				
Average	3.8	5.1	4.0	2.6
Standard deviation	2.7	2.6	3.0	1.6
Real interest rates				
Average	3.8	5.6	3.3	3.2
Standard deviation	3.5	4.9	3.2	2.5
Decreases from peak to trough				
Nominal interest rates				
Average	−6.8	−6.6	−6.7	−7.1
Standard deviation	2.7	2.2	3.0	2.8
Real interest rates				
Average	−6.2	−9.5	−5.2	−4.9
Standard deviation	4.2	6.1	2.5	2.7
G-7 countries				
Increases during 4 quarters to peak				
Nominal interest rates				
Average	4.8	6.2	5.5	2.2
Standard deviation	2.8	2.8	2.6	1.4
Real interest rates				
Average	3.3	3.2	4.3	2.1
Standard deviation	3.4	4.7	3.5	1.8
Decreases from peak to trough				
Nominal interest rates				
Average	−7.4	−7.8	−7.0	−7.6
Standard deviation	2.6	1.6	3.8	2.1
Real interest rates				
Average	−6.6	−11.3	−4.8	−4.6
Standard deviation	5.0	7.4	2.0	1.9

Source: IMF staff calculations.
[1]Only recessions during which interest rate behavior was consistent with the monetary policy cycle hypothesis are included. See text for details of the calculations.

overvaluation and falling net exports, so that the recessions could actually be related to the lack of appropriate monetary tightening.

In recession episodes when interest rates peaked before output, the magnitudes of the interest rate increases were related to the depths of recessions (Table 3.5). This suggests that the degree of monetary policy tightening may be one factor behind the magnitude of output contractions. In turn, the degree of monetary tightening was related to both the inflation rate at

---

[35]As above, the analysis involves a comparison of peaks and troughs in interest rates with peaks and troughs in aggregate economic activity. Interest rate peaks up to six quarters prior to the beginning of a recession were considered consistent with the monetary tightening hypothesis, provided that interest rate troughs occurred during the recessions.

[36]Stock and Watson (1999) have found that nominal interest rates in the United States are procyclical and in fact lead output.

Box 3.5. Capital Account Crises in Emerging Market Countries

Capital account crises in emerging market countries—characterized by a sudden cessation or reversal of capital inflows that forces a large and abrupt current account adjustment together with a large depreciation in the exchange rate—have been associated with severe output contractions (Ghosh and others, 2002). As illustrated in the table, the severity of the output collapses in such crises in emerging market countries in the 1990s has varied. On average, the swing in real GDP growth in these crises was almost 10 percentage points, compared with less than 2 percentage points in more typical IMF-supported program countries. Growth in most cases rebounded rapidly in the year following the crisis.

What underlies these steep output declines? From one perspective, they are the counterpart to the massive capital outflows experienced by these countries, which in some cases amounted to as much as 15–20 percent of GDP (at annualized rates). To the extent that these capital outflows could not be met from existing reserves or official support, they required corresponding adjustments of the current account. With only limited scope to increase exports in the short run, this adjustment took place mainly through import compression and a corresponding slump in domestic demand. The figure shows the average behavior of real GDP growth, the current account, and private capital flows during capital account crises.

The output losses in turn reflected a combination of demand- and supply-side factors. On the demand side, the salient event in all these crises was a collapse in private domestic consumption and investment spending. Net exports provided a significant positive contribution, mitigating the downturn—but as noted, this typically reflected a contraction of imports more than a large expansion of exports.[1] The recoveries, in

The main authors are Atish R. Ghosh and Timothy Lane.

[1] The high level of imports prior to the crisis reflected in part the private sector's assessment that the exchange rate policy was unsustainable, causing people to shift their demand for imports from the future to the present, when imports were relatively cheap (Calvo, 1998).

Real GDP Growth
(Percent)

Country	Crisis year	Real GDP Growth		
		Previous year	Crisis year	Following year
Argentina	1995	5.8	−2.8	5.5
Brazil	1999	0.2	0.8	4.2
Indonesia	1998	4.5	−13.1	0.8
Korea	1998	5.0	−6.7	10.9
Mexico	1995	4.4	−6.2	5.2
Philippines	1998	5.2	−0.6	3.3
Thailand	1998	−1.4	−10.8	4.2
Turkey	1994	7.7	−4.7	8.1

Sources: WEO database; IMF staff estimates.

turn, were driven mainly by a pickup in private consumption and investment, with export expansion playing only a supportive role.

Adverse shocks to aggregate supply also appear to have played a major part in the crises. Although the relative effects of supply and demand shocks are very difficult to disentangle, the behavior of inventories as well as some econometric evidence suggests that the initial sharp decline in output mostly reflected a supply shock. This may in large part have reflected high import content of domestic production and severe balance sheet effects stemming from corporate and financial sector exposures to exchange rate and interest rate changes. The large exchange rate depreciations and temporarily high interest rates forced many firms into bankruptcy and disrupted supply and credit channels. These initial supply shocks were accompanied by negative aggregate demand shocks, because the same balance sheet and credit market effects also dampened investment and consumption spending; such spending was depressed further as the initial output contractions resulted in layoffs and mounting uncertainties.

The pattern of the downturns and recoveries varied considerably across countries. In Brazil, for instance, the downturn was comparatively mild, in large part reflecting low corporate leverage and the fact that the private sector was able to hedge itself against exchange rate move-

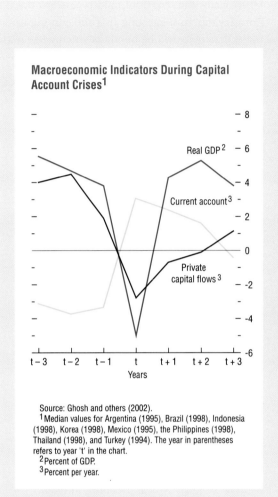

Macroeconomic Indicators During Capital Account Crises[1]

Real GDP[2]

Current account[3]

Private capital flows[3]

t − 3   t − 2   t − 1   t   t + 1   t + 2   t + 3

Years

Source: Ghosh and others (2002).
[1] Median values for Argentina (1995), Brazil (1998), Indonesia (1998), Korea (1998), Mexico (1995), the Philippines (1998), Thailand (1998), and Turkey (1994). The year in parentheses refers to year 't' in the chart.
[2] Percent of GDP.
[3] Percent per year.

ments through holdings of dollar- and inflation-indexed public debt. At the other end of the spectrum, Indonesia experienced a relatively severe and protracted downturn: the balance sheet effects of the currency depreciation were massive, owing to the corporate sector's large unhedged foreign currency exposures, and, in the absence of a framework for resolving corporate debt problems, took a long time to resolve. Indonesia's crisis was also compounded by other structural weaknesses and by political turmoil and regional fragmentation.

Macroeconomic policies played a broadly supportive or neutral role in these crises after the initial shocks (Ghosh and others, 2002). Except in Mexico and Turkey, where the fiscal contraction was substantial, fiscal impulses were either positive or modestly negative. The credit crunches that occurred appear to have reflected primarily the withdrawal of foreign financing and the heightened riskiness of lending; the timing and magnitude of changes in monetary aggregates suggest that they were not a major factor accounting for the output declines. Real interest rates typically rose to high levels temporarily, but then came down rapidly as confidence returned, contributing to the recovery.

the interest rate peaks and the increases in inflation prior to that peak. Interestingly, the magnitude of the interest rate declines during recessions remained similar across decades and does not appear related to either peak interest rate levels or recession depth. There is some evidence suggesting that more aggressive easing is associated with higher output growth during the recovery but not with the recovery duration.

Main Points About Modern Business Cycles

Overall, the analysis of modern business cycles suggests the following main points.
- In line with the broad historical trend, recessions in industrial countries were shallower in

the 1990s than in the 1970s or 1980s. The duration of recoveries was not significantly related to the duration or the severity of the preceding recession. Repeated recessions and deep recessions were unusual, and reflected mostly structural problems.
- As in previous historical episodes, synchronized recessions were fairly common after 1973—most recessions occurred when other countries were in recession too. The downturn of the early 1990s was different because the major advanced economies went into recession at somewhat different times, reflecting asymmetric shocks. Synchronized recessions were on average deeper, though not longer, than unsynchronized ones.

- In contrast to the late nineteenth century, virtually all recessions in recent decades were accompanied by contractions in private fixed investment. The investment contractions were more synchronized across countries than were the recessions, suggesting that investment busts may be stronger than other international linkages during downturns.
- While investment contractions made important contributions to recessions, upturns in consumption tended to drive recoveries. During both recessions and recoveries, the role of inventories has been falling over time, consistent with the idea that inventory management has improved, partly in response to the increased use of information technology.
- Peaks in stock prices preceded peaks in output, usually by about one year, and troughs roughly coincided. In the 1990s, stock prices fell by about 25 percent on average during recessions and usually took less than one year to regain their previous peak. Like investment contractions, stock price declines were more synchronized than recessions, underlining the role of global asset market linkages.
- Peaks in interest rates usually just preceded or just followed peaks in output, especially in larger economies where exchange rate considerations were relatively less important. The interest rate increases prior to the peaks were positively related to inflation, and also to the depths of the subsequent recessions.

The Current Cycle

The current downturn in industrial countries has so far been fairly typical of other downturns in recent decades. The synchronization of the current recessions is not unusual, though it is greater than in the early 1990s and appears to have caught some policymakers by surprise. In line with the long-term trend toward milder recessions, the output losses in the United States and Germany are proving to be smaller than usual; Italy and Canada appear to be skirting recession; and France and the United Kingdom are likely to avoid output losses altogether.

Historically, the length of mild recessions does not vary much, suggesting that the coming upturns in activity will be about as synchronized as the downturns. The forecast that the initial upturn will be sharper in the United States than in Europe is consistent with the milder downturn in Europe and the fact that—historically—it takes roughly the same amount of time for output to regain its previous peak following mild recessions, regardless of the depth of the downturn.

Japan is rather different. Its recession is deeper than the recent downturns in other major industrial countries, though still only about average compared to recessions in recent decades. Japan provides the only case of deflation in industrial countries since World War II, likely reflecting inadequate aggregate demand rather than exceptional productivity growth. And it is now in its third recession since 1993, which resembles the experience of other countries with deep structural problems that saw sequences of short cycles in recent decades. The combination of deflation and structural problems is a serious concern, underlining the urgency of additional monetary easing and aggressive structural reform.

The main drivers of the current cycle also seem to be fairly typical. Declines in fixed investment and inventories have played the largest roles in the downturns, consistent with industrial country experience after 1973, though in contrast to the more limited role of investment in the late nineteenth century. The expectation that inventories and a moderate pickup in final domestic demand will play the largest roles in the recovery is also in line with previous upturns. Even the continued growth of private consumption—indeed, it appears to be helping some European countries to avoid recession entirely—is consistent with past mild recessions. However, as discussed in Chapter I, the exceptional strength of consumption during the current downturn raises questions about its sustainability, especially in the United States, given the already low personal saving rate and relatively high levels of corporate and household debt.

The behavior of stock prices in the current downturn looks fairly typical compared to recent history, though the extraordinary stock market boom during the previous expansion was not typical. As in the past, stock price declines have been highly synchronized, underlining the importance of global asset market linkages. In the current downturn, stock prices in the United States and Germany peaked about four quarters before output did, compared with an average of five quarters in the 1990s, and stock prices fell by 25–30 percent, like in the 1990s. However, the stock market boom that preceded the current downturn has left stock prices richly valued by historical standards. The best historical parallel for the stock market boom of the late 1990s is probably that of the 1920s, which was associated in part with the introduction of electricity and other new technologies. It is difficult to make inferences about the current cycle, because the recession that followed the 1920s boom—the Great Depression—was exacerbated by serious monetary policy mistakes.

As in previous business cycles, monetary policy in G-7 countries was tightened prior to the recent downturn. Given that inflation was relatively low toward the end of the previous expansion, central banks had to raise interest rates by less than usual, which is one factor behind the relatively mild recessions. Relatively low inflation going into the downturn also allowed central banks—especially in the United States, the United Kingdom, and Canada—to cut interest rates aggressively over the past year, helping to set the stage for recovery.

Appendix 3.1. Business Cycle Turning Points

This appendix reports the business cycle turning points identified using annual data over 1881–2000 and quarterly data over 1973–2000.

Annual Data, 1881–2000

Business cycle turning points were determined using annual real GDP data for 16 industrial countries. The data sources were Bergman, Bordo, and Jonung (1998) for 1881–1950 and the WEO database, the *International Financial Statistics*, and the Penn World Tables for 1950–2000. The overall period was divided into four subperiods: 1881–1913, 1919–38, 1950–72, and 1973–2000. The years 1914–18 and 1939–49 were excluded because of the two World Wars. Data on GDP were not available for all 16 countries for all years: data for France were not available for 1919–22; data for Germany were not available for 1919–24; and data for Japan began in 1887. A year was designated as a trough *(T)* if growth in the year in question was negative and growth in the following year was positive. Similarly, a year was designated as a peak *(P)* if growth in the year in question was positive and growth in the following year was negative. In cases where a business cycle phase extended beyond the end of a subperiod, the phase was truncated at the end of that subperiod. As a result, troughs did not always follow peaks and vice versa. The turning points in each country were as follows.

Australia: *P:* 1882, *T:* 1883, *P:* 1889, *T:* 1893, *P:* 1898, *T:* 1899, *P:* 1901, *T:* 1902, *P:* 1906, *T:* 1907, *P:* 1910, *T:* 1911, *P:* 1913, *T:* 1919, *P:* 1924, *T:* 1925, *P:* 1926, *T:* 1931, *P:* 1937, *T:* 1938, *P:* 1951, *T:* 1952, *P:* 1960, *T:* 1961, *P:* 1972, *P:* 1981, *T:* 1982, *P:* 1989, *T:* 1990, *P:* 2000.

Canada: *P:* 1882, *T:* 1883, *P:* 1884, *T:* 1885, *P:* 1891, *T:* 1893, *P:* 1895, *T:* 1896, *P:* 1907, *T:* 1908, *P:* 1913, *T:* 1919, *P:* 1920, *T:* 1921, *P:* 1929, *T:* 1933, *P:* 1937, *T:* 1938, *P:* 1953, *T:* 1954, *P:* 1972, *P:* 1981, *T:* 1982, *P:* 1989, *T:* 1991, *P:* 2000.

Denmark: *T:* 1881, *P:* 1883, *T:* 1884, *P:* 1890, *T:* 1891, *P:* 1907, *T:* 1908, *P:* 1911, *T:* 1912, *P:* 1913, *P:* 1920, *T:* 1921, *P:* 1924, *T:* 1925, *P:* 1926, *T:* 1927, *P:* 1930, *T:* 1932, *P:* 1938, *P:* 1950, *T:* 1951, *P:* 1954, *T:* 1955, *P:* 1962, *T:* 1963, *P:* 1972, *P:* 1973, *T:* 1975, *P:* 1979, *T:* 1981, *P:* 1986, *T:* 1987, *P:* 2000.

Finland: *T:* 1881, *P:* 1883, *T:* 1884, *P:* 1890, *T:* 1892, *P:* 1898, *T:* 1899, *P:* 1900, *T:* 1902, *P:* 1907, *T:* 1908, *P:* 1913, *P:* 1920, *T:* 1921, *P:* 1928, *T:*

1931, *P:* 1938, *P:* 1952, *T:* 1953, *P:* 1957, *T:* 1958, *P:* 1972, *P:* 1975, *T:* 1977, *P:* 1989, *T:* 1993, *P:* 2000.

France: *P:* 1884, *T:* 1886, *P:* 1892, *T:* 1893, *P:* 1894, *T:* 1895, *P:* 1898, *T:* 1902, *P:* 1904, *T:* 1905, *P:* 1907, *T:* 1908, *P:* 1912, *T:* 1913, *P:* 1922, *T:* 1923, *P:* 1924, *T:* 1925, *P:* 1932, *T:* 1935, *P:* 1938, *P:* 1972, *P:* 1974, *T:* 1975, *P:* 1992, *T:* 1993, *P:* 2000.

Germany: *P:* 1890, *T:* 1891, *P:* 1900, *T:* 1901, *P:* 1905, *T:* 1906, *P:* 1907, *T:* 1908, *P:* 1913, *P:* 1925, *T:* 1926, *P:* 1928, *T:* 1932, *P:* 1938, *P:* 1966, *T:* 1967, *P:* 1972, *P:* 1973, *T:* 1975, *P:* 1980, *T:* 1982, *P:* 1992, *T:* 1993, *P:* 2000.

Italy: *T:* 1881, *P:* 1882, *T:* 1883, *P:* 1886, *T:* 1888, *P:* 1891, *T:* 1892, *P:* 1893, *T:* 1894, *P:* 1896, *T:* 1897, *P:* 1901, *T:* 1902, *P:* 1903, *T:* 1904, *P:* 1907, *T:* 1908, *P:* 1909, *T:* 1910, *P:* 1913, *P:* 1920, *T:* 1921, *P:* 1925, *T:* 1927, *P:* 1928, *T:* 1933, *P:* 1935, *T:* 1936, *P:* 1938, *P:* 1972, *P:* 1974, *T:* 1975, *P:* 1980, *T:* 1981, *P:* 1992, *T:* 1993, *P:* 2000.

Japan: *T:* 1887, *P:* 1892, *T:* 1893, *P:* 1896, *T:* 1897, *P:* 1902, *T:* 1903, *P:* 1904, *T:* 1905, *P:* 1909, *T:* 1910, *P:* 1913, *P:* 1923, *T:* 1924, *P:* 1930, *T:* 1933, *P:* 1936, *T:* 1937, *P:* 1938, *P:* 1972, *P:* 1973, *T:* 1974, *P:* 1997, *T:* 1999, *P:* 2000.

Netherlands: *P:* 1887, *T:* 1888, *P:* 1889, *T:* 1890, *P:* 1892, *T:* 1894, *P:* 1895, *T:* 1898, *P:* 1899, *T:* 1900, *P:* 1904, *T:* 1905, *P:* 1908, *T:* 1909, *P:* 1911, *T:* 1913, *P:* 1930, *T:* 1934, *P:* 1938, *P:* 1950, *T:* 1952, *P:* 1957, *T:* 1958, *P:* 1972, *T:* 1974, *T:* 1975, *P:* 1980, *T:* 1982, *P:* 2000.

Norway: *P:* 1882, *T:* 1883, *P:* 1902, *T:* 1903, *P:* 1913, *P:* 1920, *T:* 1921, *P:* 1923, *T:* 1924, *P:* 1930, *T:* 1931, *P:* 1938, *P:* 1972, *P:* 1987, *T:* 1988, *P:* 2000.

Portugal: *P:* 1888, *T:* 1890, *P:* 1892, *T:* 1894, *P:* 1896, *T:* 1898, *P:* 1900, *T:* 1901, *P:* 1902, *T:* 1904, *P:* 1910, *T:* 1911, *P:* 1912, *T:* 1913, *P:* 1919, *T:* 1921, *P:* 1923, *T:* 1924, *P:* 1926, *T:* 1927, *P:* 1935, *T:* 1936, *P:* 1938, *P:* 1972, *P:* 1974, *T:* 1975, *P:* 1983, *T:* 1984, *P:* 1992, *T:* 1993, *P:* 2000.

Spain: *P:* 1886, *T:* 1887, *P:* 1888, *T:* 1890, *P:* 1891, *T:* 1892, *P:* 1894, *T:* 1895, *P:* 1896, *T:* 1898,

P: 1901, *T:* 1902, *P:* 1904, *T:* 1905, *P:* 1909, *T:* 1910, *P:* 1911, *T:* 1912, *P:* 1913, *P:* 1922, *T:* 1924, *P:* 1927, *T:* 1928, *P:* 1929, *T:* 1931, *P:* 1932, *T:* 1933, *P:* 1934, *T:* 1937, *P:* 1938, *P:* 1952, *T:* 1953, *P:* 1958, *T:* 1959, *P:* 1972, *P:* 1980, *T:* 1981, *P:* 1992, *T:* 1993, *P:* 2000.

Sweden: *P:* 1881, *T:* 1882, *P:* 1885, *T:* 1886, *P:* 1894, *T:* 1895, *P:* 1901, *T:* 1902, *P:* 1907, *T:* 1908, *P:* 1911, *T:* 1912, *P:* 1913, *P:* 1920, *T:* 1922, *P:* 1930, *T:* 1933, *P:* 1938, *P:* 1972, *P:* 1976, *T:* 1977, *P:* 1980, *T:* 1981, *P:* 1990, *T:* 1993, *P:* 2000.

Switzerland: *P:* 1881, *T:* 1882, *P:* 1886, *T:* 1887, *P:* 1888, *T:* 1889, *P:* 1890, *T:* 1891, *P:* 1893, *T:* 1894, *P:* 1900, *T:* 1901, *P:* 1902, *T:* 1903, *P:* 1907, *T:* 1908, *P:* 1912, *T:* 1913, *P:* 1930, *T:* 1932, *P:* 1935, *T:* 1936, *P:* 1938, *P:* 1951, *T:* 1952, *P:* 1957, *T:* 1958, *P:* 1972, *P:* 1974, *T:* 1976, *P:* 1981, *T:* 1982, *P:* 1990, *T:* 1993, *P:* 2000.

United Kingdom: *T:* 1881, *P:* 1891, *T:* 1893, *P:* 1896, *T:* 1897, *P:* 1899, *T:* 1900, *P:* 1901, *T:* 1903, *P:* 1905, *T:* 1907, *P:* 1911, *T:* 1912, *P:* 1913, *P:* 1919, *T:* 1921, *P:* 1925, *T:* 1926, *P:* 1930, *T:* 1931, *P:* 1938, *P:* 1951, *T:* 1952, *P:* 1972, *P:* 1973, *T:* 1975, *P:* 1979, *T:* 1981, *P:* 1990, *T:* 1992, *P:* 2000.

United States: *P:* 1882, *T:* 1885, *P:* 1892, *T:* 1894, *P:* 1895, *T:* 1896, *P:* 1907, *T:* 1908, *P:* 1912, *T:* 1913, *T:* 1921, *P:* 1923, *T:* 1924, *P:* 1926, *T:* 1927, *P:* 1929, *T:* 1933, *P:* 1937, *T:* 1938, *P:* 1953, *T:* 1954, *P:* 1957, *T:* 1958, *P:* 1972, *P:* 1973, *T:* 1975, *P:* 1979, *T:* 1980, *P:* 1981, *T:* 1982, *P:* 1990, *T:* 1991, *P:* 2000.

Quarterly Data, 1973–2000

Business cycle turning points were determined using quarterly real GDP data for 21 industrial countries. The primary data source was the OECD Analytical Database. In some cases, more up-to-date data were provided by IMF country desks based on official national data sources. Turning points in the log-level of real GDP that were identified using a simplified Bry-Boschan (1971) dating algorithm, which determines peaks *(P)* and troughs *(T)* by first searching the input data for maxima and minima in five-quarter data windows and then picking pairs of adjacent, locally absolute maxima and minima that meet the rules for the minimal duration of cycles (five quarters) and phases (two quarters). The turning points in each country are as follows:

Australia: *P:* 1973Q4, *T:* 1974Q2, *P:* 1981Q3, *T:* 1983Q2, *P:* 1990Q2, *T:* 1991Q2.

Austria: *P:* 1974Q3, *T:* 1975Q2, *P:* 1980Q1, *T:* 1981Q1, *P:* 1982Q2, *T:* 1982Q4, *P:* 1983Q4, *T:* 1984Q2, *P:* 1992Q2, *T:* 1993Q1, *P:* 1996Q3, *T:* 1997Q1.

Belgium: *P:* 1974Q3, *T:* 1975Q2, *P:* 1976Q4, *T:* 1977Q2, *P:* 1980Q4, *T:* 1981Q3, *P:* 1982Q3, *T:* 1983Q1, *P:* 1992Q2, *T:* 1993Q2.

Canada: *P:* 1980Q1, *T:* 1980Q3, *P:* 1981Q2, *T:* 1982Q4, *P:* 1990Q1, *T:* 1991Q1.

Denmark: *P:* 1973Q3, *T:* 1975Q1, *P:* 1977Q3, *T:* 1978Q1, *P:* 1980Q1, *T:* 1980Q3, *P:* 1987Q2, *T:* 1988Q3, *P:* 1989Q1, *T:* 1989Q3, *P:* 1990Q3, *T:* 1991Q1, *P:* 1991Q3, *T:* 1992Q2, *P:* 1992Q4, *T:* 1993Q2.

Finland: *P:* 1975Q1, *T:* 1975Q4, *P:* 1976Q4, *T:* 1977Q2, *P:* 1980Q3, *T:* 1981Q1, *P:* 1990Q1, *T:* 1993Q1.

France: *P:* 1974Q3, *T:* 1975Q1, *P:* 1980Q1, *T:* 1980Q4, *P:* 1992Q1, *T:* 1993Q3.

Germany: *P:* 1974Q1, *T:* 1975Q2, *P:* 1980Q1, *T:* 1982Q3, *P:* 1992Q1, *T:* 1993Q2, *P:* 1995Q2, *T:* 1996Q1.

Greece: *P:* 1973Q3, *T:* 1974Q2, *P:* 1980Q4, *T:* 1981Q2, *P:* 1982Q3, *T:* 1983Q1, *P:* 1986Q3, *T:* 1987Q2, *P:* 1989Q3, *T:* 1990Q2, *P:* 1992Q1, *T:* 1993Q2.

Ireland: *P:* 1982Q3, *T:* 1983Q2, *P:* 1985Q3, *T:* 1986Q2.

Italy: *P:* 1974Q3, *T:* 1975Q2, *P:* 1977Q1, *T:* 1977Q3, *P:* 1982Q1, *T:* 1982Q3, *P:* 1992Q1, *T:* 1993Q1.

Japan: *P:* 1993Q1, *T:* 1993Q4, *P:* 1997Q1, *T:* 1999Q1.

Netherlands: *P:* 1974Q3, *T:* 1975Q2, *P:* 1980Q1, *T:* 1980Q3, *P:* 1982Q1, *T:* 1982Q4.

New Zealand: *P:* 1974Q3, *T:* 1975Q2, *P:* 1976Q4, *T:* 1979Q2, *P:* 1982Q3, *T:* 1983Q1, *P:* 1985Q1, *T:* 1986Q1, *P:* 1986Q3, *T:* 1989Q3, *P:* 1990Q4, *T:* 1992Q3, *P:* 1997Q3, *T:* 1998Q2.

Norway: *P:* 1978Q2, *T:* 1979Q1, *P:* 1981Q1, *T:* 1982Q2, *P:* 1985Q4, *T:* 1986Q2, *P:* 1987Q4, *T:* 1988Q4, *P:* 1992Q2, *T:* 1993Q1, *P:* 1998Q2, *T:* 1999Q2.

Portugal: *P:* 1974Q1, *T:* 1975Q2, *P:* 1982Q4, *T:* 1984Q2, *P:* 1992Q3, *T:* 1993Q2.

Spain: *P:* 1974Q4, *T:* 1975Q2, *P:* 1978Q2, *T:* 1979Q1, *P:* 1980Q1, *T:* 1981Q1, *P:* 1992Q1, *T:* 1993Q2.

Sweden: *P:* 1976Q2, *T:* 1977Q1, *P:* 1980Q3, *T:* 1981Q2, *P:* 1982Q3, *T:* 1983Q1, *P:* 1990Q2, *T:* 1992Q4.

Switzerland: *P:* 1974Q2, *T:* 1976Q1, *P:* 1976Q4, *T:* 1978Q1, *P:* 1981Q4, *T:* 1982Q4, *P:* 1990Q4, *T:* 1991Q2, *P:* 1992Q1, *T:* 1992Q4, *P:* 1993Q4, *T:* 1994Q2, *P:* 1996Q2, *T:* 1996Q4.

United Kingdom: *P:* 1973Q3, *T:* 1974Q1, *P:* 1974Q3, *T:* 1975Q2, *P:* 1979Q2, *T:* 1981Q1, *P:* 1990Q2, *T:* 1992Q2.

United States: *P:* 1973Q4, *T:* 1975Q1, *P:* 1980Q1, *T:* 1980Q3, *P:* 1981Q3, *T:* 1982Q3, *P:* 1990Q2, *T:* 1991Q1.

References

Artis, Michael J., Zenon G. Kontolemis, and Denise R. Osborn, 1997, "Business Cycles for G-7 and European Countries," *Journal of Business*, Vol. 70 (April), pp. 249–79.

Backus, David K., and Patrick J. Kehoe, 1992, "International Evidence of the Historical Properties of Business Cycles," *American Economic Review*, Vol. 82 (September), pp. 864–88.

———, and Finn Kydland, 1995, "International Business Cycles: Theory and Evidence," in *Frontiers of Business Cycle Research*, ed. by Thomas Cooley (Princeton, New Jersey: Princeton University Press).

Balke, Nathan S., and Robert J. Gordon, 1989, "The Estimation of Prewar Gross National Product: Methodology and New Evidence," *Journal of Political Economy*, Vol. 97 (February), pp. 38–92.

Basu, Susanto, and Alan M. Taylor, 1999, "Business Cycles in International Historical Perspective," *Journal of Economic Perspectives*, Vol. 13 (Spring), pp. 45–68.

Baxter, Marianne, 1995, "International Trade and Business Cycles," in *Handbook of International Economics*, Vol. 3, ed. by G. Grossman and K. Rogoff (New York: North-Holland), pp. 1801–64.

Bergman, U. Michael, Michael D. Bordo, and Lars Jonung, 1998, "Historical Evidence on Business Cycles: The International Experience," in *Beyond Shocks: What Causes Business Cycles?* ed. by Jeffrey C. Fuhrer and Scott Schuh (Boston, Massachusetts: Federal Reserve Bank of Boston), pp. 65–113.

Bernanke, Ben S., 1983, "Nonmonetary Effects of the Financial Crisis in the Propagation of the Great Depression," *American Economic Review*, Vol. 73 (June), pp. 257–76.

———, and Kevin Carey, 1996, "Nominal Wage Stickiness and Aggregate Supply in the Great Depression," *Quarterly Journal of Economics*, Vol. 111 (August), pp. 853–84.

Bernanke, Ben S., and Mark Gertler, 1989, "Agency Costs, Net Worth and Business Fluctuations," *American Economic Review*, Vol. 79 (March), pp. 14–31.

Bernanke, Ben S., and Harold James, 1991, "The Gold Standard, Deflation and Financial Crisis in the Great Depression: An International Comparison," in *Financial Markets and Financial Crisis*, ed. by R. Glenn Hubbard (Chicago, Illinois: University of Chicago Press), pp. 33–68.

Blanchard, Olivier J., and John Simon, 2001, "The Long and Large Decline in U.S. Output Volatility," *Brookings Papers on Economic Activity: 1,* Brookings Institution, pp. 135–74.

Blanchard, Olivier J., and Justin Wolfers, 2000, "The Role of Shocks and Institutions in the Rise of European Unemployment: The Aggregate Evidence," *Economic Journal*, Vol. 110 (March), pp. C1–33.

Boone, Laurence, Michel Juillard, Douglas Laxton, and Papa N'Diaye, 2002, "How Well Do Alternative Time-Varying Models of the NAIRU Help Policymakers Forecast Unemployment?" forthcoming IMF Working Paper (Washington: International Monetary Fund).

Bordo, Michael D., Christopher J. Erceg, and Charles L. Evans, 2000, "Money, Sticky Wages and the Great Depression," *American Economic Review*, Vol. 90 (December), pp. 1446–63.

Bordo, Michael D., Barry Eichengreen, Daniela Klingebiel, and Maria Soledad Martinez-Peria, 2001, "Is the Crisis Problem Growing More Severe?" *Economic Policy*, Vol. 32 (April), pp. 53–82.

Bry, Gerhard, and Charlotte Boschan, 1971, Cyclical Analysis of Time Series: Selected Procedures and Computer Programs (New York: NBER).

Burns, Arthur F., 1947, "Stepping Stones Towards the Future," *NBER Annual Report No. 27* (New York: National Bureau of Economic Research).

———, and Wesley C. Mitchell, 1946, *Measuring Business Cycles* (New York: National Bureau of Economic Research).

Caballero, Ricardo, 2000, "Macroeconomic Volatility in Latin America: Facts and Policy Implications," *Economia, The Journal of the Latin American and Caribbean Economic Association*, Vol. 1, No. 1, pp. 31–108.

Cagan, Philip, 1965, *Determinants and Effects of Changes in the Stock of Money, 1875–1960* (Cambridge, Massachusetts: National Bureau of Economic Research).

Calvo, Guillermo A., 1998, "Varieties of Capital-Market Crises," in *The Debt Burden and Its Consequences for Monetary Policy*, ed. by Guillermo Calvo and Mervyn King (New York: St. Martin's Press).

Campbell, John, Martin Lettau, Burton Malkiel, and Yexiao Xu, 2001, "Have Individual Stocks Become More Volatile? An Empirical Exploration of Idiosyncratic Risk," *Journal of Finance*, Vol. 56 (February), pp. 1–43.

Canova, Fabio, 1998, "Detrending and Business Cycle Facts," *Journal of Monetary Economics*, Vol. 43 (June), pp. 475–512.

Cashin, Paul, and C. John Dermott, 2002, "The Long-Run Behavior of Commodity Prices: Small Trends and Big Variability," *IMF Staff Papers*, forthcoming.

Cecchetti, Stephen G., 1992, "Prices During the Great Depression: Was the Deflation of 1930–1932 Really Unanticipated?" *American Economic Review*, Vol. 82 (March), pp. 141–56.

Choudhri, Ehsan, and Levis Kochin, 1980, "The Exchange Rate and the International Transmission of Business Cycles: Some Evidence from the Great Depression," *Journal of Money, Credit and Banking*, Vol. 12 (November), pp. 565–74.

Christiano, Larry, Martin Eichenbaum, and Charles Evans, 1999, "Monetary Policy Shocks: What Have

We Learned and to What End?" in *Handbook of Macroeconomics*, Vol. 1A, ed. by John Taylor and Michael Woodford (New York: North-Holland), pp. 65–148.

Cochrane, John H., 1994, "Shocks," *Carnegie-Rochester Conference Series on Public Policy*, Vol. 41 (December), pp. 295–364.

Cole, Harold L., and Lee E. Ohanian, 1999, "The Great Depression in the United States from a Neoclassical Perspective," *Federal Reserve Bank of Minneapolis Quarterly Review*, Vol. 23 (Winter), pp. 3–21.

Dalsgaard, Thomas, Jorgen Elmeskov, and Cyn-Young Park, 2002, "Ongoing Changes in the Business Cycle—Evidence and Causes," OECD Economics Department Working Paper 315 (Paris: Organization for Economic Cooperation and Development).

De Ferranti, David, Guillermo E. Perry, Indermit S. Gill, and Luis Serven, 2000, *Securing Our Future in a Global Economy*, Latin American and Caribbean Studies: Viewpoints Series (Washington: World Bank).

DeLong, J. Bradford, and Lawrence H. Summers, 1986, "Are Business Cycles Symmetrical?" in *The American Business Cycle: Continuity and Change*, National Bureau of Economic Research, Studies in Business Cycles, Vol. 25 (Chicago, Illinois: University of Chicago Press), pp. 166–78.

Diebold, Francis X., and Glenn D. Rudebusch, 1992, "Have Postwar Economic Fluctuations Been Stabilized?" *American Economic Review*, Vol. 82 (September), pp. 993–1005.

———, 1999, *Business Cycles: Durations, Dynamics, and Forecasting* (Princeton, New Jersey: Princeton University Press).

Dornbusch, Rudiger, 1997, "How Real Is U.S. Prosperity?" Column reprinted in *World Economic Laboratory Columns*, Massachusetts Institute of Technology, December, cited in *Beyond Shocks: What Causes Business Cycles?* ed. by Jeffrey C. Fuhrer and Scott Schuh, Federal Reserve Bank of Boston Conference Series No. 42 (Boston, Massachusetts: Federal Reserve Bank of Boston, 1998).

Du, Julan, and Shang-Jin Wei, 2002, "Does Insider Trading Raise Market Volatility?" (unpublished; Washington: International Monetary Fund, Research Department).

Edwards, Jane, and Jochen Schanz, 2001, "Faster, Higher, Stronger. An International Comparison of Structural Policies, Structural Economics," Research Papers No. 3 (London: Lehman Brothers International, Europe).

Eichengreen, Barry, 1992, *Golden Fetters: The Gold Standard and the Great Depression: 1919–1939* (New York: Oxford University Press).

———, and Ashoka Mody, 2000, "Lending Booms, Reserves, and the Sustainability of Short-Term Debt: Inferences From the Pricing of Syndicated Bank Loans," *Journal of Development Economics*, Vol. 63 (October), pp. 5–44.

Fisher, Irving, 1933, "The Debt-Deflation Theory of the Great Depression," *Econometrica*, Vol. 1 (October), pp. 337–57.

Friedman, Milton, and Anna Jacobson Schwartz, 1963, *A Monetary History of the United States, 1867–1960* (Princeton, New Jersey: Princeton University Press).

Fuhrer, Jeffrey C., and Scott Schuh, eds., 1998, *Beyond Shocks: What Causes Business Cycles?* Federal Reserve Bank of Boston Conference Series No. 42 (Boston: Federal Reserve Bank of Boston).

Galbraith, John K., 1961, *The Great Crash* (Boston, Massachusetts: Houghton Mifflin).

Ghosh, Atish, Timothy Lane, Marianne Schulze-Ghattas, Ales Bulir, Javier Hamann, and Alex Mourmouras, 2002, *IMF-Supported Programs in Capital Account Crises: Design and Experience*, IMF Occasional Paper No. 210 (Washington: International Monetary Fund).

Glasner, David, ed., 1997, *Business Cycles and Depressions: An Encyclopedia*, Garland Reference Library of Social Science, Vol. 505 (New York: Garland Publishing).

Gordon, Robert J., ed., 1986, *The American Business Cycle: Continuity and Change*, National Bureau of Economic Research, Studies in Business Cycles, Vol. 25 (Chicago, Illinois: University of Chicago Press).

Gupta, Poonam, Deepak Mishra, and Ratna Sahay, 2002, "Output Response to Currency Crises" (unpublished; Washington: International Monetary Fund).

Hamilton, James D., 1983, "Oil and the Macroeconomy since World War II," *Journal of Political Economy*, Vol. 91 (April), pp. 228–48.

———, 1989, "A New Approach to the Economic Analysis of Nonstationary Time Series and the Business Cycle," *Econometrica*, Vol. 57 (March), pp. 357–84.

———, 1996, "This Is What Happened to the Oil Price-Macroeconomy Relationship," *Journal of Monetary Economics*, Vol. 38 (October), pp. 215–20.

Harding, Don, and Adrian Pagan, 2001, "Extracting, Analyzing, and Using Cyclical Information," University of Hong Kong, School of Economics and Finance Discussion Paper Series No. 338 (Hong Kong, SAR: University of Hong Kong).

———, forthcoming, "Knowing the Cycle," *Journal of Monetary Economics.*

Helbling, Thomas, and Tamim Bayoumi, 2002, "G-7 Business Cycle Linkages Revisited," forthcoming IMF Working Paper (Washington: International Monetary Fund).

Honohan, Patrick, and Daniela Klingebiel, 2000, "Controlling the Fiscal Costs of Banking Crises," World Bank Policy Research Paper No. 2441 (Washington: World Bank).

IMF, *International Financial Statistics* (Washington: International Monetary Fund, various issues).

Kaminsky, Graciela, and Carmen Reinhart, 1998, "The Twin Crises: The Causes of Banking and Balance of Payments Problems," *American Economic Review*, Vol. 89 (June), pp. 473–500.

Keynes, John Maynard, 1936, *The General Theory of Employment, Interest, and Money* (London: Macmillan).

King, Robert G., and Charles I. Plosser, 1994, "Real Business Cycles and the Test of the Adelmans," *Journal of Monetary Economics*, Vol. 33 (April), pp. 405–38.

King, Robert G., Charles I. Plosser, James Stock, and Mark W. Watson, 1991, "Stochastic Trends and Economic Fluctuations," *American Economic Review*, Vol. 81 (September), pp. 819–40.

Kose, M. Ayhan, Christopher Otrok, and Charles H. Whiteman, 2001, "International Business Cycles: World, Region, and Country-Specific Factors," Graduate School of International Economics and Finance Working Paper, Brandeis University (Waltham, Massachusetts: Brandeis University).

Kose, M. Ayhan, Eswar Prasad, and Marco Terrones, 2002, "Dynamics of Macroeconomic Volatility in an Integrated World Economy," forthcoming IMF Working Paper (Washington: International Monetary Fund).

Kuznets, Simon, 1961, *Capital in the American Economy: Its Formation and Financing, Structures in Capital Formation and Financing* (Princeton, New Jersey: Princeton University Press).

Lumsdaine, Robin L., and Eswar S. Prasad, 1999, "Identifying the Common Component in International Economic Fluctuations: A New Approach," IMF Working Paper 99/154

(Washington: International Monetary Fund). Also forthcoming in *Economic Journal.*

McConnell, Margaret M., and Gabriel Perez-Quiros, 2000, "Output Fluctuations in the United States: What Has Changed Since the Early 1980's?" *American Economic Review,* Vol. 90 (December), pp. 1464–76.

Meltzer, Allan, 1976, "Monetary and Other Explanations of the Start of the Great Depression," *Journal of Monetary Economics*, Vol. 1 (November), pp. 455–71.

———, forthcoming, *A History of the Federal Reserve* (Chicago, Illinois: University of Chicago Press).

Milesi-Ferretti, Gian Maria, and Asaf Razin, 1998, "Current Account Reversals and Currency Crises: Empirical Regularities," NBER Working Paper No. 6620 (Cambridge, Massachusetts: National Bureau of Economic Research).

Mitchell, Wesley C., 1927, *Business Cycles: The Problem and Its Setting* (Cambridge, Massachusetts: National Bureau of Economic Research).

———, 1941, *Business Cycles and Their Causes* (Berkeley, California: University of California Press).

Moore, Geoffrey H., 1983, *Business Cycles, Inflation and Forecasting* (Cambridge, Massachusetts: National Bureau of Economic Research, published by Ballinger Publishing Company, 2nd ed.).

———, and Victor Zarnowitz, 1986, "The Development and Role of the National Bureau of Economic Research's Business Cycle Chronologies," Appendix A in *The American Business Cycle: Continuity and Change,* ed. by Robert J. Gordon, National Bureau of Economic Research, Studies in Business Cycles, Vol. 25 (Chicago, Illinois: University of Chicago Press), pp. 735–79.

Morck, Randall, Bernard Yeung, and Wayne Yu, 2000, "The Information Content of Stock Markets: Why Do Emerging Markets Have Synchronous Stock Price Movements?" *Journal of Financial Economics,* Special Issue on International Corporate Governance, Vol. 58 (October–November), pp. 215–60.

Mulder, Christian, and Manuel Rocha, 2001, "Estimating the Output Cost of External Crises" (unpublished; Washington: International Monetary Fund, Policy Development and Review Department).

Nicoletti, Giuseppe, Stefano Scarpetta, and Olivier Boylaud, 1999, "Summary Indicators of Product Market Regulation with an Extension to Employment Protection Legislation," OECD Economics Department Working Paper 226 (Paris:

Organization for Economic Cooperation and Development).

Pallage, Stéphane, and Michel Robe, 2001, "On the Welfare Cost of Business Cycles in Developing Countries," IMF Seminar Series, No. 2001–85 (Washington: International Monetary Fund).

Prasad, Eswar S., and Jeffery A. Gable, 1998, "International Evidence on the Determinants of Trade Dynamics," *IMF Staff Papers*, Vol. 45 (September), pp. 401–39.

Ramey, Garey, and Valerie A. Ramey, 1995, "Cross-Country Evidence on the Link Between Volatility and Growth," *American Economic Review*, Vol. 85 (December), pp. 1138–51.

Rodrik, Dani, 1999, "Where Did All the Growth Go? External Shocks, Social Conflict, and Growth Collapses," *Journal of Economic Growth*, Vol. 4 (December), pp. 385–412.

Rogoff, Kenneth, 2001, "Why Not a Global Currency?" *American Economic Review, Papers and Proceedings*, Vol. 91 (May), pp. 243–47.

Romer, Christina, 1994, "Remeasuring Business Cycles," *Journal of Economic History*, Vol. 54 (September), pp. 573–609.

———, 1989, "The Prewar Business Cycle Reconsidered New Estimates of Gross National Product, 1869–1908," *Journal of Political Economy*, Vol. 97 (February), pp. 1–37.

———, and David H. Romer, 1989, "Does Monetary Policy Matter? A New Test in the Spirit of Friedman and Schwartz," in *NBER Macroeconomics Annual 1989*, ed. by Olivier Jean Blanchard and Stanley Fischer (Cambridge, Massachusetts: MIT Press), pp. 121–70.

Samuelson, Paul, 1966, "Science and Stocks," *Newsweek*, September 19, cited in "Does It Pay Stock Investors to Forecast the Business Cycle?" by Jeremy J. Siegel, *Journal of Portfolio Management*, Fall 1991, pp. 27–34.

Sichel, Daniel E., 1994, "Inventories and the Three Phases of the Business Cycle," *Journal of Business and Economic Statistics*, Vol. 12 (July), pp. 269–77.

Stock, James H., and Mark W. Watson, 1999, "Business Cycle Fluctuations in U.S. Macroeconomic Time Series," in *Handbook of Macroeconomics*, Vol. 1A, ed. by John Taylor and Michael Woodford (New York: North-Holland), pp. 3–64.

Thorp, Willard Long, 1926, *Business Annals* (Cambridge, Massachusetts: National Bureau of Economic Research).

Watson, Mark W., 1994, "Business-Cycle Durations and Postwar Stabilization of the U.S. Economy," *American Economic Review*, Vol. 84 (March), pp. 24–46.

Wheelock, David C., 1991, *The Strategy and Consistency of Federal Reserve Monetary Policy 1919–1933* (Cambridge: Cambridge University Press).

Zarnowitz, Victor, 1992, *Business Cycles: Theory, History, Indicators, and Forecasting*, National Bureau of Economic Research, Studies in Business Cycles, Vol. 27 (Chicago, Illinois: University of Chicago Press).

SUMMING UP BY THE CHAIRMAN

The following remarks by the Chairman were made at the conclusion of the Executive Board's discussion of the World Economic Outlook. They were made on March 29, 2002.

Executive Directors noted that, since their discussion of the Interim World Economic Outlook in December, there have been increasing signs that the global slowdown has bottomed out, particularly in the United States and to a lesser extent in Europe, and in some countries in Asia. Financial markets have bounced back strongly since the September 11 shock; commodity prices have begun to pick up; and—with contagion effects from Argentina having so far been limited—emerging market financing conditions have also strengthened markedly. While different but serious concerns remain in a number of countries, notably Japan and Argentina, Directors believed that a global recovery is now under way.

Directors observed that the recovery is being underpinned by several factors, most importantly, the substantial easing of macroeconomic policies in advanced economies—particularly the United States—and also in a number of emerging economies, especially in Asia. They considered that the scope for such policy support owes much to earlier progress in lowering inflation, strengthening fiscal positions, and reducing other sources of vulnerability, which enabled countries across the membership to respond promptly and effectively to the difficult situation facing the world economy last year. Several Directors also noted that the adjustment in inventories appears to be well along in the United States and some other advanced economies, and that this will also help boost production in the period ahead. The recovery has also been supported by lower oil prices, although this is somewhat less of a factor following the strong pickup in prices since late February. Directors agreed that the impact of higher oil prices on the outlook will need to remain under careful assessment.

Overall, Directors agreed that the risks to the outlook have become more evenly balanced since the December 2001 Interim World Economic Outlook. Indeed, recent indicators of confidence, employment, and activity in the United States have been surprisingly positive, suggesting that the recovery may prove to be stronger than presently projected.

At the same time, Directors noted that a number of potential downside risks in the outlook require continued policy attention. First, in part because of the synchronous slowdown, relatively little progress has been made in reducing the persistent imbalances in the global economy—notably, the high U.S. current account deficit and surpluses elsewhere, the low U.S. personal saving rate, the apparent overvaluation of the dollar and undervaluation of the euro, and the relatively high household and corporate debts in a number of countries. With the United States leading the recovery, Directors considered that these imbalances could, at least in the short term, widen further.

In discussing the implications of this prospect for the global outlook, Directors observed that the risk of a disorderly unwinding of the current account imbalances might be reduced by the continued favorable outlook for U.S. productivity growth and capital inflows. Most Directors nevertheless agreed that policies, especially structural policies, should be formulated with a view to ensuring that the orderly reduction of the current imbalances enhances the sustainability of the global recovery.

As a second source of risk to the outlook, Directors noted that, following the strong rebound over recent months, global equity prices again appear richly valued and may be pricing in an excessively optimistic outlook for corporate earnings. Should earnings growth disappoint, there would be a risk of financial markets, confidence, and activity again weakening. In this context, Directors found revealing the analysis in Chapter II of the *World Economic Outlook* of the impact of asset prices on consumption, which indicates that asset prices, in particular equity prices, have become more important over time as a determinant of consumer spending. Given the aging of populations across the industrialized world, as well as continued financial market development, this trend is likely to continue, suggesting that developments in asset prices may become increasingly important in the formulation of macroeconomic policies.

Finally, Directors highlighted a number of specific risks, including the adverse effects that the continuing economic difficulties in Japan and Argentina—although of a different nature—could have on other countries in their respective regions. Regretting the recent decision by the U.S. authorities to raise tariffs on steel imports and the prospect of retaliation by other countries, Directors reiterated the critical importance for all countries to resist protectionist pressures and to ensure that substantive progress is made with multilateral trade negotiations under the Doha round.

Directors concurred that macroeconomic policies in most industrial countries should remain generally supportive of the emerging recovery. However, they noted that, with the exception of Japan, there appears little need at present for additional policy easing, and that in countries where the recovery is more advanced, attention should turn in due time toward reversing earlier monetary policy easing. Over the medium term, policy frameworks should be geared toward supporting sustainable growth, while aiming for an orderly reduction in global imbalances. This would require, in the euro area and in some Asian emerging markets, continued structural reforms to encourage growth; in Japan, decisive action to reinvigorate the economy; and in the

United States, ensuring that medium-term fiscal targets are met. Directors also underscored the importance of using the recovery to make further progress in reducing vulnerabilities, including through accelerated efforts to address looming problems from aging populations in industrial countries; a sustained effort to achieve balanced budgets in the euro area; development of a medium-term fiscal consolidation plan in Japan; reform of the corporate and financial sectors in Asia; and medium-term efforts to strengthen fiscal positions in India, China, and many Latin American countries.

Progress toward an enduring reduction in poverty in the developing countries will require sustained broad-based growth, and, in this context, Directors noted that, despite encouraging progress in a number of countries, GDP growth in sub-Saharan Africa remains well below what would be needed to reduce poverty significantly. They agreed that national policies will need to play the lead role in improving economic performance, especially policies focused on improving the conditions for savings, investment, and private sector activity. Stronger international support of sound policies will also be essential. In this connection, Directors welcomed the progress made at the Monterrey Conference on Financing for Development, including the announcement of increased aid targets by European countries and the United States. They stressed, in particular, the vital importance of phasing out trade-distorting subsidies and giving greater access to exports from developing countries in world markets.

Major Currency Areas

Turning to the prospects for the major currency areas, Directors agreed that recent indicators increasingly point to recovery in the *United States*, with confidence and equity markets picking up, household spending remaining strong, and manufacturing output stabilizing. Some Directors considered that activity could pick up even more rapidly than currently projected, especially given the size of the policy stimulus in the pipeline and the continued resilience of productivity growth. Some other Directors, however, pointed to the possibility of a less sustained or less resilient upturn—for example, if low corporate profitability or excess capacity constrain investment growth, equity prices fail to sustain recent gains, or households rebuild savings. Given the balance of risks, Directors supported the Federal Reserve's recent decision to keep interest rates on hold for the time being; while monetary policy should not be tightened prematurely, some tightening will be required in the coming months if economic activity continues to strengthen. Directors agreed that no further fiscal stimulus is warranted at this stage. While recognizing that the deterioration in the fiscal position over the past year is the result of a combination of factors, including tax cuts, the recent stimulus package, and the emergency and security spending measures taken in the aftermath of the September 11 events, Directors considered that the time has now come to turn attention to the efforts needed over the medium term to restore fiscal balance and address pressures stemming from the social security system.

Directors expressed serious concern about economic conditions and prospects in *Japan,* with the economy being in its third recession of the past decade, confidence and activity remaining very weak, and the banking sector experiencing severe strains. While welcoming recent initiatives and noting some signs of a possible bottoming out in the fall of activity, Directors urged the authorities to push ahead vigorously with measures directed at bank and corporate sector restructuring, which will remain the key to restoring confidence and prospects for solid growth. Although little scope remains for further macroeconomic stimulus, they also agreed that monetary policy needs to remain focused on ending deflation. Given the high public debt and rising long-term interest rates, Directors stressed the need for a clear and credible commitment to medium-term fiscal consolidation, backed up by reforms to the tax system, public enterprises, and the health sector. A few Directors considered that, within the context of

such a medium-term commitment, a supplementary budget to mitigate the projected withdrawal of fiscal stimulus late in 2002 should not be ruled out.

Directors were encouraged that recent business confidence surveys and a pickup in industrial production point to an emerging recovery in the *euro area.* While the recovery is likely to be somewhat slower and come later than in the United States, a number of Directors pointed to the contribution that Europe's strong fundamentals have made to global stability. Building on recent progress, further policy reforms to support a strong and sustained recovery should nevertheless continue to receive the highest priority. Directors emphasized the need for euro area economies to move ahead with structural reforms, in particular in the financial sector, labor markets, and pension systems, noting that the introduction of euro notes and coins in January has made such structural reforms all the more potentially beneficial. Directors supported the ECB's current monetary policy stance, which is to keep interest rates on hold while being ready to move in either direction as macroeconomic developments unfold, with some Directors pointing to the scope that is available for further reducing interest rates in the event of continued weakness in demand. On the fiscal side, countries with sizable structural deficits will need to strengthen their fiscal position as growth picks up, both to provide scope for the automatic stabilizers to function during subsequent slowdowns, and to help tackle rising fiscal pressures from aging populations.

Emerging Markets

Directors noted that the prospective recovery in industrial countries should play a central role in supporting activity in emerging markets, along with continued efforts aimed at strengthening economic fundamentals to reduce vulnerability and enhance productivity growth. In *Asia,* which—with the exception of China and India—was particularly hard hit by the global slowdown, clear signs of a pickup in activity have begun to emerge, aided by a nascent strengthening in the electronics sector and easier macroeconomic policies in a number of countries. Directors underscored that the emerging recovery will need to be supported by ongoing reforms across the region, especially in financial and corporate sectors. In India, structural fiscal reforms need to back the substantial consolidation that is required; and China should move ahead with reforms to address the competitive challenges arising from WTO membership and, in particular, tackle difficulties in the state-owned enterprises, the banking sector, and the pension system.

Directors considered the diverse prospects facing *Latin America*. They noted with concern that the situation in Argentina remains very difficult, with a significant contraction in output and acceleration of inflation in 2002 appearing unavoidable. They urged the authorities to move quickly to put a sustainable economic plan in place, including measures to rein in the fiscal deficit and strengthen the banking system. To date, spillovers from Argentina on other regional economies appear to have been generally limited (with the possible exception of Uruguay), although they remain a source of potential risk. Directors noted that the recovery is likely to be strongest in Mexico and Central America, which are closely linked to the United States, as well as some Andean countries, while in other countries the pace of recovery is likely to be more subdued. Directors welcomed the analysis in the *World Economic Outlook* of debt crises in Latin America and the extent to which the region's relative closure to external trade, higher macroeconomic volatility, relatively underdeveloped domestic financial markets, and low saving rates may help to explain their relatively high incidence in this region. While cautioning against generalizations across countries and across different stages of their reform processes, and noting the important progress that many have made in recent years in reducing vulnerability, including by adopting more flexible exchange rate regimes, Directors considered that this analysis nevertheless contains useful guidance for future policies. They underscored

the benefits that countries in the region would reap from further progress in strengthening fiscal positions to avoid the need for a procyclical response to shocks, as well as from continuing reforms of their trade and financial systems.

Directors noted that growth among most of the European Union candidates in *central and eastern Europe* has been generally well sustained during the global slowdown, with robust domestic demand offsetting weaker export performance, and is expected to pick up further as the global recovery takes hold. While the high current account deficits in many of these countries have so far been readily financed by direct investment and other capital inflows, they nevertheless represent a source of vulnerability that, Directors agreed, underscores the importance of ongoing fiscal discipline and structural reforms to help ensure that the climate for investment and growth remains positive. Directors welcomed the recent improvements in economic indicators in Turkey, and expected that strengthening confidence and exports should underpin a sustained recovery in 2002, provided the strong implementation of sound macroeconomic and structural policies continue.

Growth in the *CIS countries* has also remained remarkably resilient to the global slowdown, although the pace of activity in 2002 may weaken somewhat—mainly as a result of slowing demand in the region's oil exporting countries. Directors welcomed the acceleration of structural reforms in Russia, while noting that efforts to improve the investment climate remain a key priority. For the region as a whole, the central challenge continues to be to accelerate progress in structural reforms, notably institutional building and governance, enterprise and financial sector restructuring, and transforming the role of the state. Directors also stressed that the high level of external debt in a number of the poorest CIS countries continues to be a serious concern, requiring ongoing close monitoring.

Directors were encouraged that growth in *Africa* has also held up relatively well in 2001 and is expected to remain quite robust in 2002. The outlook for much of the region continues to depend heavily on commodity market developments, and on further progress in eradicating armed conflict and other sources of civil tension. Directors highlighted the central role that sound economic policies have played in raising significantly per capita income growth in strongly performing countries in recent years. They stressed that sustained economic growth and diversification will require faster structural reforms, in particular in the area of governance, including strengthened regulatory institutions, and more insecure and stable property rights. Directors welcomed the New Partnership for African Development, which emphasizes African ownership, leadership, and accountability in improving the foundations for growth and eradicating poverty. They stressed that these efforts will need to be supported by appropriate external assistance, including the further reduction of trade barriers, increased development aid, especially for HIV/AIDS, and support to capacity-building efforts.

Directors observed that growth in the *Middle East* is projected to weaken in 2002, although much will depend on oil market developments and the impact on activity of the regional security situation. They noted that the adverse impact of lower oil prices in 2001 on oil exporting countries has been limited by the prudent macroeconomic policies of recent years. Over the medium term, a key policy priority in many countries is to continue efforts to diversify production into nonenergy sectors and hence to reduce dependence on oil revenues.

Recessions and Recoveries

Directors welcomed the analysis of previous recessions and recoveries in industrial countries in Chapter III of the *World Economic Outlook*. They noted that the synchronicity of the recent global slowdown had much in common with past downturns and was indeed in line with the historical norm, whereas the relatively unsynchro-

nized recessions of the early 1990s were an exception reflecting different shocks in different countries. In the recent downturn, the collapse in investment spending associated with the bursting of the tech bubble was also consistent with the regularity of the sharp drops in business fixed investment that occurred typically in the lead-up to recessions in recent decades.

Directors also observed that the mildness of the recent global slowdown was in line with the historical trend toward shallower recessions. However, the short duration and mildness of the recent downturn does not imply that the recovery will be slow or weak. Directors observed that the increases in interest rates prior to the recent downturns were smaller than before, reflecting relatively low inflation during the previous expansion. This helps explain why the subsequent downturns have been relatively mild.

Monetary Policy in a Low Inflation Era

Turning to the essay on monetary policies in a low inflation environment, Directors agreed that a major reason for the remarkable decline in inflation among industrial countries over recent decades has been the widespread change in emphasis of central banks toward price stability and associated beneficial changes in private sector behavior. In discussing some of the policy challenges for central banks in this new environment, some Directors considered that, given the existence of the zero nominal interest rate bound, monetary policy may need to respond relatively rapidly to significant downward shocks to activity in order to minimize the possibility of a deflationary spiral. Many Directors, however, cautioned against premature policy conclusions, noting that in several countries the low inflation environment has not significantly hampered the effectiveness of monetary policy. More generally, the credibility of anti-inflationary monetary policy is an important asset that should be preserved.

STATISTICAL APPENDIX

The statistical appendix presents historical data, as well as projections. It comprises four sections: Assumptions, Data and Conventions, Classification of Countries, and Statistical Tables.

The assumptions underlying the estimates and projections for 2002–03 and the medium-term scenario for 2004–07 are summarized in the first section. The second section provides a general description of the data, and of the conventions used for calculating country group composites. The classification of countries in the various groups presented in the *World Economic Outlook* is summarized in the third section.

The last, and main, section comprises the statistical tables. Data in these tables have been compiled on the basis of information available through early April 2002. The figures for 2002 and beyond are shown with the same degree of precision as the historical figures solely for convenience; since they are projections, the same degree of accuracy is not to be inferred.

Assumptions

Real effective *exchange rates* for the advanced economies are assumed to remain constant at their average levels during the period February 11–March 11, 2002. For 2002 and 2003, these assumptions imply average U.S. dollar/SDR conversion rates of 1.249 and 1.251, U.S. dollar/euro conversion rates of 0.87 and 0.88, and U.S. dollar/yen conversion rates of 131.2 and 129.9.

Established *policies* of national authorities are assumed to be maintained. The more specific policy assumptions underlying the projections for selected advanced economies are described in Box A1.

It is assumed that the *price of oil* will average $23.00 a barrel in 2002 and $22.00 a barrel in 2003.

With regard to *interest rates*, it is assumed that the London interbank offered rate (LIBOR) on six-month U.S. dollar deposits will average 2.8 percent in 2002 and 4.5 percent in 2003; that the three-month certificate of deposit rate in Japan will average 0.1 percent in 2002 and in 2003; and that the three-month interbank deposit rate for the euro will average 3.7 percent in 2002 and 4.5 percent in 2003.

With respect to *introduction of the euro*, on December 31, 1998 the Council of the European Union decided that, effective January 1, 1999, the irrevocably fixed conversion rates between the euro and currencies of the member states adopting the euro are:

1 euro	= 13.7603	Austrian schillings
	= 40.3399	Belgian francs
	= 1.95583	Deutsche mark
	= 5.94573	Finnish markkaa
	= 6.55957	French francs
	= 340.750	Greek drachma[1]
	= 0.787564	Irish pound
	= 1,936.27	Italian lire
	= 40.3399	Luxembourg francs
	= 2.20371	Netherlands guilders
	= 200.482	Portuguese escudos
	= 166.386	Spanish pesetas

See Box 5.4 in the October 1998 *World Economic Outlook* for details on how the conversion rates were established.

Data and Conventions

Data and projections for 182 countries form the statistical basis for the *World Economic*

---

[1]The conversion rate for Greece was established prior to inclusion in the euro area on January 1, 2001.

Box A1. Economic Policy Assumptions Underlying the Projections for Selected Advanced Economies

The short-term *fiscal policy assumptions* used in the *World Economic Outlook* are based on officially announced budgets, adjusted for differences between the national authorities and the IMF staff regarding macroeconomic assumptions and projected fiscal outturns. The medium-term fiscal projections incorporate policy measures that are judged likely to be implemented. In cases where the IMF staff has insufficient information to assess the authorities' budget intentions and prospects for policy implementation, an unchanged structural primary balance is assumed, unless otherwise indicated. Specific assumptions used in some of the advanced economies follow (see also Tables 14–16 in the Statistical Appendix for data on fiscal and structural balances).[1]

United States. The fiscal projections reflect the Administration's fiscal year 2003 budget adjusted to include both the stimulus package enacted in March 2002 rather than the package in the budget, and staff assumptions based on other developments since early February when the budget was released. These include additional defense-related and other likely expenditures, extension of personal alternative minimum tax relief, and additional Medicare spending projected by the Congressional Budget Office above that in the budget.

Japan. The projections take into account the initial FY2002 budget, the first FY2001 supplementary budget of November 2001, which included additional measures of around ¥3 trillion, and the second FY2001 supplementary budget of February 2002 with measures of ¥4 trillion.

Germany. Fiscal projections for 2002–05 are based on the national authorities' updated Stability Program of December 2001, as adjusted for (1) the IMF's staff weaker macroeconomic scenario; and (2) differences between the Stability Program's estimates for fiscal developments in 2001 and the outcome in 2001, as published in January 2002. Fiscal projections for 2006–07 assume that structural revenue remains unchanged as a share of nominal potential GDP and that expenditure continues to grow as in 2004–05.

France. The projections are based on the national authorities' targets as reflected in the budget and the Stability and Growth Program (SGP). For 2002, the projections are adjusted for the IMF staff's weaker macroeconomic outlook. For the medium term, the projections are broadly consistent with France's SGP, adjusted for differences between the IMF staff's and the authorities' macroeconomic assumptions.

Italy. The fiscal projections for 2002–05 build on the authorities' program targets, as published in their Stability Program released in October 2001, adjusted for differences in macroeconomic assumptions. Projections for 2006–07 assume an unchanged fiscal balance target with respect to 2005.

United Kingdom. The fiscal projections are based on the November 2001 pre-budget report. Additionally, the projections incorporate more recent statistical releases from the Office for National Statistics, including provisional budgetary outturns through February 2002. The main difference with respect to the official budgetary projections is that the staff projections are based on potential growth of 2¾ percent rather than the 2¼ percent underlying official projections. They also include an adjustment for the proceeds of the recent UMTS license auction

[1]The output gap is actual less potential output, as a percent of potential output. Structural balances are expressed as a percent of potential output. The structural budget balance is the budgetary position that would be observed if the level of actual output coincided with potential output. Changes in the structural budget balance consequently include effects of temporary fiscal measures, the impact of fluctuations in interest rates and debt-service costs, and other noncyclical fluctuations in the budget balance. The computations of structural budget balances are based on IMF staff estimates of potential GDP and revenue and expenditure elasticities (see the October 1993 *World Economic Outlook*, Annex I). Net debt is defined as gross debt less financial assets of the general government, which include assets held by the social security insurance system. Estimates of the output gap and of the structural balance are subject to significant margins of uncertainty.

(about 2.4 percent of GDP) received in fiscal year 2000/01 to conform to the Eurostat accounting guidelines. These proceeds are not included in the computation of the structural balance.

Canada. The fiscal outlook assumes tax and expenditure policies in line with those outlined in the government's 2001 budget, announced in December 2001, adjusted for the staff's economic projections. Over the medium term, the staff assumes that the federal government budget will be in surplus in an amount that is equivalent to the contingency reserve, which is assumed to be restored to its pre-2001 budget level of Can$3 billion after FY2003/04. The consolidated fiscal position for the provinces is assumed to evolve in line with their stated medium-term targets.

Australia. The fiscal projections through the FY2004/05 are based on the Mid-Year Economic and Fiscal Outlook and on the Pre-Election Economic and Fiscal Outlook, which were published by the Australian Treasury in October 2001. For the remainder of the projection period, the IMF's staff assumes unchanged policies.

Belgium. Fiscal projections are based on existing policies and on the government's medium-term tax and expenditure plans announced in the 2001 budget and the 2002 budget. The projections incorporate the IMF staff's assumptions for economic growth and interest rates and assume that a large part of the savings on interest expenditures—resulting from ongoing large primary surpluses—are devoted to further fiscal consolidation. Revenues from UMTS licenses amounting to 0.2 percent of GDP are included in the deficit figures for 2001.

Greece. The fiscal projections are based on the authorities' policies presented in the 2002 budget, adjusted for the different macroeconomic assumptions. For the 2003–07 period, primary current expenditures are assumed to maintain their share of GDP, while the current revenue share is projected to rise slightly, as social insurance contributions—which are tied to wages—are expected to grow more rapidly

than output. Thus, the overall surplus is expected to grow by slightly more than the reduction in interest rates, which is the result of euro area membership.

Korea. The fiscal projections for 2002 are based on the government's budget, adjusted for the IMF staff's macroeconomic assumptions. For the medium term, the projections are based on the IMF staff's assumptions for economic growth and interest rates.

Netherlands. The 2000 budget balance includes revenues from the sale of mobile phone licenses of NLG 5.9 billion (0.7 percent of GDP). The fiscal projections through 2002 reflect the government's medium-term real expenditure ceilings, and a baseline path for revenues adjusted for the staff's growth projections. The revenue baseline path includes the effects of tax cuts implemented in the 2001 tax reform package as well as small additional tax cuts introduced in the 2002 budget. For 2003 and beyond, projections reflect assumptions in the 2002 Central Economic Plan and the Economic Scenario for 2003–06 adjusted for the IMF's staff macroeconomic assumptions.

Portugal. The fiscal projections for 2002 are based on the IMF staff's projection of the effects of the 2002 budget, as well as the staff's macroeconomic framework. Fiscal projections for 2003 are based on the staff's estimate of the effects of the Stability and Growth Program presented December 2001. For 2004–07 a constant structural primary balance is assumed.

Spain. Fiscal projections through 2005 are based on the policies outlined in the national authorities' updated stability program of December 2001. Projections for subsequent years assume no significant changes in those policies.

Sweden. The fiscal estimates for 2001 are based on the National Financial Management Authority's March 2002 estimate for the central government budget outturn for 2001. Projections for 2002 and beyond are based on the policies and projections for central and general government underlying the approved budget for 2002 and on the medium-term fiscal

Box A1 *(concluded)*

projections of the Ministry of Finance for 2002–04. The projections also take into account the authorities' medium-term fiscal objective of a general government surplus of 2 percent of GDP over the economic cycle, and the ceilings on nominal central government expenditures for the same period.

Monetary policy assumptions are based on the established policy framework in each country. In most cases, this implies a nonaccommodative stance over the business cycle: official interest rates will therefore increase when economic indicators suggest that prospective inflation will rise above its acceptable rate or range; and they will decrease when indicators suggest that prospective inflation will not exceed the acceptable rate or range, that prospective output growth is below its potential rate, and that the

margin of slack in the economy is significant. On this basis, the London interbank offered rate (LIBOR) on six-month U.S. dollar deposits is assumed to average 2.8 percent in 2002 and 4.5 percent in 2003. The projected path for U.S. dollar short-term interest rates reflects the assumption that the U.S. Federal Reserve will begin to raise interest rates in the summer of 2002. The interest rate on six-month Japanese yen deposits is assumed to average 0.1 percent in 2002 and 0.1 percent in 2003, with the current monetary policy framework being maintained. The rate on six-month euro deposits is assumed to average 3.7 percent in 2002 and 4.5 in 2003. Changes in interest rate assumptions compared with the December 2001 Interim *World Economic Outlook* are summarized in Table 1.1.

Outlook (the World Economic Outlook database). The data are maintained jointly by the IMF's Research Department and area departments, with the latter regularly updating country projections based on consistent global assumptions.

Although national statistical agencies are the ultimate providers of historical data and definitions, international organizations are also involved in statistical issues, with the objective of harmonizing methodologies for the national compilation of statistics, including the analytical frameworks, concepts, definitions, classifications, and valuation procedures used in the production of economic statistics. The World Economic Outlook database reflects information from both national source agencies and international organizations.

The completion in 1993 of the comprehensive revision of the standardized *System of National*

Accounts 1993 (*SNA*) and the IMF's *Balance of Payments Manual* (*BPM*) represented important improvements in the standards of economic statistics and analysis.[2] The IMF was actively involved in both projects, particularly the new *Balance of Payments Manual*, which reflects the IMF's special interest in countries' external positions. Key changes introduced with the new *Manual* were summarized in Box 13 of the May 1994 *World Economic Outlook*. The process of adapting country balance of payments data to the definitions of the new *BPM* began with the May 1995 *World Economic Outlook*. However, full concordance with the *BPM* is ultimately dependent on the provision by national statistical compilers of revised country data, and hence the *World Economic Outlook* estimates are still only partially adapted to the *BPM*.

The members of the European Union have recently adopted a harmonized system for the

---

[2]Commission of the European Communities, International Monetary Fund, Organization for Economic Cooperation and Development, United Nations, and World Bank, *System of National Accounts 1993* (Brussels/Luxembourg, New York, Paris, and Washington, 1993); and International Monetary Fund, *Balance of Payments Manual, Fifth Edition* (Washington: IMF, 1993).

compilation of the national accounts, referred to as ESA 1995. All national accounts data from 1995 onward are now presented on the basis of the new system. Revision by national authorities of data prior to 1995 to conform to the new system has progressed, but has in some cases not been completed. In such cases, historical *World Economic Outlook* data have been carefully adjusted to avoid breaks in the series. Users of EU national accounts data prior to 1995 should nevertheless exercise caution until such time as the revision of historical data by national statistical agencies has been fully completed. See Box 1.2, *Revisions in National Accounts Methodologies,* in the May 2000 *World Economic Outlook.*

Composite data for country groups in the *World Economic Outlook* are either sums or weighted averages of data for individual countries. Unless otherwise indicated, multiyear averages of growth rates are expressed as compound annual rates of change. Arithmetically weighted averages are used for all data except inflation and money growth for the developing and transition country groups, for which geometric averages are used. The following conventions apply.

- Country group composites for exchange rates, interest rates, and the growth rates of monetary aggregates are weighted by GDP converted to U.S. dollars at market exchange rates (averaged over the preceding three years) as a share of group GDP.
- Composites for other data relating to the domestic economy, whether growth rates or ratios, are weighted by GDP valued at purchasing power parities (PPPs) as a share of total world or group GDP.[3]
- Composites for data relating to the domestic economy for the euro area (12 member countries throughout the entire period unless otherwise noted) are aggregates of national

source data using weights based on 1995 ECU exchange rates.
- Composite unemployment rates and employment growth are weighted by labor force as a share of group labor force.
- Composites relating to the external economy are sums of individual country data after conversion to U.S. dollars at the average market exchange rates in the years indicated for balance of payments data and at end-of-year market exchange rates for debt denominated in currencies other than U.S. dollars. Composites of changes in foreign trade volumes and prices, however, are arithmetic averages of percentage changes for individual countries weighted by the U.S. dollar value of exports or imports as a share of total world or group exports or imports (in the preceding year).

For central and eastern European countries, external transactions in nonconvertible currencies (through 1990) are converted to U.S. dollars at the implicit U.S. dollar/ruble conversion rates obtained from each country's national currency exchange rate for the U.S. dollar and for the ruble.

Classification of Countries

Summary of the Country Classification

The country classification in the *World Economic Outlook* divides the world into three major groups: advanced economies, developing countries, and countries in transition.[4] Rather than being based on strict criteria, economic or otherwise, this classification has evolved over time with the objective of facilitating analysis by providing a reasonably meaningful organization of data. A few countries are presently not included in these groups, either because they are

---

[3]See Box A1 of the May 2000 *World Economic Outlook* for a summary of the revised PPP-based weights and Annex IV of the May 1993 *World Economic Outlook.* See also Anne-Marie Gulde and Marianne Schulze-Ghattas, "Purchasing Power Parity Based Weights for the *World Economic Outlook,*" in *Staff Studies for the World Economic Outlook* (International Monetary Fund, December 1993), pp. 106–23.

[4]As used here, the term "country" does not in all cases refer to a territorial entity that is a state as understood by international law and practice. It also covers some territorial entities that are not states, but for which statistical data are maintained on a separate and independent basis.

not IMF members, and their economies are not monitored by the IMF, or because databases have not yet been compiled. Cuba and the Democratic People's Republic of Korea are examples of countries that are not IMF members, whereas San Marino, among the advanced economies, is an example of an economy for which a database has not been completed. It should also be noted that, owing to a lack of data, only three of the former republics of the dissolved Socialist Federal Republic of Yugoslavia (Croatia, the former Yugoslav Republic of Macedonia, and Slovenia) are included in the group composites for countries in transition.

Each of the three main country groups is further divided into a number of subgroups. Among the advanced economies, the seven largest in terms of GDP, collectively referred to as the major advanced economies, are distinguished as a subgroup, and so are the 15 current members of the European Union, the 12 members of the euro area, and the four newly industrialized Asian economies. The developing countries are classified by region, as well as into a number of analytical and other groups. A regional breakdown is also used for the classification of the countries in transition. Table A provides an overview of these standard groups in the *World Economic Outlook*, showing the number of countries in each group and the average 2001 shares of groups in aggregate PPP-valued GDP, total exports of goods and services, and population.

General Features and Compositions of Groups in the *World Economic Outlook* Classification

Advanced Economies

The 29 advanced economies are listed in Table B. The seven largest in terms of GDP—the United States, Japan, Germany, France, Italy, the United Kingdom, and Canada—constitute the subgroup of *major advanced economies,* often referred to as the Group of Seven (G-7) countries. The current members of the *European Union* (15

countries), the euro area (12 countries), and the *newly industrialized Asian economies* are also distinguished as subgroups. Composite data shown in the tables for the European Union and the euro area cover the current members for all years, even though the membership has increased over time.

In 1991 and subsequent years, data for *Germany* refer to west Germany *and* the eastern Länder (i.e., the former German Democratic Republic). Before 1991, economic data are not available on a unified basis or in a consistent manner. Hence, in tables featuring data expressed as annual percent change, these apply to west Germany in years up to and including 1991, but to unified Germany from 1992 onward. In general, data on national accounts and domestic economic and financial activity through 1990 cover west Germany only, whereas data for the central government and balance of payments apply to west Germany through June 1990 and to unified Germany thereafter.

Developing Countries

The group of developing countries (125 countries) includes all countries that are not classified as advanced economies or as countries in transition, together with a few dependent territories for which adequate statistics are available.

The *regional breakdowns* of developing countries in the *World Economic Outlook* conform to the IMF's *International Financial Statistics (IFS)* classification—*Africa, Asia, Europe, Middle East,* and *Western Hemisphere*—with one important exception. Because all of the non-advanced countries in Europe except Malta and Turkey are included in the group of countries in transition, the *World Economic Outlook* classification places these two countries in a combined *Middle East and Turkey* region. In both classifications, Egypt and the Libyan Arab Jamahiriya are included in this region, not in Africa. Three additional regional groupings—two of them constituting part of Africa and one a subgroup of Asia—are included in the *World Economic Outlook* because of their analytical significance. These are *sub-*

Table A. Classification by *World Economic Outlook* Groups and Their Shares in Aggregate GDP, Exports of Goods and Services, and Population, 2001[1]

(Percent of total for group or world)

	Number of Countries	GDP		Exports of Goods and Services		Population	
		Share of total for					
		Advanced economies	World	Advanced economies	World	Advanced economies	World
Advanced Economies	**29**	**100.0**	**56.3**	**100.0**	**75.1**	**100.0**	**15.4**
Major advanced economies	7	79.4	44.7	61.9	46.5	74.3	11.5
United States		38.0	21.4	18.1	13.6	29.7	4.6
Japan		13.0	7.3	8.0	6.0	13.6	2.1
Germany		8.0	4.5	11.6	8.7	8.8	1.4
France		5.7	3.2	6.6	5.0	6.4	1.0
Italy		5.5	3.1	5.3	4.0	6.2	0.9
United Kingdom		5.6	3.1	6.8	5.1	6.4	1.0
Canada		3.5	2.0	5.4	4.1	3.3	0.5
Other advanced economies	22	20.6	11.6	38.1	28.6	25.7	4.0
Memorandum							
European Union	15	35.4	19.9	50.2	37.7	40.3	6.2
Euro area	12	28.3	15.9	40.3	30.3	32.4	5.0
Newly industrialized Asian countries	4	5.9	3.3	12.5	9.4	8.6	1.3
		Developing countries	World	Developing countries	World	Developing countries	World
Developing countries	**125**	**100.0**	**37.6**	**100.0**	**20.3**	**100.0**	**78.0**
Regional groups							
Africa	51	8.5	3.2	9.9	2.0	16.0	12.5
Sub-Sahara	48	6.6	2.5	7.2	1.5	14.5	11.3
Excluding Nigeria and South Africa	46	3.8	1.4	3.5	0.7	10.8	8.4
Developing Asia	25	59.1	22.2	46.1	9.3	66.9	52.2
China		32.2	12.1	19.7	4.0	26.9	21.0
India		12.5	4.7	4.4	0.9	21.4	16.7
Other developing Asia	23	14.4	5.4	22.1	4.5	18.6	14.5
Middle East and Turkey	16	10.6	4.0	20.7	4.2	6.4	5.0
Western Hemisphere	33	21.8	8.2	23.3	4.7	10.7	8.4
Analytical groups							
By source of export earnings							
Fuel	18	9.3	3.5	20.4	4.1	7.0	5.5
Nonfuel	109	90.7	34.1	79.6	16.1	93.0	72.5
Of which, primary products	42	6.3	2.4	6.0	1.2	11.1	8.6
By external financing source							
Net debtor countries	113	97.3	36.5	88.8	18.0	99.3	77.4
Of which, official financing	43	5.6	2.1	5.4	1.1	13.9	10.8
Net debtor countries by debt-servicing experience							
Countries with arrears and/or rescheduling during 1994–98	55	24.6	9.2	24.0	4.9	29.2	22.8
Other groups							
Heavily indebted poor countries	40	5.1	1.9	4.6	0.9	14.0	10.9
Middle East and north Africa	21	10.5	3.9	19.8	4.0	7.5	5.9
		Countries in transition	World	Countries in transition	World	Countries in transition	World
Countries in transition	**28**	**100.0**	**6.2**	**100.0**	**4.7**	**100.0**	**6.6**
Central and eastern Europe	16	37.6	2.3	52.5	2.4	28.8	1.9
CIS and Mongolia	12	62.4	3.8	47.5	2.2	71.2	4.7
Russia		42.8	2.6	32.2	1.5	36.4	2.4
Excluding Russia	11	19.6	1.2	15.3	0.7	34.7	2.3

[1]The GDP shares are based on the purchasing-power-parity (PPP) valuation of country GDPs.

Table B. Advanced Economies by Subgroup

	European Union		Euro Area	Newly Industrialized Asian Economies	Other Countries
Major advanced economies	France Germany Italy United Kingdom		France Germany Italy		Canada Japan United States
Other advanced economies	Austria Belgium Denmark Finland Greece Ireland	Luxembourg Netherlands Portugal Spain Sweden	Austria Belgium Finland Greece Ireland Luxembourg Netherlands Portugal Spain	Hong Kong SAR[1] Korea Singapore Taiwan Province of China	Australia Cyprus Iceland Israel New Zealand Norway Switzerland

[1]On July 1, 1997, Hong Kong was returned to the People's Republic of China and became a Special Administrative Region of China

Sahara, sub-Sahara excluding Nigeria and South Africa, and *Asia excluding China and India.*

The developing countries are also classified according to *analytical criteria* and into *other groups.* The analytical criteria reflect countries' composition of export earnings and other income from abroad, a distinction between net creditor and net debtor countries, and, for the net debtor countries, financial criteria based on external financing source and experience with external debt servicing. Included as "other groups" are currently the heavily indebted poor countries (HIPCs), and Middle East and north Africa (MENA). The detailed composition of developing countries in the regional, analytical, and other groups is shown in Tables C through E.

The first analytical criterion, by *source of export earnings,* distinguishes between categories: *fuel* (Standard International Trade Classification—SITC 3) and nonfuel and then focuses on *nonfuel primary products* (SITC 0, 1, 2, 4, and 68).

The financial criteria focus on *net creditor* and *net debtor countries,* which are differentiated on the basis of two additional financial criteria: by *official external financing* and by *experience with debt servicing.*[5]

The *other groups* of developing countries (see Table E) constitute the HIPCs and MENA countries. The first group comprises 40 of the countries (all except Nigeria) considered by the IMF and the World Bank for their debt initiative, known as the HIPC Initiative.[6] Middle East and north Africa, also referred to as the MENA countries, is a *World Economic Outlook* group, whose composition straddles the Africa and Middle East and Europe regions. It is defined as the Arab League countries plus the Islamic Republic of Iran.

Countries in Transition

The group of countries in transition (28 countries) is divided into two regional subgroups: *central and eastern Europe,* and *the Commonwealth of Independent States and Mongolia.* The detailed country composition is shown in Table F.

One common characteristic of these countries is the transitional state of their economies

[5]During the 1994–98 period, 55 countries incurred external payments arrears or entered into official or commercial bank debt-rescheduling agreements. This group of countries is referred to as *countries with arrears and/or rescheduling during 1994–98.*

[6]See David Andrews, Anthony R. Boote, Syed S. Rizavi, and Sukwinder Singh, *Debt Relief for Low-Income Countries: The Enhanced HIPC Initiative,* IMF Pamphlet Series, No. 51 (Washington: International Monetary Fund, November 1999).

Table C. Developing Countries by Region and Main Source of Export Earnings

	Fuel	Nonfuel, Of Which Primary Products		Fuel	Nonfuel, Of Which Primary Products
Africa **Sub-Sahara**	Angola Congo, Rep. of Equatorial Guinea Gabon Nigeria	Benin Botswana Burkina Faso Burundi Central African Rep. Chad Congo, Democratic Rep. of Côte d'Ivoire Gambia, The Ghana Guinea Guinea-Bissau Liberia Madagascar Malawi Mali Mauritania Namibia Niger Somalia Sudan Swaziland Tanzania Togo Zambia Zimbabwe	**Developing Asia**	Brunei Darussalam	Bhutan Cambodia Myanmar Papua New Guinea Solomon Islands Vanuatu Vietnam
			Middle East, and Turkey	Bahrain Iran, Islamic Rep. of Iraq Kuwait Libya Oman Qatar Saudi Arabia United Arab Emirates	
			Western Hemisphere	Trinidad and Tobago Venezuela	Belize Bolivia Chile Guyana Honduras Nicaragua Paraguay Peru Suriname
North Africa	Algeria				

from a centrally administered system to one based on market principles. Another is that this transition involves the transformation of sizable industrial sectors whose capital stocks have proven largely obsolete. Although several other countries are also "in transition" from partially command-based economic systems toward market-based systems (including China, Cambodia, the Lao People's Democratic Republic, Vietnam, and a number of African countries), most of these are largely rural, low-income economies for whom the principal challenge is one of economic development. These countries are therefore classified in the developing country group rather than in the group of countries in transition.

Table D. Developing Countries by Region and Main External Financing Source

Countries	Net Debtor Countries		Countries	Net Debtor Countries	
	By main external financing source			By main external financing source	
	Net debtor countries	Of which official financing		Net debtor countries	Of which official financing
Africa			**Developing Asia**		
Sub-Sahara			Afghanistan, Islamic State of	•	
Angola	•		Bangladesh	•	•
Benin	•	•	Bhutan	•	•
Burkina Faso	•	•	Cambodia	•	•
Burundi	•	•	China	•	
Cameroon	•	•	Fiji	•	
Cape Verde	•	•	India	•	
Central African Rep.	•	•	Indonesia	•	
Chad	•	•	Kiribati	•	
Comoros	•	•	Lao People's Democratic Rep.	•	•
Congo, Democratic Rep. of	•	•	Malaysia	•	
Congo, Rep. of	•	•	Maldives	•	
Côte d'Ivoire	•		Myanmar	•	
Djibouti	•		Nepal	•	
Equatorial Guinea	•		Pakistan	•	
Eritrea	•		Papua New Guinea	•	
Ethiopia	•	•	Philippines	•	
Gabon	•	•	Samoa	•	•
Gambia, The	•	•	Solomon Islands	•	
Ghana	•		Sri Lanka	•	•
Guinea	•	•	Thailand	•	
Guinea-Bissau	•	•	Tonga	•	•
Kenya	•		Vanuatu	•	
Lesotho	•		Vietnam	•	•
Liberia	•	•			
Madagascar	•	•	**Middle East, and Turkey**		
Malawi	•	•	Bahrain	•	
Mali	•	•	Egypt	•	
Mauritania	•	•	Iran, Islamic Rep. Of	•	
Mauritius	•		Iraq	•	
Mozambique, Rep. of	•	•	Jordan	•	
Namibia	•		Lebanon	•	•
Niger	•	•	Malta	•	
Nigeria	•		Oman		•
Rwanda	•	•	Syrian Arab Rep.	•	
São Tomé and Príncipe	•	•	Turkey	•	•
Senegal	•	•	Yemen, Rep. of	•	
Seychelles	•				
Sierra Leone	•		**Western Hemisphere**		
Somalia	•		Antigua and Barbuda	•	•
South Africa	•		Argentina	•	•
Sudan	•		Bahamas, The	•	•
Tanzania	•	•	Barbados	•	
Togo	•	•	Belize	•	•
Uganda	•	•	Bolivia	•	
Zambia	•	•	Brazil	•	•
Zimbabwe	•		Chile	•	•
North Africa			Colombia	•	
Algeria	•	•	Costa Rica	•	•
Morocco	•		Dominica	•	
Tunisia	•		Dominican Rep.	•	•
			Ecuador	•	•
			El Salvador	•	
			Grenada	•	

Table D *(concluded)*

| | Net Debtor Countries | | | Net Debtor Countries | |
| | By main external financing source | | | By main external financing source | |
Countries	Net debtor countries	Of which official financing	Countries	Net debtor countries	Of which official financing
Guatemala	•	•	Paraguay	•	
Guyana	•	•	Peru	•	
Haiti	•	•	St. Kitts and Nevis	•	
Honduras	•	•	St. Lucia	•	
Jamaica	•		St. Vincent and the Grenadines	•	
Mexico	•	•	Suriname	•	
Netherlands Antilles	•	•	Trinidad and Tobago	•	
Nicaragua	•	•	Uruguay	•	
Panama	•		Venezuela	•	

Table E. Other Developing Country Groups

Countries	Heavily Indebted Poor Countries	Middle East and North Africa	Countries	Heavily Indebted Poor Countries	Middle East and North Africa
Africa			Tanzania	•	
Sub-Sahara			Togo	•	
Angola	•		Uganda	•	
Benin	•		Zambia	•	
Burkina Faso	•		**North Africa**		
Burundi	•		Algeria		•
Cameroon	•		Morocco		•
Central African Rep.	•		Tunisia		•
Chad	•		**Developing Asia**		
Congo, Democratic Rep. of	•		Lao People's Democratic Rep.	•	
Congo, Rep. of	•		Myanmar	•	
Côte d'Ivoire	•		Vietnam	•	
Djibouti		•	**Middle East, and Turkey**		
Ethiopia	•		Bahrain		•
Gambia, The	•		Egypt		•
Ghana	•		Iran, Islamic Rep. Of		•
Guinea	•		Iraq		•
Guinea-Bissau	•		Jordan		•
Kenya	•		Kuwait		•
Liberia	•		Lebanon		•
Madagascar	•		Liberia	•	
Malawi	•		Libya		•
Mali	•		Oman		•
Mauritania	•	•	Qatar		•
Mozambique, Rep. of	•		Saudi Arabia		•
Niger	•		Syrian Arab Rep.		•
Rwanda	•		United Arab Emirates		•
São Tomé and Príncipe	•		Yemen, Rep. of	•	•
Senegal	•		**Western Hemisphere**		
Sierra Leone	•		Bolivia	•	
Somalia	•	•	Guyana	•	
Sudan	•	•	Honduras	•	
			Nicaragua	•	

Table F. Countries in Transition by Region

Central and Eastern Europe		Commonwealth of Independent States and Mongolia
Albania	Lithuania	Armenia
Belarus	Macedonia, former Yugoslav Republic of	Azerbaijan
Bosnia and Herzegovina	Poland	Belarus
Bulgaria	Romania	Georgia
Croatia	Slovak Republic	Kazakhstan
Czech Republic	Slovenia	Kyrgyz Republic
Estonia	Yugoslavia, Federal Republic of (Serbia/Montenegro)	Moldova
Hungary		Mongolia
Latvia		Russia
		Tajikistan
		Turkmenistan
		Ukraine
		Uzbekistan

List of Tables

Table 1. Summary of World Output[1]
(Annual percent change)

| | Ten-Year Averages | | 1994 | 1995 | 1996 | 1997 | 1998 | 1999 | 2000 | 2001 | 2002 | 2003 |
	1984–93	1994–2003										
World	**3.3**	**3.6**	**3.7**	**3.6**	**4.0**	**4.2**	**2.8**	**3.6**	**4.7**	**2.5**	**2.8**	**4.0**
Advanced economies	**3.2**	**2.8**	**3.4**	**2.7**	**3.0**	**3.4**	**2.7**	**3.3**	**3.9**	**1.2**	**1.7**	**3.0**
United States	3.2	3.4	4.0	2.7	3.6	4.4	4.3	4.1	4.1	1.2	2.3	3.4
European Union	2.4	2.5	2.8	2.4	1.7	2.6	3.0	2.7	3.4	1.7	1.5	2.9
Japan	3.7	0.9	1.1	1.5	3.6	1.8	–1.0	0.7	2.2	–0.4	–1.0	0.8
Other advanced economies	4.7	4.1	5.8	5.0	4.2	4.6	1.2	5.8	5.9	1.3	3.1	4.2
Developing countries	**5.1**	**5.2**	**6.7**	**6.1**	**6.5**	**5.8**	**3.5**	**3.9**	**5.7**	**4.0**	**4.3**	**5.5**
Regional groups												
Africa	2.0	3.4	2.3	3.0	5.6	3.1	3.4	2.6	3.0	3.7	3.4	4.2
Developing Asia	7.6	6.8	9.6	9.0	8.3	6.6	4.0	6.1	6.7	5.6	5.9	6.4
Middle East and Turkey[2]	3.4	3.5	0.5	4.2	4.8	5.6	3.9	1.0	5.8	2.1	3.3	4.5
Western Hemisphere	2.9	2.7	5.0	1.8	3.6	5.2	2.3	0.2	4.0	0.7	0.7	3.7
Analytical groups												
By source of export earnings												
Fuel	2.5	3.2	0.4	3.1	3.6	4.7	3.2	1.2	4.8	4.5	2.7	4.0
Nonfuel	5.4	5.4	7.4	6.5	6.8	5.9	3.6	4.2	5.8	4.0	4.6	5.6
of which, primary products	3.1	4.4	5.2	6.6	5.5	5.4	3.0	2.4	3.6	2.7	3.8	5.4
By external financing source												
Net debtor countries	5.1	5.3	6.9	6.3	6.7	5.9	3.6	4.0	5.7	4.0	4.5	5.6
of which, official financing	2.4	4.2	2.4	5.4	5.3	4.2	3.9	3.7	3.7	4.3	4.3	5.0
Net debtor countries by debt-servicing experience												
Countries with arrears and/or rescheduling during 1994–98	3.0	3.7	4.7	5.2	5.0	4.4	–0.4	2.2	4.4	3.4	3.7	4.4
Countries in transition	**–1.4**	**1.3**	**–8.5**	**–1.5**	**–0.5**	**1.6**	**–0.8**	**3.6**	**6.6**	**5.0**	**3.9**	**4.4**
Central and eastern Europe	...	3.3	3.0	5.6	4.0	2.6	2.3	2.2	3.8	3.1	3.0	4.0
Commonwealth of Independent States and Mongolia	...	0.1	–14.5	–5.5	–3.3	1.1	–2.8	4.6	8.3	6.2	4.5	4.6
Russia	...	0.2	–13.5	–4.2	–3.4	0.9	–4.9	5.4	9.0	5.0	4.4	4.9
Excluding Russia	...	–0.1	–16.6	–8.6	–3.1	1.5	1.7	2.8	7.0	8.8	4.7	4.1
Memorandum												
Median growth rate												
Advanced economies	3.1	3.2	4.1	2.9	3.6	3.7	3.5	3.7	4.0	1.4	1.6	3.0
Developing countries	3.5	3.9	3.8	4.4	4.6	4.5	3.7	3.5	3.9	3.0	3.3	4.0
Countries in transition	–1.3	2.9	–3.0	0.4	3.1	3.7	3.8	3.3	5.1	4.5	4.0	4.6
Output per capita												
Advanced economies	2.5	2.2	2.7	2.1	2.4	2.8	2.1	2.8	2.8	0.7	1.2	2.6
Developing countries	3.0	3.5	4.9	4.5	4.8	4.2	1.8	2.2	4.0	2.4	2.7	3.9
Countries in transition	–1.9	1.5	–8.4	–1.5	–0.4	1.8	–0.6	3.8	6.9	5.3	4.3	4.7
World growth based on market exchange rates	**2.9**	**2.8**	**3.1**	**2.8**	**3.3**	**3.5**	**2.3**	**3.0**	**4.0**	**1.4**	**1.8**	**3.3**
Value of world output in billions of U.S. dollars												
At market exchange rates	19,217	30,181	26,255	29,112	29,831	29,694	29,506	30,557	31,377	31,049	31,402	33,031
At purchasing power parities	24,205	41,420	32,170	33,996	36,032	38,241	39,729	41,691	44,631	46,742	48,853	52,114

[1]Real GDP.
[2]Includes Malta.

157

Table 2. Advanced Economies: Real GDP and Total Domestic Demand

(Annual percent change)

	Ten-Year Averages		1994	1995	1996	1997	1998	1999	2000	2001	2002	2003	Fourth Quarter[1]		
	1984–93	1994–2003											2001	2002	2003
Real GDP															
Advanced economies	**3.2**	**2.8**	**3.4**	**2.7**	**3.0**	**3.4**	**2.7**	**3.3**	**3.9**	**1.2**	**1.7**	**3.0**	. . .	. . .	. . .
Major advanced economies	3.0	2.6	3.1	2.3	2.8	3.2	2.8	2.9	3.5	1.1	1.5	2.8	0.2	2.7	2.8
United States	3.2	3.4	4.0	2.7	3.6	4.4	4.3	4.1	4.1	1.2	2.3	3.4	0.5	3.2	3.7
Japan	3.7	0.9	1.1	1.5	3.6	1.8	-1.0	0.7	2.2	-0.4	-1.0	0.8	-1.9	0.9	0.6
Germany	2.8	1.7	2.3	1.7	0.8	1.4	2.0	1.8	3.0	0.6	0.9	2.7	—	2.4	2.4
France	2.0	2.3	1.9	1.8	1.1	1.9	3.5	3.0	3.6	2.0	1.4	3.0	0.9	2.3	3.1
Italy	2.1	2.1	2.2	2.9	1.1	2.0	1.8	1.6	2.9	1.8	1.4	2.9	0.7	2.9	2.5
United Kingdom	2.4	2.9	4.7	2.9	2.6	3.4	3.0	2.1	3.0	2.2	2.0	2.8	1.6	3.0	2.4
Canada	2.6	3.4	4.7	2.8	1.6	4.3	3.9	5.1	4.4	1.5	2.5	3.6	0.9	3.5	3.5
Other advanced economies	3.8	3.7	4.6	4.3	3.8	4.3	2.2	5.0	5.3	1.6	2.5	3.7	. . .	. . .	. . .
Spain	2.9	3.2	2.4	2.8	2.4	4.0	4.3	4.1	4.1	2.8	2.3	3.2	2.4	2.5	3.4
Netherlands	2.7	2.9	3.2	2.3	3.0	3.8	4.3	3.7	3.5	1.1	1.4	2.7	0.2	2.5	2.5
Belgium	2.2	2.4	2.7	2.6	1.2	3.6	2.2	3.0	4.0	1.1	0.9	3.2	. . .	. . .	. . .
Sweden	1.6	2.8	4.1	3.7	1.1	2.1	3.6	4.5	3.6	1.2	1.6	2.7	0.7	2.2	2.6
Austria	2.3	2.2	2.6	1.6	2.0	1.6	3.5	2.8	3.0	1.0	1.3	2.9	. . .	. . .	. . .
Denmark	1.6	2.6	5.5	2.8	2.5	3.0	2.5	2.3	3.0	0.9	1.3	2.4	0.5	2.2	2.2
Finland	1.2	3.8	4.0	3.8	4.0	6.3	5.3	4.0	5.7	0.7	1.4	3.1	-1.2	3.5	2.5
Greece[2]	1.8	3.2	2.0	2.1	2.4	3.6	3.4	3.4	4.3	4.1	3.4	2.9	. . .	. . .	. . .
Portugal	2.9	2.9	2.4	2.9	3.7	3.8	4.7	3.4	3.2	1.6	0.8	2.0	0.7	0.8	2.0
Ireland	3.4	8.0	5.8	10.0	7.8	10.8	8.6	10.9	11.5	6.0	3.2	6.2	. . .	. . .	. . .
Luxembourg	6.2	5.3	4.1	3.5	3.6	9.0	5.8	6.0	7.5	5.1	3.0	6.0	. . .	. . .	. . .
Switzerland	1.8	1.5	0.5	0.5	0.3	1.7	2.4	1.6	3.0	1.3	0.8	2.6	0.4	1.8	2.6
Norway	2.8	3.1	5.5	3.8	4.9	4.7	2.4	1.1	2.3	1.4	2.3	2.2	. . .	. . .	. . .
Israel	4.5	3.9	8.6	6.8	4.5	3.3	2.7	2.6	6.4	-0.6	1.3	3.8	. . .	. . .	. . .
Iceland	2.1	3.1	4.5	0.1	5.2	4.6	5.3	3.9	5.0	2.1	-0.9	1.9	. . .	. . .	. . .
Cyprus	5.8	4.2	5.9	6.1	1.9	2.5	5.0	4.5	5.1	4.0	3.0	4.2	. . .	. . .	. . .
Korea	8.2	5.5	8.3	8.9	6.8	5.0	-6.7	10.9	9.3	3.0	5.0	5.5	3.7	4.6	6.4
Australia	3.7	4.0	4.6	3.9	3.9	3.7	5.2	4.8	3.2	2.4	3.9	4.0	4.1	3.3	4.4
Taiwan Province of China	8.3	4.7	7.1	6.4	6.1	6.7	4.6	5.4	5.9	-1.9	2.3	4.8	-1.9	3.0	5.5
Hong Kong SAR	6.5	3.2	5.4	3.9	4.5	5.0	-5.3	3.0	10.5	0.1	1.5	3.6	-1.8	4.3	1.9
Singapore	7.5	5.8	11.4	8.0	7.7	8.5	-0.1	6.9	10.3	-2.1	3.2	5.1	-7.0	8.2	1.8
New Zealand	2.3	3.1	5.8	4.3	3.6	2.2	-0.2	3.9	3.9	2.4	2.6	3.0	2.9	3.2	2.0
Memorandum															
European Union	2.4	2.5	2.8	2.4	1.7	2.6	3.0	2.7	3.4	1.7	1.5	2.9	. . .	. . .	. . .
Euro area	2.4	2.3	2.3	2.2	1.4	2.3	2.9	2.6	3.4	1.5	1.4	2.9	0.6	2.5	2.8
Newly industrialized Asian economies	8.0	5.0	7.7	7.5	6.3	5.8	-2.4	8.0	8.5	0.8	3.6	5.1	0.9	4.6	5.6
Real total domestic demand															
Advanced economies	**3.2**	**2.9**	**3.4**	**2.6**	**3.0**	**3.2**	**3.0**	**3.9**	**3.8**	**1.0**	**2.0**	**3.1**	. . .	. . .	. . .
Major advanced economies	3.0	2.8	3.1	2.2	2.8	3.2	3.5	3.6	3.7	1.0	1.8	3.0	—	3.1	3.0
United States	3.2	3.9	4.4	2.5	3.7	4.7	5.4	5.0	4.8	1.3	3.1	3.8	0.4	4.2	4.0
Japan	3.8	0.9	1.3	2.0	4.1	0.9	-1.4	0.8	1.8	0.3	-1.3	0.4	-1.4	0.1	0.6
Germany	2.7	1.4	2.3	1.7	0.3	0.6	2.4	2.6	2.0	-1.0	0.8	2.6	-2.0	2.2	2.4
France	2.0	2.2	1.9	1.8	0.7	0.7	4.2	3.0	3.9	1.7	1.4	3.2	0.5	2.4	3.2
Italy	2.1	2.1	1.7	2.0	0.9	2.7	3.1	3.0	2.1	1.6	1.3	2.4	0.8	3.2	1.7
United Kingdom	2.5	3.3	3.7	2.0	3.1	3.9	5.0	3.4	3.6	2.8	2.7	3.0	2.1	3.5	2.7
Canada	2.7	3.0	3.2	1.8	1.2	6.1	2.3	4.0	4.5	0.9	1.8	4.2	—	4.0	3.7
Other advanced economies	4.0	3.5	4.7	4.5	3.8	3.6	1.1	5.0	4.5	1.0	2.8	3.6	. . .	. . .	. . .
Memorandum															
European Union	2.5	2.4	2.4	2.2	1.4	2.3	4.0	3.3	3.1	1.2	1.6	2.8	. . .	. . .	. . .
Euro area	2.4	2.1	2.1	2.1	1.0	1.8	3.6	3.2	2.8	0.9	1.2	2.8	0.1	2.6	2.6
Newly industrialized Asian economies	8.3	4.1	8.5	7.8	6.9	3.9	-9.1	7.5	7.3	—	4.3	4.7	. . .	. . .	. . .

[1]From fourth quarter of preceding year.
[2]Based on revised national accounts for 1988 onward.

Table 3. Advanced Economies: Components of Real GDP
(Annual percent change)

	Ten-Year Averages		1994	1995	1996	1997	1998	1999	2000	2001	2002	2003
	1984–93	1994–2003										
Private consumer expenditure												
Advanced economies	**3.2**	**2.9**	**3.1**	**2.6**	**2.8**	**2.8**	**3.0**	**4.0**	**3.6**	**2.4**	**2.2**	**2.7**
Major advanced economies	3.1	2.8	2.8	2.3	2.5	2.6	3.4	3.7	3.4	2.3	2.1	2.5
United States	3.2	3.7	3.8	3.0	3.2	3.6	4.8	5.0	4.8	3.1	2.9	2.9
Japan	3.5	1.1	2.6	1.3	2.3	0.9	0.2	1.1	0.3	0.5	0.7	0.9
Germany	3.0	1.6	1.0	2.0	1.0	0.6	1.8	3.1	1.5	1.2	0.8	2.6
France	1.7	2.0	0.9	1.4	1.3	0.1	3.6	3.2	2.9	2.9	1.5	2.8
Italy	2.5	2.1	1.5	1.7	1.2	3.2	3.2	2.4	2.7	1.1	1.1	2.5
United Kingdom	2.9	3.4	3.3	1.9	3.8	3.8	3.8	4.2	4.1	3.9	2.7	2.8
Canada	2.8	3.1	3.0	2.1	2.6	4.6	3.0	3.4	3.6	2.5	3.0	3.3
Other advanced economies	3.8	3.5	4.1	3.7	3.9	3.6	1.7	4.9	4.4	2.5	2.8	3.2
Memorandum												
European Union	2.6	2.4	1.8	1.8	2.0	2.1	3.3	3.4	2.9	2.1	1.6	2.7
Euro area	2.5	2.1	1.3	1.9	1.6	1.6	3.0	3.2	2.5	1.8	1.4	2.7
Newly industrialized Asian economies	8.1	4.7	8.0	6.9	6.7	5.1	–4.6	7.5	6.9	3.3	4.0	4.0
Public consumption												
Advanced economies	**2.5**	**2.0**	**0.9**	**1.1**	**1.7**	**1.5**	**1.6**	**2.4**	**2.7**	**2.5**	**2.7**	**2.5**
Major advanced economies	2.2	1.9	0.8	0.8	1.2	1.2	1.3	2.5	2.8	2.8	2.9	2.7
United States	2.1	2.0	0.2	—	0.5	1.8	1.4	2.2	2.8	3.1	4.1	3.9
Japan	2.9	2.9	2.8	4.3	2.8	1.3	1.9	4.5	4.6	3.1	1.9	2.0
Germany	1.7	1.4	2.4	1.5	1.8	0.4	1.2	1.6	1.2	1.6	1.0	1.0
France	2.7	1.5	0.5	—	2.2	2.1	–0.1	2.0	2.3	2.1	1.9	2.3
Italy	2.1	0.4	–0.8	–2.1	1.1	0.3	0.3	1.4	1.7	2.3	1.2	–1.0
United Kingdom	0.9	2.0	1.0	1.7	1.2	0.1	1.5	2.8	3.3	2.7	3.2	2.6
Canada	2.3	0.8	–1.3	–0.6	–1.4	–0.8	1.8	2.6	2.2	2.2	1.8	1.7
Other advanced economies	3.7	2.2	1.3	2.0	3.7	2.4	2.6	2.2	2.2	1.7	1.8	1.8
Memorandum												
European Union	2.1	1.6	1.0	0.8	1.5	1.1	1.5	2.3	2.2	2.2	1.8	1.4
Euro area	2.2	1.5	1.2	0.7	1.7	1.3	1.2	2.1	1.9	2.0	1.5	1.3
Newly industrialized Asian economies	6.3	2.1	0.8	2.6	8.0	3.3	1.8	–0.6	1.5	0.5	1.8	1.8
Gross fixed capital formation												
Advanced economies	**3.7**	**3.9**	**4.7**	**4.0**	**5.7**	**5.6**	**5.5**	**5.0**	**5.5**	**–0.9**	**—**	**4.1**
Major advanced economies	3.5	3.8	4.3	3.1	5.8	5.6	6.2	5.3	5.4	–0.7	–0.9	3.8
United States	3.7	5.9	7.3	5.4	8.4	8.8	10.2	7.8	6.7	–0.9	0.2	5.8
Japan	4.9	–0.6	–1.3	0.1	7.3	0.8	–4.2	–0.7	3.2	–1.7	–7.2	–1.6
Germany	2.9	0.7	4.0	–0.7	–0.8	0.6	3.0	4.2	2.3	–4.8	–2.2	2.2
France	2.1	3.0	1.5	2.1	—	–0.1	7.2	6.2	6.2	2.8	0.6	3.7
Italy	1.3	3.6	0.1	6.0	3.6	2.1	4.0	5.7	6.5	2.4	2.1	4.0
United Kingdom	3.2	4.4	4.7	3.1	4.7	7.1	13.2	0.9	3.9	0.1	2.9	4.4
Canada	2.4	4.4	7.5	–2.2	4.4	15.2	2.4	7.4	6.8	1.3	–1.5	3.8
Other advanced economies	4.7	4.4	6.2	7.3	5.4	6.0	2.7	4.0	5.9	–1.7	3.4	5.0
Memorandum												
European Union	2.7	3.3	2.6	3.5	2.4	3.5	6.9	4.9	4.7	0.1	0.6	3.7
Euro area	2.6	2.7	2.3	2.5	1.4	2.4	5.2	5.5	4.4	–0.3	–0.1	3.4
Newly industrialized Asian economies	10.0	3.7	10.3	10.4	7.2	4.4	–9.0	—	10.0	–5.7	5.4	6.3

Table 3 *(concluded)*

	Ten-Year Averages		1994	1995	1996	1997	1998	1999	2000	2001	2002	2003
	1984–93	1994–2003										
Final domestic demand												
Advanced economies	**3.2**	**2.9**	**2.9**	**2.5**	**3.2**	**3.1**	**3.1**	**3.9**	**3.9**	**1.6**	**1.8**	**2.9**
Major advanced economies	3.0	2.8	2.7	2.1	3.0	2.9	3.5	3.8	3.8	1.7	1.5	2.8
United States	3.1	3.9	3.8	2.9	3.7	4.3	5.3	5.2	5.0	2.2	2.5	3.6
Japan	3.8	0.9	1.5	1.4	3.8	0.9	−0.8	1.1	1.8	0.3	−1.3	0.4
Germany	2.7	1.3	2.0	1.3	0.7	0.5	1.9	3.0	1.6	−0.1	0.2	2.2
France	2.0	2.1	0.9	1.2	1.3	0.6	3.4	3.5	3.4	2.7	1.4	2.9
Italy	2.2	2.1	0.8	1.7	1.7	2.4	2.8	2.9	3.3	1.6	1.3	2.2
United Kingdom	2.5	3.3	3.0	2.1	3.5	3.6	5.0	3.4	3.9	3.0	2.8	3.0
Canada	2.6	2.9	2.8	0.7	2.0	5.5	2.6	4.1	4.0	2.2	1.8	3.1
Other advanced economies	4.0	3.4	4.1	4.3	4.2	3.9	1.7	4.1	4.5	1.3	2.8	3.5
Memorandum												
European Union	2.5	2.4	1.8	1.9	2.0	2.2	3.6	3.5	3.1	1.7	1.4	2.6
Euro area	2.5	2.1	1.5	1.7	1.6	1.7	3.1	3.5	2.8	1.3	1.1	2.6
Newly industrialized Asian economies	8.3	4.1	7.8	7.6	7.2	4.5	−5.7	4.0	7.1	0.5	4.1	4.5
Stock building[1]												
Advanced economies	**—**	**—**	**0.5**	**0.1**	**−0.2**	**0.2**	**−0.1**	**—**	**−0.1**	**−0.7**	**0.3**	**0.2**
Major advanced economies	—	—	0.5	—	−0.2	0.3	0.1	−0.2	−0.1	−0.8	0.3	0.2
United States	0.1	—	0.7	−0.5	—	0.4	0.2	−0.2	−0.1	−1.2	0.6	0.3
Japan	—	—	−0.2	0.6	0.3	—	−0.6	−0.3	—	—	—	—
Germany	—	0.1	0.3	0.3	−0.5	—	0.5	−0.4	0.4	−0.9	0.6	0.4
France	−0.1	0.1	1.0	0.6	−0.6	0.1	0.8	−0.4	0.4	−1.0	—	0.3
Italy	—	—	0.8	0.2	−0.7	0.3	0.3	0.1	−1.1	—	—	0.2
United Kingdom	—	—	0.7	—	−0.4	0.3	0.1	0.1	−0.3	−0.2	−0.1	—
Canada	0.1	0.1	0.4	1.1	−0.7	0.7	−0.3	−0.1	0.5	−1.2	—	1.0
Other advanced economies	—	—	0.6	0.3	−0.4	−0.2	−0.6	0.7	—	−0.3	—	0.1
Memorandum												
European Union	—	0.1	0.7	0.3	−0.5	0.1	0.4	−0.2	—	−0.4	0.1	0.2
Euro area	—	0.1	0.6	0.4	−0.5	0.1	0.4	−0.2	—	−0.5	0.1	0.3
Newly industrialized Asian economies	—	−0.1	0.7	0.3	−0.3	−0.6	−3.3	2.7	0.1	−0.5	0.1	0.2
Foreign balance[1]												
Advanced economies	**—**	**−0.1**	**−0.1**	**0.1**	**—**	**0.2**	**−0.4**	**−0.5**	**—**	**0.1**	**−0.3**	**−0.1**
Major advanced economies	—	−0.2	—	0.2	−0.1	0.1	−0.8	−0.8	−0.3	—	−0.4	−0.2
United States	—	−0.6	−0.4	0.1	−0.1	−0.3	−1.3	−1.1	−0.9	−0.1	−0.9	−0.5
Japan	—	0.1	−0.2	−0.5	−0.4	1.0	0.3	−0.1	0.5	−0.7	0.3	0.4
Germany	—	0.3	0.1	0.1	0.5	0.9	−0.4	−0.7	1.1	1.6	0.1	0.2
France	—	0.1	—	0.1	0.4	1.2	−0.6	—	−0.2	0.4	0.1	−0.1
Italy	—	—	0.6	1.0	0.2	−0.6	−1.2	−1.3	0.8	0.2	0.1	0.5
United Kingdom	−0.3	−0.6	0.8	0.9	−0.4	−0.5	−2.2	−1.4	−0.7	−0.8	−0.9	−0.5
Canada	−0.1	0.5	1.6	1.1	0.4	−1.7	1.7	1.3	0.2	0.7	0.7	−0.3
Other advanced economies	−0.1	0.4	−0.1	−0.1	0.1	0.8	1.1	0.3	1.1	0.5	−0.1	0.4
Memorandum												
European Union	−0.1	0.1	0.4	0.4	0.2	0.3	−0.9	−0.6	0.3	0.4	−0.1	0.1
Euro area	—	0.2	0.3	0.2	0.4	0.6	−0.6	−0.5	0.6	0.7	0.1	0.2
Newly industrialized Asian economies	0.1	1.3	−0.8	0.1	−0.3	1.9	6.4	1.7	2.6	0.9	−0.2	0.9

[1]Changes expressed as percent of GDP in the preceding period.

Table 4. Advanced Economies: Unemployment, Employment, and Real Per Capita GDP
(Percent)

	Ten-Year Averages[1]		1994	1995	1996	1997	1998	1999	2000	2001	2002	2003
	1984–93	1994–2003										
Unemployment rate												
Advanced economies	**6.9**	**6.6**	**7.5**	**7.1**	**7.1**	**6.9**	**6.8**	**6.4**	**5.9**	**6.0**	**6.4**	**6.2**
Major advanced economies	6.8	6.4	7.1	6.7	6.8	6.6	6.4	6.2	5.8	6.0	6.5	6.3
United States[2]	6.5	5.0	6.1	5.6	5.4	4.9	4.5	4.2	4.0	4.8	5.5	5.3
Japan	2.5	4.3	2.9	3.2	3.4	3.4	4.1	4.7	4.7	5.0	5.8	5.7
Germany	7.3	8.5	8.4	8.2	8.9	9.9	9.3	8.6	7.9	7.9	8.2	8.1
France	10.1	10.8	12.3	11.7	12.3	12.3	11.8	11.2	9.5	9.0	9.2	8.7
Italy[3]	10.8	10.8	11.1	11.6	11.6	11.7	11.8	11.4	10.6	9.5	9.3	8.9
United Kingdom	9.0	6.7	9.7	8.7	8.2	7.1	6.3	6.0	5.6	5.1	5.4	5.4
Canada	9.7	8.2	10.4	9.4	9.6	9.1	8.3	7.6	6.8	7.2	7.1	6.7
Other advanced economies	7.3	7.3	8.7	8.2	8.1	7.8	8.1	7.3	6.2	6.1	6.3	6.1
Spain	19.4	17.7	24.2	22.9	22.2	20.8	18.8	15.9	14.1	13.0	13.0	12.4
Netherlands	7.4	4.4	7.6	7.1	6.6	5.5	4.2	3.2	2.6	2.0	2.5	2.7
Belgium	8.7	8.4	9.7	9.7	9.5	9.2	9.3	8.6	6.9	6.6	7.3	7.0
Sweden	3.1	6.1	8.0	7.7	8.1	8.0	6.5	5.6	4.7	4.0	4.4	4.3
Austria	3.3	4.0	3.8	3.9	4.3	4.4	4.5	3.9	3.7	3.8	4.1	3.8
Denmark	9.5	7.1	11.9	10.1	8.6	7.8	6.5	5.6	5.2	5.0	5.2	5.2
Finland	6.5	11.9	16.6	15.4	14.6	12.6	11.4	10.3	9.8	9.2	9.8	9.7
Greece	7.9	10.7	9.6	10.0	10.3	9.8	11.1	12.0	11.4	10.9	10.9	10.7
Portugal	6.5	5.4	6.8	7.2	7.3	6.7	5.0	4.4	4.0	4.1	4.2	4.3
Ireland	15.6	7.8	14.1	12.1	11.5	9.8	7.4	5.6	4.3	4.0	4.7	4.7
Luxembourg	1.6	2.9	2.7	3.0	3.3	3.3	3.1	2.9	2.6	2.5	2.9	2.7
Switzerland	1.3	3.4	4.7	4.2	4.7	5.2	3.9	2.7	2.0	1.9	2.6	2.3
Norway	4.1	4.0	5.5	5.0	4.9	4.1	3.2	3.2	3.4	3.6	3.8	3.7
Israel	8.2	8.4	7.8	6.8	6.6	7.6	8.5	8.9	8.8	9.3	10.5	9.4
Iceland	1.6	3.1	4.8	5.0	4.4	3.9	2.8	1.9	1.3	1.7	2.3	2.6
Cyprus	2.8	3.4	2.7	2.6	3.1	3.4	3.4	3.6	3.4	3.6	3.8	4.0
Korea	3.0	3.7	2.4	2.0	2.0	2.6	6.8	6.3	4.1	3.7	3.5	3.5
Australia	8.4	7.5	9.4	8.2	8.2	8.3	7.7	7.0	6.3	6.7	6.7	6.5
Taiwan Province of China	1.9	3.2	1.6	1.8	2.6	2.7	2.7	2.9	3.0	5.1	5.0	4.9
Hong Kong SAR	2.1	4.2	1.9	3.2	2.8	2.2	4.7	6.2	4.9	5.0	5.6	5.4
Singapore	3.2	3.2	2.6	2.7	2.0	1.8	3.2	3.5	3.1	4.7	4.4	3.7
New Zealand	6.9	6.4	8.2	6.3	6.1	6.7	7.5	6.8	6.0	5.3	5.5	5.6
Memorandum												
European Union	9.5	9.4	11.1	10.7	10.8	10.6	9.9	9.1	8.2	7.7	7.9	7.7
Euro area	9.6	9.9	11.3	11.1	11.3	11.3	10.7	9.8	8.8	8.3	8.5	8.2
Newly industrialized Asian economies	2.6	3.5	2.2	2.1	2.2	2.5	5.4	5.2	3.8	4.3	4.1	3.3
Growth in employment												
Advanced economies	**1.2**	**1.0**	**1.1**	**1.2**	**1.0**	**1.5**	**1.0**	**1.3**	**1.5**	**0.5**	**0.3**	**1.0**
Major advanced economies	1.2	0.9	1.0	0.9	0.8	1.4	1.0	1.1	1.2	0.2	0.1	0.9
United States	1.8	1.3	2.3	1.5	1.5	2.3	1.5	1.5	1.3	−0.1	0.5	1.4
Japan	1.2	−0.2	0.1	0.1	0.4	1.1	−0.6	−0.8	−0.2	−0.5	−1.1	0.1
Germany	0.9	0.4	−0.2	0.1	−0.3	−0.2	1.1	1.2	1.6	0.2	−0.2	0.5
France	0.1	1.0	0.1	0.9	0.1	0.6	1.3	1.9	2.3	1.5	0.4	1.3
Italy	−0.1	0.6	−1.6	−0.6	0.5	0.4	1.1	1.3	1.9	2.1	0.5	0.6
United Kingdom	0.5	1.0	1.0	1.4	1.1	2.0	1.1	1.3	1.0	0.8	−0.1	0.4
Canada	1.6	2.0	2.0	1.9	0.8	2.3	2.7	2.8	2.6	1.1	1.9	2.3
Other advanced economies	1.4	1.6	1.3	2.2	1.7	1.5	1.1	2.1	2.6	1.2	0.9	1.4
Memorandum												
European Union	0.5	1.0	−0.2	0.8	0.7	0.9	1.9	1.8	2.0	1.2	0.2	0.8
Euro area	0.5	1.0	−0.4	0.6	0.5	0.8	1.6	1.6	2.1	1.6	0.3	1.0
Newly industrialized Asian economies	2.6	1.4	2.8	2.5	2.1	1.6	−2.7	1.5	2.7	0.9	1.4	1.6

Table 4 *(concluded)*

	Ten-Year Averages[1]		1994	1995	1996	1997	1998	1999	2000	2001	2002	2003
	1984–93	1994–2003										
Growth in real per capita GDP												
Advanced economies	**2.5**	**2.2**	**2.7**	**2.1**	**2.4**	**2.8**	**2.1**	**2.8**	**2.8**	**0.7**	**1.2**	**2.6**
Major advanced economies	2.4	2.0	2.5	1.8	2.2	2.6	2.3	2.5	2.2	0.6	1.0	2.4
United States	2.3	2.3	3.1	1.7	2.6	3.5	3.3	3.3	0.9	0.2	1.4	2.5
Japan	3.3	0.7	0.8	1.2	3.3	1.6	−1.3	0.5	2.1	−0.6	−1.1	0.7
Germany	2.2	1.6	2.1	1.4	0.5	1.2	2.0	1.8	3.1	0.6	0.9	2.8
France	1.6	2.0	1.4	1.4	0.7	1.5	3.1	2.6	3.9	1.7	1.1	2.6
Italy	2.2	2.0	1.9	2.7	1.0	1.8	1.8	1.6	2.9	1.8	1.5	3.0
United Kingdom	2.1	2.6	4.3	2.5	2.3	3.1	2.6	1.7	3.0	2.0	1.8	2.6
Canada	1.3	2.5	3.5	1.7	0.5	3.2	3.1	4.3	3.6	0.6	1.7	2.8
Other advanced economies	3.2	3.1	3.8	3.5	3.0	3.6	1.5	4.3	4.9	1.1	2.0	3.2
Memorandum												
European Union	2.1	2.3	2.5	2.1	1.4	2.3	2.7	2.4	3.6	1.6	1.4	2.8
Euro area	2.1	2.1	2.0	2.0	1.2	2.1	2.7	2.5	3.5	1.4	1.3	2.9
Newly industrialized Asian economies	6.9	4.0	6.6	6.2	5.0	4.7	−3.5	7.0	7.5	−0.1	2.7	4.2

[1]Compound annual rate of change for employment and per capita GDP; arithmetic average for unemployment rate.
[2]The projections for unemployment have been adjusted to reflect the new survey techniques adopted by the U.S. Bureau of Labor Statistics in January 1994.
[3]New series starting in 1993, reflecting revisions in the labor force surveys and the definition of unemployment to bring data in line with those of other advanced economies.

Table 5. Developing Countries: Real GDP
(Annual percent change)

| | Ten-Year Averages | | 1994 | 1995 | 1996 | 1997 | 1998 | 1999 | 2000 | 2001 | 2002 | 2003 |
	1984–93	1994–2003										
Developing countries	**5.1**	**5.2**	**6.7**	**6.1**	**6.5**	**5.8**	**3.5**	**3.9**	**5.7**	**4.0**	**4.3**	**5.5**
Regional groups												
Africa	2.0	3.4	2.3	3.0	5.6	3.1	3.4	2.6	3.0	3.7	3.4	4.2
Sub-Sahara	1.9	3.4	1.8	3.8	5.1	3.7	2.7	2.7	3.1	3.4	3.5	4.2
Excluding Nigeria and South Africa	1.8	3.9	1.4	4.4	5.2	4.5	3.9	3.3	2.8	3.9	5.0	5.0
Developing Asia	7.6	6.8	9.6	9.0	8.3	6.6	4.0	6.1	6.7	5.6	5.9	6.4
China	10.5	8.6	12.6	10.5	9.6	8.8	7.8	7.1	8.0	7.3	7.0	7.4
India	5.2	6.0	6.8	7.6	7.5	5.0	5.8	6.7	5.4	4.3	5.5	5.8
Other developing Asia	5.5	3.9	7.0	7.7	6.7	3.8	–5.1	3.7	5.0	3.0	3.7	4.5
Middle East and Turkey	3.4	3.5	0.5	4.2	4.8	5.6	3.9	1.0	5.8	2.1	3.3	4.5
Western Hemisphere	2.9	2.7	5.0	1.8	3.6	5.2	2.3	0.2	4.0	0.7	0.7	3.7
Analytical groups												
By source of export earnings												
Fuel	2.5	3.2	0.4	3.1	3.6	4.7	3.2	1.2	4.8	4.5	2.7	4.0
Nonfuel	5.4	5.4	7.4	6.5	6.8	5.9	3.6	4.2	5.8	4.0	4.5	5.6
of which, primary products	3.1	4.4	5.2	6.6	5.5	5.4	3.0	2.4	3.6	2.7	3.8	5.4
By external financing source												
Net debtor countries	5.1	5.3	6.9	6.3	6.7	5.9	3.6	4.0	5.7	4.0	4.4	5.5
of which, official financing	2.4	4.2	2.4	5.4	5.3	4.2	3.9	3.7	3.7	4.3	4.3	5.0
Net debtor countries by debt-servicing experience												
Countries with arrears and/or rescheduling during 1994–98	3.0	3.7	4.7	5.2	5.0	4.4	–0.4	2.2	4.4	3.4	3.7	4.4
Other groups												
Heavily indebted poor countries	2.2	4.6	2.8	5.8	5.8	5.3	4.0	4.0	3.8	4.1	5.1	5.4
Middle East and north Africa	2.7	3.9	2.6	2.7	4.8	4.2	4.5	2.9	5.0	4.6	3.2	4.5
Memorandum												
Real per capita GDP												
Developing countries	3.0	3.5	4.9	4.5	4.8	4.2	1.8	2.2	4.0	2.4	2.7	3.9
Regional groups												
Africa	–0.9	0.8	–0.3	0.9	2.8	0.3	0.7	–0.1	0.2	1.0	0.7	1.6
Developing Asia	5.8	5.4	8.1	7.4	6.8	5.2	2.5	4.8	5.3	4.3	4.6	5.1
Middle East and Turkey	0.6	1.3	–2.5	2.3	2.4	3.6	1.7	–1.4	3.3	—	1.2	2.5
Western Hemisphere	0.9	1.1	3.3	0.3	1.8	3.7	0.6	–1.8	2.8	–0.8	–0.8	2.3

Table 6. Developing Countries—by Country: Real GDP[1]

(Annual percent change)

	Average 1984–93	1994	1995	1996	1997	1998	1999	2000	2001
Africa	**2.0**	**2.3**	**3.0**	**5.6**	**3.1**	**3.4**	**2.6**	**3.0**	**3.7**
Algeria	1.2	−0.9	3.8	3.8	1.1	5.1	3.2	2.4	3.5
Angola	0.2	−0.5	10.4	11.2	7.9	6.8	3.3	3.0	3.2
Benin	2.1	4.4	4.6	5.5	5.7	5.0	4.7	5.8	5.8
Botswana	8.6	3.5	4.5	5.7	6.7	5.9	6.1	8.7	7.1
Burkina Faso	3.7	1.2	4.0	6.0	4.8	6.2	6.2	2.2	5.7
Burundi	2.9	−3.7	−7.3	−8.4	0.4	4.5	−0.8	−2.3	3.3
Cameroon	−0.7	−2.5	3.3	5.0	5.1	5.0	4.4	4.2	5.3
Cape Verde	4.3	6.9	7.5	6.7	7.6	7.4	8.6	6.8	3.0
Central African Republic	1.4	2.6	7.6	−4.9	3.9	5.5	3.5	2.6	1.6
Chad	4.6	5.5	0.4	3.1	4.2	7.7	2.3	1.0	8.9
Comoros	1.2	−5.4	8.9	−1.3	4.2	1.2	1.9	−1.1	1.9
Congo, Dem. Rep. of	−2.9	−3.9	0.7	−1.3	−5.6	−1.6	−10.4	−7.0	−4.0
Congo, Rep. of	5.5	−5.5	4.0	4.3	−0.6	3.7	−3.0	7.9	3.3
Côte d'Ivoire	0.8	2.0	7.1	7.7	5.7	4.8	1.6	−2.3	−0.9
Djibouti	−0.7	−0.9	−3.5	−4.1	−0.7	0.1	2.2	0.7	2.0
Equatorial Guinea	2.5	5.1	14.3	29.1	71.2	22.0	50.1	16.9	46.5
Eritrea	...	9.8	2.9	6.8	13.3	3.2	1.2	−8.6	6.4
Ethiopia	0.3	1.6	6.2	10.6	5.2	−1.2	6.3	5.4	7.9
Gabon	2.1	3.7	5.0	3.6	5.7	3.5	−9.6	−1.9	1.5
Gambia, The	2.5	3.8	−3.4	6.1	4.9	3.5	6.4	5.6	5.8
Ghana	4.6	3.3	4.0	4.6	4.2	4.7	4.4	3.7	4.0
Guinea	3.8	4.0	4.7	5.1	4.8	4.6	3.6	2.0	2.9
Guinea-Bissau	3.2	3.2	4.4	4.6	5.5	−28.1	7.8	7.5	4.0
Kenya	3.3	2.7	4.4	4.2	2.1	1.6	1.3	−0.2	1.1
Lesotho	5.6	3.7	5.9	9.5	4.8	−3.0	2.4	3.2	2.9
Liberia	...	...	...	...	...	...	...	...	...
Madagascar	1.3	—	1.7	2.1	3.7	3.9	4.7	4.8	6.7
Malawi	3.2	−10.3	16.7	7.3	3.8	3.3	4.0	1.7	2.8
Mali	2.4	2.6	7.0	4.3	6.7	4.9	6.7	4.6	0.1
Mauritania	4.8	4.6	4.6	5.5	3.2	3.7	4.1	5.0	4.6
Mauritius	6.3	4.5	3.8	5.2	5.8	5.9	5.9	3.6	6.7
Morocco	3.4	10.4	−6.6	12.2	−2.2	6.8	−0.7	2.4	6.3
Mozambique, Rep. of	2.6	7.5	4.3	7.1	11.0	12.6	7.5	1.6	12.9
Namibia	2.6	7.3	4.1	3.2	4.2	3.3	3.4	3.3	2.7
Niger	−0.1	4.0	2.6	3.4	2.8	10.4	−0.6	−1.4	5.1
Nigeria	4.6	−0.6	2.6	6.4	3.1	1.9	1.1	3.8	4.0
Rwanda	1.0	−50.2	35.2	12.7	13.8	9.0	7.4	6.0	6.2
São Tomé and Príncipe	—	2.2	2.0	1.5	1.0	2.5	2.5	3.0	4.0
Senegal	1.2	2.9	5.2	5.1	5.0	5.7	5.1	5.6	5.7
Seychelles	5.9	−0.8	−0.6	4.7	4.3	2.3	−3.0	1.2	−1.0
Sierra Leone	−1.3	3.5	−10.0	−24.8	−17.6	−0.8	−8.1	3.8	5.4
Somalia	...	...	...	...	...	...	...	...	...
South Africa	1.0	3.2	3.1	4.3	2.6	0.8	2.1	3.4	2.2
Sudan	2.5	2.0	3.0	4.9	10.0	6.0	7.7	9.7	5.3
Swaziland	6.8	3.4	3.8	3.9	3.8	3.2	3.5	2.2	1.6
Tanzania	3.7	1.6	3.6	4.5	3.5	3.7	3.5	5.1	5.1
Togo	—	17.5	6.9	9.7	4.3	−2.1	2.9	−1.9	2.7
Tunisia	4.0	3.2	2.4	7.1	5.4	4.8	6.1	4.7	5.0
Uganda	3.8	6.4	11.9	8.6	5.1	4.7	8.1	4.0	4.9
Zambia	0.9	−13.3	−2.5	6.5	3.4	−1.9	2.2	3.6	5.0
Zimbabwe	2.8	5.8	0.2	10.4	2.7	2.9	−0.7	−5.1	−8.4

Table 6 *(continued)*

	Average 1984–93	1994	1995	1996	1997	1998	1999	2000	2001
Developing Asia	**7.6**	**9.6**	**9.0**	**8.3**	**6.6**	**4.0**	**6.1**	**6.7**	**5.6**
Afghanistan, Islamic State of	...	...	...	...	...	...	...	...	...
Bangladesh	4.4	4.5	4.8	5.0	5.3	5.0	5.4	5.5	4.5
Bhutan	6.4	6.4	7.4	6.1	7.3	5.5	5.9	6.1	5.9
Brunei Darussalam	...	1.8	3.1	1.0	3.6	−4.0	2.5	3.0	2.7
Cambodia	...	6.3	8.4	3.5	3.7	1.5	6.9	5.4	5.3
China	10.5	12.6	10.5	9.6	8.8	7.8	7.1	8.0	7.3
Fiji	3.1	5.1	2.5	3.1	−0.9	1.4	9.7	−2.8	—
India	5.2	6.8	7.6	7.5	5.0	5.8	6.7	5.4	4.3
Indonesia	6.7	7.5	8.2	8.0	4.5	−13.1	0.8	4.8	3.3
Kiribati	0.4	7.9	5.9	4.1	1.6	6.6	2.1	−1.7	1.5
Lao P.D. Republic	5.0	8.1	7.1	6.9	6.5	4.0	5.0	5.8	5.2
Malaysia	6.9	9.2	9.8	10.0	7.3	−7.4	6.1	8.3	0.4
Maldives	10.2	6.6	7.2	8.8	11.2	7.9	8.5	5.6	4.9
Myanmar	1.1	6.8	7.2	6.4	5.7	5.8	10.9	5.5	4.8
Nepal	5.3	8.2	3.5	5.3	5.0	3.0	4.4	6.5	5.3
Pakistan	5.5	4.4	4.9	2.9	1.8	3.1	4.1	3.9	3.4
Papua New Guinea	4.9	5.9	−3.3	7.7	−4.9	−2.8	7.6	−0.8	−3.4
Philippines	1.0	4.4	4.7	5.8	5.2	−0.6	3.4	4.0	3.4
Samoa	14.4	−0.1	6.2	7.3	0.8	2.5	3.5	6.8	5.0
Solomon Islands	3.5	9.2	10.5	3.5	−2.3	1.1	−1.3	−14.0	−3.0
Sri Lanka	4.3	5.6	5.5	3.8	6.4	4.7	4.3	6.0	0.4
Thailand	8.7	9.0	9.2	5.9	−1.4	−10.5	4.4	4.6	1.8
Tonga	2.0	5.0	3.2	−0.2	−0.1	1.6	3.1	6.2	3.0
Vanuatu	3.0	1.3	2.3	0.4	0.6	6.0	−2.5	2.5	4.0
Vietnam	6.0	8.8	9.5	9.3	8.2	3.5	4.2	5.5	4.7
Middle East and Turkey	**3.4**	**0.5**	**4.2**	**4.8**	**5.6**	**3.9**	**1.0**	**5.8**	**2.1**
Bahrain	4.1	−0.2	3.9	4.1	3.1	4.8	4.3	5.3	3.3
Egypt	3.9	3.9	4.7	5.0	5.3	5.7	6.0	5.1	3.3
Iran, Islamic Republic of	1.7	1.6	3.2	5.9	2.7	3.8	2.6	4.9	5.1
Iraq	...	...	...	...	...	...	...	...	...
Jordan	3.2	5.0	6.2	2.1	3.3	3.0	3.1	4.0	4.2
Kuwait	1.5	1.7	9.6	1.5	2.3	3.7	−1.7	1.7	2.7
Lebanon	0.8	8.0	6.5	4.0	4.0	3.0	1.0	—	1.3
Libya	−0.5	−1.3	−0.3	3.3	5.2	−3.6	0.7	4.4	0.6
Malta	4.9	5.7	6.2	4.0	4.9	3.4	4.1	5.4	0.4
Oman	6.3	3.8	4.8	2.9	6.2	2.7	−1.0	4.9	6.5
Qatar	0.7	2.3	2.9	4.8	25.4	6.2	5.3	11.6	7.2
Saudi Arabia	2.6	0.5	0.5	1.4	2.0	1.7	−0.8	4.5	2.2
Syrian Arab Republic	3.1	7.7	5.8	4.4	1.8	7.6	−2.0	2.5	3.5
Turkey	5.4	−5.0	6.9	6.9	7.6	3.1	−4.7	7.4	−6.2
United Arab Emirates	2.0	8.5	7.9	6.2	6.7	4.3	3.9	5.0	5.0
Yemen, Republic of	...	−0.5	8.6	5.9	8.1	4.9	3.7	5.1	3.3

Table 6 *(concluded)*

	Average 1984–93	1994	1995	1996	1997	1998	1999	2000	2001
Western Hemisphere	**2.9**	**5.0**	**1.8**	**3.6**	**5.2**	**2.3**	**0.2**	**4.0**	**0.7**
Antigua and Barbuda	6.4	6.2	−5.0	6.1	5.6	3.9	3.2	2.5	−0.6
Argentina	2.0	5.8	−2.8	5.5	8.1	3.8	−3.4	−0.8	−3.7
Bahamas, The	1.5	0.9	0.3	4.2	3.3	3.0	5.9	5.0	−1.0
Barbados	0.7	4.0	3.1	1.7	6.4	4.1	1.3	3.1	−2.1
Belize	6.7	1.8	3.3	1.5	3.7	2.6	3.7	9.7	2.5
Bolivia	2.1	4.7	4.7	4.4	5.0	5.2	0.4	2.4	1.0
Brazil	2.8	5.9	4.2	2.6	3.3	0.2	0.8	4.4	1.5
Chile	7.0	5.7	10.8	7.4	6.6	3.2	−1.0	4.4	2.8
Colombia	4.1	5.8	5.2	2.1	3.4	0.6	−4.1	2.8	1.5
Costa Rica	4.8	4.7	3.9	0.9	5.6	8.4	8.4	1.7	0.4
Dominica	4.1	2.1	1.6	3.1	2.0	2.4	0.9	0.5	1.0
Dominican Republic	2.5	4.3	4.7	7.2	8.3	7.3	8.0	7.8	3.0
Ecuador	2.9	4.4	2.3	2.0	3.4	0.4	−7.3	2.3	5.2
El Salvador	3.3	6.0	6.4	1.8	4.3	3.2	3.4	2.0	2.0
Grenada	3.2	3.3	3.1	3.1	4.0	7.3	7.5	6.4	3.5
Guatemala	2.7	4.0	4.9	3.0	4.1	5.1	3.8	3.6	1.8
Guyana	1.7	8.5	5.0	7.9	6.2	−1.7	3.0	−0.7	0.8
Haiti	−1.0	−11.9	9.9	4.1	2.7	2.2	2.7	0.9	−1.7
Honduras	3.9	−1.3	4.1	3.6	5.1	2.9	−1.9	5.0	2.5
Jamaica	2.4	1.0	0.2	−1.5	−1.5	−0.4	−0.1	1.1	3.0
Mexico	2.4	4.4	−6.2	5.2	6.8	5.0	3.6	6.6	−0.3
Netherlands Antilles	1.2	5.9	0.6	2.3	1.4	−2.1	−1.9	−2.3	—
Nicaragua	−2.2	3.3	4.2	4.7	5.1	4.1	7.4	4.3	3.0
Panama	2.7	2.9	1.8	2.4	4.4	4.0	4.1	2.3	2.0
Paraguay	3.5	3.1	4.7	1.3	2.6	−0.4	0.5	−0.4	0.8
Peru	0.7	12.8	8.6	2.5	6.7	−0.5	0.9	3.1	0.2
St. Kitts and Nevis	5.8	5.1	3.5	5.9	7.3	1.0	3.7	7.5	1.8
St. Lucia	6.8	2.1	4.1	1.4	0.6	3.1	3.5	0.7	0.5
St. Vincent and the Grenadines	5.7	−2.0	6.8	1.4	3.9	5.9	4.3	1.8	0.3
Suriname	−0.3	−5.4	7.1	6.7	5.6	1.9	5.0	2.9	3.4
Trinidad and Tobago	−2.2	3.6	4.0	3.8	3.1	4.8	6.8	4.8	4.5
Uruguay	3.4	7.3	−1.4	5.6	5.0	4.5	−2.8	−1.3	−3.1
Venezuela	3.0	−2.3	4.0	−0.2	6.4	0.2	−6.1	3.2	2.7

[1]For many countries, figures for recent years are IMF staff estimates. Data for some countries are for fiscal years.

Table 7. Countries in Transition: Real GDP[1]
(Annual percent change)

	Average 1984–93	1994	1995	1996	1997	1998	1999	2000	2001
Central and eastern Europe	...	**3.0**	**5.6**	**4.0**	**2.6**	**2.3**	**2.2**	**3.8**	**3.1**
Albania	−2.8	9.4	−0.9	19.8	−7.0	8.0	7.3	7.8	7.0
Bosnia and Herzegovina	...	...	32.4	85.8	39.9	10.0	10.0	5.9	5.6
Bulgaria	−2.4	−7.8	4.3	−10.9	−7.0	3.5	2.4	5.8	4.5
Croatia	...	5.9	6.8	6.0	6.6	2.5	−0.4	3.7	4.2
Czech Republic	...	2.2	5.9	4.3	−0.8	−1.2	−0.4	2.9	3.6
Estonia	...	−1.8	4.6	4.0	10.4	5.0	−0.7	6.9	5.0
Hungary	−1.1	2.9	1.5	1.3	4.6	4.9	4.5	5.2	3.8
Latvia	...	0.6	−0.8	3.3	8.6	3.9	1.1	6.6	7.0
Lithuania	...	−9.8	3.3	4.7	7.3	5.1	−3.9	3.9	4.5
Macedonia, former Yugoslav Rep. of	...	−1.8	−1.1	1.2	2.0	3.4	4.3	4.6	−4.6
Poland	0.8	5.2	6.8	6.0	6.8	4.8	4.1	4.1	1.1
Romania	−2.2	3.9	7.3	3.9	−6.1	−4.8	−1.2	1.8	5.3
Slovak Republic	...	4.9	6.7	6.2	6.2	4.1	1.9	2.2	3.3
Slovenia	...	5.3	4.1	3.5	4.6	3.8	5.2	4.6	3.0
Commonwealth of Independent States and Mongolia	...	**−14.5**	**−5.5**	**−3.3**	**1.1**	**−2.8**	**4.6**	**8.3**	**6.2**
Russia	...	−13.5	−4.2	−3.4	0.9	−4.9	5.4	9.0	5.0
Excluding Russia	...	−16.6	−8.6	−3.1	1.5	1.7	2.8	7.0	8.8
Armenia	...	5.4	6.9	5.9	3.3	7.3	3.3	6.0	7.5
Azerbaijan	...	−19.7	−11.8	1.3	5.8	10.0	7.4	11.1	9.0
Belarus	...	−9.0	−10.4	2.8	11.4	8.3	3.4	5.8	4.1
Georgia	...	−10.4	2.6	10.5	10.6	2.9	3.0	1.9	4.5
Kazakhstan	...	−12.6	−8.3	0.5	1.6	−1.9	2.7	9.8	13.2
Kyrgyz Republic	...	−19.8	−5.8	7.1	10.0	2.1	3.7	5.0	5.0
Moldova	...	−31.1	−1.4	−5.9	1.6	−6.5	−3.4	2.1	4.0
Mongolia	0.8	2.3	6.3	2.4	4.0	3.5	3.2	1.1	1.1
Tajikistan	...	−21.4	−12.5	−4.4	1.7	5.3	3.7	8.3	10.0
Turkmenistan	...	−17.3	−7.2	−6.7	−11.3	7.0	...	...	...
Ukraine	...	−22.9	−12.2	−10.0	−3.0	−1.9	−0.2	5.9	9.1
Uzbekistan	...	−4.2	−0.9	1.6	2.5	4.3	4.3	3.8	4.5
Memorandum									
EU accession candidates	...	0.6	6.0	4.7	4.1	2.5	0.1	4.9	0.4

[1]Data for some countries refer to real net material product (NMP) or are estimates based on NMP. For many countries, figures for recent years are IMF staff estimates. The figures should be interpreted only as indicative of broad orders of magnitude because reliable, comparable data are not generally available. In particular, the growth of output of new private enterprises of the informal economy is not fully reflected in the recent figures.

Table 8. Summary of Inflation

(Percent)

	Ten-Year Averages		1994	1995	1996	1997	1998	1999	2000	2001	2002	2003
	1984–93	1994–2003										
GDP deflators												
Advanced economies	**4.1**	**1.6**	**2.2**	**2.3**	**1.9**	**1.7**	**1.4**	**0.8**	**1.4**	**1.6**	**1.5**	**1.6**
United States	3.2	1.9	2.1	2.2	1.9	1.9	1.2	1.4	2.3	2.2	1.7	2.2
European Union	5.1	2.2	2.7	3.1	2.6	1.9	2.0	1.4	1.5	2.3	2.4	1.9
Japan	1.7	−0.8	0.1	−0.3	−0.8	0.3	−0.1	−1.4	−1.9	−1.5	−1.4	−1.1
Other advanced economies	7.1	1.9	3.3	3.4	3.0	2.2	1.5	−0.1	1.7	1.5	1.1	1.7
Consumer prices												
Advanced economies	**4.1**	**2.0**	**2.6**	**2.6**	**2.4**	**2.1**	**1.5**	**1.4**	**2.3**	**2.2**	**1.3**	**1.8**
United States	3.8	2.4	2.6	2.8	2.9	2.3	1.5	2.2	3.4	2.8	1.4	2.4
European Union	4.4	2.2	3.0	2.9	2.5	1.8	1.5	1.4	2.3	2.6	2.0	1.8
Japan	1.7	−0.1	0.7	−0.1	—	1.7	0.6	−0.3	−0.8	−0.7	−1.1	−0.5
Other advanced economies	7.1	2.4	3.3	3.8	3.2	2.4	2.6	1.0	2.2	2.4	1.4	1.9
Developing countries	**48.5**	**13.6**	**55.3**	**23.2**	**15.4**	**10.0**	**10.6**	**6.9**	**6.1**	**5.7**	**5.8**	**5.1**
Regional groups												
Africa	24.3	19.2	54.7	35.3	30.2	14.6	10.9	12.3	14.2	12.6	9.3	6.1
Developing Asia	10.3	6.1	16.0	13.2	8.3	4.8	7.7	2.5	1.9	2.6	2.5	3.0
Middle East and Turkey	24.3	25.0	37.3	39.1	29.6	28.3	28.1	23.7	19.6	17.2	17.5	12.3
Western Hemisphere	184.3	24.5	200.3	36.0	21.2	12.9	9.8	8.9	8.1	6.4	8.2	7.4
Analytical groups												
By source of export earnings												
Fuel	17.0	21.4	36.2	42.6	35.1	20.1	18.0	17.2	13.8	12.0	13.3	10.7
Nonfuel	53.7	12.8	57.7	21.3	13.5	9.0	9.8	5.9	5.3	5.1	5.0	4.5
of which, primary products	75.5	19.1	63.0	29.8	27.0	16.0	13.9	12.7	13.5	11.7	7.3	5.7
By external financing source												
Net debtor countries	50.6	14.0	57.5	23.9	15.8	10.2	10.9	7.1	6.3	5.9	5.9	5.2
of which, official financing	38.9	16.8	64.2	30.2	22.6	11.4	10.7	11.2	10.5	8.2	5.3	4.4
Net debtor countries by debt-servicing experience												
Countries with arrears and/or rescheduling during 1994–98	125.2	28.2	221.6	40.1	21.1	12.2	18.6	13.8	11.4	11.3	9.6	7.0
Countries in transition	**73.1**	**46.0**	**252.5**	**133.8**	**42.5**	**27.3**	**21.8**	**44.1**	**20.2**	**15.9**	**10.8**	**8.7**
Central and eastern Europe	...	19.1	45.6	24.7	23.2	41.7	17.2	11.0	12.8	9.6	6.7	5.6
Commonwealth of Independent States and Mongolia	...	63.7	455.5	235.6	55.9	19.1	25.0	70.5	25.0	19.8	13.4	10.5
Russia	...	56.8	307.5	198.0	47.9	14.7	27.8	85.7	20.8	20.7	14.1	10.8
Excluding Russia	...	79.9	978.9	338.8	75.5	29.7	19.3	41.7	34.7	17.9	11.8	10.0
Memorandum												
Median inflation rate												
Advanced economies	4.2	2.1	2.4	2.5	2.2	1.8	1.7	1.5	2.7	2.6	1.8	2.1
Developing countries	9.4	6.0	10.7	10.0	7.3	6.2	5.8	4.0	4.2	4.4	4.0	3.9
Countries in transition	133.5	25.6	131.6	40.1	24.1	14.8	10.0	8.0	10.0	7.4	5.0	5.0

Table 9. Advanced Economies: GDP Deflators and Consumer Prices
(Annual percent change)

	Ten-Year Averages		1994	1995	1996	1997	1998	1999	2000	2001	2002	2003	Fourth Quarter[1]		
	1984–93	1994–2003											2001	2002	2003
GDP deflators															
Advanced economies	**4.1**	**1.6**	**2.2**	**2.3**	**1.9**	**1.7**	**1.4**	**0.8**	**1.4**	**1.6**	**1.5**	**1.6**	...	...	...
Major advanced economies	3.4	1.4	1.8	1.9	1.6	1.5	1.1	0.9	1.2	1.4	1.3	1.5	1.4	1.5	1.6
United States	3.2	1.9	2.1	2.2	1.9	1.9	1.2	1.4	2.3	2.2	1.7	2.2	1.9	2.1	2.2
Japan	1.7	–0.8	0.1	–0.3	–0.8	0.3	–0.1	–1.4	–1.9	–1.5	–1.4	–1.1	–1.1	–1.7	–0.8
Germany	2.9	1.2	2.5	2.0	1.0	0.7	1.1	0.5	–0.4	1.3	1.7	1.2	2.0	1.5	1.2
France	3.7	1.2	1.8	1.7	1.4	1.2	0.9	0.3	0.8	1.6	1.4	1.3	1.6	1.4	1.4
Italy	7.2	2.9	3.5	5.0	5.3	2.4	2.7	1.7	2.1	2.6	2.4	1.6	3.3	2.3	1.3
United Kingdom	5.3	2.7	1.4	2.6	3.3	2.9	2.9	2.6	1.7	2.4	4.0	3.1	2.7	3.5	3.4
Canada	3.2	1.4	1.2	2.3	1.7	1.1	–0.4	1.4	3.7	1.2	–0.2	1.8	–0.9	1.7	1.9
Other advanced economies	7.3	2.5	3.8	3.9	3.0	2.5	2.3	0.8	2.0	2.4	2.1	1.9	...	...	...
Spain	7.4	3.3	3.9	4.9	3.5	2.3	2.4	2.9	3.4	3.9	2.8	2.5	3.5	2.5	2.5
Netherlands	1.4	2.5	2.3	1.8	1.2	2.0	1.7	1.7	3.7	4.7	3.4	2.4	4.2	3.0	2.1
Belgium	3.4	1.4	1.8	1.8	1.2	1.3	1.6	1.2	1.3	1.1	1.0	1.1	...	...	...
Sweden	5.7	1.8	2.4	3.5	1.4	1.7	0.9	0.2	1.5	2.0	2.0	2.1	2.8	1.8	1.8
Austria	3.1	1.5	2.7	2.5	1.3	0.9	0.5	0.7	1.2	1.8	1.8	1.2	...	...	...
Denmark	3.8	2.2	1.7	1.8	2.5	2.2	1.0	2.7	3.7	2.7	2.2	2.2	2.3	1.4	1.8
Finland	4.7	1.9	2.0	4.1	–0.2	2.1	3.0	–0.1	3.4	1.1	1.8	1.7	...	...	...
Greece	16.9	5.7	11.2	11.2	7.4	6.8	5.2	3.0	3.4	3.2	3.0	2.6	...	...	...
Portugal	14.0	4.1	6.1	7.4	3.8	3.1	4.3	3.4	2.8	4.4	3.0	2.4	...	...	...
Ireland	3.8	3.5	1.7	3.0	2.2	4.1	5.9	4.2	4.3	3.5	3.3	2.9	...	...	...
Luxembourg	2.6	2.7	4.9	4.3	1.8	2.8	2.6	2.5	3.7	0.9	1.8	2.0	...	...	...
Switzerland	3.3	0.8	1.6	1.2	0.3	–0.2	—	0.6	1.0	1.7	0.8	1.1	1.1	0.9	1.3
Norway	3.6	3.4	–0.2	3.1	4.3	3.0	–0.7	6.3	16.3	1.9	–0.1	1.3	...	...	...
Israel	55.5	6.4	11.8	10.1	10.8	9.0	7.0	6.5	2.0	1.8	3.2	2.1	...	...	...
Iceland	17.2	3.9	1.9	2.7	2.0	3.7	4.5	3.8	2.8	6.9	6.3	4.1	...	...	...
Cyprus	5.0	2.7	5.1	3.6	1.9	2.5	2.3	2.1	4.1	2.0	1.8	2.2	...	...	...
Korea	7.0	2.9	7.7	7.1	3.9	3.1	5.1	–2.0	–1.1	1.3	2.5	1.4	...	...	...
Australia	4.8	1.9	1.1	1.6	2.4	1.5	0.4	0.6	4.3	3.2	1.3	2.2	2.2	1.7	2.2
Taiwan Province of China	2.4	1.4	2.0	2.0	3.1	1.7	2.6	–1.4	–1.7	0.7	2.6	2.5	0.6	3.0	3.0
Hong Kong SAR	8.5	0.6	6.9	2.6	5.9	5.8	0.4	–5.4	–6.5	–0.5	–2.1	–0.1	0.5	–2.5	1.3
Singapore	2.1	0.7	2.9	2.2	1.2	0.8	–1.8	–4.8	3.5	1.0	1.1	1.6	–1.3	2.7	0.9
New Zealand	6.7	1.6	1.4	2.1	1.9	0.9	1.0	–0.2	2.3	4.1	0.8	1.8	3.6	0.9	1.6
Memorandum															
European Union	5.1	2.2	2.7	3.1	2.6	1.9	2.0	1.4	1.5	2.3	2.4	1.9	...	...	...
Euro area	4.6	1.7	2.0	2.4	2.9	–0.1	1.2	1.8	1.3	2.3	2.0	1.6	2.5	1.9	1.6
Newly industrialized Asian economies	5.5	2.0	5.5	4.7	3.7	2.9	3.2	–2.4	–1.6	0.9	1.9	1.6	...	...	...
Consumer prices															
Advanced economies	**4.1**	**2.0**	**2.6**	**2.6**	**2.4**	**2.1**	**1.5**	**1.4**	**2.3**	**2.2**	**1.3**	**1.8**	...	...	...
Major advanced economies	3.6	1.9	2.2	2.2	2.2	2.0	1.3	1.4	2.3	2.1	1.1	1.7	1.4	1.5	1.8
United States	3.8	2.4	2.6	2.8	2.9	2.3	1.5	2.2	3.4	2.8	1.4	2.4	1.9	2.0	2.5
Japan	1.7	–0.1	0.7	–0.1	—	1.7	0.6	–0.3	–0.8	–0.7	–1.1	–0.5	–1.0	–0.7	–0.4
Germany[2]	2.4	1.6	2.7	1.7	1.2	1.5	0.6	0.7	2.1	2.4	1.5	1.2	1.7	1.5	1.1
France[2]	3.6	1.5	1.7	1.8	2.1	1.3	0.7	0.6	1.8	1.8	1.5	1.4	1.5	1.5	1.5
Italy[2]	6.4	2.8	4.1	5.2	4.1	1.9	2.0	1.7	2.6	2.7	2.2	1.6	2.3	2.0	1.5
United Kingdom[3]	5.0	2.5	2.4	2.8	3.0	2.8	2.7	2.3	2.1	2.1	2.4	2.5	2.0	2.3	2.8
Canada	3.9	1.6	0.2	1.9	1.6	1.6	1.0	1.8	2.7	2.5	0.9	1.8	1.1	1.5	2.0
Other advanced economies	6.5	2.6	4.1	3.8	3.2	2.3	2.4	1.3	2.4	2.9	2.0	2.1	...	...	...
Memorandum															
European Union[2]	4.4	2.2	3.0	2.9	2.5	1.8	1.5	1.4	2.3	2.6	2.0	1.8	...	...	...
Euro area[2]	4.2	2.0	3.0	2.7	2.3	1.6	1.2	1.1	2.4	2.6	1.9	1.6	2.2	1.8	1.6
Newly industrialized Asian economies	4.2	2.9	5.7	4.6	4.3	3.4	4.4	—	1.1	1.9	1.3	1.9	...	...	...

[1]From fourth quarter of preceding year.
[2]Based on Eurostat's harmonized index of consumer prices.
[3]Retail price index excluding mortgage interest.

Table 10. Advanced Economies: Hourly Earnings, Productivity, and Unit Labor Costs in Manufacturing
(Annual percent change)

| | Ten-Year Averages | | 1994 | 1995 | 1996 | 1997 | 1998 | 1999 | 2000 | 2001 | 2002 | 2003 |
	1984–93	1994–2003										
Hourly earnings												
Advanced economies	**5.8**	**3.3**	**3.3**	**3.2**	**3.1**	**2.6**	**3.2**	**3.3**	**4.5**	**4.6**	**2.5**	**3.2**
Major advanced economies	4.9	3.1	2.7	2.7	2.4	2.2	3.3	2.9	4.5	4.9	2.2	3.0
United States	4.1	3.9	2.8	2.1	1.3	1.9	5.4	4.0	7.0	7.3	3.4	3.9
Japan	3.9	0.6	2.1	2.2	1.8	3.0	0.9	−0.7	−0.1	1.0	−3.1	−0.7
Germany	5.5	3.0	2.4	4.1	4.7	1.5	2.1	2.8	2.7	3.3	3.0	3.0
France	5.1	2.2	1.7	2.4	2.3	−1.6	0.8	3.7	2.9	3.4	3.2	3.0
Italy	8.5	2.9	3.1	4.7	5.8	4.2	−1.4	2.9	2.7	2.3	2.4	2.6
United Kingdom	8.0	4.3	5.0	4.4	4.3	4.2	4.5	4.0	4.6	4.3	3.4	4.1
Canada	4.5	2.4	1.6	2.2	1.0	2.2	2.1	1.3	3.5	2.9	2.9	4.9
Other advanced economies	9.8	4.5	5.8	5.2	6.1	4.4	2.9	4.9	4.6	3.4	3.8	3.9
Memorandum												
European Union	6.8	3.3	3.4	4.1	4.3	2.6	2.1	3.3	3.4	3.7	3.3	3.2
Euro area	7.4	3.3	3.2	4.1	4.4	2.2	1.7	3.2	3.1	3.8	3.6	3.3
Newly industrialized Asian economies	13.4	6.1	11.4	7.9	10.2	5.6	0.8	9.4	7.0	1.0	3.7	5.0
Productivity												
Advanced economies	**3.1**	**3.2**	**4.8**	**3.8**	**3.2**	**4.4**	**2.4**	**4.1**	**5.6**	**0.7**	**1.2**	**2.3**
Major advanced economies	3.0	3.2	4.3	3.8	3.2	4.3	2.6	3.8	5.8	0.6	1.0	2.2
United States	2.9	3.7	3.0	3.9	3.5	4.3	5.3	4.6	6.1	1.1	2.3	2.9
Japan	2.5	1.1	3.1	4.5	3.9	4.7	−4.2	3.5	6.7	−4.4	−5.0	−0.9
Germany	3.7	5.1	9.0	4.5	6.0	7.3	4.8	3.1	6.5	4.1	3.2	3.0
France	3.1	3.9	6.9	6.0	1.0	5.6	5.5	2.9	5.4	0.9	1.2	3.4
Italy	2.8	2.6	6.0	3.6	3.7	2.3	−1.5	2.0	4.5	1.8	2.0	1.9
United Kingdom	4.5	1.9	4.5	−0.5	−0.6	0.9	0.9	3.6	5.7	1.9	0.8	2.0
Canada	2.5	1.7	4.5	1.5	−1.1	2.8	—	1.6	1.2	1.0	2.5	2.9
Other advanced economies	3.3	3.6	6.6	4.0	3.1	4.7	1.5	5.5	4.4	1.3	2.1	2.6
Memorandum												
European Union	3.3	3.4	7.3	3.6	2.6	4.4	2.7	2.8	4.9	1.9	1.8	2.5
Euro area	4.2	4.0	8.0	4.8	3.6	5.4	3.4	2.8	4.9	2.3	2.4	3.0
Newly industrialized Asian economies	7.3	6.0	7.1	7.9	6.3	7.1	−1.6	14.9	9.4	2.2	3.1	4.3
Unit labor costs												
Advanced economies	**2.7**	**0.1**	**−1.4**	**−0.6**	**−0.1**	**−1.7**	**0.9**	**−0.7**	**−1.0**	**3.8**	**1.3**	**0.9**
Major advanced economies	1.9	−0.1	−1.5	−1.0	−0.8	−2.1	0.7	−0.8	−1.3	4.3	1.2	0.8
United States	1.2	0.2	−0.2	−1.7	−2.1	−2.3	0.1	−0.5	0.8	6.2	1.1	1.0
Japan	1.4	−0.5	−0.9	−2.2	−1.9	−1.6	5.3	−4.1	−6.4	5.7	2.1	0.2
Germany	1.7	−2.1	−6.1	−0.4	−1.2	−5.5	−2.6	−0.3	−3.6	−0.7	−0.2	—
France	1.9	−1.6	−4.8	−3.4	1.3	−6.8	−4.5	0.8	−2.3	2.5	2.0	−0.4
Italy	5.6	0.3	−2.7	1.0	2.0	1.9	0.2	0.9	−1.7	0.5	0.4	0.7
United Kingdom	3.3	2.4	0.5	4.9	5.0	3.3	3.6	0.4	−1.0	2.4	2.6	2.0
Canada	2.0	0.8	−2.8	0.7	2.1	−0.6	2.2	−0.3	2.2	1.9	0.5	1.9
Other advanced economies	6.1	0.9	−0.8	0.9	2.6	−0.4	1.6	−0.4	0.2	2.1	1.7	1.2
Memorandum												
European Union	3.4	−0.1	−3.6	0.6	1.8	−1.7	−0.5	0.5	−1.4	1.7	1.5	0.7
Euro area	3.1	−0.7	−4.4	−0.6	0.7	−3.0	−1.6	0.4	−1.7	1.5	1.2	0.3
Newly industrialized Asian economies	4.7	−0.1	2.6	−1.0	2.6	−1.5	2.7	−4.1	−2.3	−0.9	0.6	0.7

Table 11. Developing Countries: Consumer Prices
(Annual percent change)

| | Ten-Year Averages | | 1994 | 1995 | 1996 | 1997 | 1998 | 1999 | 2000 | 2001 | 2002 | 2003 |
	1984–93	1994–2003										
Developing countries	**48.5**	**13.6**	**55.3**	**23.2**	**15.4**	**10.0**	**10.6**	**6.9**	**6.1**	**5.7**	**5.8**	**5.1**
Regional groups												
Africa	24.3	19.2	54.7	35.3	30.2	14.6	10.9	12.3	14.2	12.6	9.3	6.1
Sub-Sahara	28.7	23.3	68.5	40.9	36.6	17.8	13.0	15.5	18.3	15.7	11.1	6.9
Excluding Nigeria and South Africa	38.6	34.0	121.6	57.5	58.8	25.5	17.2	23.4	28.5	20.9	12.0	7.0
Developing Asia	10.3	6.1	16.0	13.2	8.3	4.8	7.7	2.5	1.9	2.6	2.5	3.0
China	8.9	5.0	24.1	17.1	8.3	2.8	−0.8	−1.4	0.4	0.7	0.3	1.5
India	8.8	7.0	10.2	10.2	9.0	7.2	13.2	4.7	4.0	3.8	4.1	4.0
Other developing Asia	13.0	8.3	8.1	9.1	7.6	6.8	22.0	9.1	3.3	5.9	6.3	5.5
Middle East and Turkey	24.3	25.0	37.3	39.1	29.6	28.3	28.1	23.7	19.6	17.2	17.5	12.3
Western Hemisphere	184.3	24.5	200.3	36.0	21.2	12.9	9.8	8.9	8.1	6.4	8.2	7.4
Analytical groups												
By source of export earnings												
Fuel	17.0	21.4	36.2	42.6	35.1	20.1	18.0	17.2	13.8	12.0	13.3	10.7
Nonfuel	53.7	12.8	57.7	21.3	13.5	9.0	9.8	5.9	5.3	5.1	5.0	4.5
of which, primary products	75.5	19.1	63.0	29.8	27.0	16.0	13.9	12.7	13.5	11.7	7.3	5.7
By external financing source												
Net debtor countries	50.6	14.0	57.5	23.9	15.8	10.2	10.9	7.1	6.3	5.9	5.9	5.2
of which, official financing	38.9	16.8	64.2	30.2	22.6	11.4	10.7	11.2	10.5	8.2	5.3	4.4
Net debtor countries by debt-servicing experience												
Countries with arrears and/or rescheduling during 1994–98	125.2	28.2	221.6	40.1	21.1	12.2	18.6	13.8	11.4	11.3	9.6	7.0
Other groups												
Heavily indebted poor countries	54.0	27.5	91.8	49.6	46.5	21.7	17.6	18.2	20.0	14.8	9.1	6.0
Middle East and north Africa	16.3	12.5	21.8	24.2	16.8	11.7	11.1	10.7	8.1	6.9	8.3	7.3
Memorandum												
Median												
Developing countries	9.4	6.0	10.7	10.0	7.3	6.2	5.8	4.0	4.2	4.4	4.0	3.9
Regional groups												
Africa	9.5	8.2	24.7	12.4	7.8	7.8	5.8	4.4	5.7	5.0	4.5	4.0
Developing Asia	8.2	5.9	8.4	7.9	7.6	6.4	8.4	4.4	3.6	3.8	4.5	4.2
Middle East and Turkey	6.7	3.5	4.9	6.4	6.8	3.4	3.0	2.2	1.5	2.0	2.9	2.4
Western Hemisphere	14.7	5.7	8.3	10.2	7.4	7.0	5.1	3.5	4.8	3.8	3.8	3.8

Table 12. Developing Countries—by Country: Consumer Prices[1]
(Annual percent change)

	Average 1984–93	1994	1995	1996	1997	1998	1999	2000	2001
Africa	**24.3**	**54.7**	**35.3**	**30.2**	**14.6**	**10.9**	**12.3**	**14.2**	**12.6**
Algeria	13.6	29.0	29.8	18.7	5.7	5.0	2.6	0.3	4.1
Angola	62.0	949.8	2,672.2	4,146.0	221.5	107.4	248.2	325.0	152.6
Benin	2.3	38.5	14.5	4.9	3.8	5.8	0.3	4.2	3.8
Botswana	12.6	12.3	10.5	10.3	9.4	7.6	6.9	7.9	7.2
Burkina Faso	—	24.7	7.8	6.1	2.3	5.0	−1.1	−0.2	3.0
Burundi	7.3	14.7	19.4	26.4	31.1	12.5	7.9	24.3	8.0
Cameroon	2.5	12.7	25.8	6.6	5.1	—	2.9	0.8	2.8
Cape Verde	7.6	3.3	8.4	6.0	8.6	4.4	4.4	−2.4	3.7
Central African Republic	−0.3	24.5	19.2	3.7	1.6	−1.9	−1.5	3.1	3.7
Chad	0.5	41.3	5.4	11.3	5.6	4.3	−8.4	3.7	12.4
Comoros	0.4	25.3	7.1	2.0	3.0	3.5	3.5	4.5	5.0
Congo, Dem. Rep. of	282.8	23,760.5	541.8	616.8	198.5	106.9	269.6	553.7	299.0
Congo, Rep. of	−1.1	42.9	8.6	10.2	13.2	1.8	3.1	0.4	−0.5
Côte d'Ivoire	3.5	26.0	14.3	2.7	4.2	4.5	0.7	2.5	4.4
Djibouti	5.7	6.5	4.9	3.5	2.5	2.2	2.0	2.4	1.8
Equatorial Guinea	8.0	38.9	11.4	6.0	3.0	3.0	6.5	6.0	12.0
Eritrea	...	13.1	12.0	10.3	3.7	9.5	8.4	19.9	15.1
Ethiopia	7.9	1.2	13.4	0.9	−6.4	3.6	3.9	4.2	−7.2
Gabon	1.2	36.1	10.0	4.5	4.1	2.3	−0.7	1.0	2.6
Gambia, The	17.3	4.0	4.0	4.8	3.1	1.1	3.8	0.9	4.0
Ghana	25.7	24.9	59.5	46.6	27.9	14.6	12.4	25.2	33.0
Guinea	25.7	4.2	5.6	3.0	1.9	5.1	4.6	6.8	6.8
Guinea-Bissau	64.9	15.2	45.4	50.7	49.1	8.0	−2.1	8.6	5.0
Kenya	16.7	28.8	1.6	8.9	11.4	6.6	3.5	6.2	0.8
Lesotho	14.7	7.2	9.9	9.1	8.5	7.8	8.7	6.1	7.8
Liberia	...	...	...	...	...	...	...	...	...
Madagascar	12.9	39.0	49.0	19.8	4.5	6.2	9.9	11.9	5.0
Malawi	18.0	34.7	83.1	37.7	9.1	29.8	44.8	29.6	27.2
Mali	0.1	24.8	12.4	6.5	−0.7	4.1	−1.2	−0.7	5.0
Mauritania	8.5	4.1	6.5	4.7	4.5	8.0	4.1	3.3	4.7
Mauritius	7.1	9.4	6.0	5.9	7.9	5.4	7.9	5.3	4.4
Morocco	6.3	5.1	6.1	3.0	1.0	2.7	0.7	1.9	0.5
Mozambique, Rep. of	49.6	63.1	54.4	44.6	6.4	0.6	2.9	12.7	9.0
Namibia	9.1	10.8	10.0	8.1	8.8	6.2	8.6	9.3	9.2
Niger	−1.1	24.8	21.9	5.3	2.9	4.5	−2.3	2.9	4.0
Nigeria	25.3	57.0	72.8	29.3	8.5	10.0	6.6	6.9	18.9
Rwanda	6.1	47.3	48.2	13.4	11.7	6.8	−2.4	3.9	3.5
Sâo Tomé and Príncipe	26.6	51.2	36.8	42.0	69.0	42.1	16.3	11.0	9.3
Senegal	2.2	32.0	8.1	2.8	1.7	1.1	0.8	0.7	3.0
Seychelles	2.2	1.8	−0.3	−1.1	0.7	2.6	6.2	7.6	6.2
Sierra Leone	75.5	24.2	26.0	23.1	14.9	35.5	34.1	−0.9	6.0
Somalia	...	...	...	...	...	...	...	...	...
South Africa	14.4	8.8	8.7	7.3	8.6	6.9	5.2	5.4	5.7
Sudan	67.3	115.5	68.4	132.8	46.7	17.1	16.0	8.0	5.0
Swaziland	13.0	13.8	12.3	6.4	7.9	7.5	5.9	9.9	7.5
Tanzania	29.3	37.1	26.5	21.0	16.1	9.8	9.0	6.2	5.2
Togo	1.0	48.5	6.4	2.5	5.5	−1.4	4.5	−2.5	6.8
Tunisia	6.9	4.5	6.3	4.6	3.7	3.1	2.7	3.0	1.9
Uganda	80.1	6.5	6.1	7.5	7.8	5.8	−0.2	6.3	4.6
Zambia	82.6	54.6	34.9	43.1	24.4	24.5	26.8	26.1	22.5
Zimbabwe	18.2	22.2	22.6	21.5	18.8	31.7	58.5	55.9	76.7

Table 12 *(continued)*

	Average 1984–93	1994	1995	1996	1997	1998	1999	2000	2001
Developing Asia	**10.3**	**16.0**	**13.2**	**8.3**	**4.8**	**7.7**	**2.5**	**1.9**	**2.6**
Afghanistan, Islamic State of	...	...	...	...	...	...	...	...	...
Bangladesh	8.5	6.1	7.7	3.9	5.1	8.5	6.4	2.3	1.8
Bhutan	9.3	7.0	9.5	8.8	6.5	10.6	6.8	4.8	5.0
Brunei Darussalam	...	2.4	6.0	2.0	1.7	-0.4	-0.1	1.5	2.1
Cambodia	...	9.4	1.3	7.2	8.0	14.8	4.0	-0.8	-0.6
China	8.9	24.1	17.1	8.3	2.8	-0.8	-1.4	0.4	0.7
Fiji	5.8	1.2	2.2	2.4	2.9	8.3	0.2	3.0	5.0
India	8.8	10.2	10.2	9.0	7.2	13.2	4.7	4.0	3.8
Indonesia	7.9	8.5	9.4	7.9	6.2	58.0	20.7	3.8	11.5
Kiribati	2.8	4.0	4.1	-1.5	2.2	4.7	0.4	1.0	2.5
Lao P.D. Republic	29.1	6.8	19.4	13.0	19.3	87.4	134.0	27.1	8.0
Malaysia	2.6	4.1	3.5	3.5	2.6	5.1	2.8	1.6	1.4
Maldives	7.6	3.4	5.5	6.2	7.6	-1.4	3.0	-1.1	3.7
Myanmar	19.5	22.4	28.9	20.0	33.9	49.1	11.4	10.3	15.0
Nepal	10.8	8.9	7.7	7.2	8.1	8.3	11.4	3.4	2.4
Pakistan	7.7	12.4	12.3	10.4	11.4	6.2	4.1	4.4	3.8
Papua New Guinea	5.3	2.9	17.3	11.6	3.9	13.6	14.9	15.6	10.0
Philippines	14.2	8.4	8.0	9.0	5.9	9.7	6.6	4.3	6.1
Samoa	2.0	12.1	-2.9	5.4	6.9	2.2	0.3	1.0	1.5
Solomon Islands	12.0	13.3	9.6	11.8	8.1	12.4	8.3	6.0	7.0
Sri Lanka	11.5	8.4	7.7	15.9	9.6	9.4	4.7	6.2	14.0
Thailand	3.6	5.1	5.8	5.9	5.6	8.1	0.3	1.6	1.7
Tonga	9.4	2.4	-0.5	2.7	2.0	3.0	3.9	5.3	7.0
Vanuatu	6.3	2.3	2.2	0.9	2.9	3.2	2.0	2.0	2.0
Vietnam	117.5	9.5	17.4	5.7	3.2	7.3	4.1	-1.7	0.1
Middle East and Turkey	**24.3**	**37.3**	**39.1**	**29.6**	**28.3**	**28.1**	**23.7**	**19.6**	**17.2**
Bahrain	-0.2	0.4	3.1	-0.1	4.6	-0.4	-1.3	-0.7	-0.2
Egypt	18.1	9.0	9.4	7.1	6.2	4.7	3.8	2.8	2.4
Iran, Islamic Republic of	18.9	35.2	49.4	23.2	17.3	20.0	20.4	12.6	11.7
Iraq	...	...	...	...	...	...	...	...	...
Jordan	4.9	3.6	2.3	6.5	3.0	3.1	0.6	0.7	1.8
Kuwait	7.6	2.5	2.7	3.6	0.7	0.1	3.0	1.7	2.5
Lebanon	92.8	8.0	10.6	8.9	7.7	4.5	0.2	-0.4	—
Libya	7.4	10.7	8.3	4.0	3.6	3.7	2.6	-2.9	-8.5
Malta	1.5	4.1	4.0	2.0	3.1	2.4	2.1	2.4	2.9
Oman	1.8	-0.7	-1.1	0.3	-0.2	-0.5	0.5	-1.0	-2.6
Qatar	2.6	1.4	3.0	7.1	2.7	2.9	2.2	1.7	-0.7
Saudi Arabia	-0.4	0.6	5.0	0.9	-0.4	-0.2	-1.3	-0.6	-1.4
Syrian Arab Republic	22.4	3.9	7.7	8.9	1.9	-0.4	-2.1	-0.6	1.0
Turkey	56.1	106.2	93.6	82.3	85.7	84.6	64.9	54.9	54.4
United Arab Emirates	4.0	5.7	4.4	3.0	2.9	2.0	2.1	1.4	2.2
Yemen, Republic of	...	71.3	62.5	40.0	4.6	11.5	8.0	10.9	11.9

Table 12 *(concluded)*

	Average 1984–93	1994	1995	1996	1997	1998	1999	2000	2001
Western Hemisphere	**184.3**	**200.3**	**36.0**	**21.2**	**12.9**	**9.8**	**8.9**	**8.1**	**6.4**
Antigua and Barbuda	3.7	6.5	2.7	3.0	0.3	3.3	1.1	0.7	1.0
Argentina	346.5	4.2	3.4	0.2	0.5	0.9	−1.2	−0.9	−1.1
Bahamas, The	5.0	1.3	2.1	1.4	0.5	1.3	1.3	1.6	1.0
Barbados	4.1	−0.1	1.9	2.4	7.7	−1.3	1.6	2.5	2.2
Belize	2.5	2.5	2.9	6.4	1.0	−0.8	−1.2	0.6	1.2
Bolivia	163.8	7.9	10.2	12.4	4.7	7.7	2.2	4.6	1.6
Brazil	614.2	2,075.8	66.0	15.8	6.9	3.2	4.9	7.0	6.8
Chile	19.7	11.4	8.2	7.4	6.1	5.1	3.3	3.8	3.6
Colombia	24.5	22.8	20.9	20.8	18.5	18.7	10.9	9.2	8.0
Costa Rica	17.1	13.5	23.2	17.6	13.3	11.7	10.1	11.5	11.0
Dominica	3.7	—	1.3	1.7	2.4	0.9	1.6	1.9	1.8
Dominican Republic	27.0	8.3	12.5	5.4	8.3	4.8	6.5	7.7	8.9
Ecuador	43.4	27.3	22.9	24.4	30.6	36.1	52.2	96.2	37.0
El Salvador	19.5	10.6	10.1	9.8	4.5	2.5	0.5	2.3	3.8
Grenada	2.9	2.6	2.2	2.8	1.3	1.4	0.5	2.2	2.5
Guatemala	16.2	12.5	8.4	11.0	9.2	6.6	4.9	5.1	8.7
Guyana	38.0	12.4	12.2	7.1	3.6	4.6	7.5	6.1	2.4
Haiti	11.0	37.4	30.2	21.9	16.2	12.7	8.1	11.5	16.7
Honduras	10.4	18.2	29.5	23.8	20.2	13.7	11.6	11.0	9.7
Jamaica	28.4	33.2	21.7	21.5	8.8	6.0	8.4	6.4	5.0
Mexico	49.9	7.0	35.0	34.4	20.6	15.9	16.6	9.5	6.4
Netherlands Antilles	2.4	1.9	2.8	3.4	3.1	1.2	0.8	4.7	3.9
Nicaragua	901.7	7.7	11.2	11.6	9.2	13.0	11.2	11.6	8.3
Panama	0.8	1.3	0.9	1.3	1.3	0.6	1.3	1.4	1.8
Paraguay	24.2	20.6	13.4	9.8	7.0	11.6	6.8	9.0	7.7
Peru	367.0	23.7	11.1	11.5	8.5	7.3	3.5	3.8	2.0
St. Kitts and Nevis	2.5	1.4	3.0	2.0	8.7	3.7	3.4	2.1	2.1
St. Lucia	3.0	2.7	5.9	1.2	0.3	2.8	3.5	3.6	2.5
St. Vincent and the Grenadines	3.3	1.0	1.7	4.4	0.5	2.1	1.0	0.2	0.9
Suriname	28.4	368.5	235.5	−0.8	7.3	19.0	98.8	59.1	50.2
Trinidad and Tobago	9.3	3.7	5.3	3.3	3.6	5.6	3.4	5.6	2.5
Uruguay	73.9	45.0	42.6	28.6	19.8	10.8	5.7	4.8	4.4
Venezuela	30.8	60.8	59.9	99.9	50.0	35.8	23.6	16.2	12.5

[1]For many countries, figures for recent years are IMF staff estimates. Data for some countries are for fiscal years.

Table 13. Countries in Transition: Consumer Prices[1]

(Annual percent change)

	Average 1984–93	1994	1995	1996	1997	1998	1999	2000	2001
Central and eastern Europe	...	**45.6**	**24.7**	**23.2**	**41.7**	**17.2**	**11.0**	**12.8**	**9.6**
Albania	23.4	22.6	7.8	12.7	32.1	20.9	0.4	—	3.1
Bosnia and Herzegovina	...	...	0.2	-13.7	9.5	0.6	3.2	5.4	3.3
Bulgaria	35.3	96.0	62.1	121.6	1,061.2	18.8	2.6	10.4	7.5
Croatia	...	97.5	2.0	3.5	3.6	5.7	4.1	6.2	4.9
Czech Republic	...	10.0	9.1	8.8	8.5	10.7	2.1	3.9	4.7
Estonia	...	49.3	29.0	23.1	11.2	8.1	3.3	4.0	5.8
Hungary	16.7	18.8	28.3	23.5	18.3	14.3	10.0	9.8	9.2
Latvia	...	35.9	25.0	17.6	8.4	4.6	2.4	2.6	2.5
Lithuania	...	72.1	39.5	24.7	8.8	5.1	0.8	1.0	1.3
Macedonia, former Yugoslav Rep. of	...	126.4	15.8	1.9	2.5	-0.1	-0.7	5.8	5.3
Poland	73.6	32.2	27.9	19.9	14.9	11.8	7.3	10.1	5.4
Romania	52.7	136.7	32.3	38.8	154.8	59.1	45.8	45.7	34.5
Slovak Republic	...	13.4	9.9	5.8	6.1	6.7	10.7	12.0	7.3
Slovenia	...	21.5	13.5	9.9	8.4	8.0	6.1	8.9	8.4
Commonwealth of Independent States and Mongolia	...	**455.5**	**235.6**	**55.9**	**19.1**	**25.0**	**70.5**	**25.0**	**19.8**
Russia	...	307.5	198.0	47.9	14.7	27.8	85.7	20.8	20.7
Excluding Russia	...	978.9	338.8	75.5	29.7	19.3	41.7	34.7	17.9
Armenia	...	5,273.4	176.7	18.7	14.0	8.7	0.7	-0.8	3.4
Azerbaijan	...	1,664.0	411.8	19.8	3.7	-0.8	-8.5	1.8	1.5
Belarus	...	2,434.1	709.3	52.7	63.9	73.2	293.8	168.9	61.3
Georgia	...	15,606.5	162.7	39.3	7.0	3.6	19.1	4.0	4.7
Kazakhstan	...	1,879.9	176.3	39.1	17.4	7.3	8.4	13.3	8.3
Kyrgyz Republic	...	190.1	40.7	31.3	22.6	12.0	35.9	18.7	7.0
Moldova	...	329.6	30.2	23.5	11.8	7.7	39.3	31.3	9.8
Mongolia	29.6	87.6	56.8	46.8	36.6	9.4	7.6	11.6	8.2
Tajikistan	...	350.4	610.0	418.2	88.0	43.2	27.5	32.9	38.6
Turkmenistan	...	1,748.3	1,005.2	992.4	83.7	16.8	...	...	...
Ukraine	...	418.5	376.4	80.2	15.9	10.6	22.7	28.2	12.0
Uzbekistan	...	1,568.3	304.6	54.0	70.9	29.0	29.1	25.0	27.2
Memorandum									
EU accession candidates	...	59.1	42.7	39.4	55.4	35.6	25.3	24.7	21.1

[1]For many countries, inflation for the earlier years is measured on the basis of a retail price index. Consumer price indices with a broader and more up-to-date coverage are typically used for more recent years.

Table 14. Summary Financial Indicators

(Percent)

	1994	1995	1996	1997	1998	1999	2000	2001	2002	2003
Advanced economies										
Central government fiscal balance[1]										
Advanced economies	−3.7	−3.4	−2.7	−1.6	−1.7	−0.9	0.2	−0.8	−1.4	−1.1
United States	−3.0	−2.6	−1.8	−0.6	0.5	1.3	2.2	0.8	−0.7	−0.5
Japan	−3.5	−4.1	−4.4	−4.0	−9.0	−8.0	−7.6	−6.3	−5.6	−5.0
European Union	−5.3	−4.7	−4.0	−2.4	−1.8	−1.0	0.5	−1.0	−1.3	−1.1
Euro area	−4.5	−4.1	−3.8	−2.6	−2.3	−1.6	−0.4	−1.4	−1.5	−1.2
Other advanced economies	−1.4	−1.0	−0.2	0.7	−0.1	0.1	1.7	0.7	0.3	0.5
General government fiscal balance[1]										
Advanced economies	−4.1	−3.9	−3.1	−1.7	−1.4	−1.0	—	−1.2	−2.0	−1.6
United States	−3.8	−3.3	−2.4	−1.3	−0.1	0.6	1.5	0.1	−1.4	−1.2
Japan	−2.8	−4.3	−4.9	−3.7	−5.6	−7.6	−8.5	−8.5	−8.7	−7.6
European Union	−5.6	−5.3	−4.3	−2.4	−1.6	−0.7	0.9	−0.8	−1.3	−1.0
Euro area	−5.1	−5.0	−4.2	−2.5	−2.2	−1.3	0.2	−1.4	−1.6	−1.1
Other advanced economies	−1.7	−0.8	0.1	0.8	−0.1	0.3	1.7	1.4	0.8	0.8
General government structural balance[2]										
Advanced economies	−3.5	−3.4	−2.6	−1.4	−1.0	−0.8	−0.8	−1.2	−1.6	−1.4
Growth of broad money[3]										
Advanced economies	2.6	5.0	4.8	5.0	6.7	5.8	5.1	8.7	...	...
United States	0.6	3.9	4.5	5.6	8.5	6.3	6.1	10.3	...	...
Japan	2.9	3.2	2.9	3.8	4.4	2.6	2.0	3.4	...	...
Euro area[4]	2.3	5.5	4.0	4.6	4.8	5.5	4.1	11.0	...	...
Other advanced economies	9.5	8.8	8.6	6.3	10.3	10.8	8.2	7.4	...	...
Short-term interest rates[5]										
United States	3.1	4.4	5.7	5.1	4.9	4.8	6.0	3.5	2.3	4.0
Japan	1.9	0.8	0.3	0.3	0.2	0.0	0.2	0.0	0.0	0.0
Euro area[4]	6.4	6.1	4.8	4.3	4.0	3.1	4.5	4.2	3.3	3.8
LIBOR	5.1	6.1	5.6	5.8	5.5	5.5	6.6	3.7	2.8	4.5
Developing countries										
Central government fiscal balance[1]										
Weighted average	−2.8	−2.6	−2.2	−2.5	−3.8	−4.1	−3.2	−3.8	−3.9	−3.3
Median	−3.8	−3.3	−2.4	−2.4	−3.0	−3.3	−3.2	−3.4	−3.5	−2.8
General government fiscal balance[1]										
Weighted average	−3.7	−3.2	−3.3	−3.5	−4.9	−5.3	−4.1	−4.8	−4.8	−4.1
Median	−3.5	−3.3	−2.8	−2.4	−3.1	−3.3	−3.2	−3.3	−3.2	−2.6
Growth of broad money										
Weighted average	68.4	24.4	22.5	22.4	17.3	15.2	11.4	12.5	10.4	11.2
Median	18.8	16.3	13.6	15.5	10.5	13.1	12.0	10.5	9.2	9.3
Countries in transition										
Central government fiscal balance[1]	−7.4	−4.6	−4.6	−4.7	−3.5	−2.1	−0.1	−0.1	−0.8	−0.6
General government fiscal balance[1]	−7.5	−4.7	−5.9	−5.4	−4.9	−2.1	0.1	−0.5	−1.2	−1.4
Growth of broad money	149.7	75.3	32.3	33.1	20.5	38.8	37.2	25.5	13.9	15.2

[1]Percent of GDP.

[2]Percent of potential GDP.

[3]M2, defined as M1 plus quasi-money, except for Japan, for which the data are based on M2 plus certificates of deposit (CDs), and M4, respectively. Quasi-money is essentially private term deposits and other notice deposits. The United States also includes money market mutual fund balances, money market deposit accounts, overnight repurchase agreements, and overnight Eurodollars issued to U.S. residents by foreign branches of U.S. banks. For Japan, M2 plus CDs is currency in circulation plus total private and public sector deposits and installments of Sogo Bank plus CDs. For the euro area, M3 is composed of M2 plus marketable instruments held by euro area residents, which comprise repurchase agreements, money market fund shares/units, money market paper, and debt securities up to two years.

[4]Excludes Greece prior to 2001.

[5]For the United States, three-month treasury bills; for Japan, three-month certificates of deposit; for the euro area, a weighted average of national three-month money market interest rates through 1998 and three-month EURIBOR thereafter; for LIBOR, London interbank offered rate on six-month U.S. dollar deposits.

Table 15. Advanced Economies: General and Central Government Fiscal Balances and Balances Excluding Social Security Transactions[1]

(Percent of GDP)

	1994	1995	1996	1997	1998	1999	2000	2001	2002	2003
General government fiscal balance										
Advanced economies	**−4.1**	**−3.9**	**−3.1**	**−1.7**	**−1.4**	**−1.0**	**—**	**−1.2**	**−2.0**	**−1.6**
Major advanced economies	−4.3	−4.2	−3.6	−2.0	−1.6	−1.2	−0.3	−1.7	−2.6	−2.1
United States	−3.8	−3.3	−2.4	−1.3	−0.1	0.6	1.5	0.1	−1.4	−1.2
Japan	−2.8	−4.3	−4.9	−3.7	−5.6	−7.6	−8.5	−8.5	−8.7	−7.6
Germany[2]	−2.4	−3.3	−3.4	−2.7	−2.2	−1.6	1.2	−2.7	−2.7	−2.0
France[2,3]	−5.5	−5.5	−4.1	−3.0	−2.7	−1.8	−1.4	−1.4	−2.1	−1.9
Italy[2,4]	−9.3	−7.6	−7.1	−2.7	−2.8	−1.8	−0.5	−1.4	−1.2	−0.2
United Kingdom[2,5]	−6.8	−5.4	−4.1	−1.5	0.3	1.5	4.4	0.4	−0.9	−1.2
Canada	−6.7	−5.3	−2.8	0.2	0.5	1.6	3.2	2.4	1.7	1.7
Other advanced economies	−2.9	−2.5	−1.4	−0.5	−0.7	−0.1	1.1	0.8	0.3	0.2
Spain	−6.1	−7.0	−5.1	−3.2	−2.5	−1.2	−0.3	−0.1	−0.5	−0.6
Netherlands[2]	−3.6	−4.2	−1.8	−1.1	−0.8	0.4	2.2	0.2	—	−0.5
Belgium[2]	−5.0	−4.3	−3.7	−2.0	−0.8	−0.6	0.1	0.2	−0.3	0.1
Sweden	−10.8	−7.9	−3.4	−2.0	1.8	1.9	4.0	4.7	2.1	2.1
Austria[2,6]	−5.0	−5.2	−3.8	−1.9	−2.5	−2.3	−1.6	−0.1	−0.1	−0.1
Denmark	−2.4	−2.3	−1.0	0.5	1.1	3.1	2.5	1.7	1.6	1.5
Finland	−5.7	−3.7	−3.2	−1.5	1.3	1.9	6.9	4.0	1.8	1.9
Greece	−10.0	−10.2	−7.4	−4.0	−2.4	−1.7	−0.8	0.1	0.6	1.2
Portugal	−6.0	−4.6	−4.0	−2.6	−1.9	−2.1	−1.5	−3.0	−3.0	−2.5
Ireland	−1.7	−2.2	−0.3	1.2	2.3	4.1	4.5	1.7	0.4	−0.8
Luxembourg	3.0	2.7	2.0	2.8	3.2	3.8	5.8	5.0	1.0	1.1
Switzerland	−2.8	−1.9	−2.0	−2.4	−0.4	−0.2	2.4	−0.2	—	−0.5
Norway	0.4	3.5	6.6	7.9	3.5	5.9	14.9	15.6	14.0	10.3
Israel	−3.2	−4.5	−5.8	−4.3	−3.8	−4.8	−2.2	−3.8	−3.6	−2.0
Iceland	−4.7	−3.0	−1.6	—	0.4	2.2	2.8	1.9	1.9	2.2
Cyprus	−1.4	−1.0	−3.4	−5.3	−5.5	−4.0	−2.7	−3.0	−2.8	−1.9
Korea[7]	1.0	1.3	1.0	−0.9	−3.8	−2.7	2.7	2.9	2.5	1.6
Australia[8]	−3.5	−2.1	−0.9	−0.1	0.3	0.9	0.9	0.3	0.1	0.2
Taiwan Province of China	1.5	2.7	2.3	2.3	3.7	0.8	−5.5	−2.6	−4.4	−2.5
Hong Kong SAR	1.1	−0.3	2.2	6.6	−1.8	0.8	−0.6	−5.2	−3.6	−3.0
Singapore	13.9	12.2	9.3	9.2	3.6	4.5	7.9	6.2	3.1	5.4
New Zealand[9]	2.2	3.6	2.7	1.6	0.9	0.4	0.8	0.8	0.7	1.2
Memorandum										
European Union[2]	−5.6	−5.3	−4.3	−2.4	−1.6	−0.7	0.9	−0.8	−1.3	−1.0
Euro area[2]	−5.1	−5.0	−4.2	−2.5	−2.2	−1.3	0.2	−1.4	−1.6	−1.1
Newly industrialized Asian economies	2.1	2.3	2.2	1.8	−0.6	−0.7	0.2	0.5	−0.2	0.1
Fiscal balance excluding social security transactions										
United States	−4.2	−3.7	−2.7	−1.7	−0.7	−0.4	−0.1	−0.9	−1.9	−1.7
Japan	−5.1	−6.5	−7.0	−5.8	−7.2	−9.0	−9.2	−8.8	−8.7	−7.4
Germany	−2.5	−2.9	−3.1	−2.8	−2.3	−1.8	1.2	−2.6	−2.7	−2.0
France	−5.0	−4.8	−3.6	−2.6	−2.5	−2.1	−2.0	−1.8	−2.7	−2.9
Italy	−7.1	−5.6	−5.3	−0.7	1.3	2.6	3.5	2.5	3.1	3.8
Canada	−3.9	−2.7	—	3.0	3.0	3.9	5.1	4.1	3.5	3.3

Table 15 *(concluded)*

	1994	1995	1996	1997	1998	1999	2000	2001	2002	2003
Central government fiscal balance										
Advanced economies	**-3.7**	**-3.4**	**-2.7**	**-1.6**	**-1.7**	**-0.9**	**0.2**	**-0.8**	**-1.4**	**-1.1**
Major advanced economies	-3.9	-3.5	-3.0	-1.7	-1.9	-1.0	0.1	-1.0	-1.7	-1.4
United States[10]	-3.0	-2.6	-1.8	-0.6	0.5	1.3	2.2	0.8	-0.7	-0.5
Japan[11]	-3.5	-4.1	-4.4	-4.0	-9.0	-8.0	-7.6	-6.3	-5.6	-5.0
Germany[12]	-1.5	-1.4	-2.2	-1.7	-1.5	-1.3	1.3	-1.1	-1.2	-0.8
France[12]	-4.8	-4.1	-3.7	-3.6	-3.8	-2.5	-2.4	-2.3	-2.8	-2.4
Italy	-9.1	-8.0	-7.0	-2.9	-2.7	-1.6	-1.0	-2.4	-1.9	-1.3
United Kingdom	-6.9	-5.4	-4.1	-1.5	0.3	1.4	4.3	0.4	-0.8	-1.1
Canada	-4.5	-3.9	-2.0	0.7	1.0	0.9	1.8	1.2	1.2	1.2
Other advanced economies	-3.2	-2.8	-1.8	-1.0	-1.0	-0.6	0.9	0.2	-0.3	-0.2
Memorandum										
European Union	-5.3	-4.7	-4.0	-2.4	-1.8	-1.0	0.5	-1.0	-1.3	-1.1
Euro area	-4.5	-4.1	-3.8	-2.6	-2.3	-1.6	-0.4	-1.4	-1.5	-1.2
Newly industrialized Asian economies	1.0	1.0	1.0	0.8	-1.3	-1.2	1.0	-0.3	-1.0	-0.6

[1]On a national income accounts basis except as indicated in footnotes. See Box A1 for a summary of the policy assumptions underlying the projections.
[2]Includes one-off receipts from the sale of mobile telephone licenses equivalent to 2.5 percent of GDP in 2000 for Germany, 0.1 percent of GDP in 2001 and 2002 for France, 1.2 percent of GDP in 2000 for Italy, 2.4 percent of GDP in 2000 for the United Kingdom, 0.7 percent of GDP in 2000 for the Netherlands, 0.2 percent of GDP in 2001 for Belgium, and 0.4 percent of GDP in 2000 for Austria.
[3]Adjusted for valuation changes of the foreign exchange stabilization fund.
[4]Includes asset sales equivalent to 0.6 percent of GDP in 2001 and 2002 and 0.5 percent of GDP in 2003.
[5]Excludes asset sales.
[6]Based on ESA95 methodology, according to which swap income is not included. Data on swap income are not yet available for other countries in the European Union.
[7]Data include social security transactions (that is, the operations of the public pension plan).
[8]Data exclude net advances (primarily privatization receipts and net policy-related lending).
[9]Data from 1992 onward are on an accrual basis and are not strictly comparable with previous cash-based data.
[10]Data are on a budget basis.
[11]Data are on a national income basis and exclude social security transactions.
[12]Data are on an administrative basis and exclude social security transactions.

Table 16. Advanced Economies: General Government Structural Balances[1]

(Percent of potential GDP)

	1994	1995	1996	1997	1998	1999	2000	2001	2002	2003
Structural balance[2]										
Advanced economies	**−3.5**	**−3.4**	**−2.6**	**−1.4**	**−1.0**	**−0.8**	**−0.8**	**−1.2**	**−1.6**	**−1.4**
Major advanced economies	−3.4	−3.3	−2.7	−1.4	−1.0	−0.9	−1.0	−1.5	−2.0	−1.7
United States	−2.8	−2.3	−1.5	−0.7	0.1	0.5	1.0	0.1	−1.2	−1.0
Japan	−2.5	−3.9	−5.2	−4.1	−5.0	−6.9	−8.3	−7.8	−7.3	−6.1
Germany[3,4]	−2.5	−3.4	−2.7	−1.6	−1.3	−0.8	−1.3	−2.0	−1.4	−1.1
France[4]	−3.5	−3.7	−1.9	−1.0	−1.6	−1.0	−1.2	−1.3	−1.4	−1.3
Italy[4]	−8.1	−7.0	−6.2	−1.7	−1.7	−0.6	−2.1	−1.2	−0.7	−0.1
United Kingdom[4]	−5.7	−4.6	−3.3	−0.9	0.5	1.6	2.1	0.3	−0.7	−0.8
Canada	−3.8	−2.8	—	2.1	2.4	2.4	3.1	2.9	2.3	1.9
Other advanced economies	−4.2	−3.7	−2.0	−1.2	−0.8	−0.3	0.3	0.3	0.3	0.3
Spain	−5.2	−5.1	−2.2	−1.8	−1.8	−1.2	−0.9	−0.3	—	0.1
Netherlands	−2.7	−3.1	−0.9	−0.8	−1.4	−0.7	0.2	−0.4	—	−0.4
Belgium	−3.1	−2.7	−1.6	−0.7	0.5	0.3	−0.2	0.3	0.8	0.7
Sweden	−11.8	−8.8	−4.9	−3.7	0.6	1.8	4.6	4.3	1.8	2.0
Austria[4]	−4.6	−4.7	−3.6	−1.4	−2.2	−2.3	−2.2	0.4	1.0	0.6
Denmark	−1.4	−2.0	−1.0	0.3	0.8	2.8	1.9	2.1	2.0	1.7
Finland	−0.7	0.3	0.3	0.1	2.0	2.4	6.9	5.1	3.6	3.7
Greece	−9.4	−9.5	−6.9	−3.9	−2.5	−1.9	−1.3	−0.6	—	0.8
Portugal	−5.0	−3.4	−3.2	−2.3	−2.3	−2.7	−2.5	−3.1	−2.4	−1.7
Ireland	0.2	−1.7	0.2	0.7	1.8	3.1	2.9	0.5	−0.1	−0.9
Norway[5]	−6.7	−4.5	−3.4	−2.6	−3.6	−3.5	−3.3	−2.9	−2.9	−2.9
Australia[6]	−2.3	−1.7	−0.8	0.1	0.2	0.6	0.8	0.5	0.4	0.4
New Zealand[7]	0.9	1.7	1.3	1.6	1.7	0.9	1.1	1.0	0.8	1.7
Memorandum										
European Union[8]	−4.7	−4.5	−3.1	−1.4	−1.0	−0.3	−0.4	−0.7	−0.6	−0.5
Euro area[8]	−4.1	−4.2	−3.0	−1.4	−1.4	−0.8	−1.1	−1.1	−0.8	−0.5

[1]On a national income accounts basis.

[2]The structural budget position is defined as the actual budget deficit (or surplus) less the effects of cyclical deviations of output from potential output. Because of the margin of uncertainty that attaches to estimates of cyclical gaps and to tax and expenditure elasticities with respect to national income, indicators of structural budget positions should be interpreted as broad orders of magnitude. Moreover, it is important to note that changes in structural budget balances are not necessarily attributable to policy changes but may reflect the built-in momentum of existing expenditure programs. In the period beyond that for which specific consolidation programs exist, it is assumed that the structural deficit remains unchanged.

[3]The estimate of the fiscal impulse for 1995 is affected by the assumption by the federal government of the debt of the Treuhandanstalt and various other agencies, which were formerly held outside the general government sector. At the public sector level, there would be an estimated withdrawal of fiscal impulse amounting to just over 1 percent of GDP.

[4]Excludes mobile telephone license receipts.

[5]Excludes oil.

[6]Excludes commonwealth government privatization receipts.

[7]Excludes privatization proceeds.

[8]Excludes Luxembourg.

Table 17. Advanced Economies: Monetary Aggregates

(Annual percent change)[1]

	1994	1995	1996	1997	1998	1999	2000	2001
Narrow money[2]								
Advanced economies	**4.4**	**5.1**	**4.7**	**4.7**	**6.0**	**8.2**	**2.6**	**8.5**
United States	2.5	−1.6	−4.4	−1.2	2.1	1.9	−1.7	6.8
Japan	4.9	12.8	10.0	8.9	6.1	11.8	4.1	13.6
Euro area[3]	4.2	5.8	8.0	7.5	10.8	11.0	5.1	6.2
United Kingdom	6.8	5.6	6.7	6.4	5.3	11.7	4.8	8.3
Canada	8.7	7.8	18.0	10.8	8.7	7.5	14.1	15.1
Memorandum								
Newly industrialized Asian economies	9.3	10.5	5.8	−3.8	0.9	19.7	4.5	7.4
Broad money[4]								
Advanced economies	**2.6**	**5.0**	**4.8**	**5.0**	**6.7**	**5.8**	**5.1**	**8.7**
United States	0.6	3.9	4.5	5.6	8.5	6.3	6.1	10.3
Japan	2.9	3.2	2.9	3.8	4.4	2.6	2.0	3.4
Euro area[3]	2.3	5.5	4.0	4.6	4.8	5.5	4.1	11.0
United Kingdom	4.2	9.9	9.6	5.7	8.4	4.1	8.5	6.8
Canada	2.9	4.2	1.9	−1.5	1.0	5.0	6.3	5.8
Memorandum								
Newly industrialized Asian economies	16.5	13.0	11.4	11.3	19.8	16.9	14.2	6.4

[1]Based on end-of-period data except for Japan, which is based on monthly averages.

[2]M1 except for the United Kingdom, where M0 is used here as a measure of narrow money; it comprises notes in circulation plus bankers' operational deposits. M1 is generally currency in circulation plus private demand deposits. In addition, the United States includes traveler's checks of nonbank issues and other checkable deposits and excludes private sector float and demand deposits of banks. Japan includes government demand deposits and excludes float. Canada excludes private sector float.

[3]Excludes Greece prior to 2001.

[4]M2, defined as M1 plus quasi-money, except for Japan, and the United Kingdom, for which the data are based on M2 plus certificates of deposit (CDs), and M4, respectively. Quasi-money is essentially private term deposits and other notice deposits. The United States also includes money market mutual fund balances, money market deposit accounts, overnight repurchase agreements, and overnight Eurodollars issued to U.S. residents by foreign branches of U.S. banks. For Japan, M2 plus CDs is currency in circulation plus total private and public sector deposits and installments of Sogo Bank plus CDs. For the United Kingdom, M4 is composed of non-interest-bearing M1, private sector interest-bearing sterling sight bank deposits, private sector sterling time banks deposits, private sector holdings of sterling bank CDs, private sector holdings of building society shares and deposites, and sterling CDs less building society of banks deposits and bank CDs and notes and coins. For the euro area, M3 is composed of M2 plus marketable instruments held by euro-area residents, which comprise repurchase agreements, money market fund shares/units, money market paper, and debt securities up to two years.

Table 18. Advanced Economies: Interest Rates

(Percent a year)

	1994	1995	1996	1997	1998	1999	2000	2001	March 2002
Policy-related interest rate[1]									
United States	5.5	5.6	5.3	5.5	4.7	5.3	6.4	1.8	1.7
Japan	2.2	0.4	0.4	0.4	0.3	0.0	0.2	0.0	0.0
Euro area[2]	...	...	...	...	...	3.0	4.8	3.3	3.3
United Kingdom	6.1	6.4	5.9	7.3	6.3	5.5	6.0	4.0	4.0
Canada	5.5	5.7	3.0	4.3	5.1	4.8	5.8	2.2	2.0
Short-term interest rate[3]									
Advanced economies	**4.5**	**4.6**	**4.3**	**4.0**	**4.0**	**3.5**	**4.5**	**3.2**	**2.3**
United States	3.1	4.4	5.7	5.1	4.9	4.8	6.0	3.5	1.8
Japan	1.9	0.8	0.3	0.3	0.2	0.0	0.2	0.0	0.0
Euro area[2]	6.4	6.1	4.8	4.3	4.0	3.1	4.5	4.2	3.4
United Kingdom	5.6	6.8	6.1	6.9	7.4	5.5	6.1	5.0	4.1
Canada	5.4	7.0	4.3	3.2	4.7	4.7	5.5	3.9	2.1
Memorandum									
Newly industrialized Asian economies	9.1	9.2	8.7	9.2	9.9	5.4	5.6	4.4	3.3
Long-term interest rate[4]									
Advanced economies	**7.1**	**6.8**	**6.1**	**5.5**	**4.5**	**4.6**	**5.0**	**4.4**	**4.7**
United States	7.1	6.6	6.4	6.4	5.3	5.6	6.0	5.0	5.1
Japan	4.2	3.3	3.0	2.1	1.3	1.7	1.7	1.3	1.5
Euro area[2]	8.3	8.5	7.2	6.0	4.8	4.6	5.4	4.9	5.1
United Kingdom	8.4	8.4	8.1	7.4	5.4	5.4	5.4	5.1	4.9
Canada	8.4	8.1	7.2	6.1	5.3	5.6	5.9	5.5	5.8
Memorandum									
Newly industrialized Asian economies	9.4	9.4	8.5	9.2	9.4	7.1	5.9	6.2	6.2

[1]Annual data are end of period. For the United States, federal funds rate; for Japan, overnight call rate; for the euro area, main refinancing rate; for the United Kingdom, base lending rate; and for Canada, overnight money market financing rate.

[2]Excludes Greece prior to 2001.

[3]Annual data are period average. For the United States, three-month treasury bill market bid yield at constant maturity; for Japan, three-month bond yield with repurchase agreement; for the euro area, a weighted average of national three-month money market interest rates through 1998 and three-month EURIBOR thereafter; for the United Kingdom, three-month London interbank offered rate; and for Canada, three-month treasury bill yield.

[4]Annual data are period average. For the United States, ten-year treasury bond yield at constant maturity; for Japan, ten-year government bond yield; for euro area, a weighted average of national ten-year government bond yields through 1998 and ten-year euro bond yield thereafter; for the United Kingdom, ten-year government bond yield; and for Canada, government bond yield of ten years and over.

Table 19. Advanced Economies: Exchange Rates

	1994	1995	1996	1997	1998	1999	2000	2001	Exchange Rate Assumption[1] 2002
					U.S. dollars per national currency unit				
U.S. dollar nominal exchange rates									
Euro	...	...	...	...	...	1.067	0.924	0.895	0.874
ECU	1.188	1.308	1.269	1.134	1.120	...	...	...	...
Pound sterling	1.532	1.578	1.562	1.638	1.656	1.618	1.516	1.440	1.417
Irish pound	1.180	1.263	1.261	1.195	1.123	1.067	0.924	0.895	0.874
					National currency units per U.S. dollar				
Deutsche mark	1.623	1.433	1.505	1.734	1.760	1.833	2.117	2.184	...
French franc	5.552	4.991	5.116	5.837	5.900	6.149	7.101	7.324	...
Italian lira	1,612.4	1,628.9	1,542.9	1,703.1	1,736.2	1,815.0	2,096.2	2,161.8	...
Spanish peseta	134.0	124.7	126.7	146.4	149.4	156.0	180.1	185.8	...
Netherlands guilder	1.820	1.606	1.686	1.951	1.984	2.066	2.386	2.460	...
Belgian franc	33.456	29.480	30.962	35.774	36.299	37.813	43.671	45.039	...
Austrian schilling	11.422	10.081	10.587	12.204	12.379	12.898	14.897	15.363	...
Finnish markka	5.224	4.367	4.594	5.191	5.344	5.573	6.437	6.638	...
Greek drachma	242.6	231.7	240.7	273.1	295.5	305.1	360.9	380.4	...
Portuguese escudo	166.0	151.1	154.2	175.3	180.1	187.9	217.0	223.8	...
Japanese yen	102.2	94.1	108.8	121.0	130.9	113.9	107.8	121.5	131.2
Canadian dollar	1.366	1.372	1.363	1.385	1.483	1.486	1.485	1.549	1.594
Swedish krona	7.716	7.133	6.706	7.635	7.950	8.262	9.162	10.329	10.451
Danish krone	6.361	5.602	5.799	6.604	6.701	6.976	8.083	8.323	8.548
Swiss franc	1.368	1.182	1.236	1.451	1.450	1.502	1.689	1.688	1.698
Norwegian krone	7.058	6.335	6.450	7.073	7.545	7.799	8.802	8.992	8.926
Israeli new sheqel	3.011	3.011	3.192	3.449	3.800	4.140	4.077	4.206	4.715
Icelandic krona	69.94	64.69	66.50	70.90	70.96	72.34	78.62	97.42	101.60
Cyprus pound	0.492	0.452	0.466	0.514	0.518	0.543	0.622	0.643	0.658
Korean won	803.4	771.3	804.5	951.3	1,401.4	1,188.8	1,131.0	1,291.0	1,291.0
Australian dollar	1.367	1.349	1.277	1.344	1.589	1.550	1.717	1.932	1.927
New Taiwan dollar	26.456	26.486	27.458	28.703	33.456	32.270	31.234	33.809	35.154
Hong Kong dollar	7.728	7.736	7.734	7.742	7.745	7.757	7.767	7.800	7.800
Singapore dollar	1.527	1.417	1.410	1.485	1.674	1.695	1.724	1.792	1.832
									Percent change from previous assumption[2]
					Index, 1990 = 100				
Real effective exchange rates[3]									
United States	93.7	86.4	89.6	94.8	101.0	99.6	107.3	117.6	1.3
Japan	138.8	145.8	124.1	117.9	109.2	123.1	130.7	114.1	−1.3
Euro[4]	97.2	101.6	102.2	92.1	89.1	84.8	75.8	75.8	−0.6
Germany	113.7	122.3	120.9	113.9	111.3	108.3	102.4	101.9	−0.2
France	96.4	97.3	94.3	90.4	90.0	89.2	85.8	84.9	−0.2
United Kingdom	96.1	92.7	96.2	114.8	122.2	124.6	131.8	131.9	0.6
Italy	80.0	73.6	84.3	86.2	84.6	84.3	81.6	81.2	−0.2
Canada	88.6	88.0	88.9	91.4	85.9	85.3	85.8	82.9	−0.2
Spain	94.8	93.9	96.3	93.9	95.7	95.9	94.7	96.9	−0.2
Netherlands	102.4	104.8	101.7	97.1	98.3	97.6	95.5	97.3	−0.2
Belgium	100.8	103.7	99.3	95.8	95.1	91.5	88.5	89.4	−0.2
Sweden	80.0	80.5	90.8	88.5	87.1	84.4	83.8	76.0	1.1
Austria	95.4	91.9	87.3	82.8	81.3	79.3	77.3	76.4	−0.1
Denmark	99.4	102.4	100.5	97.9	99.3	98.9	95.5	96.4	−0.3
Finland	67.4	74.3	68.7	64.7	63.8	61.4	58.5	58.8	−0.4
Greece	100.4	106.4	109.3	113.3	109.6	110.3	106.8	107.2	−0.1
Portugal	115.0	119.7	120.1	119.4	120.6	121.0	119.7	122.3	−0.2
Ireland	75.1	70.2	66.8	62.6	56.7	53.0	47.9	47.4	−0.4
Switzerland	104.9	111.5	111.6	108.0	114.0	113.2	112.4	117.4	−0.3
Norway	97.4	103.0	105.4	110.2	111.6	117.2	119.8	127.1	1.1
Australia	93.5	92.6	108.7	113.5	102.1	104.3	98.8	94.2	0.9
New Zealand	96.5	102.4	114.6	119.1	103.5	101.2	89.9	87.9	1.2

[1]Average exchange rates for the period February 11-March 11, 2002. See "Assumptions" in the Introduction to the Statistical Appendix.

[2]In nominal effective terms. Average February 11-March 11, 2002 rates compared with December 3, 2001-January 17, 2002 rates.

[3]Defined as the ratio, in common currency, of the normalized unit labor costs in the manufacturing sector to the weighted average of those of its industrial country trading partners, using 1989–91 trade weights.

[4]A synthetic euro for the period prior to January 1, 1999 is used in the calculation of real effective exchange rates for the euro. See Box 5.5 in the *World Economic Outlook*, October 1998.

Table 20. Developing Countries: Central Government Fiscal Balances
(Percent of GDP)

	1994	1995	1996	1997	1998	1999	2000	2001	2002	2003
Developing countries	**−2.8**	**−2.6**	**−2.2**	**−2.5**	**−3.8**	**−4.1**	**−3.2**	**−3.8**	**−3.9**	**−3.3**
Regional groups										
Africa	−5.3	−4.1	−2.7	−3.0	−3.9	−3.7	−1.4	−1.6	−3.3	−2.4
Sub-Sahara	−5.8	−4.3	−3.4	−3.7	−3.9	−4.4	−2.4	−2.0	−3.6	−2.7
Excluding Nigeria and South Africa	−6.3	−5.3	−3.9	−4.2	−3.7	−4.9	−3.6	−2.6	−2.7	−2.5
Developing Asia	−2.6	−2.5	−2.0	−2.5	−3.6	−4.2	−4.2	−4.1	−4.1	−3.7
China	−1.6	−2.1	−1.6	−1.9	−3.0	−4.0	−3.6	−3.3	−3.4	−3.1
India	−5.5	−4.6	−4.2	−4.7	−5.3	−5.5	−5.7	−5.9	−6.2	−5.9
Other developing Asia	−2.1	−1.4	−1.0	−2.0	−3.0	−3.3	−4.3	−4.3	−3.7	−2.9
Middle East and Turkey	−5.5	−3.6	−3.1	−3.5	−5.9	−3.9	−0.2	−5.4	−5.5	−3.8
Western Hemisphere	−1.0	−1.9	−1.8	−1.7	−3.3	−4.3	−2.7	−3.1	−2.7	−2.2
Analytical groups										
By source of export earnings										
Fuel	−6.6	−3.3	—	−1.0	−5.8	−1.9	5.6	0.2	−2.2	−1.5
Nonfuel	−2.3	−2.5	−2.4	−2.7	−3.6	−4.4	−4.1	−4.2	−4.0	−3.5
of which, primary products	−3.4	−1.8	−1.1	−1.8	−1.6	−2.8	−3.1	−2.9	−2.9	−2.6
By external financing source										
Net debtor countries	−2.6	−2.6	−2.3	−2.6	−3.7	−4.3	−3.5	−3.9	−4.0	−3.3
of which, official financing	−5.3	−3.5	−2.1	−2.7	−3.6	−3.3	−2.0	−2.5	−3.7	−3.4
Net debtor countries by debt-servicing experience										
Countries with arrears and/or rescheduling during 1994–98	−2.2	−1.9	−1.2	−2.0	−4.1	−3.9	−1.1	−2.4	−2.8	−1.9
Other groups										
Heavily indebted poor countries	−5.9	−3.7	−2.6	−3.5	−2.5	−3.6	−2.7	−3.1	−3.3	−3.1
Middle East and north Africa	−5.6	−3.4	−1.1	−1.7	−4.9	−1.4	3.1	−0.8	−2.7	−2.5
Memorandum										
Median										
Developing countries	−3.8	−3.3	−2.4	−2.4	−3.0	−3.3	−3.2	−3.4	−3.5	−2.8
Regional groups										
Africa	−4.8	−3.9	−4.1	−3.0	−3.2	−3.3	−3.1	−3.2	−2.9	−2.8
Developing Asia	−3.4	−3.4	−2.1	−2.2	−2.5	−4.0	−4.5	−4.6	−5.0	−3.1
Middle East and Turkey	−4.8	−4.3	−2.2	−2.5	−5.8	−2.4	2.0	−0.7	−2.5	−3.5
Western Hemisphere	−1.0	−1.7	−1.7	−1.6	−2.4	−3.2	−2.7	−3.5	−2.6	−2.0

Table 21. Developing Countries: Broad Money Aggregates
(Annual percent change)

	1994	1995	1996	1997	1998	1999	2000	2001	2002	2003
Developing countries	**68.4**	**24.4**	**22.5**	**22.4**	**17.3**	**15.2**	**11.4**	**12.5**	**10.4**	**11.2**
Regional groups										
Africa	43.5	23.8	12.0	18.1	16.7	19.6	20.9	19.6	11.3	10.2
Sub-Sahara	53.5	28.8	12.4	19.3	18.2	21.5	23.9	22.4	12.6	11.2
Developing Asia	25.0	22.6	20.4	17.9	18.3	14.2	12.1	12.9	13.0	13.0
China	34.9	29.5	25.3	19.6	14.8	14.7	12.3	14.4	13.5	13.0
India	20.2	13.7	16.9	17.6	20.2	18.2	15.5	14.9	15.3	15.1
Other developing Asia	18.5	20.8	17.6	16.5	21.3	11.4	9.6	9.1	10.4	11.4
Middle East and Turkey	43.6	33.2	36.9	27.5	26.9	29.6	18.9	22.6	12.1	10.7
Western Hemisphere	156.0	22.8	22.1	26.3	12.9	10.3	6.0	6.7	6.5	9.5
Analytical groups										
By source of export earnings										
Fuel	25.8	17.0	22.1	16.5	13.1	16.2	17.6	13.9	6.7	9.8
Nonfuel	76.3	25.5	22.6	23.1	17.8	15.0	10.6	12.3	10.9	11.4
of which, primary products	61.7	32.8	12.7	21.2	13.5	22.6	20.4	18.1	12.5	12.6
By external financing source										
Net debtor countries	73.7	25.8	23.5	23.4	18.1	15.7	11.7	12.8	11.1	11.6
of which, official financing	45.6	22.8	0.8	16.6	16.1	22.0	25.8	20.2	12.4	11.8
Net debtor countries by debt-servicing experience										
Countries with arrears and/or rescheduling during 1994–98	229.3	27.4	15.5	22.9	18.6	14.4	11.9	14.2	11.0	11.1
Other groups										
Heavily indebted poor countries	91.6	39.9	13.5	22.8	19.8	33.3	34.8	25.1	15.9	14.0
Middle East and north Africa	14.4	12.7	12.9	10.3	10.2	11.3	12.4	12.5	7.6	8.9
Memorandum										
Median										
Developing countries	18.8	16.3	13.6	15.5	10.5	13.1	12.0	10.5	9.2	9.3
Regional groups										
Africa	31.0	16.2	14.1	14.3	9.6	13.5	14.2	11.9	9.9	9.3
Developing Asia	19.4	16.7	15.0	16.8	12.4	14.9	12.4	11.6	11.0	11.7
Middle East and Turkey	11.4	9.9	9.0	9.7	8.5	11.4	10.2	9.2	6.5	6.7
Western Hemisphere	18.3	20.0	16.7	17.3	11.5	12.2	8.9	9.1	7.8	9.0

Table 22. Summary of World Trade Volumes and Prices

(Annual percent change)

	Ten-Year Averages		1994	1995	1996	1997	1998	1999	2000	2001	2002	2003
	1984–93	1994–2003										
Trade in goods and services												
World trade[1]												
Volume	5.5	6.6	8.8	9.7	6.8	10.5	4.2	5.3	12.4	−0.2	2.5	6.6
Price deflator												
In U.S. dollars	2.4	−0.7	2.7	8.9	−1.3	−6.1	−4.6	−2.0	−0.7	−3.3	−1.3	1.0
In SDRs	−0.3	0.3	0.2	2.8	3.2	−0.9	−3.2	−2.8	2.9	0.1	0.6	0.8
Volume of trade												
Exports												
Advanced economies	5.8	6.0	8.6	8.3	6.0	10.5	4.0	5.2	11.7	−1.3	0.9	6.3
Developing countries	6.7	8.4	11.6	11.0	9.6	13.8	4.8	4.3	15.0	3.0	4.8	7.0
Imports												
Advanced economies	6.3	6.6	9.5	8.7	6.4	9.3	5.9	7.8	11.6	−1.5	2.1	6.6
Developing countries	4.4	7.9	6.5	19.1	9.6	11.7	−0.8	1.3	16.0	2.9	6.4	7.7
Terms of trade												
Advanced economies	1.1	—	0.1	0.2	−0.2	−0.6	1.4	−0.1	−2.2	0.2	0.9	0.4
Developing countries	−2.8	0.3	0.9	2.8	1.8	−0.7	−6.7	4.5	7.0	−2.8	−1.6	−1.2
Trade in goods												
World trade[1]												
Volume	5.7	6.8	10.0	10.4	6.4	10.6	4.6	5.6	12.8	−0.7	2.6	6.7
Price deflator												
In U.S. dollars	2.1	−0.7	2.6	9.3	−1.2	−6.3	−5.4	−2.0	0.3	−3.5	−1.5	1.0
In SDRs	−0.6	0.3	0.1	3.2	3.2	−1.1	−4.1	−2.7	4.0	—	0.4	0.9
World trade prices in U.S. dollars[2]												
Manufactures	4.4	−0.9	3.1	10.3	−3.1	−8.0	−1.8	−1.9	−5.1	−2.4	−0.5	1.2
Oil	−5.5	2.7	−5.0	7.9	18.4	−5.4	−32.1	37.5	57.0	−14.0	−5.3	−4.4
Nonfuel primary commodities	0.3	−0.4	13.4	8.4	−1.3	−3.0	−14.7	−7.0	1.8	−5.5	−0.1	7.2
World trade prices in SDRs[2]												
Manufactures	1.6	0.2	0.6	4.1	1.2	−2.9	−0.4	−2.7	−1.6	1.1	1.4	1.0
Oil	−8.0	3.9	−7.3	1.8	23.7	−0.2	−31.2	36.5	62.8	−10.9	−3.4	−4.5
Nonfuel primary commodities	−2.4	0.7	10.6	2.3	3.1	2.4	−13.4	−7.8	5.6	−2.1	1.8	7.0
World trade prices in euros[2]												
Manufactures	1.4	1.4	2.1	0.2	−0.6	5.0	−0.2	2.5	7.9	−1.3	−1.6	0.1
Oil	−8.2	5.1	−6.0	−2.0	21.6	7.9	−31.0	43.6	78.6	−13.0	−6.3	−5.4
Nonfuel primary commodities	−2.6	1.9	12.2	−1.5	1.3	10.7	−13.3	−2.9	15.8	−4.4	−1.2	6.1

Table 22 *(concluded)*

	Ten-Year Averages		1994	1995	1996	1997	1998	1999	2000	2001	2002	2003
	1984–93	1994–2003										
Trade in goods												
Volume of trade												
Exports												
Advanced economies	6.1	6.1	9.6	9.0	5.7	10.9	4.4	5.2	12.0	−1.9	1.2	6.3
Developing countries	6.9	8.4	12.0	12.3	9.1	12.7	4.7	4.8	15.3	2.4	4.8	6.7
Fuel exporters	5.8	4.1	3.1	16.7	6.8	5.0	2.0	1.0	5.8	−0.1	−1.7	3.3
Nonfuel exporters	7.5	9.6	15.1	11.0	9.7	15.1	5.5	5.6	17.8	3.3	6.7	7.4
Imports												
Advanced economies	6.6	6.8	11.1	9.2	5.8	10.0	6.0	8.7	11.9	−2.0	1.8	6.7
Developing countries	4.6	8.1	8.2	20.0	9.6	10.2	0.5	0.7	16.5	1.8	6.8	8.2
Fuel exporters	−2.4	9.6	−11.3	71.2	7.7	14.1	3.3	−0.5	10.8	8.4	4.6	4.0
Nonfuel exporters	7.4	7.7	12.7	10.8	10.0	9.5	—	0.9	17.5	0.8	7.2	8.9
Price deflators in SDRs												
Exports												
Advanced economies	0.1	−0.1	0.3	3.4	1.8	−2.2	−3.4	−3.4	1.0	0.1	0.6	1.1
Developing countries	−3.2	1.6	0.3	2.8	7.6	1.4	−10.7	4.9	13.9	−1.9	−0.4	0.1
Fuel exporters	−7.9	2.8	−3.0	−1.8	18.8	1.4	−26.5	26.6	48.3	−7.4	−5.6	−4.9
Nonfuel exporters	−0.7	1.2	1.5	4.2	4.4	1.3	−6.2	0.2	4.9	−0.1	1.1	1.2
Imports												
Advanced economies	−1.0	−0.1	−0.2	3.0	2.6	−1.6	−4.9	−3.4	3.7	−0.3	0.1	0.7
Developing countries	0.2	1.2	−1.0	0.6	4.8	2.2	−4.5	0.4	6.1	1.1	1.3	1.2
Fuel exporters	0.3	—	−2.2	−7.7	1.3	1.0	−1.1	−1.9	3.4	3.5	2.5	1.3
Nonfuel exporters	—	1.4	−0.7	2.1	5.5	2.4	−5.0	0.7	6.5	0.7	1.0	1.2
Terms of trade												
Advanced economies	1.2	—	0.5	0.4	−0.8	−0.6	1.6	0.1	−2.5	0.4	0.6	0.4
Developing countries	−3.3	0.4	1.2	2.2	2.6	−0.9	−6.5	4.5	7.4	−3.0	−1.6	−1.1
Fuel exporters	−8.3	2.8	−0.9	6.4	17.3	0.5	−25.7	29.0	43.4	−10.5	−7.9	−6.2
Nonfuel exporters	−0.7	−0.2	2.1	2.1	−1.0	−1.1	−1.2	−0.5	−1.5	−0.8	0.1	0.1
Memorandum												
World exports in billions of												
U.S. dollars												
Goods and services	3,564	6,953	5,282	6,260	6,584	6,848	6,791	6,959	7,744	7,465	7,516	8,078
Goods	2,849	5,566	4,203	5,035	5,271	5,474	5,399	5,543	6,252	5,985	6,025	6,475

[1]Average of annual percent change for world exports and imports. The estimates of world trade comprise, in addition to trade of advanced economies and developing countries (which is summarized in the table), trade of countries in transition.

[2]As represented, respectively, by the export unit value index for the manufactures of the advanced economies; the average of U.K. Brent, Dubai, and West Texas Intermediate crude oil spot prices; and the average of world market prices for nonfuel primary commodities weighted by their 1987–89 shares in world commodity exports.

Table 23. Nonfuel Commodity Prices[1]
(Annual percent change; U.S. dollar terms)

| | Ten-Year Averages | | 1994 | 1995 | 1996 | 1997 | 1998 | 1999 | 2000 | 2001 | 2002 | 2003 |
	1984–93	1994–2003										
Nonfuel primary commodities	**0.3**	**−0.4**	**13.4**	**8.4**	**−1.3**	**−3.0**	**−14.7**	**−7.0**	**1.8**	**−5.5**	**−0.1**	**7.2**
Food	−1.0	−0.6	5.1	8.1	12.2	−10.7	−12.6	−15.6	−0.5	3.0	3.9	5.4
Beverages	−6.0	−0.2	74.9	0.9	−17.4	32.6	−15.2	−21.3	−16.6	−19.1	3.9	8.5
Agricultural raw materials	4.6	−1.3	9.5	4.3	−3.1	−6.1	−16.2	2.3	2.0	−7.2	−4.6	9.3
Metals	−1.0	1.3	16.5	19.6	−11.8	3.0	−16.3	−1.5	12.1	−9.5	0.3	6.7
Fertilizers	−1.4	2.1	8.0	10.6	13.7	1.1	2.8	−4.0	−5.3	−5.8	−0.9	2.4
Advanced economies	**−0.3**	**−0.2**	**13.3**	**11.2**	**−2.4**	**−3.9**	**−15.7**	**−6.8**	**4.1**	**−5.9**	**0.7**	**6.9**
Developing countries	**−0.4**	**−0.5**	**15.8**	**9.6**	**−2.6**	**−1.4**	**−16.2**	**−9.2**	**1.8**	**−7.0**	**1.2**	**7.3**
Regional groups												
Africa	−0.3	−0.7	16.6	8.1	−5.3	−1.0	−14.6	−8.4	0.6	−7.2	0.5	7.6
Sub-Sahara	−0.3	−0.7	16.9	8.0	−5.9	−0.7	−14.7	−8.2	0.7	−7.6	0.5	7.7
Developing Asia	0.1	−0.7	13.5	8.2	−1.4	−3.4	−14.3	−8.0	0.3	−6.9	0.7	7.3
Excluding China and India	0.1	−1.0	13.9	7.4	−1.5	−3.9	−13.7	−9.3	−1.4	−6.8	1.3	7.3
Middle East and Turkey	−0.6	—	15.2	12.5	−3.5	−2.7	−15.4	−7.8	4.2	−6.3	0.8	7.1
Western Hemisphere	−1.1	−0.3	17.8	11.0	−2.8	0.4	−18.3	−10.6	3.3	−7.2	1.8	7.1
Analytical groups												
By source of export earnings												
Fuel	0.4	−0.4	10.5	11.6	−7.2	−0.4	−16.9	−3.5	7.3	−8.4	0.4	6.7
Nonfuel	−0.5	−0.5	16.0	9.5	−2.5	−1.5	−16.1	−9.3	1.6	−7.0	1.2	7.3
of which, primary products	−0.6	−0.5	18.8	14.0	−8.7	−1.0	−16.2	−11.4	3.1	−7.6	2.2	7.8
By external financing source												
Net debtor countries	−0.5	−0.5	15.8	9.6	−2.6	−1.5	−16.1	−9.2	1.8	−7.0	1.1	7.3
of which, official financing	−0.4	−1.3	21.1	9.2	−8.1	−0.3	−13.9	−12.0	−2.5	−10.1	1.4	7.8
Net debtor countries by debt-servicing experience												
Countries with arrears and/or rescheduling during 1994–98	−1.1	−0.5	18.5	9.3	−4.2	0.5	−15.9	−10.7	1.2	−7.6	1.5	7.1
Other groups												
Heavily indebted poor countries	−1.9	−0.7	24.9	7.8	−7.0	2.0	−12.0	−14.6	−4.5	−8.1	2.5	7.5
Middle East and north Africa	−0.6	−0.2	15.3	11.4	−2.8	−2.8	−15.0	−8.6	3.2	−6.1	0.7	7.1
Memorandum												
Average oil spot price[2]	−5.5	2.7	−5.0	7.9	18.4	−5.4	−32.1	37.5	57.0	−14.0	−5.3	−4.4
In U.S. dollars a barrel	19.91	20.14	15.95	17.20	20.37	19.27	13.07	17.98	28.24	24.28	23.00	22.00
Export unit value of manufactures[3]	4.4	−0.9	3.1	10.3	−3.1	−8.0	−1.8	−1.9	−5.1	−2.4	−0.5	1.2

[1]Averages of world market prices for individual commodities weighted by 1987–89 exports as a share of world commodity exports and total commodity exports for the indicated country group, respectively.
[2]Average of U.K. Brent, Dubai, and West Texas Intermediate crude oil spot prices.
[3]For the manufactures exported by the advanced economies.

Table 24. Advanced Economies: Export Volumes, Import Volumes, and Terms of Trade in Goods and Services
(Annual percent change)

| | Ten-Year Averages | | 1994 | 1995 | 1996 | 1997 | 1998 | 1999 | 2000 | 2001 | 2002 | 2003 |
	1984–93	1994–2003										
Export volume												
Advanced economies	**5.8**	**6.0**	**8.6**	**8.3**	**6.0**	**10.5**	**4.0**	**5.2**	**11.7**	**−1.3**	**0.9**	**6.3**
Major advanced economies	5.6	5.5	8.0	8.1	5.8	10.6	3.7	4.0	11.1	−1.5	−0.5	6.3
United States	8.2	5.0	8.9	10.3	8.2	12.3	2.1	3.2	9.5	−4.6	−4.6	5.9
Japan	4.3	3.8	3.4	4.1	6.4	11.3	−2.3	1.3	12.4	−6.5	1.7	7.4
Germany	4.7	6.9	7.6	5.7	5.1	11.2	6.8	5.6	13.2	4.7	2.6	6.9
France	4.7	6.0	7.7	7.7	3.5	11.8	8.2	3.9	13.3	1.1	−2.4	5.9
Italy	5.2	5.3	9.8	12.6	0.6	6.4	3.4	0.3	11.7	0.8	2.4	6.2
United Kingdom	4.2	6.0	9.2	9.0	8.2	8.3	3.0	5.4	10.3	1.0	1.1	5.5
Canada	6.4	6.4	12.8	8.5	5.6	8.3	8.8	10.0	7.7	−3.6	0.4	6.3
Other advanced economies	6.2	6.7	9.7	8.7	6.4	10.4	4.3	7.2	12.7	−0.8	3.1	6.3
Memorandum												
European Union	4.7	6.5	8.8	7.9	5.0	10.2	6.4	5.3	11.9	2.1	1.7	6.3
Euro area	4.9	6.6	8.6	7.7	4.5	10.6	7.0	5.1	12.3	2.5	1.6	6.5
Newly industrialized Asian economies	9.6	7.2	11.3	12.7	7.6	10.8	0.4	8.4	16.1	−5.2	4.7	7.0
Import volume												
Advanced economies	**6.3**	**6.6**	**9.5**	**8.7**	**6.4**	**9.3**	**5.9**	**7.8**	**11.6**	**−1.5**	**2.1**	**6.6**
Major advanced economies	5.9	6.6	8.8	7.9	6.5	9.5	7.8	7.8	11.6	−1.2	1.1	6.6
United States	7.0	8.3	12.0	8.2	8.6	13.7	11.8	10.5	13.4	−2.7	2.0	7.1
Japan	5.9	4.1	7.7	12.8	13.2	1.2	−6.8	3.0	9.6	−0.4	−1.8	4.7
Germany	4.8	6.1	7.4	5.6	3.1	8.3	8.9	8.5	10.0	0.1	2.5	7.0
France	4.5	5.9	8.2	8.0	1.6	6.9	11.9	4.2	15.4	−0.2	−3.0	7.0
Italy	5.7	5.7	8.1	9.7	−0.3	10.1	8.9	5.3	9.4	0.2	2.1	4.8
United Kingdom	5.2	7.1	5.7	5.4	9.6	9.7	9.6	8.9	10.9	2.8	3.3	5.7
Canada	7.3	5.3	8.1	5.8	5.1	14.3	4.9	7.3	8.1	−5.6	−1.4	8.2
Other advanced economies	7.0	6.5	10.6	10.0	6.1	9.0	2.6	7.8	11.6	−2.1	4.0	6.6
Memorandum												
European Union	5.1	6.5	7.9	7.1	4.1	9.3	9.9	7.3	11.1	0.9	1.8	6.2
Euro area	5.2	6.4	8.0	7.4	3.3	9.1	9.9	7.2	11.1	0.7	1.4	6.4
Newly industrialized Asian economies	13.0	6.3	13.1	14.4	7.8	8.1	−9.0	8.5	15.2	−7.0	7.2	8.0
Terms of trade												
Advanced economies	**1.1**	**—**	**0.1**	**0.2**	**−0.2**	**−0.6**	**1.4**	**−0.1**	**−2.2**	**0.2**	**0.9**	**0.4**
Major advanced economies	0.8	0.1	0.1	−0.1	−0.3	−0.4	2.2	−0.1	−2.8	0.6	1.1	0.5
United States	−0.1	0.9	—	−0.5	0.6	1.6	3.5	−0.9	−2.5	2.5	2.9	1.6
Japan	3.1	−0.8	1.5	−0.1	−5.4	−3.7	3.2	−0.6	−4.5	−1.6	3.2	0.1
Germany	−0.4	−0.3	0.2	0.8	−0.7	−1.9	2.0	0.6	−4.5	0.1	0.2	—
France	0.7	−0.2	0.2	0.1	−1.2	—	1.1	−0.3	−2.5	1.1	−0.4	−0.4
Italy	1.9	−0.4	−0.9	−2.3	4.3	−1.5	2.0	−0.6	−6.3	1.8	0.5	−0.3
United Kingdom	0.4	0.7	−1.7	−2.8	1.4	3.1	3.2	1.9	2.1	−0.5	0.7	−0.4
Canada	−0.5	−0.2	−0.7	2.9	1.7	−0.7	−4.1	1.1	4.2	−1.3	−4.6	0.2
Other advanced economies	1.5	−0.1	0.1	0.6	−0.1	−0.7	0.2	−0.2	−1.1	−0.5	0.4	0.2
Memorandum												
European Union	0.7	−0.1	−0.4	−0.3	0.3	−0.4	1.6	0.1	−2.2	0.5	0.1	−0.1
Euro area	0.8	−0.2	−0.2	—	0.1	−0.9	1.5	−0.2	−3.1	0.6	—	−0.1
Newly industrialized Asian economies	3.5	−0.6	—	0.1	−0.7	−1.1	0.3	−1.1	−4.2	−1.4	2.0	0.5
Memorandum												
Trade in goods												
Advanced economies												
Export volume	6.1	6.1	9.6	9.0	5.7	10.9	4.4	5.2	12.0	−1.9	1.2	6.3
Import volume	6.6	6.8	11.1	9.2	5.8	10.0	6.0	8.7	11.9	−2.0	1.8	6.7
Terms of trade	1.2	—	0.5	0.4	−0.8	−0.6	1.6	0.1	−2.5	0.4	0.6	0.4

Table 25. Developing Countries—by Region: Total Trade in Goods
(Annual percent change)

	Ten-Year Averages		1994	1995	1996	1997	1998	1999	2000	2001	2002	2003
	1984–93	1994–2003										
Developing countries												
Value in U.S. dollars												
Exports	5.0	8.5	15.1	20.5	11.8	8.1	−7.8	9.6	25.5	−2.9	2.5	6.8
Imports	6.6	7.2	9.8	18.9	9.5	6.6	−5.2	0.7	18.9	−0.8	6.2	9.6
Volume												
Exports	6.9	8.4	12.0	12.3	9.1	12.7	4.7	4.8	15.3	2.4	4.8	6.7
Imports	4.6	8.1	8.2	20.0	9.6	10.2	0.5	0.7	16.5	1.8	6.8	8.2
Unit value in U.S. dollars												
Exports	−0.5	0.5	2.8	9.0	3.0	−3.9	−11.9	5.7	9.9	−5.3	−2.3	0.3
Imports	2.9	0.1	1.6	6.6	0.3	−3.1	−5.8	1.2	2.3	−2.4	−0.7	1.4
Terms of trade	−3.3	0.4	1.2	2.2	2.6	−0.9	−6.5	4.5	7.4	−3.0	−1.6	−1.1
Memorandum												
Real GDP growth in developing country trading partners	4.0	3.2	4.3	3.6	3.9	4.1	1.7	3.4	4.7	1.2	1.9	3.4
Market prices of nonfuel commodities exported by developing countries	−0.4	−0.5	15.8	9.6	−2.6	−1.4	−16.2	−9.2	1.8	−7.0	1.2	7.3
Regional groups												
Africa												
Value in U.S. dollars												
Exports	1.8	4.5	3.6	18.4	11.6	1.9	−13.5	6.9	25.1	−4.5	−3.4	4.2
Imports	2.0	4.3	5.1	20.3	1.0	4.2	−0.6	−0.7	5.3	2.5	2.6	4.8
Volume												
Exports	2.8	4.1	3.0	8.9	8.2	5.5	1.0	2.7	5.5	2.5	0.7	3.6
Imports	1.6	4.8	4.7	11.9	4.7	7.1	5.5	0.4	4.3	3.9	2.2	4.0
Unit value in U.S. dollars												
Exports	−0.2	0.4	0.9	8.9	3.2	−3.3	−14.4	4.4	18.8	−7.1	−4.1	0.8
Imports	1.3	−0.1	1.3	7.7	−2.7	−2.5	−5.4	−1.0	2.1	−1.3	0.4	1.1
Terms of trade	−1.6	0.5	−0.4	1.1	6.1	−0.9	−9.5	5.5	16.4	−5.9	−4.5	−0.2
Sub-Sahara												
Value in U.S. dollars												
Exports	2.0	4.1	4.7	18.4	11.0	1.5	−13.7	5.4	21.6	−4.5	−2.2	3.8
Imports	1.7	4.2	3.1	21.7	3.4	6.8	−2.6	−2.1	5.7	1.4	2.0	4.3
Volume												
Exports	3.2	4.0	3.3	10.0	9.9	5.2	0.3	0.9	4.7	2.6	1.0	3.0
Imports	2.1	4.7	2.8	13.7	9.5	8.1	3.6	−1.0	3.6	2.3	1.3	3.5
Unit value in U.S. dollars												
Exports	−0.3	0.3	2.0	7.8	1.1	−3.3	−14.0	4.9	16.6	−7.2	−3.2	1.0
Imports	0.6	—	1.1	7.2	−4.9	−0.8	−5.6	−1.1	3.4	−0.9	0.7	1.1
Terms of trade	−0.9	0.3	0.8	0.6	6.3	−2.6	−8.9	6.0	12.8	−6.4	−3.9	—

Table 25 *(concluded)*

| | Ten-Year Averages | | 1994 | 1995 | 1996 | 1997 | 1998 | 1999 | 2000 | 2001 | 2002 | 2003 |
	1984–93	1994–2003										
Developing Asia												
Value in U.S. dollars												
Exports	11.8	10.8	23.9	23.2	10.0	12.2	−2.2	8.4	22.2	−1.2	5.3	9.4
Imports	10.9	8.8	17.8	23.7	10.5	1.1	−13.5	9.0	27.2	−0.6	7.9	10.7
Volume												
Exports	9.5	10.8	20.8	11.5	9.2	18.3	5.9	5.5	22.8	2.1	6.3	8.0
Imports	8.2	8.7	16.2	12.9	9.8	6.0	−6.6	6.5	23.7	3.1	8.7	9.7
Unit value in U.S. dollars												
Exports	2.5	0.2	2.6	10.6	1.1	−5.0	−7.5	4.7	−0.2	−3.3	−1.0	1.3
Imports	2.9	0.4	1.5	9.6	1.0	−4.5	−7.8	5.4	3.4	−3.3	−0.7	0.9
Terms of trade	−0.4	−0.2	1.1	0.9	0.1	−0.5	0.4	−0.7	−3.5	−0.1	−0.3	0.4
Excluding China and India												
Value in U.S. dollars												
Exports	11.4	7.7	18.8	22.4	5.7	7.4	−3.9	10.2	18.8	−8.3	2.1	7.9
Imports	10.1	5.7	20.3	26.8	5.7	−0.7	−22.9	6.2	22.7	−5.5	4.9	9.3
Volume												
Exports	10.4	7.0	16.5	10.3	2.0	11.1	8.1	3.4	15.7	−5.0	3.6	6.5
Imports	8.5	4.8	19.7	16.4	3.7	1.7	−14.1	−0.1	18.1	−5.8	5.9	8.1
Unit value in U.S. dollars												
Exports	1.2	1.0	2.1	11.0	3.8	−3.2	−11.0	10.1	2.8	−3.6	−1.4	1.4
Imports	1.8	1.4	0.7	9.1	2.4	−2.4	−10.6	11.8	4.1	0.4	−0.9	1.2
Terms of trade	−0.6	−0.4	1.4	1.7	1.4	−0.9	−0.4	−1.6	−1.3	−4.0	−0.5	0.2
Middle East and Turkey												
Value in U.S. dollars												
Exports	0.5	5.2	6.4	14.3	16.9	1.1	−21.6	22.4	40.1	−7.2	−5.8	−1.5
Imports	1.7	4.0	−10.6	17.5	10.9	6.7	−1.6	−4.6	14.8	−3.3	6.3	7.5
Volume												
Exports	6.5	5.2	5.5	17.6	7.9	6.0	1.8	1.8	7.3	1.6	0.6	3.1
Imports	−0.5	9.2	−12.3	64.7	14.1	12.6	4.3	−2.6	13.9	−1.8	7.6	6.2
Unit value in U.S. dollars												
Exports	−5.0	1.0	0.8	4.0	9.9	−4.5	−22.7	20.2	31.6	−8.8	−6.4	−4.4
Imports	3.1	−1.4	1.3	−0.5	−2.1	−4.8	−5.2	−1.8	1.0	−1.4	−1.2	1.3
Terms of trade	−7.8	2.4	−0.4	4.5	12.3	0.4	−18.4	22.4	30.3	−7.5	−5.2	−5.5
Western Hemisphere												
Value in U.S. dollars												
Exports	4.8	9.0	15.4	22.2	10.5	10.0	−3.8	4.3	20.1	−1.5	6.9	9.3
Imports	9.8	8.0	17.2	10.7	10.6	18.3	4.5	−6.7	13.5	−0.6	4.5	10.6
Volume												
Exports	7.1	8.5	8.6	10.6	10.3	12.2	6.8	6.5	11.3	3.8	7.4	7.8
Imports	7.8	7.2	14.9	4.8	8.4	17.7	7.7	−5.0	11.6	1.3	4.6	8.2
Unit value in U.S. dollars												
Exports	0.4	0.6	6.3	10.7	0.2	−1.7	−10.0	−1.8	8.4	−5.2	−0.5	1.3
Imports	3.6	0.7	2.1	5.8	2.3	0.7	−3.0	−1.9	1.6	−1.9	−0.6	2.5
Terms of trade	−3.1	−0.1	4.2	4.6	−2.0	−2.4	−7.2	0.1	6.7	−3.4	0.1	−1.2

Table 26. Developing Countries—by Source of Export Earnings: Total Trade in Goods
(Annual percent change)

| | Ten-Year Averages | | 1994 | 1995 | 1996 | 1997 | 1998 | 1999 | 2000 | 2001 | 2002 | 2003 |
	1984–93	1994–2003										
Fuel												
Value in U.S. dollars												
Exports	−0.6	4.9	2.5	13.8	20.6	0.8	−26.5	28.8	50.8	−10.7	−9.0	−1.9
Imports	−0.2	4.0	−10.9	13.1	3.4	8.9	0.3	−1.7	10.2	8.4	5.2	5.4
Volume												
Exports	5.8	4.1	3.1	16.7	6.8	5.0	2.0	1.0	5.8	−0.1	−1.7	3.3
Imports	−2.4	9.6	−11.3	71.2	7.7	14.1	3.3	−0.5	10.8	8.4	4.6	4.0
Unit value in U.S. dollars												
Exports	−5.4	1.7	−0.6	4.0	13.7	−3.8	−27.6	27.7	43.1	−10.6	−7.4	−4.8
Imports	3.1	−1.1	0.3	−2.3	−3.1	−4.3	−2.5	−1.1	−0.2	—	0.5	1.5
Terms of trade	−8.3	2.8	−0.9	6.4	17.3	0.5	−25.7	29.0	43.4	−10.5	−7.9	−6.2
Nonfuel												
Value in U.S. dollars												
Exports	8.2	9.5	19.5	22.5	9.3	10.3	−2.5	5.5	18.9	−0.3	5.9	9.0
Imports	9.2	7.8	14.6	19.9	10.5	6.3	−6.0	1.1	20.3	−2.2	6.4	10.3
Volume												
Exports	7.5	9.6	15.1	11.0	9.7	15.1	5.5	5.6	17.8	3.3	6.7	7.4
Imports	7.4	7.7	12.7	10.8	10.0	9.5	—	0.9	17.5	0.8	7.2	8.9
Unit value in U.S. dollars												
Exports	2.0	0.1	4.0	10.5	−0.1	−3.9	−7.5	1.0	1.2	−3.6	−0.8	1.4
Imports	2.7	0.3	1.8	8.2	0.9	−2.9	−6.4	1.5	2.8	−2.8	−0.9	1.4
Terms of trade	−0.7	−0.2	2.1	2.1	−1.0	−1.1	−1.2	−0.5	−1.5	−0.8	0.1	0.1
Primary products												
Value in U.S. dollars												
Exports	5.3	7.8	17.7	25.2	4.0	6.4	−5.6	3.9	12.6	0.9	5.5	10.3
Imports	6.0	6.9	11.5	25.3	8.9	7.8	−1.7	−8.4	9.7	0.9	7.1	10.9
Volume												
Exports	4.2	7.3	8.1	9.3	10.0	8.2	4.8	7.2	7.0	5.6	5.5	7.6
Imports	4.3	7.0	10.1	18.8	10.0	9.5	6.4	−8.2	5.2	3.5	7.5	9.7
Unit value in U.S. dollars												
Exports	1.8	0.5	10.0	15.1	−5.3	−1.3	−10.1	−3.2	5.1	−5.4	−0.1	2.5
Imports	2.4	0.1	2.2	5.6	−0.1	−1.8	−7.9	−0.5	5.4	−2.4	−0.4	1.2
Terms of trade	−0.6	0.4	7.6	8.9	−5.2	0.5	−2.4	−2.6	−0.3	−3.1	0.3	1.3

Table 27. Summary of Payments Balances on Current Account
(Billions of U.S. dollars)

	1994	1995	1996	1997	1998	1999	2000	2001	2002	2003
Advanced economies	**24.2**	**47.8**	**30.9**	**79.5**	**24.3**	**−138.6**	**−256.2**	**−186.4**	**−192.6**	**−191.5**
United States	−118.2	−109.9	−120.9	−139.8	−217.5	−324.4	−444.7	−417.4	−435.3	−451.8
European Union	10.1	46.1	77.4	107.3	61.7	5.1	−28.3	28.5	29.6	29.8
Euro area[1]	17.0	53.6	81.3	102.5	64.4	24.3	−11.0	41.9	50.1	53.8
Japan	130.6	111.4	65.7	96.6	119.1	114.5	119.6	87.6	110.2	127.0
Other advanced economies	1.8	0.2	8.7	15.4	61.0	66.2	97.2	114.9	103.0	103.5
Memorandum										
Newly industrialized Asian economies	16.1	6.4	−1.1	10.8	67.4	60.9	45.8	60.1	57.3	56.6
Developing countries	**−85.1**	**−96.7**	**−74.9**	**−58.0**	**−85.3**	**−11.2**	**65.6**	**27.3**	**−23.2**	**−50.6**
Regional groups										
Africa	−11.6	−17.3	−6.0	−7.2	−20.0	−15.3	3.1	−2.1	−10.8	−9.9
Developing Asia	−19.0	−43.1	−38.9	8.9	47.3	45.9	45.9	39.1	20.4	11.1
Excluding China and India	−25.0	−39.2	−40.1	−25.0	22.7	33.5	29.8	19.6	9.9	6.7
Middle East and Turkey	−2.3	0.2	10.4	7.3	−21.9	14.7	64.5	44.5	12.3	−3.6
Western Hemisphere	−52.2	−36.5	−40.5	−67.1	−90.7	−56.7	−47.9	−54.3	−45.0	−48.0
Analytical groups										
By source of export earnings										
Fuel	−2.8	2.3	30.6	21.3	−27.9	18.6	102.0	56.1	21.4	7.0
Nonfuel	−82.3	−99.0	−105.5	−79.4	−57.4	−29.8	−36.4	−28.8	−44.6	−57.6
of which, primary products	−11.5	−14.6	−16.9	−18.9	−19.0	−9.6	−9.4	−8.8	−11.4	−13.4
By external financing source										
Net debtor countries	−78.2	−99.2	−87.9	−69.8	−71.2	−24.7	4.7	−10.2	−37.2	−52.7
of which, official financing	−9.7	−12.1	−8.8	−4.7	−10.1	−6.1	3.5	−0.3	−7.4	−9.5
Net debtor countries by debt-servicing experience										
Countries with arrears and/or rescheduling during 1994–98	−18.3	−46.4	−42.1	−48.8	−58.0	−23.1	8.5	−11.2	−26.4	−33.7
Countries in transition	**2.2**	**−2.4**	**−16.9**	**−24.0**	**−29.4**	**−2.2**	**27.1**	**15.6**	**2.2**	**−6.1**
Central and eastern Europe	−3.3	−3.2	−15.0	−17.0	−20.4	−23.3	−19.9	−18.8	−19.7	−21.9
Commonwealth of Independent States and Mongolia	5.5	0.8	−1.9	−7.0	−9.0	21.1	47.1	34.4	21.9	15.8
Russia	8.2	4.9	3.8	−0.4	−1.6	22.7	45.2	35.1	24.4	19.3
Excluding Russia	−2.7	−4.1	−5.7	−6.6	−7.4	−1.6	1.8	−0.6	−2.6	−3.5
Total[1]	**−58.6**	**−51.3**	**−60.9**	**−2.6**	**−90.4**	**−152.0**	**−163.5**	**−143.6**	**−213.6**	**−248.2**
In percent of total world current account transactions	−0.6	−0.4	−0.5	—	−0.7	−1.1	−1.0	−1.0	−1.4	−1.5
In percent of world GDP	−0.2	−0.2	−0.2	—	−0.3	−0.5	−0.5	−0.5	−0.7	−0.8
Memorandum										
Emerging market countries, excluding Asian countries in surplus[2]	−74.1	−76.3	−76.3	−105.5	−171.5	−61.5	45.4	5.8	−47.1	−75.8

[1]Reflects errors, omissions, and asymmetries in balance of payments statistics on current account, as well as the exclusion of data for international organizations and a limited number of countries. Calculated as the sum of the balance of individual euro area countries. See "Classification of Countries" in the introduction to this Statistical Appendix.
[2]All developing and transition countries excluding China, Hong Kong SAR, Korea, Malaysia, the Philippines, Singapore, Taiwan Province of China, and Thailand.

Table 28. Advanced Economies: Balance of Payments on Current Account

	1994	1995	1996	1997	1998	1999	2000	2001	2002	2003
					Billions of U.S. dollars					
Advanced economies	**24.2**	**47.8**	**30.9**	**79.5**	**24.3**	**−138.6**	**−256.2**	**−186.4**	**−192.6**	**−191.5**
Major advanced economies	−14.4	−1.9	−12.9	14.8	−63.7	−214.1	−333.4	−289.9	−293.6	−295.0
United States	−118.2	−109.9	−120.9	−139.8	−217.5	−324.4	−444.7	−417.4	−435.3	−451.8
Japan	130.6	111.4	65.7	96.6	119.1	114.5	119.6	87.6	110.2	127.0
Germany	−24.0	−20.7	−7.9	−2.7	−6.7	−17.9	−18.8	10.0	9.4	12.2
France	7.4	10.9	20.5	39.5	37.6	37.2	23.8	32.3	32.7	30.7
Italy	13.2	25.1	40.0	32.4	20.0	6.3	−5.7	4.0	8.3	11.7
United Kingdom	−10.4	−14.2	−13.6	−2.8	−8.0	−30.9	−25.8	−25.1	−31.1	−36.1
Canada	−13.0	−4.4	3.4	−8.2	−8.3	1.1	18.1	18.8	12.3	11.4
Other advanced economies	38.6	49.7	43.8	64.6	88.0	75.5	77.2	103.4	101.1	103.4
Spain	−6.6	0.2	0.4	2.5	−2.9	−14.0	−17.5	−11.7	−10.1	−9.9
Netherlands	17.3	25.8	21.4	25.1	13.3	13.0	11.0	11.8	14.5	13.7
Belgium-Luxembourg	12.6	14.3	13.8	14.0	12.1	13.4	11.8	12.1	12.0	12.2
Sweden	0.8	4.9	6.5	7.0	6.8	8.8	5.9	7.0	6.5	6.7
Austria	−3.3	−6.1	−5.4	−6.5	−5.2	−6.8	−5.3	−4.6	−3.1	−2.8
Denmark	2.7	1.8	3.2	0.7	−1.5	2.9	2.5	4.7	4.0	5.4
Finland	1.1	5.3	5.1	6.8	7.3	7.8	9.0	6.5	5.8	6.2
Greece	−0.1	−2.9	−4.6	−4.8	−3.6	−5.1	−7.7	−7.2	−7.4	−7.7
Portugal	−2.2	−0.1	−4.4	−6.2	−8.2	−9.9	−11.1	−10.6	−10.3	−10.4
Ireland	1.6	1.9	2.4	2.5	0.8	0.4	−0.6	−0.6	−1.5	−1.9
Switzerland	17.3	21.0	21.9	25.5	26.1	28.4	30.9	25.2	26.9	28.8
Norway	3.7	4.9	10.2	8.7	−1.3	6.3	23.1	24.2	23.5	22.5
Israel	−3.4	−5.2	−5.4	−4.0	−1.4	−3.0	−1.4	−1.6	−1.8	−2.2
Iceland	0.1	0.1	−0.1	−0.1	−0.6	−0.6	−0.9	−0.5	−0.4	−0.3
Cyprus	0.1	−0.2	−0.5	−0.3	−0.6	−0.2	−0.5	−0.4	−0.4	−0.4
Korea	−3.9	−8.5	−23.0	−8.2	40.4	24.5	12.2	8.6	6.9	3.0
Australia	−17.0	−19.3	−15.8	−12.5	−18.1	−23.0	−15.3	−9.3	−12.1	−10.7
Taiwan Province of China	6.5	5.5	10.9	7.1	3.4	8.4	8.9	19.0	18.7	20.2
Hong Kong SAR	2.1	−5.5	−1.6	−6.2	3.9	11.5	8.9	12.0	12.4	12.9
Singapore	11.4	14.9	12.6	18.1	19.7	16.5	15.8	20.5	19.3	20.5
New Zealand	−2.1	−3.1	−3.9	−4.4	−2.2	−3.7	−2.8	−1.6	−2.3	−2.3
Memorandum										
European Union	10.1	46.1	77.4	107.3	61.7	5.1	−28.3	28.5	29.6	29.8
Euro area[1]	17.0	53.6	81.3	102.5	64.4	24.3	−11.0	41.9	50.1	53.8
Newly industrialized Asian economies	16.1	6.4	−1.1	10.8	67.4	60.9	45.8	60.1	57.3	56.6
					Percent of GDP					
United States	−1.7	−1.5	−1.5	−1.7	−2.5	−3.5	−4.5	−4.1	−4.1	−4.0
Japan	2.7	2.1	1.4	2.2	3.0	2.5	2.5	2.1	2.9	3.4
Germany	−1.1	−0.8	−0.3	−0.1	−0.3	−0.9	−1.0	0.5	0.5	0.6
France	0.5	0.7	1.3	2.8	2.6	2.6	1.8	2.5	2.5	2.2
Italy	1.3	2.3	3.2	2.8	1.7	0.5	−0.5	0.4	0.7	1.0
United Kingdom	−1.0	−1.3	−1.1	−0.2	−0.6	−2.1	−1.8	−1.8	−2.1	−2.3
Canada	−2.3	−0.8	0.5	−1.3	−1.3	0.2	2.5	2.7	1.8	1.6
Spain	−1.3	—	0.1	0.5	−0.5	−2.3	−3.1	−2.0	−1.7	−1.6
Netherlands	4.9	6.2	5.2	6.6	3.4	3.2	3.0	3.1	3.7	3.3
Belgium-Luxembourg	5.1	4.8	4.8	5.3	4.5	4.9	4.8	4.9	4.9	4.7
Sweden	0.4	2.1	2.5	2.9	2.8	3.7	2.6	3.3	3.0	3.0
Austria	−1.6	−2.6	−2.3	−3.2	−2.5	−3.2	−2.8	−2.4	−1.6	−1.4
Denmark	1.8	1.0	1.8	0.4	−0.9	1.7	1.6	2.9	2.5	3.2
Finland	1.1	4.1	4.0	5.6	5.6	6.0	7.4	5.4	4.8	4.9
Greece	−0.1	−2.4	−3.7	−4.0	−3.0	−4.0	−6.8	−6.2	−6.1	−6.0
Portugal	−2.5	−0.1	−3.9	−5.8	−7.2	−8.5	−10.4	−9.7	−9.3	−8.9
Ireland	2.9	2.8	3.3	3.1	0.9	0.4	−0.6	−0.6	−1.4	−1.6
Switzerland	6.6	6.8	7.4	9.9	10.0	11.0	12.9	10.2	10.8	11.3
Norway	3.0	3.3	6.5	5.6	−0.9	4.1	14.3	14.8	13.9	13.1
Israel	−4.5	−5.8	−5.5	−3.9	−1.4	−3.0	−1.2	−1.5	−1.7	−2.1
Iceland	1.9	0.8	−1.8	−1.5	−6.9	−7.0	−10.3	−6.9	−5.2	−3.9
Cyprus	1.2	−1.8	−5.2	−4.0	−6.7	−2.4	−5.2	−4.3	−3.9	−3.7
Korea	−1.0	−1.7	−4.4	−1.7	12.7	6.0	2.7	2.0	1.5	0.6
Australia	−5.1	−5.4	−3.9	−3.1	−5.0	−5.9	−4.0	−2.6	−3.2	−2.7
Taiwan Province of China	2.7	2.1	3.9	2.4	1.3	2.9	2.9	6.7	6.6	6.6
Hong Kong SAR	1.6	−3.9	−1.0	−3.6	2.4	7.3	5.5	7.4	7.7	7.7
Singapore	16.3	17.9	13.8	19.2	24.0	20.0	17.0	23.3	21.4	21.4
New Zealand	−4.1	−5.1	−6.0	−6.6	−4.1	−6.7	−5.6	−3.2	−4.5	−4.2

[1]Calculated as the sum of the balances of individual euro area countries.

Table 29. Advanced Economies: Current Account Transactions

(Billions of U.S. dollars)

	1994	1995	1996	1997	1998	1999	2000	2001	2002	2003
Exports	3,318.6	3,956.5	4,075.1	4,189.2	4,161.7	4,261.8	4,646.5	4,406.2	4,402.0	4,742.2
Imports	3,245.2	3,866.3	4,016.4	4,119.1	4,100.6	4,339.7	4,859.2	4,583.5	4,579.0	4,926.1
Trade balance	73.4	90.2	58.7	70.1	61.1	−78.0	−212.7	−177.3	−177.0	−183.9
Services, credits	894.3	1,008.4	1,067.2	1,100.6	1,116.6	1,164.5	1,214.4	1,193.5	1,194.9	1,281.8
Services, debits	825.1	940.9	988.9	1,006.6	1,043.6	1,087.4	1,131.5	1,114.0	1,133.2	1,215.1
Balance on services	69.1	67.5	78.3	94.1	73.0	77.1	82.9	79.5	61.8	66.7
Balance on goods and services	142.5	157.7	137.0	164.2	134.1	−0.9	−129.9	−97.8	−115.2	−117.2
Income, net	−29.4	−28.1	−13.3	2.3	−17.0	−34.3	−24.0	10.6	18.7	25.9
Current transfers, net	−88.9	−81.8	−92.8	−87.0	−92.9	−103.5	−102.3	−99.2	−96.0	−100.2
Current account balance	**24.2**	**47.8**	**30.9**	**79.5**	**24.3**	**−138.6**	**−256.2**	**−186.4**	**−192.6**	**−191.5**
Balance on goods and services										
Advanced economies	**142.5**	**157.7**	**137.0**	**164.2**	**134.1**	**−0.9**	**−129.9**	**−97.8**	**−115.2**	**−117.2**
Major advanced economies	73.9	86.1	59.6	77.8	22.0	−104.1	−237.8	−216.6	−229.8	−236.3
United States	−96.7	−96.4	−101.8	−107.8	−166.8	−261.8	−375.7	−347.8	−379.2	−399.4
Japan	96.4	74.7	21.2	47.3	73.2	69.2	69.0	26.4	54.9	69.7
Germany	10.1	18.1	25.2	29.1	30.9	18.3	7.4	37.0	39.7	42.8
France	25.0	28.9	31.2	45.8	42.1	39.3	23.1	31.3	31.3	28.8
Italy	37.0	45.3	62.2	47.6	39.8	23.2	11.3	18.3	20.7	25.5
United Kingdom	−4.2	−2.9	−2.9	3.6	−8.1	−13.7	−8.4	−17.2	−22.9	−26.7
Canada	6.3	18.4	24.4	12.1	10.9	21.5	35.4	35.3	25.8	23.0
Other advanced economies	68.6	71.6	77.4	86.3	112.2	103.3	108.0	118.8	114.6	119.1
Memorandum										
European Union	113.6	146.7	176.4	186.3	151.2	104.4	65.0	109.7	109.2	113.9
Euro area	99.7	125.2	152.5	158.3	141.3	95.9	53.1	105.0	111.3	119.1
Newly industrialized Asian economies	11.9	4.6	−1.0	7.0	63.3	59.8	45.4	43.6	43.1	42.4
Income, net										
Advanced economies	**−29.4**	**−28.1**	**−13.3**	**2.3**	**−17.0**	**−34.3**	**−24.0**	**10.6**	**18.7**	**25.9**
Major advanced economies	3.1	−5.5	16.4	20.1	4.3	−15.4	−4.3	14.1	19.7	28.5
United States	16.7	20.5	21.0	8.8	−6.2	−13.6	−14.8	−19.1	−8.1	−3.4
Japan	40.3	44.4	53.5	58.1	54.7	57.4	60.4	69.1	64.1	68.2
Germany	3.0	0.1	0.9	−1.4	−7.2	−8.8	−1.1	−3.2	−6.2	−6.0
France	−6.9	−9.0	−2.7	2.6	8.6	11.0	13.4	13.9	14.3	15.5
Italy	−16.7	−15.6	−15.0	−11.2	−12.3	−11.5	−12.4	−10.5	−8.7	−9.8
United Kingdom	−14.4	−23.2	−19.8	−16.0	−13.5	−28.9	−31.6	−18.4	−21.0	−23.2
Canada	−19.0	−22.7	−21.6	−20.9	−19.7	−21.1	−18.3	−17.7	−14.7	−12.8
Other advanced economies	−32.5	−22.6	−29.7	−17.8	−21.2	−18.8	−19.8	−3.5	−1.0	−2.7
Memorandum										
European Union	−59.7	−64.6	−57.2	−43.9	−49.4	−59.0	−57.4	−44.3	−44.8	−48.5
Euro area	−32.9	−27.7	−24.7	−15.9	−28.2	−26.1	−20.6	−22.1	−19.6	−21.2
Newly industrialized Asian economies	5.1	5.4	3.5	8.2	5.1	4.2	5.3	22.6	20.4	20.5

Table 30. Developing Countries: Payments Balances on Current Account

	1994	1995	1996	1997	1998	1999	2000	2001	2002	2003
					Billions of U.S. dollars					
Developing countries	**−85.1**	**−96.7**	**−74.9**	**−58.0**	**−85.3**	**−11.2**	**65.6**	**27.3**	**−23.2**	**−50.6**
Regional groups										
Africa	−11.6	−17.3	−6.0	−7.2	−20.0	−15.3	3.1	−2.1	−10.8	−9.9
Sub-Sahara	−8.4	−13.1	−6.8	−10.0	−18.3	−14.7	−4.4	−8.4	−12.7	−12.0
Excluding Nigeria and South Africa	−6.9	−9.6	−7.7	−10.0	−13.1	−10.8	−6.0	−7.8	−9.2	−10.4
Developing Asia	−19.0	−43.1	−38.9	8.9	47.3	45.9	45.9	39.1	20.4	11.1
China	7.7	1.6	7.2	37.0	31.5	15.7	20.5	19.6	13.1	7.1
India	−1.7	−5.6	−6.0	−3.0	−6.9	−3.2	−4.3	−0.1	−2.6	−2.7
Other developing Asia	−25.0	−39.2	−40.1	−25.0	22.7	33.5	29.8	19.6	9.9	6.7
Middle East and Turkey	−2.3	0.2	10.4	7.3	−21.9	14.7	64.5	44.5	12.3	−3.6
Western Hemisphere	−52.2	−36.5	−40.5	−67.1	−90.7	−56.7	−47.9	−54.3	−45.0	−48.0
Analytical groups										
By source of export earnings										
Fuel	−2.8	2.3	30.6	21.3	−27.9	18.6	102.0	56.1	21.4	7.0
Nonfuel	−82.3	−99.0	−105.5	−79.4	−57.4	−29.8	−36.4	−28.8	−44.6	−57.6
of which, primary products	−11.5	−14.6	−16.9	−18.9	−19.0	−9.6	−9.4	−8.8	−11.4	−13.4
By external financing source										
Net debtor countries	−78.2	−99.2	−87.9	−69.8	−71.2	−24.7	4.7	−10.2	−37.2	−52.7
of which, official financing	−9.7	−12.1	−8.8	−4.7	−10.1	−6.1	3.5	−0.3	−7.4	−9.5
Net debtor countries by debt-servicing experience										
Countries with arrears and/or rescheduling during 1994–98	−18.3	−46.4	−42.1	−48.8	−58.0	−23.1	8.5	−11.2	−26.4	−33.7
Other groups										
Heavily indebted poor countries	−9.8	−13.2	−12.9	−13.8	−15.4	−12.3	−7.1	−8.8	−12.1	−14.6
Middle East and north Africa	−10.9	−4.5	12.4	11.2	−27.5	14.0	80.6	47.5	15.0	−0.7

Table 30 (concluded)

	Ten-Year Averages		1994	1995	1996	1997	1998	1999	2000	2001	2002	2003
	1984–93	1994–2003										
	Percent of exports of goods and services											
Developing countries	**−15.7**	**−3.0**	**−9.8**	**−9.3**	**−6.5**	**−4.6**	**−7.3**	**−0.9**	**4.2**	**1.8**	**−1.5**	**−3.0**
Regional groups												
Africa	−11.4	−6.6	−11.4	−14.5	−4.5	−5.3	−16.6	−11.9	2.0	−1.4	−7.4	−6.6
Sub-Sahara	−13.7	−10.8	−10.8	−14.3	−6.7	−9.6	−20.0	−15.3	−3.9	−7.8	−11.9	−10.8
Excluding Nigeria and South Africa	−26.2	−17.9	−18.1	−21.5	−15.7	−19.8	−28.4	−21.9	−10.9	−14.6	−16.7	−17.9
Developing Asia	−11.1	1.4	−5.1	−9.5	−7.7	1.6	8.8	7.9	6.6	5.6	2.8	1.4
China	−13.8	2.0	−16.0	−29.3	−22.6	4.3	22.8	21.0	16.4	13.0	6.3	3.1
India	−6.1	−3.6	−60.0	−113.1	−94.3	19.9	103.3	89.4	74.9	59.5	29.6	14.6
Other developing Asia	−10.6	1.8	−11.4	−14.5	−13.7	−8.0	7.9	10.9	8.3	5.9	2.9	1.8
Middle East and Turkey	−15.9	−1.2	−1.2	0.1	4.2	2.8	−9.9	5.9	19.1	14.1	4.1	−1.2
Western Hemisphere	−25.2	−11.8	−25.1	−14.8	−14.8	−22.4	−31.1	−18.8	−13.4	−15.4	−12.0	−11.8
Analytical groups												
By source of export earnings												
Fuel	−13.6	2.5	−1.6	1.1	12.7	8.7	−15.1	8.0	29.6	18.0	7.5	2.5
Nonfuel	−16.3	−4.2	−5.9	−6.4	−6.0	−2.3	—	0.2	−0.9	−0.3	−1.6	−2.3
of which, primary products	−25.1	−12.5	−19.3	−19.6	−21.5	−22.7	−23.8	−11.7	−10.4	−9.5	−11.7	−12.5
By external financing source												
Net debtor countries	−15.8	−3.5	−10.2	−10.8	−8.6	−6.3	−6.7	−2.2	0.3	−0.8	−2.7	−3.5
of which, official financing	−18.8	−11.0	−21.9	−22.5	−14.5	−7.2	−16.6	−9.2	4.1	−0.3	−9.0	−11.0
Net debtor countries by debt-servicing experience												
Countries with arrears and/or rescheduling during 1994–98	−14.1	−8.7	−8.3	−18.4	−14.8	−15.7	−20.5	−7.6	2.2	−3.1	−7.2	−8.7
Other groups												
Heavily indebted poor countries	−40.2	−19.1	−25.7	−28.2	−24.2	−24.9	−28.7	−21.3	−10.4	−12.7	−16.9	−19.1
Middle East and north Africa	−14.5	−0.3	−6.1	−2.2	5.3	4.7	−14.4	6.0	24.8	15.8	5.3	−0.3
Memorandum												
Median												
Developing countries	−19.5	−10.3	−13.9	−12.6	−14.6	−11.7	−15.4	−10.8	−10.8	−9.7	−11.0	−10.3

Table 31. Developing Countries—by Region: Current Account Transactions
(Billions of U.S. dollars)

	1994	1995	1996	1997	1998	1999	2000	2001	2002	2003
Developing countries										
Exports	716.8	863.5	965.0	1,042.7	961.5	1,054.1	1,322.6	1,284.2	1,316.4	1,406.1
Imports	731.3	869.2	951.7	1,014.8	962.5	969.5	1,152.4	1,143.5	1,214.5	1,330.8
Trade balance	−14.6	−5.8	13.3	27.9	−1.0	84.6	170.1	140.7	101.8	75.3
Services, net	−40.0	−47.7	−54.5	−59.6	−48.9	−48.7	−52.7	−60.4	−67.0	−69.0
Balance on goods and services	−54.5	−53.4	−41.2	−31.6	−49.9	35.9	117.4	80.3	34.9	6.3
Income, net	−59.0	−76.6	−71.6	−72.1	−76.8	−92.7	−99.3	−100.5	−106.0	−108.7
Current transfers, net	28.4	33.3	37.9	45.7	41.4	45.5	47.5	47.5	47.9	51.8
Current account balance	**−85.1**	**−96.7**	**−74.9**	**−58.0**	**−85.3**	**−11.2**	**65.6**	**27.3**	**−23.2**	**−50.6**
Memorandum										
Exports of goods and services	866.5	1,035.1	1,160.8	1,261.9	1,172.3	1,259.0	1,550.1	1,515.5	1,553.4	1,664.5
Interest payments	84.2	99.2	103.4	104.5	112.7	117.5	123.2	121.5	120.2	121.6
Oil trade balance	105.1	120.1	151.4	141.8	90.7	134.1	222.0	185.3	154.5	148.5
Regional groups										
Africa										
Exports	85.1	100.8	112.4	114.5	99.1	105.9	132.4	126.4	122.2	127.3
Imports	82.7	99.5	100.5	104.8	104.1	103.4	108.9	111.6	114.5	120.1
Trade balance	2.4	1.3	11.9	9.8	−5.1	2.4	23.6	14.9	7.7	7.3
Services, net	−8.3	−9.9	−8.6	−8.2	−8.5	−8.3	−8.4	−8.4	−10.2	−10.1
Balance on goods and services	−5.9	−8.6	3.3	1.5	−13.5	−5.8	15.2	6.4	−2.5	−2.9
Income, net	−16.5	−19.1	−20.1	−20.0	−18.7	−21.1	−24.7	−22.5	−21.5	−21.5
Current transfers, net	10.8	10.4	10.9	11.3	12.3	11.6	12.7	14.0	13.2	14.4
Current account balance	**−11.6**	**−17.3**	**−6.0**	**−7.2**	**−20.0**	**−15.3**	**3.1**	**−2.1**	**−10.8**	**−9.9**
Memorandum										
Exports of goods and services	102.1	120.0	133.4	136.1	120.7	128.1	154.7	149.0	145.3	151.7
Interest payments	13.6	16.5	16.2	15.8	15.9	15.6	16.6	16.0	14.7	15.0
Oil trade balance	18.8	22.2	30.8	29.3	19.6	25.4	46.9	41.5	35.8	35.6
Developing Asia										
Exports	307.1	378.4	416.3	467.0	456.6	494.9	605.0	597.6	629.1	688.2
Imports	327.4	404.9	447.2	452.3	391.2	426.3	542.2	538.9	581.4	643.3
Trade balance	−20.3	−26.5	−30.9	14.7	65.4	68.6	62.8	58.7	47.7	44.8
Services, net	−4.6	−11.6	−7.6	−12.1	−12.7	−11.2	−10.0	−13.2	−16.1	−18.7
Balance on goods and services	−24.9	−38.0	−38.5	2.7	52.7	57.5	52.8	45.5	31.6	26.1
Income, net	−13.3	−25.1	−24.5	−23.4	−28.4	−38.1	−36.2	−35.0	−39.7	−44.9
Current transfers, net	19.2	20.0	24.1	29.7	23.0	26.6	29.4	28.6	28.5	29.9
Current account balance	**−19.0**	**−43.1**	**−38.9**	**8.9**	**47.3**	**45.9**	**45.9**	**39.1**	**20.4**	**11.1**
Memorandum										
Exports of goods and services	370.5	454.7	505.1	565.4	539.7	578.0	699.8	698.1	734.8	803.3
Interest payments	24.5	26.8	29.5	26.9	31.3	33.5	33.5	31.3	32.0	34.9
Oil trade balance	−10.4	−12.2	−18.0	−20.6	−12.7	−21.5	−39.3	−36.8	−38.1	−38.9

Table 31 *(concluded)*

	1994	1995	1996	1997	1998	1999	2000	2001	2002	2003
Middle East and Turkey										
Exports	157.2	179.8	210.2	212.5	166.6	203.9	285.7	265.1	249.8	246.0
Imports	133.3	156.7	173.8	185.3	182.5	174.1	199.9	193.4	205.5	221.0
Trade balance	23.9	23.1	36.5	27.1	−15.9	29.8	85.7	71.7	44.3	25.0
Services, net	−18.4	−17.8	−27.4	−23.7	−12.7	−19.1	−22.5	−26.5	−32.2	−30.1
Balance on goods and services	5.5	5.3	9.0	3.4	−28.5	10.6	63.2	45.2	12.0	−5.1
Income, net	7.5	8.2	13.8	15.1	18.1	16.9	16.7	17.8	18.3	18.6
Current transfers, net	−15.3	−13.3	−12.4	−11.2	−11.4	−12.8	−15.4	−18.5	−18.0	−17.1
Current account balance	**−2.3**	**0.2**	**10.4**	**7.3**	**−21.9**	**14.7**	**64.5**	**44.5**	**12.3**	**−3.6**
Memorandum										
Exports of goods and services	186.4	214.1	249.2	261.1	220.1	251.2	338.1	315.3	297.7	300.8
Interest payments	9.5	11.6	11.9	12.8	12.8	12.8	14.3	15.2	15.9	17.7
Oil trade balance	81.0	91.1	113.3	109.1	68.6	106.5	175.2	151.7	132.5	126.0
Western Hemisphere										
Exports	167.4	204.5	226.0	248.7	239.2	249.4	299.4	295.0	315.3	344.6
Imports	188.0	208.2	230.2	272.4	284.7	265.6	301.4	299.6	313.1	346.4
Trade balance	−20.6	−3.7	−4.2	−23.7	−45.5	−16.2	−2.0	−4.6	2.2	−1.8
Services, net	−8.7	−8.4	−10.9	−15.5	−15.1	−10.1	−11.8	−12.3	−8.5	−10.0
Balance on goods and services	−29.3	−12.1	−15.1	−39.2	−60.6	−26.4	−13.8	−16.8	−6.2	−11.8
Income, net	−36.6	−40.6	−40.8	−43.8	−47.8	−50.4	−55.0	−60.8	−63.0	−60.9
Current transfers, net	13.7	16.2	15.3	16.0	17.6	20.1	20.9	23.4	24.2	24.7
Current account balance	**−52.2**	**−36.5**	**−40.5**	**−67.1**	**−90.7**	**−56.7**	**−47.9**	**−54.3**	**−45.0**	**−48.0**
Memorandum										
Exports of goods and services	207.5	246.2	273.0	299.2	291.8	301.7	357.5	353.2	375.6	408.7
Interest payments	36.7	44.3	45.7	49.0	52.6	55.5	58.9	58.9	57.7	54.0
Oil trade balance	15.7	19.0	25.3	24.0	15.3	23.7	39.1	28.9	24.3	25.8

Table 32. Developing Countries—by Analytical Criteria: Current Account Transactions
(Billions of U.S. dollars)

	1994	1995	1996	1997	1998	1999	2000	2001	2002	2003
By source of export earnings										
Fuel										
Exports	166.1	188.9	227.8	229.6	168.7	217.3	327.8	292.7	266.4	261.4
Imports	111.1	125.7	130.0	141.5	142.0	139.6	153.8	166.8	175.5	185.0
Trade balance	55.0	63.3	97.8	88.1	26.7	77.7	173.9	126.0	90.9	76.4
Services, net	−33.7	−35.1	−47.9	−48.4	−38.1	−39.0	−46.2	−46.4	−47.8	−48.4
Balance on goods and services	21.3	28.2	49.9	39.7	−11.4	38.7	127.7	79.6	43.1	28.0
Income, net	−0.9	−3.1	1.8	2.3	5.8	3.7	0.7	3.6	5.6	5.6
Current transfers, net	−23.2	−22.9	−21.1	−20.7	−22.3	−23.8	−26.4	−27.1	−27.2	−26.6
Current account balance	**−2.8**	**2.3**	**30.6**	**21.3**	**−27.9**	**18.6**	**102.0**	**56.1**	**21.4**	**7.0**
Memorandum										
Exports of goods and services	176.1	199.9	240.5	245.1	184.5	232.9	344.5	310.8	285.7	282.5
Interest payments	12.2	14.8	14.1	15.4	15.4	14.0	15.7	14.7	14.2	14.4
Oil trade balance	115.8	132.8	169.8	165.2	108.5	156.2	259.1	223.4	194.7	190.4
Nonfuel exports										
Exports	550.7	674.5	737.2	813.1	792.8	836.8	994.8	991.4	1,050.0	1,144.7
Imports	620.3	743.6	821.8	873.3	820.5	829.9	998.6	976.8	1,039.0	1,145.9
Trade balance	−69.6	−69.0	−84.5	−60.2	−27.7	6.9	−3.8	14.7	11.0	−1.1
Services, net	−6.3	−12.6	−6.6	−11.2	−10.8	−9.7	−6.5	−14.0	−19.2	−20.5
Balance on goods and services	−75.8	−81.6	−91.1	−71.4	−38.5	−2.7	−10.3	0.6	−8.2	−21.7
Income, net	−58.1	−73.5	−73.4	−74.4	−82.7	−96.4	−100.0	−104.1	−111.6	−114.3
Current transfers, net	51.6	56.2	59.0	66.5	63.8	69.3	73.9	74.6	75.1	78.5
Current account balance	**−82.3**	**−99.0**	**−105.5**	**−79.4**	**−57.4**	**−29.8**	**−36.4**	**−28.8**	**−44.6**	**−57.6**
Memorandum										
Exports of goods and services	690.4	835.2	920.3	1,016.7	987.8	1,026.1	1,205.6	1,204.8	1,267.6	1,382.0
Interest payments	72.1	84.4	89.3	89.1	97.3	103.5	107.5	106.8	106.0	107.3
Oil trade balance	−10.7	−12.6	−18.4	−23.4	−17.8	−22.1	−37.1	−38.1	−40.2	−41.9
Nonfuel primary products										
Exports	48.6	60.9	63.3	67.3	63.6	66.1	74.4	75.0	79.1	87.3
Imports	52.9	66.2	72.2	77.8	76.5	70.1	76.9	77.5	83.0	92.1
Trade balance	−4.3	−5.4	−8.9	−10.5	−12.9	−4.0	−2.5	−2.5	−3.9	−4.8
Services, net	−5.2	−6.3	−6.6	−6.9	−6.3	−5.8	−6.2	−5.8	−6.1	−6.8
Balance on goods and services	−9.5	−11.7	−15.5	−17.4	−19.2	−9.8	−8.6	−8.3	−10.0	−11.7
Income, net	−8.8	−9.6	−9.5	−9.6	−9.0	−9.3	−10.4	−10.3	−11.0	−12.2
Current transfers, net	6.8	6.8	8.1	8.1	9.2	9.4	9.6	9.8	9.6	10.5
Current account balance	**−11.5**	**−14.6**	**−16.9**	**−18.9**	**−19.0**	**−9.6**	**−9.4**	**−8.8**	**−11.4**	**−13.4**
Memorandum										
Exports of goods and services	59.6	74.6	78.4	83.3	80.1	82.1	90.5	92.0	97.2	106.7
Interest payments	7.6	9.2	8.9	8.7	9.3	9.0	9.3	8.8	8.4	9.6
Oil trade balance	−2.4	−3.0	−4.0	−4.3	−3.7	−3.4	−4.6	−4.3	−3.8	−4.0

Table 32 *(continued)*

	1994	1995	1996	1997	1998	1999	2000	2001	2002	2003
By external financing source										
Net debtor countries										
Exports	618.3	748.8	831.4	905.5	863.0	932.6	1,142.2	1,124.9	1,175.8	1,271.1
Imports	665.6	797.2	876.4	934.0	883.0	896.0	1,075.8	1,064.8	1,131.8	1,243.0
Trade balance	−47.3	−48.4	−45.0	−28.5	−20.0	36.6	66.4	60.0	44.0	28.2
Services, net	−17.7	−23.6	−18.4	−22.8	−21.5	−20.0	−17.4	−24.9	−30.5	−31.5
Balance on goods and services	−65.0	−72.0	−63.3	−51.3	−41.5	16.6	49.0	35.2	13.4	−3.4
Income, net	−67.7	−85.0	−85.6	−87.4	−94.5	−109.8	−116.4	−118.8	−125.6	−128.4
Current transfers, net	54.5	57.8	61.0	68.9	64.9	68.4	72.1	73.4	74.9	79.1
Current account balance	**−78.2**	**−99.2**	**−87.9**	**−69.8**	**−71.2**	**−24.7**	**4.7**	**−10.2**	**−37.2**	**−52.7**
Memorandum										
Exports of goods and services	763.1	915.3	1,021.2	1,116.5	1,065.0	1,128.0	1,359.6	1,345.3	1,401.3	1,517.2
Interest payments	81.9	96.4	100.3	100.7	108.8	114.2	119.6	118.1	116.8	118.1
Oil trade balance	39.5	45.7	59.5	52.1	36.3	56.9	90.3	74.5	63.5	60.6
Official financing										
Exports	32.8	40.6	47.0	51.2	46.1	51.0	67.5	66.6	64.3	67.9
Imports	42.8	51.6	54.8	54.8	56.2	57.4	64.6	68.3	73.3	79.5
Trade balance	−9.9	−11.0	−7.8	−3.7	−10.1	−6.4	2.8	−1.7	−9.0	−11.6
Services, net	−3.0	−3.8	−3.8	−3.2	−4.4	−4.3	−3.3	−3.5	−4.4	−4.5
Balance on goods and services	−13.0	−14.8	−11.6	−6.9	−14.5	−10.7	−0.5	−5.2	−13.4	−16.1
Income, net	−5.8	−6.7	−6.8	−7.1	−6.1	−6.4	−8.2	−7.0	−6.2	−6.5
Current transfers, net	9.2	9.4	9.7	9.3	10.5	11.0	12.2	11.9	12.2	13.1
Current account balance	**−9.7**	**−12.1**	**−8.8**	**−4.7**	**−10.1**	**−6.1**	**3.5**	**−0.3**	**−7.4**	**−9.5**
Memorandum										
Exports of goods and services	44.1	53.7	61.0	66.0	60.9	66.3	83.8	83.4	81.6	86.4
Interest payments	6.3	7.0	7.0	7.1	7.0	6.4	7.2	6.7	5.8	5.8
Oil trade balance	9.4	10.9	14.1	14.4	10.2	13.3	22.8	19.9	16.2	15.9
Net debtor countries by debt-servicing experience										
Countries with arrears and/or rescheduling during 1994–98										
Exports	183.3	208.2	233.4	252.9	232.8	259.6	329.1	314.0	315.4	332.5
Imports	176.3	221.4	240.8	259.5	241.8	232.6	266.4	271.4	286.1	308.4
Trade balance	6.9	−13.2	−7.4	−6.6	−9.0	27.1	62.7	42.5	29.3	24.0
Services, net	−13.6	−17.3	−22.5	−28.7	−32.3	−22.2	−23.4	−24.0	−25.8	−26.2
Balance on goods and services	−6.6	−30.5	−30.0	−35.3	−41.3	4.9	39.3	18.6	3.5	−2.2
Income, net	−28.3	−32.9	−28.9	−31.3	−34.6	−45.6	−48.4	−48.2	−49.7	−53.2
Current transfers, net	16.7	17.1	16.8	17.8	17.8	17.7	17.6	18.5	19.8	21.6
Current account balance	**−18.3**	**−46.4**	**−42.1**	**−48.8**	**−58.0**	**−23.1**	**8.5**	**−11.2**	**−26.4**	**−33.7**
Memorandum										
Exports of goods and services	220.2	251.6	284.5	311.3	282.5	303.8	377.0	362.8	367.1	388.3
Interest payments	29.4	36.1	37.8	39.1	43.3	45.2	47.3	45.2	44.8	45.2
Oil trade balance	35.0	39.2	50.0	47.9	36.7	55.6	87.8	80.0	75.5	73.7

Table 32 *(concluded)*

	1994	1995	1996	1997	1998	1999	2000	2001	2002	2003
Other groups										
Heavily indebted poor countries										
Exports	29.9	37.0	42.5	44.9	42.6	46.6	56.7	56.7	58.7	62.3
Imports	35.2	42.4	47.4	50.6	51.6	52.6	57.4	59.6	64.2	70.6
Trade balance	−5.3	−5.4	−4.8	−5.7	−9.0	−6.0	−0.7	−3.0	−5.5	−8.4
Services, net	−4.0	−5.2	−5.5	−6.1	−6.0	−5.5	−5.3	−5.5	−6.5	−6.7
Balance on goods and services	−9.3	−10.5	−10.4	−11.8	−15.0	−11.5	−5.9	−8.5	−12.0	−15.1
Income, net	−8.6	−10.7	−11.4	−10.8	−10.6	−11.2	−12.6	−11.7	−11.5	−11.7
Current transfers, net	8.1	8.0	8.9	8.7	10.2	10.4	11.4	11.4	11.3	12.2
Current account balance	**−9.8**	**−13.2**	**−12.9**	**−13.8**	**−15.4**	**−12.3**	**−7.1**	**−8.8**	**−12.1**	**−14.6**
Memorandum										
Exports of goods and services	38.1	46.8	53.1	55.5	53.7	58.0	68.7	69.2	71.8	76.3
Interest payments	6.2	7.3	7.3	6.7	7.3	6.8	6.5	6.1	5.5	5.8
Oil trade balance	3.6	4.8	6.0	6.1	3.7	6.8	11.7	10.1	10.7	10.0
Middle East and north Africa										
Exports	154.0	175.1	203.0	205.8	157.8	199.6	289.0	263.5	244.1	239.1
Imports	133.5	147.9	156.2	162.2	163.6	161.1	173.5	182.8	193.0	205.7
Trade balance	20.5	27.1	46.7	43.7	−5.8	38.5	115.6	80.7	51.1	33.4
Services, net	−20.1	−21.2	−30.6	−30.9	−22.7	−22.6	−29.4	−29.1	−32.2	−31.2
Balance on goods and services	0.4	5.9	16.2	12.7	−28.5	15.9	86.2	51.6	18.9	2.3
Income, net	2.4	2.6	7.8	9.5	12.9	11.1	10.2	12.1	12.6	12.8
Current transfers, net	−13.7	−13.0	−11.6	−11.0	−11.8	−13.0	−15.7	−16.2	−16.5	−15.8
Current account balance	**−10.9**	**−4.5**	**12.4**	**11.2**	**−27.5**	**14.0**	**80.6**	**47.5**	**15.0**	**−0.7**
Memorandum										
Exports of goods and services	178.0	201.1	232.6	238.4	190.9	234.0	324.8	301.6	281.7	280.7
Interest payments	−10.1	−12.5	−12.9	−13.1	−12.7	−11.9	−12.6	−11.6	−11.8	−12.2
Oil trade balance	92.2	103.6	129.2	125.6	81.9	121.3	201.3	173.9	152.4	146.8

Table 33. Summary of Balance of Payments, Capital Flows, and External Financing
(Billions of U.S. dollars)

	1994	1995	1996	1997	1998	1999	2000	2001	2002	2003
Developing countries										
Balance of payments[1]										
Balance on current account	−85.1	−96.7	−74.9	−58.0	−85.3	−11.2	65.6	27.3	−23.2	−50.6
Balance on goods and services	−54.5	−53.4	−41.2	−31.6	−49.9	35.9	117.4	80.3	34.9	6.3
Income, net	−59.0	−76.6	−71.6	−72.1	−76.8	−92.7	−99.3	−100.5	−106.0	−108.7
Current transfers, net	28.4	33.3	37.9	45.7	41.4	45.5	47.5	47.5	47.9	51.8
Balance on capital and financial account	114.5	125.5	105.0	117.1	111.7	41.8	−38.4	0.4	44.1	65.4
Balance on capital account[2]	5.3	7.6	3.4	13.3	6.1	8.6	5.5	4.9	5.6	8.6
Balance on financial account	109.2	118.0	101.6	103.8	105.6	33.2	−43.9	−4.5	38.5	56.9
Direct investment, net	74.7	84.3	106.7	129.5	130.2	131.9	126.1	149.5	119.3	129.4
Portfolio investment, net	99.1	21.8	73.1	42.3	6.6	20.0	−12.9	−38.3	−3.1	8.8
Other investment, net	−14.8	78.2	15.6	−13.8	−36.7	−88.9	−96.4	−32.5	−32.3	−53.0
Reserve assets	−49.9	−66.4	−93.8	−54.2	5.5	−29.8	−60.7	−83.2	−45.4	−28.3
Errors and omissions, net	−29.4	−28.8	−30.1	−59.1	−26.4	−30.6	−27.2	−27.7	−20.9	−14.9
Capital flows										
Total capital flows, net[3]	159.1	184.4	195.3	157.9	100.1	63.1	16.8	78.7	83.9	85.2
Net official flows	20.8	33.8	2.9	20.7	36.8	29.8	12.8	50.1	41.7	24.9
Net private flows[4]	138.3	150.5	192.5	137.3	63.2	33.3	4.0	28.6	42.2	60.3
Direct investment, net	74.7	84.3	106.7	129.5	130.2	131.9	126.1	149.5	119.3	129.4
Private portfolio investment, net	93.5	15.2	61.1	36.3	−2.2	12.2	−18.1	−35.7	−1.8	6.5
Other private flows, net	−29.9	51.0	24.6	−28.5	−64.8	−110.8	−104.0	−85.2	−75.3	−75.6
External financing[5]										
Net external financing[6]	174.0	217.5	236.6	247.3	200.1	164.3	144.8	161.6	188.3	190.7
Nondebt-creating flows	100.2	113.6	143.9	169.4	143.5	156.8	152.7	152.4	140.3	157.9
Capital transfers[7]	5.3	7.6	3.4	13.3	6.1	8.6	5.5	4.9	5.6	8.6
Foreign direct investment and equity security liabilities[8]	94.8	106.0	140.5	156.1	137.4	148.2	147.2	147.5	134.7	149.3
Net external borrowing[9]	73.9	103.9	92.7	77.9	56.5	7.5	−7.9	9.3	47.9	32.8
Borrowing from official creditors[10]	21.6	32.2	7.5	12.9	32.2	31.9	19.3	48.1	35.5	22.1
Of which,										
Credit and loans from IMF[11]	−0.8	12.6	−2.9	0.8	8.5	1.3	−6.7	23.3	. . .	. . .
Borrowing from banks[12]	−28.5	18.9	20.7	26.0	32.0	5.1	9.1	2.8	6.7	13.9
Borrowing from other private creditors	80.8	52.8	64.5	38.9	−7.6	−29.5	−36.4	−41.7	5.7	−3.2
Memorandum										
Balance on goods and services in percent of GDP[13]	−1.4	−1.2	−0.8	−0.6	−1.0	0.7	2.2	1.5	0.6	0.1
Scheduled amortization of external debt	127.6	154.8	197.7	243.7	245.3	274.5	282.4	279.0	239.9	250.5
Gross external financing[14]	301.7	372.2	434.3	491.0	445.3	438.8	427.2	440.6	428.1	441.3
Gross external borrowing[15]	201.5	258.7	290.4	321.5	301.8	282.0	274.5	288.2	287.8	283.3
Exceptional external financing, net	19.8	21.6	22.0	19.1	20.5	22.0	5.3	18.0	24.5	6.3
Of which,										
Arrears on debt service	−14.3	−2.5	−2.9	−7.0	1.0	8.3	−29.9	3.9	. . .	. . .
Debt forgiveness	1.2	2.5	9.1	14.9	1.7	3.3	2.0	3.4	. . .	. . .
Rescheduling of debt service	25.1	20.5	15.1	10.5	6.8	9.6	31.8	9.0	. . .	. . .
Countries in transition										
Balance of payments[1]										
Balance on current account	2.2	−2.4	−16.9	−24.0	−29.4	−2.2	27.1	15.6	2.2	−6.1
Balance on goods and services	1.0	−5.4	−18.0	−19.1	89.3	3.4	31.5	16.4	5.2	−3.4
Income, net	−3.1	−2.0	−4.7	−10.8	−131.9	−13.6	−12.5	−9.9	−11.4	−11.7
Current transfers, net	4.3	5.0	5.8	5.9	13.3	8.0	8.1	9.0	8.4	9.0
Balance on capital and financial account	−1.6	6.0	24.6	27.9	37.2	7.5	−20.2	−12.9	−2.5	5.9
Balance on capital account[2]	10.2	0.7	1.2	0.4	0.6	0.2	0.1	0.3	0.1	0.2
Balance on financial account	−11.8	5.3	23.5	27.5	36.6	7.3	−20.3	−13.3	−2.6	5.7
Direct investment, net	5.3	13.1	12.5	15.8	21.4	23.4	22.8	24.0	31.9	30.3
Portfolio investment, net	16.1	14.6	13.3	24.0	12.8	2.1	5.9	5.5	7.2	6.4
Other investment, net	−28.2	15.1	−0.1	−2.9	3.8	−11.2	−27.6	−24.0	−21.9	−18.3
Reserve assets	−5.1	−37.5	−2.3	−9.4	−1.4	−7.0	−21.5	−18.8	−19.9	−12.8
Errors and omissions, net	−0.6	−3.6	−7.7	−3.9	−7.8	−5.3	−6.9	−2.6	0.3	0.2

Table 33 *(concluded)*

	1994	1995	1996	1997	1998	1999	2000	2001	2002	2003
Capital flows										
Total capital flows, net[3]	−6.8	42.8	25.8	36.8	38.0	14.3	1.2	5.5	17.3	18.4
Net official flows	−11.2	−5.8	2.3	32.9	18.2	0.4	0.4	1.4	3.5	0.3
Net private flows[4]	4.4	48.6	23.5	3.9	19.8	13.9	0.8	4.2	13.8	18.1
Direct investment, net	5.3	13.1	12.5	15.8	21.4	23.4	22.8	24.0	31.9	30.3
Private portfolio investment, net	16.1	14.6	13.3	7.5	4.5	3.1	2.8	2.4	3.8	4.3
Other private flows, net	−17.0	20.9	−2.4	−19.4	−6.1	−12.6	−24.8	−22.2	−22.0	−16.5
External financing[5]										
Net external financing[6]	13.4	32.4	36.4	75.7	56.7	43.3	25.5	34.0	43.5	45.1
Nondebt-creating flows	16.3	15.0	14.0	20.9	24.1	24.5	26.4	25.5	34.0	32.6
Capital transfers[7]	10.2	0.7	1.2	0.4	0.6	0.2	0.1	0.3	0.1	0.2
Foreign direct investment and equity security liabilities[8]	6.1	14.3	12.8	20.5	23.5	24.3	26.2	25.2	33.9	32.4
Net external borrowing[9]	−2.9	17.4	22.4	54.8	32.6	18.8	−0.9	8.4	9.5	12.5
Borrowing from official creditors[10]	−5.8	−2.5	2.6	32.9	18.2	0.3	0.3	1.4	3.5	0.3
Of which,										
Credit and loans from IMF[11]	2.4	4.7	3.7	2.5	5.5	−3.6	−4.2	−4.3	. . .	. . .
Borrowing from banks[12]	3.8	−0.8	4.4	4.7	5.2	−1.1	−0.4	0.4	1.2	4.0
Borrowing from other private creditors	−0.9	20.7	15.4	17.2	9.1	19.6	−0.8	6.7	4.8	8.3
Memorandum										
Balance on goods and services in percent of GDP[13]	0.2	−0.7	−2.0	−2.1	11.1	0.5	4.2	2.0	0.6	−0.4
Scheduled amortization of external debt	22.4	26.7	26.0	20.0	24.0	28.6	28.4	29.6	30.0	37.3
Gross external financing[14]	35.7	59.1	62.4	95.7	80.7	71.9	53.9	63.6	73.5	82.4
Gross external borrowing[15]	19.5	44.1	48.4	74.7	56.6	47.4	27.5	38.1	39.5	49.8
Exceptional external financing, net	17.3	14.9	13.6	−20.8	7.8	7.7	5.2	1.1	0.6	0.3
Of which,										
Arrears on debt service	3.8	−0.5	1.1	−24.8	5.0	1.8	1.6	0.1	. . .	. . .
Debt forgiveness	—	0.9	0.9	—	—	—	—	—	. . .	. . .
Rescheduling of debt service	13.3	13.9	9.9	3.3	2.4	4.7	3.7	1.2	. . .	. . .

[1]Standard presentation in accordance with the fifth edition of the International Monetary Fund's *Balance of Payments Manual* (1993).

[2]Comprises capital transfers—including debt forgiveness—and acquisition/disposal of nonproduced, nonfinancial assets.

[3]Comprise net direct investment, net portfolio investment, and other long- and short-term net investment flows, including official and private borrowing. In the standard balance of payments presentation above, total net capital flows are equal to the balance on financial account minus the change in reserve assets.

[4]Because of limitations on the data coverage for net official flows, the residually derived data for net private flows may include some official flows.

[5]As defined in the *World Economic Outlook* (see footnote 6). It should be noted that there is no generally accepted standard definition of external financing.

[6]Defined as the sum of—with opposite sign—the goods and services balance, net income and current transfers, direct investment abroad, the change in reserve assets, the net acquisition of other assets (such as recorded private portfolio assets, export credit, and the collateral for debt-reduction operations), and the net errors and omissions. Thus, net external financing, according to the definition adopted in the *World Economic Outlook*, measures the total amount required to finance the current account, direct investment outflows, net reserve transactions (often at the discretion of the monetary authorities), the net acquisition of nonreserve external assets, and the net transactions underlying the errors and omissions (not infrequently reflecting capital flight).

[7]Including other transactions on capital account.

[8]Debt-creating foreign direct investment liabilities are not included.

[9]Net disbursement of long- and short-term credits, including exceptional financing, by both official and private creditors.

[10]Net disbursement by official creditors, based on directly reported flows and flows derived from information on external debt.

[11]Comprise use of International Monetary Fund resources under the General Resources Account, Trust Fund, and Poverty Reduction and Growth Facility (PRGF). For further detail, see Table 37.

[12]Net disbursement by commercial banks, based on directly reported flows and cross-border claims and liabilities reported in the International Banking section of the International Monetary Fund's *International Financial Statistics*.

[13]This is often referred to as the "resource balance" and, with opposite sign, the "net resource transfer."

[14]Net external financing plus amortization due on external debt.

[15]Net external borrowing plus amortization due on external debt.

Table 34. Developing Countries—by Region: Balance of Payments and External Financing[1]

(Billions of U.S. dollars)

	1994	1995	1996	1997	1998	1999	2000	2001	2002	2003
Africa										
Balance of payments										
Balance on current account	−11.6	−17.3	−6.0	−7.2	−20.0	−15.3	3.1	−2.1	−10.8	−9.9
Balance on capital account	2.3	2.5	−2.1	9.1	3.2	5.5	2.4	2.9	2.9	5.1
Balance on financial account	11.2	14.6	6.0	−0.9	16.5	9.1	−8.4	−1.5	7.7	4.0
Change in reserves (− = increase)	−5.5	−1.4	−8.9	−11.0	1.5	−3.4	−13.7	−10.5	−0.5	−5.5
Other official flows, net	3.3	4.1	−1.9	1.9	3.1	1.9	1.4	1.1	1.0	1.1
Private flows, net	13.4	11.9	16.8	8.2	11.9	10.6	3.9	7.9	7.3	8.4
External financing										
Net external financing	19.5	24.6	17.3	28.4	26.8	27.5	14.8	16.2	21.9	24.6
Nondebt-creating inflows	6.7	10.5	5.7	25.4	20.2	25.3	12.2	19.8	19.9	23.0
Net external borrowing	12.8	14.0	11.7	3.0	6.6	2.2	2.5	−3.5	1.9	1.6
From official creditors	3.2	4.5	−1.6	2.1	3.5	2.2	1.8	1.7	1.5	1.7
Of which,										
Credit and loans from IMF	0.9	0.8	0.6	−0.5	−0.4	−0.2	−0.1	−0.4	. . .	. . .
From banks	2.4	0.9	−0.4	0.4	3.7	1.5	0.3	0.9	−0.2	0.6
From other private creditors	7.2	8.7	13.6	0.6	−0.6	−1.5	0.4	−6.2	0.6	−0.6
Memorandum										
Exceptional financing	14.2	13.7	15.4	14.7	4.3	12.6	9.0	10.8	8.0	5.5
Sub-Sahara										
Balance of payments										
Balance on current account	−8.4	−13.1	−6.8	−10.0	−18.3	−14.7	−4.4	−8.4	−12.7	−12.0
Balance on capital account	2.2	2.5	−2.2	9.0	3.0	5.2	2.4	2.9	2.8	5.0
Balance on financial account	8.0	10.6	7.1	2.1	14.8	8.3	−0.7	5.6	9.6	6.2
Change in reserves (− = increase)	−3.4	−2.8	−6.2	−6.0	0.4	−3.7	−7.1	−1.7	1.6	−2.2
Other official flows, net	3.5	4.4	−1.6	3.0	3.6	2.5	2.3	1.8	1.9	2.1
Private flows, net	7.9	8.9	14.9	5.1	10.8	9.5	4.0	5.5	6.1	6.4
External financing										
Net external financing	15.0	22.4	16.0	26.7	25.9	27.1	15.9	15.1	21.8	23.9
Nondebt-creating inflows	5.3	9.8	4.4	23.5	18.5	23.5	10.9	16.0	17.5	19.8
Net external borrowing	9.7	12.6	11.5	3.2	7.4	3.7	5.1	−0.9	4.3	4.1
From official creditors	3.5	4.8	−1.2	3.1	4.0	2.8	2.7	2.4	2.4	2.7
Of which,										
Credit and loans from IMF	0.5	0.6	0.1	−0.5	−0.3	−0.1	—	−0.2	. . .	. . .
From banks	2.1	0.4	−0.7	−0.4	3.6	0.1	—	0.5	−0.4	0.3
From other private creditors	4.1	7.3	13.4	0.6	−0.1	0.8	2.3	−3.8	2.2	1.1
Memorandum										
Exceptional financing	8.5	7.6	10.8	11.1	3.3	11.9	9.0	10.7	8.0	5.5
Developing Asia										
Balance of payments										
Balance on current account	−19.0	−43.1	−38.9	8.9	47.3	45.9	45.9	39.1	20.4	11.1
Balance on capital account	1.6	2.5	2.9	2.8	1.6	0.5	−0.2	0.7	1.1	1.9
Balance on financial account	29.2	63.7	65.3	29.2	−29.6	−28.2	−20.5	−25.6	−6.0	−0.9
Change in reserves (− = increase)	−43.8	−31.2	−37.1	−19.4	−16.2	−28.9	−17.1	−61.0	−32.4	−27.4
Other official flows, net	11.8	8.6	−0.6	4.3	15.2	19.6	13.5	13.4	18.6	19.6
Private flows, net	61.2	86.3	103.0	44.2	−28.6	−18.9	−16.8	22.0	7.8	6.9
External financing										
Net external financing	76.2	96.5	106.5	93.5	41.9	45.6	47.1	62.6	83.6	86.5
Nondebt-creating inflows	48.0	64.5	76.6	66.7	57.0	54.7	64.9	58.5	63.3	65.5
Net external borrowing	28.3	32.0	29.8	26.8	−15.0	−9.1	−17.8	4.0	20.3	21.0
From official creditors	11.2	7.4	−1.5	3.7	14.9	19.0	12.9	12.9	18.2	19.5
Of which,										
Credit and loans from IMF	−0.8	−1.5	−1.7	5.0	6.6	1.7	0.9	−2.2	. . .	. . .
From banks	10.8	14.6	19.7	21.3	2.6	−6.3	−0.6	5.4	7.9	8.6
From other private creditors	6.3	10.0	11.6	1.8	−32.6	−21.8	−30.1	−14.2	−5.9	−7.1
Memorandum										
Exceptional financing	1.2	0.4	0.7	0.5	14.6	7.1	−3.7	6.4	6.5	9.6

Table 34 *(concluded)*

	1994	1995	1996	1997	1998	1999	2000	2001	2002	2003
Excluding China and India										
Balance of payments										
Balance on current account	−25.0	−39.2	−40.1	−25.0	22.7	33.5	29.8	19.6	9.9	6.7
Balance on capital account	1.6	2.5	2.9	2.9	1.6	0.6	−0.2	0.7	1.1	1.9
Balance on financial account	27.0	42.7	48.9	39.6	−22.5	−30.3	−16.5	−14.0	−5.0	−4.0
Change in reserves (− = increase)	−3.9	−10.8	−2.7	21.0	−7.2	−14.3	−0.5	−7.6	−6.2	−8.5
Other official flows, net	3.1	4.7	−2.9	2.8	9.7	12.5	11.7	8.4	10.8	10.4
Private flows, net	27.8	48.9	54.5	15.8	−25.0	−28.5	−27.7	−14.7	−9.6	−5.8
External financing										
Net external financing	27.9	51.0	49.3	19.1	−3.4	−10.0	−15.6	−6.0	4.4	7.6
Nondebt-creating inflows	8.8	24.7	30.0	13.8	12.1	11.5	6.8	3.1	7.3	9.7
Net external borrowing	19.1	26.2	19.3	5.3	−15.5	−21.5	−22.4	−9.0	−2.8	−2.1
From official creditors	2.5	3.5	−3.7	2.2	9.4	12.0	11.1	7.9	10.4	10.2
Of which,										
Credit and loans from IMF	0.4	−0.3	−0.4	5.7	7.0	2.1	0.9	−2.2	. . .	. . .
From banks	7.1	8.9	15.8	14.0	−0.3	−4.4	−2.7	−0.3	−0.5	−0.3
From other private creditors	9.5	13.8	7.2	−10.8	−24.6	−29.1	−30.8	−16.6	−12.8	−12.0
Memorandum										
Exceptional financing	1.2	0.4	0.7	0.5	14.6	7.1	−3.7	6.4	6.5	9.6
Middle East and Turkey										
Balance of payments										
Balance on current account	−2.3	0.2	10.4	7.3	−21.9	14.7	64.5	44.5	12.3	−3.6
Balance on capital account	1.5	2.1	0.7	0.4	0.4	1.1	2.2	0.2	0.3	0.4
Balance on financial account	13.0	0.3	−10.6	5.0	22.6	−6.0	−54.1	−35.4	−7.2	6.0
Change in reserves (− = increase)	−4.6	−10.5	−18.8	−10.0	11.5	−5.4	−27.0	−13.4	−7.0	4.4
Other official flows, net	0.9	2.6	1.9	0.7	2.3	0.9	−1.6	6.6	10.3	2.1
Private flows, net	16.7	8.3	6.3	14.3	8.8	−1.5	−25.6	−28.5	−10.6	−0.5
External financing										
Net external financing	8.5	8.7	18.3	26.7	29.1	11.7	18.1	−10.4	13.3	14.4
Nondebt-creating inflows	5.8	7.1	7.4	4.8	4.9	5.2	9.4	3.7	7.1	9.8
Net external borrowing	2.7	1.6	10.9	21.8	24.2	6.5	8.6	−14.2	6.2	4.6
From official creditors	−1.1	−0.1	0.3	−0.7	−1.0	−1.7	2.9	8.0	9.3	—
Of which,										
Credit and loans from IMF	0.4	0.4	0.1	0.2	−0.1	0.6	3.3	10.3	. . .	. . .
From banks	−9.5	−1.9	−1.6	0.3	9.6	7.5	2.7	−7.8	−3.9	0.8
From other private creditors	13.3	3.6	12.2	22.2	15.6	0.8	3.0	−14.4	0.8	3.7
Memorandum										
Exceptional financing	4.3	3.3	1.0	0.3	0.4	0.2	0.4	0.3	0.4	0.5
Western Hemisphere										
Balance of payments										
Balance on current account	−52.2	−36.5	−40.5	−67.1	−90.7	−56.7	−47.9	−54.3	−45.0	−48.0
Balance on capital account	—	0.5	1.9	1.0	0.9	1.4	1.1	1.1	1.2	1.1
Balance on financial account	55.9	39.4	40.8	70.5	96.1	58.4	39.1	57.9	44.0	47.8
Change in reserves (− = increase)	4.0	−23.3	−29.0	−13.8	8.7	7.8	−2.8	1.7	−5.5	0.2
Other official flows, net	4.7	18.6	3.4	13.7	16.1	7.4	−0.5	29.1	11.8	2.2
Private flows, net	47.1	44.0	66.4	70.6	71.3	43.2	42.5	27.1	37.7	45.4
External financing										
Net external financing	69.8	87.7	94.5	98.7	102.3	79.5	64.9	93.3	69.5	65.2
Nondebt-creating inflows	39.8	31.5	54.2	72.5	61.6	71.7	66.1	70.4	49.9	59.5
Net external borrowing	30.0	56.2	40.2	26.2	40.8	7.8	−1.2	22.9	19.6	5.7
From official creditors	8.2	20.4	10.2	7.8	14.7	12.4	1.7	25.5	6.5	0.9
Of which,										
Credit and loans from IMF	−1.3	12.9	−2.0	−4.0	2.5	−0.9	−10.7	15.6	. . .	. . .
From banks	−32.2	5.2	2.9	4.1	16.1	2.4	6.8	4.4	2.9	3.9
From other private creditors	54.0	30.6	27.1	14.3	9.9	−7.0	−9.7	−6.9	10.1	0.8
Memorandum										
Exceptional financing	0.1	4.1	4.9	3.5	1.2	2.0	−0.4	0.4	9.6	−9.2

[1]For definitions, see footnotes to Table 33.

Table 35. Developing Countries—by Analytical Criteria: Balance of Payments and External Financing[1]
(Billions of U.S. dollars)

	1994	1995	1996	1997	1998	1999	2000	2001	2002	2003
By source of export earnings										
Fuel										
Balance of payments										
Balance on current account	−2.8	2.3	30.6	21.3	−27.9	18.6	102.0	56.1	21.4	7.0
Balance on capital account	0.5	1.0	−5.0	0.6	0.7	1.2	2.5	−0.5	0.4	2.3
Balance on financial account	21.2	4.8	−26.0	−6.2	29.8	−8.2	−90.3	−45.9	−16.5	−6.6
Change in reserves (− = increase)	1.0	0.5	−23.0	−13.3	17.4	4.6	−41.6	−21.0	−2.1	1.4
Other official flows, net	6.6	6.5	1.0	5.0	6.3	2.1	−9.4	−3.9	6.4	3.8
Private flows, net	13.6	−2.1	−3.9	2.1	6.1	−14.9	−39.4	−21.0	−20.8	−11.8
External financing										
Net external financing	17.0	1.4	4.3	20.9	30.6	4.1	6.9	−5.3	5.4	10.7
Nondebt-creating inflows	3.1	3.8	1.2	7.2	8.3	10.5	13.9	10.0	11.4	14.7
Net external borrowing	14.0	−2.4	3.1	13.6	22.3	−6.4	−7.1	−15.3	−6.0	−4.0
From official creditors	4.9	3.1	0.9	2.4	1.4	1.0	0.2	−1.0	0.8	0.7
Of which,										
Credit and loans from IMF	0.4	−0.2	0.7	−0.3	−0.6	−0.5	−0.6	−0.4	. . .	. . .
From banks	−2.6	−4.0	−7.6	−3.7	7.3	0.9	−0.3	−0.6	−1.1	−1.1
From other private creditors	11.7	−1.5	9.9	14.9	13.7	−8.3	−7.0	−13.6	−5.7	−3.6
Memorandum										
Exceptional financing	11.7	11.9	9.4	7.4	5.4	4.7	3.7	4.8	2.7	1.2
Nonfuel										
Balance of payments										
Balance on current account	−82.3	−99.0	−105.5	−79.4	−57.4	−29.8	−36.4	−28.8	−44.6	−57.6
Balance on capital account	4.9	6.6	8.4	12.7	5.5	7.3	3.0	5.5	5.1	6.2
Balance on financial account	88.0	113.1	127.5	110.0	75.8	41.4	46.4	41.4	55.0	63.5
Change in reserves (− = increase)	−50.9	−66.9	−70.7	−40.8	−11.9	−34.4	−19.1	−62.2	−43.3	−29.7
Other official flows, net	14.2	27.4	1.9	15.6	30.5	27.7	22.2	54.0	35.3	21.1
Private flows, net	124.7	152.7	196.3	135.2	57.2	48.2	43.3	49.6	63.0	72.1
External financing										
Net external financing	157.0	216.1	232.3	226.4	169.5	160.2	137.9	166.9	182.8	180.1
Nondebt-creating inflows	97.1	109.8	142.8	162.2	135.3	146.3	138.8	142.4	128.9	143.3
Net external borrowing	59.9	106.3	89.5	64.2	34.2	13.8	−0.9	24.5	53.9	36.8
From official creditors	16.7	29.1	6.6	10.5	30.8	30.9	19.2	49.2	34.7	21.4
Of which,										
Credit and loans from IMF	−1.2	12.8	−3.6	1.2	9.1	1.8	−6.1	23.6	. . .	. . .
From banks	−25.9	22.9	28.3	29.8	24.7	4.2	9.4	3.5	7.8	15.0
From other private creditors	69.1	54.4	54.6	24.0	−21.3	−21.2	−29.4	−28.1	11.4	0.4
Memorandum										
Exceptional financing	8.2	9.7	12.5	11.7	15.1	17.3	1.5	13.1	21.8	5.2
By external financing source										
Net debtor countries										
Balance of payments										
Balance on current account	−78.2	−99.2	−87.9	−69.8	−71.2	−24.7	4.7	−10.2	−37.2	−52.7
Balance on capital account	5.5	7.8	3.7	13.5	6.0	7.9	3.6	4.8	5.5	8.5
Balance on financial account	90.9	110.7	108.0	107.4	89.0	37.4	9.1	27.1	48.3	56.3
Change in reserves (− = increase)	−51.8	−66.5	−85.2	−46.8	−5.5	−33.5	−39.8	−71.2	−45.1	−35.3
Other official flows, net	18.6	31.0	0.7	19.4	33.6	28.0	18.1	51.9	40.9	23.0
Private flows, net	124.1	146.2	192.5	134.8	60.9	42.9	30.8	46.3	52.6	68.6
External financing										
Net external financing	169.5	216.1	229.6	241.1	195.5	165.8	142.8	167.8	187.3	189.0
Nondebt-creating inflows	100.9	114.0	144.3	169.9	143.7	155.9	149.0	150.8	137.3	153.8
Net external borrowing	68.7	102.1	85.3	71.2	51.9	10.0	−6.2	17.0	50.0	35.1
From official creditors	21.4	32.0	7.0	13.0	32.3	32.8	20.1	48.5	35.7	22.2
Of which,										
Credit and loans from IMF	−0.8	12.6	−2.9	0.8	8.5	1.3	−6.7	23.3	. . .	. . .
From banks	−28.3	18.9	21.2	26.0	29.8	2.6	7.9	3.2	6.9	14.8
From other private creditors	75.6	51.1	57.2	32.2	−10.3	−25.5	−34.3	−34.6	7.4	−1.9
Memorandum										
Exceptional financing	19.8	21.6	22.0	19.1	20.5	22.0	5.3	18.0	24.5	6.3

Table 35 *(continued)*

	1994	1995	1996	1997	1998	1999	2000	2001	2002	2003
Official financing										
Balance of payments										
Balance on current account	−9.7	−12.1	−8.8	−4.7	−10.1	−6.1	3.5	−0.3	−7.4	−9.5
Balance on capital account	4.3	5.5	7.3	12.0	4.5	6.4	3.2	4.7	4.2	6.9
Balance on financial account	4.7	6.9	1.6	−7.6	5.9	0.8	−7.2	−4.9	3.2	2.3
Change in reserves (− = increase)	−3.1	−0.3	−3.5	−6.5	1.2	−0.9	−10.3	−7.6	−3.5	−4.8
Other official flows, net	4.3	5.7	2.4	6.9	5.6	4.7	6.1	7.0	5.3	5.9
Private flows, net	3.5	1.5	2.7	−7.9	−0.9	−3.0	−3.0	−4.3	1.4	1.2
External financing										
Net external financing	11.5	13.3	11.7	10.4	8.6	7.7	5.7	6.9	10.1	13.2
Nondebt-creating inflows	6.3	7.7	9.8	15.1	7.7	10.6	7.7	8.9	9.6	13.1
Net external borrowing	5.2	5.6	1.9	−4.7	0.9	−2.9	−2.0	−1.9	0.6	0.1
From official creditors	4.1	5.5	2.3	6.8	5.5	4.6	6.1	6.9	5.3	5.8
Of which,										
Credit and loans from IMF	1.1	1.1	0.9	0.2	—	—	—	−0.2	...	...
From banks	−0.2	−0.1	0.5	0.7	−0.3	1.1	0.4	0.2	0.6	0.8
From other private creditors	1.4	0.3	−0.8	−12.3	−4.4	−8.6	−8.5	−9.1	−5.3	−6.5
Memorandum										
Exceptional financing	12.3	12.2	13.6	10.1	6.1	8.0	−5.4	4.5	3.4	2.7
Net debtor countries by debt-servicing experience										
Countries with arrears and/or rescheduling during 1994–98										
Balance of payments										
Balance on current account	−18.3	−46.4	−42.1	−48.8	−58.0	−23.1	8.5	−11.2	−26.4	−33.7
Balance on capital account	4.7	7.0	2.0	11.9	4.5	5.8	2.2	3.1	3.6	6.4
Balance on financial account	25.2	38.8	43.4	54.5	60.8	28.3	2.8	22.3	30.1	31.1
Change in reserves (− = increase)	−16.1	−22.2	−22.0	−3.6	8.0	1.6	−23.7	−18.8	−3.3	−9.6
Other official flows, net	2.0	3.0	−8.9	3.5	10.5	14.2	4.1	12.9	8.0	7.6
Private flows, net	39.2	57.9	74.2	54.7	42.2	12.5	22.3	28.2	25.4	33.1
External financing										
Net external financing	46.0	73.2	70.1	69.0	60.4	37.9	31.2	44.3	40.2	47.5
Nondebt-creating inflows	27.4	31.4	41.4	49.3	46.4	56.4	52.7	49.4	44.7	52.1
Net external borrowing	18.6	41.9	28.7	19.8	14.0	−18.5	−21.5	−5.1	−4.5	−4.6
From official creditors	1.8	2.8	−9.0	3.4	10.4	14.2	4.1	13.0	8.2	8.0
Of which,										
Credit and loans from IMF	1.0	0.5	0.7	3.9	10.9	5.6	−5.5	5.0	...	...
From banks	−37.3	4.0	7.1	13.5	11.7	−1.7	1.1	2.0	1.2	1.9
From other private creditors	54.1	35.1	30.6	2.9	−8.1	−30.9	−26.8	−20.2	−14.0	−14.5
Memorandum										
Exceptional financing	18.6	20.9	21.7	18.8	18.2	17.2	1.1	13.2	11.2	12.8
Other groups										
Heavily indebted poor countries										
Balance of payments										
Balance on current account	−9.8	−13.2	−12.9	−13.8	−15.4	−12.3	−7.1	−8.8	−12.1	−14.6
Balance on capital account	4.3	5.7	1.9	11.8	4.2	5.8	1.8	3.9	4.1	7.2
Balance on financial account	5.8	6.0	6.2	1.6	11.3	6.5	5.3	6.2	7.8	6.6
Change in reserves (− = increase)	−2.4	−0.4	−3.3	−0.9	1.0	−2.9	−3.6	−2.2	−2.7	−3.1
Other official flows, net	2.6	4.2	−1.8	4.0	4.4	3.3	3.5	3.5	2.2	2.6
Private flows, net	5.6	2.2	11.3	−1.5	5.9	6.1	5.4	4.9	8.3	7.1
External financing										
Net external financing	12.1	15.0	12.6	15.4	15.5	16.7	12.1	14.6	16.1	18.7
Nondebt-creating inflows	7.2	9.2	5.8	17.3	10.0	13.5	7.8	10.7	12.4	14.4
Net external borrowing	4.9	5.7	6.8	−1.8	5.6	3.2	4.3	3.9	3.7	4.3
From official creditors	2.9	4.9	−1.3	4.4	4.8	3.6	3.9	4.0	2.8	3.2
Of which,										
Credit and loans from IMF	0.5	0.6	0.3	—	0.2	0.2	—	−0.1	...	...
From banks	1.3	0.7	0.8	0.3	0.5	0.7	0.5	1.0	−0.1	0.6
From other private creditors	0.7	0.2	7.3	−6.6	0.3	−1.1	−0.1	−1.2	1.0	0.4
Memorandum										
Exceptional financing	9.5	7.9	12.5	9.0	1.0	9.3	−2.4	8.7	6.0	4.4

Table 35 *(concluded)*

	1994	1995	1996	1997	1998	1999	2000	2001	2002	2003
Middle East and north Africa										
Balance of payments										
Balance on current account	−10.9	−4.5	12.4	11.2	−27.5	14.0	80.6	47.5	15.0	−0.7
Balance on capital account	1.6	2.1	0.8	0.5	0.6	1.4	2.2	0.3	0.4	0.5
Balance on financial account	21.5	4.9	−13.0	0.7	28.4	−5.1	−70.8	−39.5	−10.2	2.6
Change in reserves (− = increase)	−5.8	−4.5	−17.1	−11.8	13.0	1.1	−33.5	−26.3	−6.2	2.6
Other official flows, net	1.9	2.6	2.3	0.1	2.9	1.5	−6.7	−3.1	−0.2	0.9
Private flows, net	25.4	6.8	1.8	12.4	12.5	−7.7	−30.6	−10.0	−3.8	−0.8
External financing										
Net external financing	20.3	5.2	13.1	21.0	28.7	1.1	4.2	−4.0	6.7	9.8
Nondebt-creating inflows	5.5	6.6	7.1	5.7	5.8	6.0	10.0	8.4	8.5	11.1
Net external borrowing	14.8	−1.4	6.0	15.3	22.9	−5.0	−5.8	−12.4	−1.8	−1.4
From official creditors	−0.1	−0.1	0.6	−1.3	−0.4	−1.1	−2.2	−1.7	−1.2	−1.1
Of which,										
Credit and loans from IMF	0.5	0.2	0.6	0.3	−0.1	—	−0.3	−0.2	. . .	. . .
From banks	−2.2	−3.4	−4.4	−1.1	6.4	6.2	−0.7	1.3	0.5	−0.1
From other private creditors	17.2	2.1	9.7	17.7	16.9	−10.1	−2.9	−12.1	−1.1	−0.2
Memorandum										
Exceptional financing	10.2	9.5	6.9	5.4	2.9	2.4	1.9	1.5	1.6	1.7

[1]For definitions, see footnotes to Table 33.

Table 36. Developing Countries: Reserves[1]

	1994	1995	1996	1997	1998	1999	2000	2001	2002	2003
					Billions of U.S. dollars					
Developing countries	**419.8**	**483.3**	**577.2**	**634.2**	**637.1**	**664.4**	**721.9**	**804.9**	**850.1**	**878.0**
Regional groups										
Africa	24.8	26.4	31.4	43.0	41.3	42.0	53.3	63.9	64.3	69.5
Sub-Sahara	15.9	18.9	21.1	28.7	27.9	29.3	34.3	36.2	34.4	36.4
Developing Asia	174.3	200.8	246.5	264.9	289.8	322.9	336.9	394.5	426.8	454.1
Excluding China and India	100.4	106.2	118.0	96.3	112.1	131.3	129.7	133.9	140.0	148.4
Middle East and Turkey	115.4	125.7	142.5	156.1	144.5	145.3	175.1	190.2	197.2	192.8
Western Hemisphere	105.4	130.4	156.9	170.3	161.5	154.2	156.6	156.2	161.7	161.6
Analytical groups										
By source of export earnings										
Fuel	92.9	91.0	110.6	129.4	112.9	107.1	151.7	175.4	177.4	175.7
Nonfuel	326.9	392.4	466.6	504.9	524.2	557.3	570.2	629.5	672.7	702.3
of which, primary products	48.9	53.5	58.1	62.0	58.8	59.5	59.8	61.0	63.4	66.5
By external financing source										
Net debtor countries	355.6	419.3	504.8	553.3	568.9	599.3	637.3	706.0	751.0	785.9
of which, official financing	30.7	30.8	33.4	38.4	37.0	37.2	46.6	53.7	57.2	61.9
Net debtor countries by debt-servicing experience										
Countries with arrears and/or rescheduling during 1994–98	110.7	128.7	155.4	153.9	150.2	148.7	174.8	193.4	196.5	205.9
Other groups										
Heavily indebted poor countries	24.3	26.6	28.5	30.0	29.6	32.3	34.9	37.5	40.1	43.0
Middle East and north Africa	115.2	119.3	134.8	150.4	137.0	133.3	170.6	198.6	204.8	202.2
					Ratio of reserves to imports of goods and services[2]					
Developing countries	**45.6**	**44.4**	**48.0**	**49.0**	**52.1**	**54.3**	**50.4**	**56.1**	**56.0**	**52.9**
Regional groups										
Africa	22.9	20.5	24.1	31.9	30.8	31.4	38.2	44.9	43.5	45.0
Sub-Sahara	19.8	19.5	21.2	27.3	27.1	28.9	32.3	33.7	31.0	31.5
Developing Asia	44.1	40.7	45.3	47.1	59.5	62.0	52.1	60.4	60.7	58.4
Excluding China and India	40.9	34.4	35.3	28.3	42.4	49.0	40.4	43.7	43.6	42.5
Middle East and Turkey	63.8	60.2	59.3	60.6	58.1	60.4	63.7	70.4	69.0	63.0
Western Hemisphere	44.5	50.5	54.5	50.3	45.8	47.0	42.2	42.2	42.4	38.4
Analytical groups										
By source of export earnings										
Fuel	60.0	53.0	58.1	63.0	57.6	55.2	70.0	75.9	73.1	69.0
Nonfuel	42.7	42.8	46.1	46.4	51.1	54.2	46.9	52.3	52.7	50.0
of which, primary products	70.7	62.1	61.9	61.6	59.2	64.7	60.3	60.8	59.1	56.2
By external financing source										
Net debtor countries	42.9	42.5	46.5	47.4	51.4	53.9	48.6	53.9	54.1	51.7
of which, official financing	53.8	44.9	46.0	52.8	49.1	48.3	55.3	60.6	60.2	60.4
Net debtor countries by debt-servicing experience										
Countries with arrears and/or rescheduling during 1994–98	48.8	45.6	49.4	44.4	46.4	49.7	51.8	56.2	54.0	52.7
Other groups										
Heavily indebted poor countries	51.4	46.4	44.9	44.6	43.1	46.5	46.8	48.3	47.9	47.1
Middle East and north Africa	64.8	61.1	62.3	66.6	62.4	61.1	71.5	79.4	77.9	72.6

[1]In this table, official holdings of gold are valued at SDR 35 an ounce. This convention results in a marked underestimate of reserves for countries that have substantial gold holdings.

[2]Reserves at year-end in percent of imports of goods and services for the year indicated.

Table 37. Net Credit and Loans from IMF[1]
(Billions of U.S. dollars)

	1993	1994	1995	1996	1997	1998	1999	2000	2001
Advanced economies	—	—	**−0.1**	**−0.1**	**11.3**	**5.2**	**−10.3**	—	**−5.7**
Newly industrialized Asian economies	—	—	—	—	11.3	5.2	−10.3	—	−5.7
Developing countries	**−0.1**	**−0.8**	**12.6**	**−2.9**	**0.8**	**8.5**	**1.3**	**−6.7**	**23.3**
Regional groups									
Africa	0.2	0.9	0.8	0.6	−0.5	−0.4	−0.2	−0.1	−0.4
Sub-Sahara	0.7	0.5	0.6	0.1	−0.5	−0.3	−0.1	—	−0.2
Developing Asia	0.6	−0.8	−1.5	−1.7	5.0	6.6	1.7	0.9	−2.2
Excluding China and India	0.1	0.4	−0.3	−0.4	5.7	7.0	2.1	0.9	−2.2
Middle East and Turkey	—	0.4	0.4	0.1	0.2	−0.1	0.6	3.3	10.3
Western Hemisphere	−0.9	−1.3	12.9	−2.0	−4.0	2.5	−0.9	−10.7	15.6
Analytical groups									
By source of export earnings									
Fuel	−0.8	0.4	−0.2	0.7	−0.3	−0.6	−0.5	−0.6	−0.4
Nonfuel	0.6	−1.2	12.8	−3.6	1.2	9.1	1.8	−6.1	23.6
of which, primary products	−0.1	0.2	0.4	0.1	—	—	—	−0.2	−0.2
By external financing source									
Net debtor countries	−0.1	−0.8	12.6	−2.9	0.8	8.5	1.3	−6.7	23.3
of which, official financing	−0.5	1.1	1.1	0.9	0.2	—	—	—	−0.2
Net debtor countries by debt-servicing experience									
Countries with arrears and/or rescheduling during 1994–98	−0.8	1.0	0.5	0.7	3.9	10.9	5.6	−5.5	5.0
Other groups									
Heavily indebted poor countries	−0.2	0.5	0.6	0.3	—	0.2	0.2	—	−0.1
Middle East and north Africa	−0.5	0.5	0.2	0.6	0.3	−0.1	—	−0.3	−0.2
Countries in transition	**3.7**	**2.4**	**4.7**	**3.7**	**2.5**	**5.5**	**−3.6**	**−4.2**	**−4.3**
Central and eastern Europe	1.9	0.1	−2.7	−0.8	0.4	−0.3	—	—	−0.3
Commonwealth of Independent States and Mongolia	1.9	2.3	7.5	4.5	2.1	5.8	−3.6	−4.1	−4.0
Russia	1.5	1.5	5.5	3.2	1.5	5.3	−3.6	−2.9	−3.8
Excluding Russia	0.3	0.7	2.0	1.3	0.5	0.5	—	−1.2	−0.2
Memorandum									
Total									
Net credit provided under:									
General Resources Account	3.374	0.594	15.633	0.291	14.355	18.811	−12.856	−10.741	13.213
Trust Fund	−0.060	−0.014	−0.015	—	−0.007	−0.001	−0.001	—	—
PRGF	0.253	0.998	1.619	0.325	0.179	0.374	0.194	−0.111	0.102
Disbursements at year-end under:[2]									
General Resources Account	34.503	37.276	53.275	51.824	62.703	84.961	69.913	55.756	66.822
Trust Fund	0.157	0.153	0.141	0.137	0.121	0.126	0.122	0.116	0.111
PRGF	5.285	6.634	8.342	8.392	8.049	8.788	8.761	8.207	8.017

[1]Includes net disbursements from programs under the General Resources Account, Trust Fund, and Poverty Reduction and Growth Facility (formerly ESAF—Enhanced Structural Adjustment Facility). The data are on a transactions basis, with conversion to U.S. dollar values at annual average exchange rates.
[2]Converted to U.S. dollar values at end-of-period exchange rates.

Table 38. Summary of External Debt and Debt Service

	1994	1995	1996	1997	1998	1999	2000	2001	2002	2003
					Billions of U.S. dollars					
External debt										
Developing countries	**1,727.2**	**1,873.3**	**1,944.8**	**2,036.8**	**2,195.3**	**2,239.8**	**2,208.1**	**2,190.4**	**2,232.0**	**2,236.7**
Regional groups										
Africa	286.8	303.0	300.1	290.8	289.8	289.9	277.6	276.1	268.4	265.2
Developing Asia	518.8	579.1	615.4	669.3	696.9	702.2	674.9	675.8	688.7	716.8
Middle East and Turkey	356.5	371.9	383.0	404.6	452.0	468.9	486.7	486.1	502.4	510.1
Western Hemisphere	565.1	619.2	646.3	672.1	756.7	778.8	768.9	752.4	772.5	744.5
Analytical groups										
By external financing source										
Net debtor countries	1,687.1	1,830.1	1,896.8	1,975.0	2,119.9	2,160.4	2,127.0	2,109.1	2,148.6	2,151.3
of which, official financing	174.8	181.9	180.3	171.1	172.4	172.0	165.6	166.0	161.4	161.9
Net debtor countries by debt-servicing experience										
Countries with arrears and/or rescheduling during 1994–98	726.2	766.0	796.5	829.3	895.7	901.0	880.5	857.0	851.6	852.2
Countries in transition	**253.0**	**276.0**	**301.3**	**311.1**	**362.7**	**359.7**	**361.4**	**362.9**	**370.7**	**373.4**
Central and eastern Europe	114.7	125.5	138.7	145.3	167.8	173.8	179.4	187.2	197.9	210.5
Commonwealth of Independent States and Mongolia	138.3	150.5	162.6	165.8	194.9	185.9	181.9	175.7	172.8	162.8
Russia	127.5	128.0	136.1	134.6	158.2	144.3	140.7	131.2	126.0	114.0
Excluding Russia	10.8	22.5	26.5	31.2	36.7	41.6	41.2	44.5	46.9	48.9
Debt-service payments[1]										
Developing countries	**195.6**	**238.9**	**281.2**	**308.7**	**318.8**	**345.4**	**351.5**	**352.4**	**322.4**	**342.9**
Regional groups										
Africa	28.4	32.2	32.2	28.8	27.0	25.9	26.9	26.6	34.1	26.4
Developing Asia	64.2	74.2	77.7	85.2	98.7	96.7	99.5	102.6	100.3	104.8
Middle East and Turkey	26.3	33.5	43.1	38.0	36.8	38.7	41.1	44.1	40.7	44.9
Western Hemisphere	76.7	98.9	128.2	156.6	156.2	184.1	184.1	179.0	147.3	166.7
Analytical groups										
By external financing source										
Net debtor countries	187.7	229.7	268.2	300.0	310.4	338.2	343.9	343.6	313.4	333.8
of which, official financing	16.8	18.0	15.9	14.6	13.0	12.4	12.7	12.5	20.6	12.0
Net debtor countries by debt-servicing experience										
Countries with arrears and/or rescheduling during 1994–98	65.9	83.3	94.9	117.0	133.3	149.2	136.1	130.0	130.5	129.0
Countries in transition	**19.8**	**29.5**	**31.6**	**33.1**	**50.1**	**46.9**	**48.3**	**50.9**	**49.4**	**57.8**
Central and eastern Europe	14.8	19.5	21.7	23.7	29.5	28.9	32.2	32.7	31.6	34.3
Commonwealth of Independent States and Mongolia	5.0	10.0	9.9	9.4	20.6	18.1	16.1	18.2	17.8	23.6
Russia	4.3	6.4	6.9	5.9	16.3	12.9	9.8	12.4	12.6	18.4
Excluding Russia	0.7	3.6	3.0	3.5	4.3	5.2	6.3	5.8	5.2	5.1

Table 38 *(concluded)*

	1994	1995	1996	1997	1998	1999	2000	2001	2002	2003
					Percent of exports of goods and services					
External debt[2]										
Developing countries	**199.3**	**181.0**	**167.5**	**161.4**	**187.3**	**177.9**	**142.5**	**144.5**	**143.7**	**134.4**
Regional groups										
Africa	280.9	252.5	225.0	213.6	240.2	226.3	179.5	185.3	184.7	174.8
Developing Asia	140.0	127.4	121.8	118.4	129.1	121.5	96.4	96.8	93.7	89.2
Middle East and Turkey	191.2	173.7	153.7	155.0	205.3	186.6	144.0	154.2	168.8	169.6
Western Hemisphere	272.3	251.5	236.7	224.6	259.3	258.2	215.1	213.0	205.7	182.2
Analytical groups										
By external financing source										
Net debtor countries	221.1	199.9	185.7	176.9	199.1	191.5	156.4	156.8	153.3	141.8
of which, official financing	396.2	338.6	295.7	259.4	282.9	259.4	197.5	199.0	197.8	187.2
Net debtor countries by debt-servicing experience										
Countries with arrears and/or rescheduling during 1994–98	329.9	304.5	280.0	266.4	317.1	296.6	233.6	236.2	232.0	219.5
Countries in transition	**124.8**	**106.3**	**107.1**	**104.9**	**106.6**	**131.5**	**108.3**	**103.6**	**101.5**	**95.9**
Central and eastern Europe	119.9	100.0	103.6	98.8	79.0	116.0	107.3	101.9	99.9	97.5
Commonwealth of Independent States and Mongolia	129.2	112.2	110.4	111.0	152.3	150.2	109.4	105.6	103.4	93.9
Russia	166.1	134.2	132.4	130.6	181.3	170.3	122.1	115.9	113.0	100.3
Excluding Russia	35.5	58.0	59.5	67.3	90.1	106.5	80.7	83.6	84.1	81.8
Debt-service payments										
Developing countries	**22.6**	**23.1**	**24.2**	**24.5**	**27.2**	**27.4**	**22.7**	**23.2**	**20.8**	**20.6**
Regional groups										
Africa	27.8	26.8	24.1	21.2	22.4	20.2	17.4	17.8	23.5	17.4
Developing Asia	17.3	16.3	15.4	15.1	18.3	16.7	14.2	14.7	13.7	13.0
Middle East and Turkey	14.1	15.7	17.3	14.6	16.7	15.4	12.2	14.0	13.7	14.9
Western Hemisphere	36.9	40.2	47.0	52.3	53.5	61.0	51.5	50.7	39.5	40.9
Analytical groups										
By external financing source										
Net debtor countries	24.6	25.1	26.3	26.9	29.1	30.0	25.3	25.5	22.4	22.0
of which, official financing	38.1	33.5	26.1	22.1	21.3	18.7	15.1	15.0	25.2	13.9
Net debtor countries by debt-servicing experience										
Countries with arrears and/or rescheduling during 1994–98	29.9	33.1	33.4	37.6	47.2	49.1	36.1	35.8	35.5	33.2
Countries in transition	**9.8**	**11.4**	**11.2**	**11.2**	**14.7**	**17.2**	**14.5**	**14.5**	**13.5**	**14.9**
Central and eastern Europe	15.5	15.5	16.2	16.1	13.9	19.3	19.2	17.8	15.9	15.9
Commonwealth of Independent States and Mongolia	4.7	7.5	6.7	6.3	16.1	14.6	9.7	10.9	10.7	13.6
Russia	5.6	6.7	6.7	5.7	18.7	15.2	8.5	11.0	11.3	16.2
Excluding Russia	2.4	9.3	6.7	7.5	10.6	13.3	12.3	10.8	9.3	8.6

[1]Debt-service payments refer to actual payments of interest on total debt plus actual amortization payments on long-term debt. The projections incorporate the impact of exceptional financing items.

[2]Total debt at year-end in percent of exports of goods and services in year indicated.

Table 39. Developing Countries—by Region: External Debt, by Maturity and Type of Creditor
(Billions of U.S. dollars)

	1994	1995	1996	1997	1998	1999	2000	2001	2002	2003
Developing countries										
Total debt	**1,727.2**	**1,873.3**	**1,944.8**	**2,036.8**	**2,195.3**	**2,239.8**	**2,208.1**	**2,190.4**	**2,232.0**	**2,236.7**
By maturity										
Short-term	230.1	284.9	305.3	317.3	290.6	275.5	251.9	239.6	251.5	257.1
Long-term	1,497.0	1,588.4	1,639.5	1,719.5	1,904.7	1,964.3	1,956.2	1,950.8	1,980.5	1,979.6
By type of creditor										
Official	786.5	814.2	873.5	838.6	886.0	911.0	893.6	926.2	957.7	972.5
Banks	364.1	436.4	459.9	520.3	554.3	546.7	526.4	524.9	535.4	536.7
Other private	576.6	622.7	611.5	677.9	755.0	782.1	788.1	739.3	738.9	727.5
Regional groups										
Africa										
Total debt	**286.8**	**303.0**	**300.1**	**290.8**	**289.8**	**289.9**	**277.6**	**276.1**	**268.4**	**265.2**
By maturity										
Short-term	32.1	35.4	37.4	45.3	46.9	48.8	24.3	25.7	26.5	26.7
Long-term	254.7	267.6	262.7	245.5	242.9	241.2	253.4	250.4	241.9	238.5
By type of creditor										
Official	198.1	210.4	213.6	200.8	206.0	204.9	198.8	196.5	191.1	190.4
Banks	35.2	37.0	34.6	35.2	31.7	32.1	29.9	30.9	29.9	29.5
Other private	53.5	55.6	52.0	54.8	52.1	52.9	48.9	48.7	47.4	45.3
Sub-Sahara										
Total debt	**224.9**	**236.2**	**233.6**	**228.7**	**227.2**	**230.1**	**222.7**	**224.6**	**219.0**	**217.5**
By maturity										
Short-term	30.1	33.5	35.1	43.0	44.4	45.9	21.5	22.8	23.5	23.5
Long-term	194.8	202.6	198.5	185.7	182.8	184.2	201.1	201.7	195.5	194.0
By type of creditor										
Official	157.7	164.2	165.5	155.8	159.5	161.0	158.0	157.9	153.1	153.0
Banks	25.9	27.1	24.6	24.3	20.7	20.0	18.5	19.8	19.3	19.2
Other private	41.2	44.9	43.5	48.6	47.0	49.1	46.1	46.9	46.6	45.3
Developing Asia										
Total debt	**518.8**	**579.1**	**615.4**	**669.3**	**696.9**	**702.2**	**674.9**	**675.8**	**688.7**	**716.8**
By maturity										
Short-term	76.3	110.1	114.9	105.3	89.2	73.2	62.7	64.2	67.4	72.2
Long-term	442.4	469.0	500.5	564.0	607.7	629.0	612.2	611.7	621.3	644.6
By type of creditor										
Official	252.6	238.7	249.0	262.1	284.7	305.3	300.9	309.5	322.2	337.8
Banks	122.7	193.5	203.3	220.0	215.4	197.1	172.1	172.4	176.2	183.2
Other private	143.5	146.9	163.1	187.1	196.8	199.8	201.8	194.0	190.3	195.8
Middle East and Turkey										
Total debt	**356.5**	**371.9**	**383.0**	**404.6**	**452.0**	**468.9**	**486.7**	**486.1**	**502.4**	**510.1**
By maturity										
Short-term	42.0	44.3	46.2	52.1	60.5	61.6	64.8	54.5	52.6	56.3
Long-term	314.5	327.6	336.8	352.5	391.5	407.3	421.8	431.6	449.8	453.8
By type of creditor										
Official	161.4	173.6	173.3	166.7	168.3	168.6	173.2	184.2	199.9	201.1
Banks	90.0	91.1	110.3	149.2	175.5	188.4	197.5	190.2	189.1	193.4
Other private	105.0	107.3	99.3	88.7	108.2	111.9	115.9	111.7	113.4	115.6
Western Hemisphere										
Total debt	**565.1**	**619.2**	**646.3**	**672.1**	**756.7**	**778.8**	**768.9**	**752.4**	**772.5**	**744.5**
By maturity										
Short-term	79.6	95.0	106.8	114.6	94.1	92.0	100.1	95.3	105.0	101.8
Long-term	485.5	524.2	539.5	557.5	662.6	686.9	668.8	657.1	667.5	642.7
By type of creditor										
Official	174.3	191.5	237.6	208.9	227.1	232.2	220.6	236.0	244.4	243.2
Banks	116.2	114.8	111.6	115.9	131.7	129.1	126.9	131.4	140.3	130.5
Other private	274.6	312.9	297.1	347.3	397.9	417.5	421.4	384.9	387.8	370.8

Table 40. Developing Countries—by Analytical Criteria: External Debt, by Maturity and Type of Creditor

(Billions of U.S. dollars)

	1994	1995	1996	1997	1998	1999	2000	2001	2002	2003
By source of export earnings										
Fuel										
Total debt	**358.5**	**365.9**	**366.9**	**383.9**	**423.1**	**432.1**	**434.9**	**433.3**	**437.3**	**436.9**
By maturity										
Short-term	37.9	37.0	40.0	48.7	56.6	58.3	35.7	35.3	36.5	39.3
Long-term	320.6	328.9	326.9	335.3	366.4	373.8	399.2	398.0	400.8	397.6
By type of creditor										
Official	146.9	162.0	161.3	160.6	165.3	167.0	165.7	166.8	168.9	167.1
Banks	76.0	73.6	90.5	102.0	114.7	118.4	120.4	121.9	123.8	122.6
Other private	135.6	130.2	115.2	121.3	143.0	146.8	148.8	144.6	144.5	147.2
Nonfuel										
Total debt	**1,368.7**	**1,507.4**	**1,577.9**	**1,652.8**	**1,772.2**	**1,807.7**	**1,773.2**	**1,757.0**	**1,794.7**	**1,799.7**
By maturity										
Short-term	192.3	247.9	265.3	268.6	233.9	217.2	216.2	204.3	215.0	217.7
Long-term	1,176.4	1,259.6	1,312.6	1,384.2	1,538.3	1,590.5	1,557.0	1,552.8	1,579.7	1,582.0
By type of creditor										
Official	639.6	652.2	712.2	678.0	720.7	744.1	727.9	759.4	788.8	805.4
Banks	288.1	362.8	369.4	418.2	439.6	428.4	406.0	403.0	411.6	414.0
Other private	441.0	492.4	496.2	556.7	612.0	635.3	639.3	594.6	594.4	580.3
Nonfuel primary products										
Total debt	**194.5**	**201.3**	**200.6**	**199.0**	**205.2**	**209.6**	**208.2**	**211.6**	**210.8**	**215.8**
By maturity										
Short-term	19.0	18.6	18.2	18.1	15.6	13.2	14.1	13.7	13.8	14.4
Long-term	175.5	182.8	182.3	181.0	189.7	196.4	194.1	197.9	196.9	201.4
By type of creditor										
Official	134.2	139.4	136.0	134.2	138.0	141.3	139.7	142.2	139.7	142.6
Banks	32.2	34.2	33.3	30.6	30.2	30.5	29.0	29.0	28.8	28.5
Other private	28.1	27.7	31.2	34.1	37.0	37.8	39.5	40.3	42.2	44.7
By external financing source										
Net debtor countries										
Total debt	**1,687.1**	**1,830.1**	**1,896.8**	**1,975.0**	**2,119.9**	**2,160.4**	**2,127.0**	**2,109.1**	**2,148.6**	**2,151.3**
By maturity										
Short-term	210.6	267.8	286.6	293.8	261.7	247.3	224.9	212.7	224.2	229.3
Long-term	1,476.5	1,562.3	1,610.3	1,681.1	1,858.2	1,913.1	1,902.1	1,896.4	1,924.5	1,922.0
By type of creditor										
Official	781.8	809.3	867.8	833.0	879.9	905.6	888.8	922.0	953.5	968.4
Banks	345.2	418.8	425.8	476.7	500.6	489.9	468.8	467.2	477.3	478.6
Other private	560.1	602.0	603.2	665.3	739.4	764.8	769.4	719.9	717.8	704.3
Official financing										
Total debt	**174.8**	**181.9**	**180.3**	**171.1**	**172.4**	**172.0**	**165.6**	**166.0**	**161.4**	**161.9**
By maturity										
Short-term	8.6	6.8	4.6	3.9	3.8	3.4	3.6	3.9	3.9	4.0
Long-term	166.3	175.0	175.7	167.2	168.6	168.6	162.0	162.2	157.5	157.8
By type of creditor										
Official	141.6	150.0	152.1	145.0	147.7	148.3	143.9	145.1	142.6	144.3
Banks	14.0	13.0	10.8	10.0	9.3	9.3	9.1	9.7	8.8	8.4
Other private	19.2	18.9	17.4	16.1	15.3	14.5	12.6	11.2	10.0	9.1

Table 40 *(concluded)*

	1994	1995	1996	1997	1998	1999	2000	2001	2002	2003
Net debtor countries by debt-servicing experience										
Countries with arrears and/or rescheduling during 1994–98										
Total debt	**726.2**	**766.0**	**796.5**	**829.3**	**895.7**	**901.0**	**880.5**	**857.0**	**851.6**	**852.2**
By maturity										
Short-term	78.1	88.3	99.7	98.5	85.3	84.6	63.0	59.4	59.0	60.4
Long-term	648.1	677.7	696.7	730.8	810.3	816.4	817.6	797.6	792.6	791.7
By type of creditor										
Official	406.2	424.2	493.5	476.3	506.7	525.1	505.3	514.4	517.4	519.0
Banks	146.1	147.2	141.4	150.2	154.7	149.3	134.5	137.3	136.9	136.3
Other private	173.9	194.6	161.6	202.8	234.3	226.6	240.7	205.4	197.3	196.9
Other groups										
Heavily indebted poor countries										
Total debt	**202.4**	**205.5**	**200.4**	**187.6**	**188.7**	**191.7**	**184.5**	**187.4**	**184.1**	**186.3**
By maturity										
Short-term	9.7	8.9	7.4	7.0	4.0	3.6	3.1	3.2	3.2	3.3
Long-term	192.7	196.6	192.9	180.7	184.6	188.1	181.4	184.2	180.8	183.0
By type of creditor										
Official	166.7	171.5	168.1	155.0	158.2	161.4	156.8	158.6	156.5	158.9
Banks	23.6	23.4	21.5	20.5	17.6	17.1	15.9	17.4	16.4	16.3
Other private	12.1	10.5	10.8	12.2	12.8	13.2	11.8	11.4	11.1	11.1
Middle East and north Africa										
Total debt	**371.6**	**387.6**	**395.4**	**407.8**	**445.1**	**453.6**	**452.6**	**450.7**	**460.6**	**464.5**
By maturity										
Short-term	32.7	30.4	31.0	36.2	41.3	40.4	38.1	37.2	38.6	40.3
Long-term	338.9	357.2	364.4	371.6	403.7	413.2	414.5	413.5	421.9	424.3
By type of creditor										
Official	189.8	208.7	210.2	201.2	206.5	206.2	203.0	203.7	210.1	211.6
Banks	77.8	77.9	96.3	110.2	123.7	130.0	129.6	132.2	134.8	135.9
Other private	104.0	101.0	88.9	96.5	114.9	117.4	119.9	114.8	115.7	117.1

Table 41. Developing Countries: Ratio of External Debt to GDP[1]

	1994	1995	1996	1997	1998	1999	2000	2001	2002	2003
Developing countries	**43.4**	**41.8**	**39.5**	**39.1**	**43.6**	**44.9**	**40.8**	**40.8**	**40.8**	**38.2**
Regional groups										
Africa	77.8	73.6	68.9	65.4	67.6	67.8	64.0	65.1	65.0	60.7
Sub-Sahara	80.2	74.1	70.2	66.5	69.8	71.0	68.0	71.1	72.2	67.5
Developing Asia	35.3	32.9	31.1	32.7	36.6	34.2	30.8	29.7	28.0	26.9
Excluding China and India	53.3	52.8	51.8	59.7	83.9	72.3	65.5	66.2	60.1	56.5
Middle East and Turkey	65.0	59.6	55.9	56.5	64.6	63.8	59.3	62.8	67.4	63.6
Western Hemisphere	35.5	36.8	35.3	33.6	37.7	44.0	39.2	39.7	41.6	38.1
Analytical groups										
By source of export earnings										
Fuel	80.6	72.4	64.9	64.5	76.2	71.7	61.5	60.2	64.9	61.8
Nonfuel	38.7	37.9	36.2	35.9	39.6	41.2	37.7	37.8	37.4	35.0
of which, primary products	86.7	75.5	70.0	66.0	69.2	73.6	71.9	73.8	70.5	67.2
By external financing source										
Net debtor countries	45.1	43.3	40.8	40.2	44.4	46.0	42.0	41.9	41.7	38.9
of which, official financing	95.7	89.9	81.4	75.3	75.0	72.6	67.3	66.5	62.3	58.7
Net debtor countries by debt-servicing experience										
Countries with arrears and/or rescheduling during 1994–98	62.1	54.4	50.9	51.9	62.4	72.9	65.8	67.5	63.0	58.5
Other groups										
Heavily indebted poor countries	131.4	124.3	114.6	102.7	100.8	99.8	94.1	93.4	85.7	80.9
Middle East and north Africa	72.8	70.3	64.0	64.1	73.2	69.5	61.3	60.2	65.0	61.8

[1]Debt at year-end in percent of GDP in year indicated.

Table 42. Developing Countries: Debt-Service Ratios[1]
(Percent of exports of goods and services)

	1994	1995	1996	1997	1998	1999	2000	2001	2002	2003
Interest payments[2]										
Developing countries	**8.9**	**8.9**	**8.3**	**7.7**	**8.8**	**8.6**	**7.4**	**7.4**	**7.3**	**6.8**
Regional groups										
Africa	10.0	9.7	9.2	8.6	8.8	8.3	6.9	7.0	9.5	6.7
Sub-Sahara	8.4	7.9	7.9	7.6	7.7	7.6	6.4	6.8	10.2	6.7
Developing Asia	6.4	6.2	6.0	5.1	6.0	5.8	5.0	4.6	4.4	4.4
Excluding China and India	6.1	6.3	6.3	6.7	7.5	6.5	6.1	5.7	5.7	5.5
Middle East and Turkey	5.1	4.9	4.0	4.0	4.8	4.2	3.6	4.0	4.5	5.0
Western Hemisphere	16.2	16.9	16.0	15.4	17.2	17.8	16.0	16.1	14.2	12.8
Analytical groups										
By source of export earnings										
Fuel	5.2	5.6	4.6	4.2	5.1	3.9	3.0	3.2	3.3	3.7
Nonfuel	9.8	9.6	9.3	8.5	9.5	9.6	8.7	8.5	8.2	7.4
of which, primary products	8.3	7.7	7.1	7.3	8.0	7.6	7.7	9.4	12.9	7.3
By external financing source										
Net debtor countries	9.8	9.7	9.2	8.4	9.4	9.4	8.2	8.1	7.8	7.3
of which, official financing	11.4	9.6	9.8	8.8	8.5	7.4	6.2	6.0	10.7	5.3
Net debtor countries by debt-servicing experience										
Countries with arrears and/or rescheduling during 1994–98	10.7	11.8	11.6	11.1	13.1	13.0	10.8	10.8	12.1	10.4
Other groups										
Heavily indebted poor countries	12.0	9.0	9.1	7.2	7.0	6.2	5.5	5.3	10.5	4.3
Middle East and north Africa	4.8	5.2	4.3	4.0	4.9	3.6	2.8	2.7	2.9	3.1
Amortization[2]										
Developing countries	13.7	14.2	15.9	16.8	18.4	18.8	15.3	15.9	13.5	13.8
Regional groups										
Africa	17.8	17.1	14.9	12.6	13.6	11.9	10.5	10.8	14.0	10.7
Sub-Sahara	10.6	11.2	11.6	9.6	11.3	9.6	9.2	9.9	14.1	9.7
Developing Asia	10.9	10.2	9.3	10.0	12.3	11.0	9.2	10.1	9.2	8.6
Excluding China and India	12.5	10.9	9.9	12.8	17.2	14.5	12.4	15.8	14.5	12.6
Middle East and Turkey	9.0	10.8	13.3	10.6	11.9	11.2	8.6	10.0	9.2	9.9
Western Hemisphere	20.7	23.3	30.9	37.0	36.3	43.2	35.5	34.6	25.2	28.0
Analytical groups										
By source of export earnings										
Fuel	11.4	13.9	15.4	12.8	13.1	10.0	6.3	7.5	7.5	8.7
Nonfuel	14.3	14.3	16.0	17.8	19.3	20.9	17.8	18.0	14.8	14.8
of which, primary products	12.6	14.1	14.1	11.5	12.0	13.0	12.8	12.9	16.6	11.4
By external financing source										
Net debtor countries	14.8	15.4	17.0	18.5	19.7	20.6	17.1	17.4	14.5	14.7
of which, official financing	26.7	23.9	16.3	13.2	12.8	11.4	8.9	9.0	14.4	8.7
Net debtor countries by debt-servicing experience										
Countries with arrears and/or rescheduling during 1994–98	19.2	21.3	21.8	26.5	34.1	36.1	25.3	25.1	23.5	22.9
Other groups										
Heavily indebted poor countries	17.4	16.5	13.5	10.9	12.8	10.9	10.6	10.3	16.0	8.0
Middle East and north Africa	12.1	13.8	15.4	12.1	12.8	10.2	6.5	7.1	7.0	7.8

[1]Excludes service payments to the International Monetary Fund.
[2]Interest payments on total debt and amortization on long-term debt. Estimates through 2001 reflect debt-service payments actually made. The estimates for 2002 and 2003 take into account projected exceptional financing items, including accumulation of arrears and rescheduling agreements. In some cases, amortization on account of debt-reduction operations is included.

Table 43. IMF Charges and Repurchases to the IMF[1]

(Percent of exports of goods and services)

	1994	1995	1996	1997	1998	1999	2000	2001
Developing countries	**0.7**	**0.9**	**0.6**	**0.6**	**0.5**	**0.9**	**1.1**	**0.5**
Regional groups								
Africa	0.8	2.4	0.4	0.9	1.1	0.5	0.2	0.3
Sub-Sahara	0.5	2.8	0.2	0.7	0.7	0.2	0.1	0.1
Developing Asia	0.5	0.4	0.4	0.2	0.2	0.2	0.2	0.6
Excluding China and India	0.2	0.2	0.2	0.2	0.2	0.3	0.4	1.2
Middle East and Turkey	—	0.1	0.1	—	0.1	0.2	0.1	0.5
Western Hemisphere	1.5	1.6	1.6	1.9	1.1	3.2	4.2	0.6
Analytical groups								
By source of export earnings								
Fuel	0.4	0.5	0.3	0.4	0.6	0.4	0.2	0.1
Nonfuel	0.8	1.0	0.7	0.7	0.5	1.1	1.3	0.6
By external financing source								
Net debtor countries	0.8	1.0	0.7	0.7	0.6	1.1	1.2	0.6
of which, official financing	1.0	4.9	0.6	0.9	1.3	0.9	0.4	0.4
Net debtor countries by debt-servicing experience								
Countries with arrears and/or rescheduling during 1994–98	0.6	1.4	0.4	0.4	0.5	1.3	2.2	0.9
Other groups								
Heavily indebted poor countries	1.0	5.4	0.5	0.5	0.5	0.3	0.3	0.3
Middle East and north Africa	0.3	0.3	0.2	0.3	0.4	0.3	0.1	0.1
Countries in transition	**1.2**	**1.4**	**0.8**	**0.6**	**0.8**	**2.4**	**1.8**	**1.6**
Central and eastern Europe	2.3	2.6	0.8	0.3	0.4	0.3	0.3	0.3
Commonwealth of Independent States and Mongolia	0.2	0.3	0.8	0.9	1.7	4.9	3.2	3.0
Russia	0.2	0.3	1.0	1.0	1.9	5.9	3.1	3.8
Excluding Russia	0.1	0.3	0.4	0.5	1.2	2.9	3.4	1.4
Memorandum								
Total, billions of U.S. dollars								
General Resources Account	8.336	12.721	9.489	9.966	8.783	18.508	22.836	13.835
Charges	1.790	2.762	2.258	2.180	2.483	2.806	2.819	2.624
Repurchases	6.546	9.960	7.231	7.786	6.300	15.702	20.017	11.211
Trust Fund	0.015	0.015	—	0.007	0.001	0.001	—	—
Interest	—	—	—	—	—	—	—	—
Repayments	0.014	0.015	—	0.007	0.001	0.001	—	—
PRGF[2]	0.330	0.585	0.750	0.866	0.881	0.855	0.812	1.046
Interest	0.024	0.033	0.046	0.039	0.040	0.042	0.038	0.038
Repayments	0.306	0.552	0.703	0.827	0.842	0.813	0.776	1.009

[1]Excludes advanced economies. Charges on, and repurchases (or repayments of principal) for, use of International Monetary Fund credit.
[2]Poverty Reduction and Growth Facility (formerly ESAF—Enhanced Structural Adjustment Facility).

Table 44. Summary of Sources and Uses of World Saving
(Percent of GDP)

	Averages		1996	1997	1998	1999	2000	2001	2002	2003	Average 2004–07
	1980–87	1988–95									
World											
Saving	22.8	23.3	23.5	23.9	23.1	23.2	23.7	22.8	22.7	23.1	23.7
Investment	23.7	24.2	24.2	24.3	23.5	23.2	23.4	22.8	22.7	23.1	23.7
Advanced economies											
Saving	21.7	21.7	21.4	22.0	22.0	21.6	21.6	20.5	20.7	21.0	21.7
Private	21.4	21.1	20.7	20.1	20.3	18.7	18.3	17.7	18.4	18.6	18.6
Public	0.3	0.6	0.7	1.8	1.7	2.9	3.3	2.8	2.2	2.4	3.1
Investment	22.7	22.1	21.6	21.9	21.8	21.8	22.2	20.9	20.5	20.7	20.9
Private	18.2	18.1	17.7	18.2	18.1	18.1	18.6	17.3	16.8	17.2	17.5
Public	4.4	4.1	3.9	3.7	3.6	3.7	3.6	3.6	3.6	3.5	3.4
Net lending	−1.0	−0.4	−0.2	0.1	0.3	−0.3	−0.5	−0.3	0.2	0.3	0.8
Private	3.2	3.0	3.0	1.9	2.1	0.6	−0.3	0.4	1.6	1.4	1.1
Public	−4.1	−3.4	−3.2	−1.9	−1.9	−0.9	−0.2	−0.7	−1.4	−1.1	−0.3
Current transfers	−0.2	−0.3	−0.3	−0.3	−0.3	−0.4	−0.4	−0.4	−0.4	−0.4	−0.4
Factor income	−0.5	−0.3	−0.3	−0.2	—	0.1	0.4	0.3	0.8	0.9	1.3
Resource balance	−0.2	0.1	0.4	0.6	0.6	—	−0.5	−0.2	−0.3	−0.2	−0.2
United States											
Saving	18.6	16.8	17.3	18.1	18.8	18.4	18.1	16.1	17.1	17.6	18.8
Private	19.6	17.7	16.5	16.2	15.7	14.5	13.4	12.7	15.1	15.3	15.8
Public	−1.0	−0.9	0.8	1.9	3.1	3.9	4.7	3.4	2.0	2.2	3.0
Investment	20.7	18.4	19.1	19.9	20.7	20.9	21.1	19.3	19.2	19.6	19.8
Private	17.1	14.9	15.9	16.7	17.5	17.7	17.9	16.0	15.8	16.2	16.3
Public	3.6	3.5	3.2	3.2	3.2	3.3	3.2	3.3	3.4	3.5	3.4
Net lending	−2.1	−1.6	−1.8	−1.8	−1.9	−2.5	−3.0	−3.3	−2.2	−2.1	−1.0
Private	2.5	2.8	0.6	−0.6	−1.9	−3.1	−4.5	−3.3	−0.7	−0.9	−0.5
Public	−4.6	−4.4	−2.4	−1.3	−0.1	0.6	1.5	0.1	−1.4	−1.2	−0.4
Current transfers	−0.5	−0.4	−0.5	−0.5	−0.5	−0.5	−0.5	−0.5	−0.5	−0.4	−0.4
Factor income	0.3	0.1	—	−0.1	0.5	0.8	1.3	0.6	1.9	1.9	2.8
Resource balance	−1.9	−1.3	−1.3	−1.3	−1.9	−2.8	−3.8	−3.4	−3.6	−3.6	−3.4
European Union											
Saving	20.3	20.8	20.4	21.0	21.0	20.8	21.0	20.8	20.8	21.1	21.8
Private	20.9	22.0	21.8	20.9	19.9	18.9	18.8	18.5	18.5	18.6	19.1
Public	−0.5	−1.2	−1.4	0.1	1.1	1.9	2.2	2.3	2.3	2.5	2.7
Investment	21.4	21.3	19.6	19.7	20.5	20.7	21.3	20.3	20.3	20.6	21.1
Private	17.6	18.1	17.1	17.4	18.2	18.3	18.9	17.9	17.8	18.1	18.6
Public	3.8	3.2	2.5	2.3	2.3	2.4	2.4	2.4	2.5	2.5	2.5
Net lending	−1.1	−0.5	0.8	1.2	0.5	0.1	−0.3	0.5	0.5	0.5	0.6
Private	3.2	3.9	4.7	3.5	1.8	0.6	−0.1	0.6	0.7	0.5	0.5
Public	−4.3	−4.4	−3.9	−2.3	−1.2	−0.5	−0.2	−0.2	−0.2	—	0.2
Current transfers	−0.3	−0.3	−0.3	−0.3	−0.4	−0.4	−0.4	−0.4	−0.4	−0.4	−0.4
Factor income	−1.2	−0.8	−0.7	−0.6	−0.7	−0.6	−0.5	−0.4	−0.3	−0.4	−0.3
Resource balance	0.4	0.6	1.9	2.1	1.7	1.1	0.7	1.3	1.3	1.3	1.4
Japan											
Saving	31.4	32.8	30.6	30.9	29.8	28.4	28.5	27.6	26.6	26.3	26.3
Private	27.0	26.0	27.8	27.8	33.3	28.1	28.6	27.9	27.1	26.7	24.3
Public	4.4	6.8	2.8	3.2	−3.5	0.3	−0.2	−0.3	−0.5	−0.4	2.0
Investment	29.4	30.5	29.2	28.7	26.9	25.9	26.0	25.5	23.6	22.8	22.7
Private	21.5	23.2	20.6	21.1	19.4	18.1	19.1	18.9	17.1	17.1	17.8
Public	7.9	7.3	8.6	7.6	7.4	7.8	6.8	6.6	6.5	5.6	4.9
Net lending	2.0	2.3	1.4	2.2	3.0	2.5	2.5	2.1	3.1	3.5	3.6
Private	5.5	2.9	7.2	6.7	13.8	10.0	9.5	9.0	10.0	9.5	6.5
Public	−3.5	−0.5	−5.8	−4.5	−10.9	−7.4	−7.0	−6.9	−6.9	−6.1	−2.9
Current transfers	−0.1	−0.2	−0.2	−0.2	−0.2	−0.3	−0.2	−0.2	−0.2	−0.3	−0.4
Factor income	0.3	0.8	1.1	1.3	1.3	1.3	1.2	1.6	1.8	1.9	2.0
Resource balance	1.8	1.7	0.5	1.1	1.9	1.5	1.4	0.6	1.5	1.8	2.0

Table 44 (continued)

| | Averages | | 1996 | 1997 | 1998 | 1999 | 2000 | 2001 | 2002 | 2003 | Average 2004–07 |
	1980–87	1988–95									
Newly industrialized Asian economies											
Saving	...	34.6	32.3	32.3	32.6	31.7	30.6	29.4	29.3	29.6	29.1
Private	...	26.7	25.4	25.2	25.4	25.2	23.9	22.5	22.8	22.9	22.2
Public	...	7.9	6.9	7.1	7.3	6.6	6.7	6.9	6.6	6.7	6.9
Investment	...	31.6	32.8	31.6	24.2	25.8	26.7	24.4	24.0	24.3	23.8
Private	...	25.2	26.2	25.1	17.5	19.5	20.8	18.4	17.8	18.1	17.8
Public	...	6.4	6.6	6.5	6.7	6.4	6.0	6.0	6.3	6.2	5.9
Net lending	...	3.0	−0.5	0.7	8.4	5.9	3.9	4.9	5.3	5.4	5.3
Private	...	1.5	−0.8	0.2	7.8	5.7	3.1	4.1	5.0	4.9	4.3
Public	...	1.5	0.3	0.6	0.5	0.2	0.8	0.9	0.3	0.5	1.0
Current transfers	...	—	−0.4	−0.4	0.1	−0.2	−0.4	−0.6	−0.6	−0.5	−0.5
Factor income	...	0.4	0.1	0.6	−0.1	−0.1	0.2	1.2	1.8	2.2	2.6
Resource balance	...	2.7	−0.2	0.5	8.4	6.3	4.1	4.3	4.1	3.7	3.2
Developing countries											
Saving	21.6	25.0	27.0	27.5	25.8	25.9	26.6	26.0	25.6	25.9	26.5
Investment	23.9	26.7	28.4	28.2	26.6	25.7	25.8	25.8	25.9	26.4	27.3
Net lending	−2.4	−1.7	−1.4	−0.7	−0.8	0.2	0.8	0.2	−0.3	−0.5	−0.8
Current transfers	0.8	1.0	1.1	1.1	0.8	0.9	1.1	1.3	1.2	1.2	1.1
Factor income	−2.1	−1.5	−1.5	−1.7	−1.9	−2.3	−2.6	−2.4	−2.2	−1.9	−1.8
Resource balance	−1.0	−1.1	−0.9	−0.1	0.4	1.6	2.2	1.4	0.7	0.2	−0.1
Memorandum											
Acquisition of foreign assets	0.6	1.5	3.1	4.3	2.8	3.2	3.8	3.6	3.2	2.7	2.2
Change in reserves	−0.1	1.1	2.1	1.4	0.1	0.8	1.1	2.0	1.0	0.8	0.7
Regional groups											
Africa											
Saving	18.6	16.3	17.5	16.5	15.1	16.3	19.7	19.5	17.9	18.4	20.3
Investment	21.9	19.5	19.7	19.5	20.6	20.8	20.0	20.8	21.6	22.0	22.4
Net lending	−3.3	−3.2	−2.1	−2.9	−5.4	−4.5	−0.3	−1.3	−3.7	−3.5	−2.1
Current transfers	1.6	3.2	3.1	3.1	3.3	3.2	3.5	3.9	3.5	3.7	3.3
Factor income	−3.8	−4.7	−5.0	−5.5	−4.9	−5.5	−5.5	−4.9	−5.3	−5.0	−4.2
Resource balance	−1.1	−1.6	−0.2	−0.5	−3.9	−2.2	1.6	−0.2	−1.9	−2.2	−1.1
Memorandum											
Acquisition of foreign assets	0.3	0.6	2.3	3.6	0.7	1.8	3.3	3.8	2.2	2.8	2.6
Change in reserves	−0.1	0.4	2.2	2.5	−0.4	0.6	2.8	2.3	0.3	1.2	1.4
Developing Asia											
Saving	24.7	30.4	32.5	33.4	32.1	31.4	31.7	31.2	30.4	30.2	30.3
Investment	27.0	31.7	33.9	32.8	30.0	29.4	29.3	29.3	29.2	29.5	30.3
Net lending	−2.3	−1.3	−1.4	0.6	2.2	2.0	2.5	1.9	1.1	0.7	—
Current transfers	1.1	0.9	1.3	1.6	1.3	1.4	1.4	1.4	1.3	1.3	1.1
Factor income	−0.7	−0.8	−1.1	−1.3	−1.5	−1.8	−1.0	−1.3	−1.2	−1.3	−1.4
Resource balance	−2.6	−1.5	−1.6	0.4	2.4	2.4	2.1	1.8	1.1	0.7	0.3
Memorandum											
Acquisition of foreign assets	0.6	2.4	3.4	5.6	4.4	4.2	4.1	4.3	4.1	3.5	2.8
Change in reserves	−0.6	1.4	2.1	1.6	0.8	1.3	0.9	2.8	1.3	1.0	0.8
Middle East and Turkey											
Saving	21.3	23.5	24.8	24.8	20.6	23.0	22.1	21.8	21.2	23.8	24.1
Investment	23.4	24.5	24.1	24.9	24.1	22.1	22.8	22.8	22.5	24.5	25.9
Net lending	−2.1	−1.1	0.7	−0.1	−3.5	0.9	−0.7	−1.0	−1.2	−0.7	−1.8
Current transfers	—	−0.7	−1.3	−2.8	−4.0	−4.8	−2.8	−1.5	−1.1	−0.9	−0.7
Factor income	−0.5	1.8	1.4	0.6	−0.6	−1.0	−7.8	−4.7	−2.0	0.6	0.4
Resource balance	−1.7	−2.1	0.6	2.1	1.1	6.7	9.9	5.2	1.9	−0.4	−1.4
Memorandum											
Acquisition of foreign assets	0.6	−1.4	1.9	3.5	2.0	3.9	9.2	4.1	3.8	1.6	0.6
Change in reserves	−0.6	0.9	2.6	0.7	−1.5	0.9	3.3	1.7	2.0	0.4	0.2

Table 44 *(continued)*

	Averages		1996	1997	1998	1999	2000	2001	2002	2003	Average 2004–07
	1980–87	1988–95									
Western Hemisphere											
Saving	18.8	19.1	19.1	19.1	17.4	17.1	18.0	16.7	17.5	17.7	18.5
Investment	21.0	21.1	21.0	22.3	22.1	20.1	20.4	19.7	20.0	20.2	20.6
Net lending	−2.2	−2.0	−1.9	−3.3	−4.6	−3.0	−2.4	−3.1	−2.4	−2.5	−2.1
Current transfers	0.5	1.1	1.0	1.0	1.1	1.3	1.3	1.4	1.3	1.3	1.2
Factor income	−4.0	−3.1	−2.5	−2.3	−2.4	−2.9	−3.0	−3.4	−3.7	−3.5	−3.1
Resource balance	1.4	0.1	−0.5	−1.9	−3.2	−1.4	−0.7	−1.0	—	−0.3	−0.3
Memorandum											
Acquisition of foreign assets	0.6	1.5	3.1	1.6	0.3	0.9	0.7	1.7	1.1	0.7	1.2
Change in reserves	−0.2	0.9	1.8	0.9	−0.5	−0.6	0.1	0.1	0.2	—	0.5
Analytical groups											
By source of export earnings											
Fuel											
Saving	23.6	24.0	28.0	26.4	19.4	24.4	27.5	25.1	23.9	27.0	28.0
Investment	23.8	23.7	23.1	24.0	24.6	22.5	21.9	23.6	23.7	26.0	28.2
Net lending	−0.2	0.3	4.9	2.4	−5.2	1.9	5.6	1.4	0.2	1.0	−0.2
Current transfers	−2.4	−2.9	−3.0	−4.7	−6.2	−7.0	−4.7	−2.9	−2.6	−2.3	−1.9
Factor income	−0.2	1.3	−0.7	−1.7	−2.9	−3.1	−10.8	−6.6	−3.8	−0.8	−1.0
Resource balance	2.5	1.9	8.5	8.8	3.9	12.0	21.1	10.9	6.6	4.0	2.8
Memorandum											
Acquisition of foreign assets	0.9	−1.7	3.7	5.7	1.4	3.6	14.4	6.9	4.0	2.5	1.7
Change in reserves	−1.0	0.2	4.3	1.8	−2.7	−0.5	6.5	3.5	1.5	1.0	0.8
Nonfuel											
Saving	21.2	25.2	26.9	27.6	26.5	26.0	26.5	26.1	25.8	25.8	26.3
Investment	24.0	27.1	29.0	28.7	26.8	26.1	26.2	26.0	26.1	26.4	27.2
Net lending	−2.8	−1.9	−2.0	−1.0	−0.3	—	0.3	0.1	−0.3	−0.6	−0.8
Current transfers	1.3	1.5	1.5	1.7	1.6	1.7	1.7	1.7	1.6	1.6	1.4
Factor income	−2.5	−1.9	−1.6	−1.7	−1.8	−2.2	−1.7	−2.0	−1.9	−1.9	−1.8
Resource balance	−1.7	−1.5	−2.0	−1.0	—	0.5	0.3	0.4	—	−0.3	−0.4
Memorandum											
Acquisition of foreign assets	0.5	1.9	3.0	4.1	3.0	3.2	2.8	3.3	3.1	2.7	2.3
Change in reserves	—	1.2	1.8	1.4	0.4	0.9	0.6	1.9	1.0	0.7	0.7
By external financing source											
Net debtor countries											
Saving	21.2	25.4	27.2	27.6	26.2	26.0	26.4	26.0	25.6	25.9	26.5
Investment	24.0	26.9	28.7	28.5	26.8	25.9	26.0	26.0	26.1	26.5	27.3
Net lending	−2.7	−1.5	−1.5	−0.8	−0.6	—	0.4	—	−0.4	−0.6	−0.8
Current transfers	1.2	1.4	1.4	1.3	1.1	1.1	1.3	1.5	1.5	1.5	1.3
Factor income	−2.3	−1.8	−1.7	−1.9	−2.2	−2.5	−2.7	−2.6	−2.3	−2.1	−1.9
Resource balance	−1.6	−1.2	−1.2	−0.2	0.5	1.4	1.8	1.0	0.4	—	−0.2
Memorandum											
Acquisition of foreign assets	0.4	1.7	3.0	4.2	3.0	3.2	3.5	3.5	3.2	2.7	2.3
Change in reserves	−0.1	1.2	2.0	1.4	0.3	0.8	1.0	2.0	1.0	0.8	0.7
Official financing											
Saving	13.8	14.4	18.3	18.8	17.1	19.5	22.0	21.7	20.4	20.1	21.7
Investment	19.7	19.2	22.9	21.8	22.5	22.4	22.0	22.9	24.1	24.5	24.0
Net lending	−5.9	−4.8	−4.6	−3.0	−5.5	−2.9	—	−1.3	−3.7	−4.4	−2.3
Current transfers	4.4	4.3	4.7	4.3	4.7	4.8	5.3	5.3	5.1	5.4	4.8
Factor income	−4.7	−3.2	−2.9	−3.2	−3.6	−2.8	−3.0	−2.7	−2.2	−2.2	−2.0
Resource balance	−5.6	−5.9	−6.4	−4.1	−6.6	−4.9	−2.3	−3.8	−6.6	−7.5	−5.0
Memorandum											
Acquisition of foreign assets	−0.1	0.3	1.5	2.4	−0.5	1.1	2.9	2.4	0.9	1.2	1.1
Change in reserves	0.1	0.6	1.5	2.6	−0.5	0.6	3.2	2.5	1.3	1.6	1.3

Table 44 *(concluded)*

	Averages		1996	1997	1998	1999	2000	2001	2002	2003	Average 2004–07
	1980–87	1988–95									
Net debtor countries by debt-servicing experience											
Countries with arrears and/or rescheduling during 1994–98											
Saving	17.6	21.8	21.8	21.1	17.6	19.0	20.9	19.9	20.0	21.3	22.4
Investment	21.4	23.3	24.5	24.7	21.5	19.8	20.6	21.3	21.9	22.9	24.0
Net lending	−3.8	−1.5	−2.7	−3.6	−3.9	−0.8	0.3	−1.5	−1.9	−1.7	−1.6
Current transfers	0.7	1.4	1.2	0.5	0.1	−0.1	0.6	1.4	1.5	1.6	1.5
Factor income	−2.9	−2.9	−1.6	−2.4	−3.3	−3.9	−5.7	−4.9	−3.8	−2.9	−2.6
Resource balance	−1.6	−0.8	−2.3	−1.7	−0.8	3.3	5.4	2.1	0.4	−0.4	−0.4
Memorandum											
Acquisition of foreign assets	−0.3	0.4	1.4	1.8	1.0	2.1	4.1	2.9	1.4	1.1	1.0
Change in reserves	−0.5	0.8	1.3	0.5	−0.1	0.2	2.0	1.5	0.5	0.8	0.8
Countries in transition											
Saving	...	...	22.2	21.2	17.1	22.2	26.4	24.2	23.4	23.4	23.4
Investment	...	...	24.5	24.2	21.0	19.9	20.9	21.8	23.0	23.8	24.4
Net lending	...	...	−2.3	−2.9	−3.9	2.3	5.5	2.4	0.4	−0.3	−1.0
Current transfers	...	...	0.7	0.7	1.7	1.1	1.1	1.1	1.0	1.0	0.9
Factor income	...	...	−0.7	−1.2	−19.3	−2.6	−2.5	−2.2	−2.2	−2.0	−1.9
Resource balance	...	...	−2.4	−2.5	13.7	3.9	6.9	3.5	1.6	0.8	—
Memorandum											
Acquisition of foreign assets	...	...	2.0	5.1	3.3	6.9	7.7	6.0	4.8	3.7	3.7
Change in reserves	...	...	0.2	1.1	−0.3	1.0	3.4	2.5	2.2	1.4	1.4

Note: The estimates in this table are based on individual countries' national accounts and balance of payments statistics. For many countries, the estimates of national saving are built up from national accounts data on gross domestic investment and from balance-of-payments-based data on net foreign investment. The latter, which is equivalent to the current account balance, comprises three components: current transfers, net factor income, and the resource balance. The mixing of data sources, which is dictated by availability, implies that the estimates for national saving that are derived incorporate the statistical discrepancies. Furthermore, errors, omissions, and asymmetries in balance of payments statistics affect the estimates for net lending; at the global level, net lending, which in theory would be zero, equals the world current account discrepancy. Notwithstanding these statistical shortcomings, flow of funds estimates, such as those presented in this table, provide a useful framework for analyzing development in saving and investment, both over time and across regions and countries. Country group composites are weighted by GDP valued at purchasing power parities (PPPs) as a share of total world GDP.

Table 45. Summary of World Medium-Term Baseline Scenario

	Eight-Year Averages		Four-Year Average					Four-Year Average
	1984–91	1992–99	2000–03	2000	2001	2002	2003	2004–07
	Annual percent change unless otherwise noted							
World real GDP	**3.6**	**3.3**	**3.5**	**4.7**	**2.5**	**2.8**	**4.0**	**4.4**
Advanced economies	3.5	2.8	2.4	3.9	1.2	1.7	3.0	3.1
Developing countries	4.7	5.7	4.9	5.7	4.0	4.3	5.5	6.0
Countries in transition	1.2	–3.7	5.0	6.6	5.0	3.9	4.4	5.0
Memorandum								
Potential output								
Major advanced economies	2.9	2.5	2.4	2.5	2.4	2.3	2.5	2.6
World trade, volume[1]	**5.9**	**6.6**	**5.3**	**12.4**	**–0.2**	**2.5**	**6.6**	**7.0**
Imports								
Advanced economies	7.2	6.6	4.6	11.6	–1.5	2.1	6.6	6.7
Developing countries	3.1	8.1	8.1	16.0	2.9	6.4	7.7	8.5
Countries in transition	–0.2	1.5	9.9	13.2	10.8	8.0	7.7	7.4
Exports								
Advanced economies	6.3	6.3	4.3	11.7	–1.3	0.9	6.3	6.6
Developing countries	6.1	9.1	7.4	15.0	3.0	4.8	7.0	8.1
Countries in transition	0.2	1.7	8.0	14.6	6.3	5.2	6.1	6.5
Terms of trade								
Advanced economies	1.1	0.3	–0.2	–2.2	0.2	0.9	0.4	0.3
Developing countries	–3.2	—	0.2	7.0	–2.8	–1.6	–1.2	–0.0
Countries in transition	–1.0	–0.7	1.3	8.0	–1.1	–0.8	–0.8	–0.1
World prices in U.S. dollars								
Manufactures	5.8	–0.6	–1.7	–5.1	–2.4	–0.5	1.2	1.0
Oil	–5.2	–0.9	5.2	57.0	–14.0	–5.3	–4.4	–1.2
Nonfuel primary commodities	0.1	–0.6	0.8	1.8	–5.5	–0.1	7.2	3.4
Consumer prices								
Advanced economies	4.4	2.3	1.9	2.3	2.2	1.3	1.8	2.0
Developing countries	49.1	25.5	5.5	6.1	5.7	5.5	4.7	4.2
Countries in transition	17.9	153.5	13.8	20.2	15.9	10.8	8.7	6.2
Interest rates (in percent)								
Real six-month LIBOR[2]	4.9	3.2	2.3	4.4	1.5	1.1	2.3	3.7
World real long-term interest rate[3]	5.1	3.8	2.9	2.8	2.3	3.3	3.0	3.5
	Percent of GDP							
Balances on current account								
Advanced economies	–0.3	0.1	–0.8	–1.0	–0.8	–0.8	–0.7	–0.7
Developing countries	–1.8	–1.8	0.1	1.2	0.5	–0.4	–0.9	–1.2
Countries in transition	0.1	–1.4	1.3	3.6	1.9	0.2	–0.6	–1.5
Total external debt								
Developing countries	39.1	42.0	40.1	40.8	40.8	40.8	38.2	33.5
Countries in transition	9.4	44.2	43.0	48.3	43.3	41.5	38.8	33.2
Debt service								
Developing countries	4.7	5.6	6.2	6.5	6.6	5.9	5.9	4.9
Countries in transition	2.3	4.8	6.0	6.5	6.1	5.5	6.0	4.7

[1]Data refer to trade in goods and services.
[2]London interbank offered rate on U.S. dollar deposits less percent change in U.S. GDP deflator.
[3]GDP-weighted average of ten-year (or nearest maturity) government bond rates for the United States, Japan, Germany, France, Italy, the United Kingdom, and Canada.

Table 46. Developing Countries—Medium-Term Baseline Scenario: Selected Economic Indicators

	Eight-Year Averages		Four-Year Average					Four-Year Average
	1984–91	1992–99	2000–03	2000	2001	2002	2003	2004–07
	Annual percent change							
Developing countries								
Real GDP	4.7	5.7	4.9	5.7	4.0	4.3	5.5	6.0
Export volume[1]	6.1	9.1	7.4	15.0	3.0	4.8	7.0	8.1
Terms of trade[1]	–3.2	—	0.2	7.0	–2.8	–1.6	–1.2	—
Import volume[1]	3.1	8.1	8.1	16.0	2.9	6.4	7.7	8.5
Regional groups								
Africa								
Real GDP	2.6	2.4	3.6	3.0	3.7	3.4	4.2	5.0
Export volume[1]	5.6	4.8	3.4	5.2	3.0	1.5	4.1	6.1
Terms of trade[1]	–2.2	–0.6	0.6	16.0	–5.9	–4.6	–1.6	–0.7
Import volume[1]	2.4	4.8	3.4	4.7	3.4	3.0	2.6	4.3
Developing Asia								
Real GDP	7.1	7.8	6.1	6.7	5.6	5.9	6.4	6.8
Export volume[1]	9.0	11.8	9.8	22.2	3.6	6.5	7.9	10.0
Terms of trade[1]	–1.0	—	–0.4	–2.8	0.8	–0.1	0.5	0.4
Import volume[1]	5.8	9.7	11.5	22.1	5.8	9.0	9.7	11.1
Middle East and Turkey								
Real GDP	3.0	3.7	3.9	5.8	2.1	3.3	4.5	5.0
Export volume[1]	5.5	7.9	3.2	6.2	1.2	0.6	4.9	4.8
Terms of trade[1]	–6.8	0.3	1.5	29.9	–9.1	–5.6	–4.9	–0.2
Import volume[1]	–0.4	7.0	6.0	15.8	–2.8	6.3	5.5	5.7
Western Hemisphere								
Real GDP	2.7	3.2	2.4	4.0	0.7	0.7	3.7	4.3
Export volume[1]	4.3	7.6	7.6	12.8	3.4	6.7	7.8	7.4
Terms of trade[1]	–1.9	0.5	–0.3	3.6	–2.6	0.1	–1.6	–0.6
Import volume[1]	5.7	9.2	5.8	11.0	1.6	3.1	7.8	7.0
Analytical groups								
Net debtor countries by debt-servicing experience								
Countries with arrears and/or rescheduling during 1994–98								
Real GDP	3.0	3.4	4.0	4.4	3.4	3.7	4.4	5.2
Export volume[1]	4.6	9.1	5.8	10.1	1.1	5.6	6.6	7.1
Terms of trade[1]	–3.4	–1.5	0.3	11.4	–3.8	–3.6	–2.1	–0.5
Import volume[1]	0.1	8.8	6.5	11.2	3.2	6.2	5.9	6.7

Table 46 (*concluded*)

	1991	1995	1999	2000	2001	2002	2003	2007
	Percent of exports of good and services							
Developing countries								
Current account balance	−15.2	−9.3	−0.9	4.2	1.8	−1.5	−3.0	−4.5
Total external debt	210.6	181.0	177.9	142.5	144.5	143.7	134.4	103.6
Debt-service payments[2]	24.0	23.1	27.4	22.7	23.2	20.8	20.6	15.2
Interest payments	10.4	8.9	8.6	7.4	7.4	7.3	6.8	5.9
Amortization	13.6	14.2	18.8	15.3	15.9	13.5	13.8	9.3
Regional groups								
Africa								
Current account balance	−7.6	−14.5	−11.9	2.0	−1.4	−7.4	−6.6	−2.4
Total external debt	254.3	252.5	226.3	179.5	185.3	184.7	174.8	135.1
Debt-service payments[2]	26.0	26.8	20.2	17.4	17.8	23.5	17.4	13.2
Interest payments	9.8	9.7	8.3	6.9	7.0	9.5	6.7	5.5
Amortization	16.2	17.1	11.9	10.5	10.8	14.0	10.7	7.7
Developing Asia								
Current account balance	−5.2	−9.5	7.9	6.6	5.6	2.8	1.4	−2.2
Total external debt	161.9	127.4	121.5	96.4	96.8	93.7	89.2	68.5
Debt-service payments[2]	17.3	16.3	16.7	14.2	14.7	13.7	13.0	8.7
Interest payments	7.9	6.2	5.8	5.0	4.6	4.4	4.4	3.8
Amortization	9.4	10.2	11.0	9.2	10.1	9.2	8.6	4.9
Middle East and Turkey								
Current account balance	−39.4	0.1	5.9	19.1	14.1	4.1	−1.2	−5.5
Total external debt	182.1	173.7	186.6	144.0	154.2	168.8	169.6	142.7
Debt-service payments[2]	15.6	15.7	15.4	12.2	14.0	13.7	14.9	14.2
Interest payments	6.3	4.9	4.2	3.6	4.0	4.5	5.0	4.9
Amortization	9.4	10.8	11.2	8.6	10.0	9.2	9.9	9.3
Western Hemisphere								
Current account balance	−10.0	−14.8	−18.8	−13.4	−15.4	−12.0	−11.8	−9.6
Total external debt	278.9	251.5	258.2	215.1	213.0	205.7	182.2	142.8
Debt-service payments[2]	40.3	40.2	61.0	51.5	50.7	39.2	40.8	30.6
Interest payments	18.2	16.9	17.8	16.0	16.1	14.2	12.8	11.2
Amortization	22.1	23.3	43.2	35.5	34.6	25.0	28.0	19.4
Analytical groups								
Net debtor countries by debt-servicing experience								
Countries with arrears and/or rescheduling during 1994–98								
Current account balance	−17.5	−18.4	−7.6	2.2	−3.1	−7.2	−8.7	−7.7
Total external debt	341.0	304.5	296.6	233.6	236.2	232.0	219.5	166.1
Debt-service payments[2]	34.2	33.1	49.1	36.1	35.8	35.5	33.2	22.8
Interest payments	13.8	11.8	13.0	10.8	10.8	12.1	10.4	8.2
Amortization	20.4	21.3	36.1	25.3	25.1	23.5	22.9	14.6

[1]Data refer to trade in goods and services.
[2]Interest payments on total debt plus amortization payments on long-term debt only. Projections incorporate the impact of exceptional financing items. Excludes service payments to the International Monetary Fund.

WORLD ECONOMIC OUTLOOK AND STAFF STUDIES FOR THE WORLD ECONOMIC OUTLOOK, SELECTED TOPICS, 1992–2002

I. Methodology—Aggregation, Modeling, and Forecasting

II. Historical Surveys

III. Economic Growth—Sources and Patterns

IV. Inflation and Deflation; Commodity Markets

VII. Labor Market Issues

VIII. Exchange Rate Issues

IX. External Payments, Trade, Capital Movements, and Foreign Debt

X. Regional Issues

XI. Country-Specific Analyses

***Staff Studies for the
World Economic Outlook***

World Economic and Financial Surveys

This series (ISSN 0258-7440) contains biannual, annual, and periodic studies covering monetary and financial issues of importance to the global economy. The core elements of the series are the *World Economic Outlook* report, usually published in May and October, and the quarterly *Global Financial Stability Report*. Other studies assess international trade policy, private market and official financing for developing countries, exchange and payments systems, export credit policies, and issues discussed in the *World Economic Outlook*. Please consult the IMF *Publications Catalog* for a complete listing of currently available World Economic and Financial Surveys.

World Economic Outlook: A Survey by the Staff of the International Monetary Fund

The *World Economic Outlook,* published twice a year in English, French, Spanish, and Arabic, presents IMF staff economists' analyses of global economic developments during the near and medium term. Chapters give an overview of the world economy; consider issues affecting industrial countries, developing countries, and economies in transition to the market; and address topics of pressing current interest.

ISSN 0256-6877.

$42.00 (academic rate: $35.00); paper.
2002. (April). ISBN 1-58906-107-1. **Stock #WEO EA 0012002.**
2001. (Dec.). ISBN 1-58906-087-3. **Stock #WEO EA 0172001.**
2001. (Oct.). ISBN 1-58906-073-3. **Stock #WEO EA 0022001.**
2001. (May). ISBN 1-58906-032-6. **Stock #WEO EA 0012001.**
2000. (Oct.). ISBN 1-55775-975-8. **Stock #WEO EA 0022000.**
2000. (May). ISBN 1-55775-936-7. **Stock #WEO EA 012000.**
1999. (Oct.). ISBN 1-55775-839-5. **Stock #WEO EA 299.**

Official Financing for Developing Countries
by a staff team in the IMF's Policy Development and Review Department led by Anthony R. Boote and Doris C. Ross

This study provides information on official financing for developing countries, with the focus on low-income countries. It updates the 1995 edition and reviews developments in direct financing by official and multilateral sources.

$25.00 (academic rate: $20.00); paper.
2001. ISBN 1-58906-038-5. **Stock #WEO EA 0132001.**
1998. ISBN 1-55775-702-X. **Stock #WEO-1397.**
1995. ISBN 1-55775-527-2. **Stock #WEO-1395.**

Exchange Rate Arrangements and Currency Convertibility: Developments and Issues
by a staff team led by R. Barry Johnston

A principal force driving the growth in international trade and investment has been the liberalization of financial transactions, including the liberalization of trade and exchange controls. This study reviews the developments and issues in the exchange arrangements and currency convertibility of IMF members.

$20.00 (academic rate: $12.00); paper.
1999. ISBN 1-55775-795-X. **Stock #WEO EA 0191999.**

World Economic Outlook Supporting Studies
by the IMF's Research Department

These studies, supporting analyses and scenarios of the *World Economic Outlook*, provide a detailed examination of theory and evidence on major issues currently affecting the global economy.

$25.00 (academic rate: $20.00); paper.
2000. ISBN 1-55775-893-X. **Stock #WEO EA 0032000.**

Global Financial Stability Report: Market Developments and Issues

The *Global Financial Stability Report,* published four times a year, examines trends and issues that influence world financial markets. It replaces two IMF publications—the annual *International Capital Markets* report and the electronic quarterly *Emerging Market Financing* report. The report is designed to deepen understanding of international capital flows and explores developments that could pose a risk to international financial market stability.

$42.00 (academic rate: $35.00); paper.
March 2002 ISBN 1-58906-105-5. **Stock #GFSR EA0012002.**

International Capital Markets: Developments, Prospects, and Key Policy Issues (back issues)
$42.00 (academic rate: $35.00); paper.
2001. ISBN 1-58906-056-3. **Stock #WEO EA 0062001.**
2000. (Sep.). ISBN 1-55775-949-9. **Stock #WEO EA 0062000.**
1999. (Sep.). ISBN 1-55775-852-2. **Stock #WEO EA 699.**

Toward a Framework for Financial Stability
by a staff team led by David Folkerts-Landau and Carl-Johan Lindgren

This study outlines the broad principles and characteristics of stable and sound financial systems, to facilitate IMF surveillance over banking sector issues of macroeconomic significance and to contribute to the general international effort to reduce the likelihood and diminish the intensity of future financial sector crises.

$25.00 (academic rate: $20.00); paper.
1998. ISBN 1-55775-706-2. **Stock #WEO-016.**

Trade Liberalization in IMF-Supported Programs
by a staff team led by Robert Sharer

This study assesses trade liberalization in programs supported by the IMF by reviewing multiyear arrangements in the 1990s and six detailed case studies. It also discusses the main economic factors affecting trade policy targets.

$25.00 (academic rate: $20.00); paper.
1998. ISBN 1-55775-707-0. **Stock #WEO-1897.**

Private Market Financing for Developing Countries
by a staff team from the IMF's Policy Development and Review Department led by Steven Dunaway

This study surveys recent trends in flows to developing countries through banking and securities markets. It also analyzes the institutional and regulatory framework for developing country finance; institutional investor behavior and pricing of developing country stocks; and progress in commercial bank debt restructuring in low-income countries.

$20.00 (academic rate: $12.00); paper.
1995. ISBN 1-55775-526-4. **Stock #WEO-1595.**

Available by series subscription or single title (including back issues); academic rate available only to full-time university faculty and students. For earlier editions please inquire about prices.

The IMF *Catalog of Publications* is available on-line at the Internet address listed below.

Please send orders and inquiries to:
International Monetary Fund, Publication Services, 700 19th Street, N.W.
Washington, D.C. 20431, U.S.A.
Tel.: (202) 623-7430   Telefax: (202) 623-7201
E-mail: publications@imf.org
Internet: http://www.imf.org

DARASSE • BOSSE • ZIDROU

7

tamara
MA PREMIÈRE FOIS !

Couleurs : Benoît Bekaert

Merci à Louise,
sans qui cet album
ne serait pas ce qu'il est.

DUPUIS

À Simon. À Émile.
À coup sûr, Tamara serait tombée amoureuse de vous
si elle avait eu la chance de vous connaître.

Zidrou

D.2009/0089/103 — R.3/2012.
ISBN 978-2-8001-4426-9
© Dupuis, 2009.
Tous droits réservés.
✆ Imprimé en R.P.C. par Book Partners China Ltd.

Cet album a été imprimé sur papier issu de forêts
gérées de manière durable et équitable.

www.DUPUIS.com

AAARGH! JE HAIS LA RENTRÉE!

VA FALLOIR RETROUVER LES AUTRES BOUTONNEUX ET LEURS STUPIDES VANNES ANTI-GROSSES!

LE GROS EST LE LÉPREUX DU MONDE MODERNE.

ALLONS, ALLONS! QU'EST-CE QUE TU RACONTES LÀ, MA TAMOUNETTE?!

IL EST LOIN, LE TEMPS OÙ LES GR... HEU LES PERSONNES SOUFFRANT D'UNE LÉGÈRE SURCHARGE PONDÉRALE ÉTAIENT L'OBJET DE BLAGUES CRUELLES!

NOUS VIVONS DANS UN MONDE OÙ PLUS PERSONNE N'EST JUGÉ OU DISCRIMINÉ À CAUSE DE SON APPARENCE PHYSIQUE...

228

... UN MONDE DE TOLÉRANCE, D'OUVERTURE, UN MONDE ENFIN LARGE D'ESPRIT!

JE LE HAIS!... HOOO, COMME JE LE HAIS!

OUF! BONNE RENTRÉE DES GRASSES, TAMARA!

3

" AVIS DE TEMPÊTE SUR LE DÉTROIT DE GIBRALTAR..." ON EST BLOQUÉS À TANGER POUR QUELQUES HEURES ENCORE!

...ET TOI?

REVIENS VIIIITE! L'ANNÉE SCOLAIRE EST À PEINE COMMENCÉE QUE J'AI DÉJÀ ENVIE DE ME JETER PAR LA FENÊTRE!

LE MÊME LOCAL MALSAIN! LES MÊMES PROFS PÉRIMÉS! LES MÊMES TÊTES D'ANCHOIS... TU LES CONNAIS, HEIN!?

ANAÏS QUI SE LA JOUE "REINE DU KAMASOUTRA" MAIS QUI N'A JAMAIS COUCHÉ QU'AVEC SON NOUNOURS EN PELUCHE...

JOY, LA GAIE-LURONNE!

...BRIAN "WARHAMMER-MAN" QUI PASSE SES NUITS À JOUER À "VIRTUAL-HAMMER" ET SES JOURNÉES À "REAL-SLEEPER"!

RZZZZ

ZZZZ!

229A

...SANS OUBLIER WAGNER ET SON HUMOUR DE FIN DE SÉRIE!

CHAPEAU, TAMARA! VRAIMENT EFFICACE TON RÉGIME!

...MAIS LA PROCHAINE FOIS, CHOISIS UN RÉGIME AMAIGRISSANT, PAS UN RÉGIME GROSSISSANT!

JE LE HAIS! HOOO COMME JE LE HAIS!

WARF! WARF!

UN PEU DE SILENCE, JE VOUS PRIE!

OUPS! LE PROF! JE VAIS TE LAISSER, JELILAH!

230

EUH... COMMENT TE LE DIRE?... CELA VA ÊTRE DOULOUREUX POUR TOI, MAIS...

NOUS DEUX... C'EST FINI! VOILÀ!...

JE... J'EN AIME UN AUTRE! IL S'APPELLE DIEGO, ET...

TU SAIS, POUR MOI TU N'AURAS PAS ÉTÉ UNE DE CES AMOURETTES D'ADOLESCENCE TROP VITE OUBLIÉES!...

JE ME SOUVIENDRAI TOUJOURS DE CES HEURES PASSÉES ENSEMBLE À JOUER OU À REGARDER DES ÉPISODES INÉDITS DE " GROSSEGIRL "...

JE N'AVAIS D'YEUX QUE POUR TOI! JE TE DONNAIS LA MAIN, ET TOI, TU RONRONNAIS DE BONHEUR!

TU TE SOUVIENS QUAND, DÉSOBÉISSANT À MES PARENTS QUI ME CROYAIENT AU GYMNASE, JE VENAIS TE REJOINDRE DANS MA CHAMBRE? JE TE CONFIAIS TOUS MES SECRETS...

JE TE CONSACRAIS L'ESSENTIEL DE MES JOURNÉES ET... PAS MAL DE MES NUITS AUSSI...

NON! N'ESSAIE PAS DE ME RETENIR! MA DÉCISION EST IRRÉVOCABLE!

231

ON GARDE LE CONTACT, HEIN!...

C'EST ÇA! VA TE JETER DANS LES GIGABITS DU PREMIER VENU!

MAL ARO-BASÉE!

Quelques grands moments dans la vie d'une maman...

SYMPA, BEAU GARS, VIRIL, BIEN DOTÉ DU CIBOULOT... PFFF, CE DIEGO A VRAIMENT TOUS LES DÉFAUTS!

CE MEC DOIT BIEN AVOIR **UN** TRUC QUI CLOCHE!

IL EST HOMO...

QUOI?!

BEN OUI! LES BEAUX MECS QUI AFFOLENT LES FILLES SONT TOUS HOMOS... J'AI LU ÇA DANS LES NOMBRILS!

MAIS OUI! LA VOILÀ L'EXPLICATION! CETTE GENTILLESSE DANS LE REGARD, CE SOUCI SUSPECT DE SON HYGIÈNE CORPORELLE! CE GARS-LÀ EST TOTAL HOMO!

FAUDRAIT EN ÊTRE SÛR...

MÛT MÛT

HEIN! POURQUOI MOI?

QUI A LANCÉ CETTE RUMEUR NAUSÉEUSE, HMMM?

JOUE-LA SUBTIL, INVITE-LE CE SOIR AU "GAY PIED"!

HE, HE SALUT, DIEGO! J'AI UN TRUC À TE DEMANDER... ÇA T'EMBÊTE SI JE M'ASSIEDS LÀ?

NON, NON! AU CONTRAIRE!

233

TU VOULAIS PAS ME DEMANDER QUELQUE CHOSE?

OUI, HEU, NON HEUUU, GLUPS!...

ALORS! ALORS! IL EST HOMO!?

LUI, JE NE SAIS PAS MAIS MOI... JE NE SUIS PLUS TRÈS SÛR!...

J'AI DÉCIDÉ DE DÉCLARER MA FLAMME À DIEGO!

C'EST PAS TROP TÔT!

JE LUI AI ÉCRIT UN POÈME...

"... et j'arrive au rythme de tes reins, mes yeux orphelins sans les tiens."

MAIS, C'EST MAGNIFIQUE! JE NE SAVAIS PAS QUE TU ÉCRIVAIS AUSSI BIEN!

L'AMOUR DONNE TOUS LES TALENTS!

IL EST LÀ! VAS-Y!

HEUUU, TIENS, DIEGO!

C'EST POUR MOI? GRACIAS, GUAPA!

ÇA ALORS?! TOI AUSSI, TU ES UNE ADMIRATRICE DE OLGA DE LA TORRE, LA GRANDE POÉTESSE CHILIENNE!

OUI, HEUU... JE POSSÈDE TOUTE SON OEUVRE!

SUR INTERNET...

234

MAIS, HEUU... CETTE TRADUCTION N'EST PAS DES PLUS HEUREUSES... DANS CE CAS "VENGO" SE TRADUI-RAIT PLUTÔT PAR "JE JOUIS"...

AH, HEU!...GLUPS! V... VRAIMENT?

" L'AMOUR DONNE TOUS LES TALENTS," HEIN?!

FAIS-MOI PENSER À ACHETER L'INTÉGRALE DES POÈMES DE CETTE ALGO DE LA CHICORÉE, LÀ!

10

BABACAR! PSSIIIT! BABA?!

UN MESSAGE POUR TOI, DE LA PART DE TAMARA!

UN... MESSAGE?!

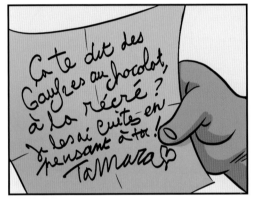

Ça te dit des gaufres au chocolat, à la récré ? Je les ai cuites en pensant à toi ! TaMaRa ♥

UN AUTRE MESSAGE! DE FATOU, CETTE FOIS!

?

ta bouche sur ma bouche ! tes mains sur ma peau, je n'en dors plus ! Fatou

ENCORE UN! D'ANAÏS, CETTE FOIS!

DADADA... D'ANAÏS!?

MARRE À LA FIN! Y A PAS ÉCRIT FACTEUR, ICI!

RENDEZ-VOUS DANS LE DÉBARRAS DU CONCIERGE PENDANT LA RÉCRÉATION... JE SERAI TON ESCLAVE, TA CHOSE! ANAÏS.

235

"JE N'EN DORS PLUS!" "TON ESCLAVE, TA CHOSE..." VAYA! VAYA! QUEL CASANOVA!

ET T'AS PAS VU LE MEILLEUR! Y EN A UNE QUI M'INVITE À MANGER DES GAUFRES AU CHOCOLAT, MIAM!

À DIEGO!

JE T'AVAIS DIT DE PASSER LE MESSAGE À DIEGO!

PAS À CE GROS NIGAUD DE BABACAR!

$\pi = \frac{3}{4}\sqrt{3} \, \frac{1}{4}$

TAMARA! DEPUIS QUE TU M'AS OUVERT TON COEUR, J'AI PERDU JUSQU'À L'APPÉTIT!

?

COMBIEN DE FOIS FAUDRA-T-IL TE LE RÉPÉTER, BABACAR, CE MOT DOUX NE S'ADRESSAIT PAS À TOI MAIS À DIEGO!

TOUT ÇA, C'EST LA FAUTE DE CE 東 DE WAGNER!

DIEGO! DIEGO! QU'EST-CE QU'IL A DE PLUS QUE MOI?

DE PLUS, JE NE SAIS PAS...

DE MOINS PAR CONTRE...

ET C'EST TOI QUI ME DIS ÇA?! ON TE CROIRAIT ENCEINTE DE PLUSIEURS MOIS!

JE SUIS UN PEU BOULOTTE, C'EST VRAI. MAIS PAS ÉLÉPHANTESQUE COMME CERTAINS!

JE NE VISE PERSONNE.

SUIVEZ MON REGARD.

"UN PEU BOULOTTE"? BEN VOYONS! COMBIEN TU PÈSES? ALLEZ! DIS VOIR! SANS TRICHER, HEIN!

83

COMBIEN? J'AI PAS BIEN ENTENDU!

83... ENFIN, CE MATIN DU MOINS. J'AI BEAUCOUP PERDU DEPUIS!

83? PILE POIL COMME MOI!

?!

237

ON EST TOUS LE GROS DE QUEL-QU'UN, PAS VRAI?

"L'ÉLÉPHANT" TE SALUE BIEN!

QU'EST-CE-QU' ELLE A, TAMARA?

D'APRÈS CE QUE J'AI PU COMPRENDRE, TAMARA EST ENCEINTE DE DIEGO, DE 83 JOURS. CE SERAIT WAGNER QUI AURAIT VENDU LA MÈCHE. ELLE ESSAIERAIT DE FAIRE ASSUMER LA PATERNITÉ À BABACAR QUI N'EN DORT PLUS.

PFF, ELLE CACHAIT BIEN SON JEU, CELLE-LÀ!

236

C'EST LUI, TON "DIEGO" ? C'EST VRAI QU'IL EST MIAM-MIOUM TOUT PLEIN !

SI SEULEMENT J'OSAIS L'INVITER AU CINÉMA...

MA MAIN GLISSE-RAIT, L'AIR DE RIEN, DE L'ACCOUDOIR VERS SA CUISSE ET ...

ARRÊTE DE SOUPIRER COMME UN CLOCHARD DEVANT LE MENU D'UN RESTAURANT CINQ ÉTOILES ET MANGE TA PART DU GÂTEAU !

HÉLAS... LES MECS MIAM-MIOUM TOUT PLEIN COMME ÇA, CE N'EST PAS POUR MOI !...

ET POURQUOI DONC ?!

PARCE QUE LUI, IL EST...

ET MOI, JE SUIS...

ET PUIS REGARDE LE GENRE DE FILLES QUI LUI TOURNENT AUTOUR ! IL N'A MÊME PAS À SE BAISSER POUR LES RAMASSER !...

JUSTEMENT ! LE ROI QUI MANGE DU CAVIAR AU PETIT DÉJEUNER RÊVE D'UNE BONNE CHOUCROUTE !

MERCI POUR LA COMPA-RAISON !

LA SEULE FAÇON DE SAVOIR S'IL VEUT SE TAPER UNE TOILE, C'EST DE LUI DEMANDER !

YOLI ! NON ! T'ES FOLLE !

238

ARGH ! PLUS JAMAIS JE N'OSERAI LE REGARDER EN CACHETTE !

TU VOIS ? LUI AUSSI IL AVAIT ENVIE D'ALLER AU CINÉ !

ADIOS, GUAPA !

14

HA, HA! LÀ, ELLE VA FULMINER GRAVE!

POUR DAMER LES PISTES, ENGAGEZ UNE GROSSE!

LA VOILÀ!

BONJOUR, WAGNER! SALUT, ZAK! RIGOLO, VOTRE BANDEROLE!

? ?

MONSIEUR, PAR ÉGARD POUR NOTRE CAMARADE OBÈSE ICI PRÉSENTE, POURRAIT-ON ÉVITER LE SUJET DÉLICAT DE LA REPRODUCTION DES BALEINES?

HIHI, CE WAGNER! IL N'EN RATE PAS UNE!

? ?

ET CE N'EST PAS SANS ÉMOTION QUE JE REMETS AUJOURD'HUI À TAMARA LE TITRE QUI LUI REVIENT POUR LA QUATRIÈME ANNÉE CONSÉCUTIVE...

SACRÉ WAGNER, TOUJOURS À TAQUINER LES AUTRES!

?

MISS BABAR 2009

ET POUR NOTRE TAMARA, UN PAQUET DE FRITES MAYO SPÉCIAL "RÉGIME DÉSESPÉRÉ"... **SANS** FRITES ET **SANS** MAYONNAISE!

FRICADELLES. VIANDELLES POULY...

239

TU AS BIEN FAIT, MERCI, WAGNER!

?

PFFF! DEPUIS QU'ELLE KIFFE CE DE DIEGO, IL N'Y A PLUS MOYEN DE LA FAIRE SORTIR DE SES GONDS!

15

C'EST QUOI CE SOUK? TU ORGANISES UNE BROCANTE INDOOR, OU QUOI?!

LE MUSÉE DE L'AMOUR! J'Y AI RASSEMBLÉ TOUT CE QUE JE POSSÈDE DE DIEGO!

BIGZOUILLE! ELLE EST ENCORE PLUS ATTEINTE QUE JE CRAIGNAIS!

UN PEU DE L'EAU DE LA PISCINE DANS LAQUELLE DIEGO A NAGÉ...

LE FLACON DE GEL DOUCHE "ÉVEIL DES SENS" QUE DIEGO A OUBLIÉ DANS LES VESTIAIRES...

LE BONBON QUE DIEGO M'A OFFERT UN JOUR À LA RÉCRÉ...

PAS TOUCHE, LARVE DE MOUCHE!

LA PAILLE AVEC LAQUELLE DIEGO A BU SON JUS D'ORANGE...

... ET LE CLOU DE MA COLLECTION: L'HEUREUX SPARADRAP QUI, PENDANT TOUTE UNE JOURNÉE, A CONNU LE CONTACT ÉLECTRISANT DE LA PEAU DE DIEGO!

ÇA, LE CLOU DE TA COLLECTION? PEUH, J'AI MIEUX, BÔÔÔCOUP MIEUX!

HEIN, QUE!? QUOI?! MONTRE! MONTRE!

PTOUY

240

UN AUTHENTIQUE CHEWING-GUM QUE LA BOUCHE DE DIEGO A MASTIQUÉ SENSUELLEMENT PENDANT DE LONGUES MINUTES!

POUR DEUX SUCETTES, JE T'APPORTE DEMAIN UN KLEENEX DANS LEQUEL DIEGO A MOUCHÉ SON AMOUR DE PETIT NEZ!

UN NAMOURA-QUOI?

UN NAMOURAGOUTCHI.® C'EST LE DERNIER JEU JAPONAIS À LA MODE!...

LES FILLES ONT DES NAMOURAGOUTCHIS ROSES ET LES GARÇONS DES BLEUS!

SI TON NAMOURAGOUTCHI ROSE PASSE À PROXIMITÉ D'UN NAMOURAGOUTCHI BLEU EN PHASE AVEC LE TIEN, ILS VIBRENT À L'UNISSON!

HA, HA! J'AI VU PAS MAL DE MODES DÉBILES, MAIS CELLE-LÀ LES ENFONCE TOUTES!

MA PAUVRE PETITE YOLI, JAMAIS PERSONNE NE LAISSERA À UN VULGAIRE GADGET LE SOIN DE DÉSIGNER L'ÉLU DE SON CŒUR!

L'AMOUR, CE NE SONT PAS DES PUCES ÉLECTRONIQUES EN CHALEUR! L'AMOUR, C'EST...

PIUWWWW

?

COOL!

241

J'EMBARQUE DANS LA PREMIÈRE FUSÉE POUR MARS!...

PIUWW PIUWW PIUWW PIUWW PIUWW PIUWW PIUWW PIUW

PIUWW

PIUWW

17

JE CROYAIS QUE LE NAMOURAGOUTCHI ÉTAIT L'INVENTION LA PLUS STUPIDE DEPUIS CELLE DU CAMEMBERT À VAPEUR!

BAH, UN ESSAI NE COÛTE RIEN...

SI! 13 EUROS ET 95 CENTS, PRÉCISÉMENT...

NAMOU RAGOU TCHI

PFFF! LE MODE D'EMPLOI EST EN JAPONAIS!

LAISSE-MOI FAIRE.

LA PREMIÈRE CHOSE À FAIRE, C'EST ENCODER TES GOÛTS: LES DESSINS ANIMÉS DE GROSSEGIRL, LES CHIPS AU PAPRIKA, LE HARD-ROCK...

...LES POUTOUS TOUT PARTOUT!

SI TON NAMOURAGOUTCHI PASSE À CÔTÉ DE CELUI D'UN GARÇON EN PHASE AVEC LE TIEN, VOUS DEVEZ VITE LES... EUH, ACCOUPLER!

SINON, LES NAMOURAGOUTCHI PERDENT PEU À PEU LEUR VITALITÉ...

MON NAMOURA-GOUTCHI! IL... IL...

TON ÂME SOEUR NE DOIT PAS ÊTRE BIEN LOIN...

PIUWW PIUUWW PIUWW

Y A TON "RAGOÛT CHICHI", LÀ, QUI COUINE!

LA MEUF DE MA VIE, ENFIN!

NOOOON! N'IMPORTE QUI, MAIS PAS... LUI!

PIUWW PIUWW

PIUW PIUWW

242

BEN, OÙ QU'ELLE EST, LA MEUF DE MA VIE!?

QUELLE ARNAQUE, CE NAMOURA-GOUTCHIOTTE!

PIUW PIUWW

SI TU VEUX ENCORE QUE JE TE PRÊTE MON NAMOURAGOUTCHI, N'HÉSITE PAS!

BOARF! POUR TOMBER LES MEUFS, C'EST PAS DEMAIN QU'ON TROUVERA MIEUX QUE LE SEX-APPEAL!

18

243

RHAAA, DIEGO! JE L'AIME, MAMAN!

EH BIEN, QU'EST-CE QUE TU ATTENDS POUR LUI ÉCRIRE, MA TAMOUNETTE?!

LUI ÉCRIRE, MAIS OUI, BON SANG!

TU PRENDS DU PAPIER PARFUMÉ À LA LAVANDE, TON PLUS BEAU STYLO...

...SUR UNE FEUILLE, TU ÉCRIS TA DÉCLARATION D'AMOUR! QUELQUE CHOSE DE TERRRIIIIBLEMENT ROMANTIQUE, AVEC UN ZESTE DE PULSION ANIMALE DIFFICILEMENT RÉFRÉNÉE!...

QU'IL SENTE QUE TU EN AS SOUS LE CAPOT!

...TU PLIES ALORS LA FEUILLE QUE TU GLISSES DANS UNE ENVELOPPE COUVERTE DE PETITS CŒURS, TU FERMES L'ENVELOPPE ET TU Y ÉCRIS L'ADRESSE DU BEAU DIEGO...

...MALGRÉ LA PLUIE TORRENTIELLE, TU COURS JUSQU'À LA POSTE ACHETER UN TIMBRE (ILS EN ONT ÉMIS UNE SÉRIE UN RIEN COQUINE À L'OCCASION DE LA SAINT-VALENTIN) QUE TU COLLES SUR L'ENVELOPPE D'UNE LANGUE SENSUELLE...

...LE CŒUR BATTANT, TU GLISSES ALORS LA LETTRE PORTEUSE DE TOUS TES ESPOIRS DANS LA BOÎTE AUX LETTRES...

IL NE TE RESTE PLUS QU'À ATTENDRE TROIS JOURS, QUATRE MAXI, AVANT QUE LE FACTEUR NE T'APPORTE UNE LETTRE ENFLAMMÉE QUI...

TU DISAIS?

244

J'AI ENVOYÉ UN E-MAIL À DIEGO POUR LUI PROPOSER DE SORTIR ENSEMBLE... IL M'A RÉPONDU DANS LA SECONDE! ON A RENDEZ-VOUS CE SOIR POUR ALLER AU CINÉMA!

OH, MAMAN, COMME JE SUIS HEUREUSE!

BOUHOUHOU! JE ME SENS VIEILLE, MAIS VIEIIIILLE!

?

JE N'EN CROIS PAS MES YEUX! MON PREMIER CINÉ **AVEC DIEGO!**

18H30-20H30 22H30-

SEX-CRIME 2

DIEGÔÔÔÔ!

OH NOOON! PAS ANAÏS!

QUELLE CHANCE! J'ÉTAIS JUSTEMENT SEULE!...

ET JE DÉTESTE ALLER AU CINÉMA TOUTE SEULE!

TIENS, T'ÉTAIS LÀ AUSSI, TAMARA?

ÇA ALORS, DIEGO! TU VAS AUSSI VOIR "SEX-CRIME 2"?

PARAÎT QU'IL EST ENCORE PLUS TORRIDE QUE LE **1**...

RAPPELEZ-MOI VOS PRÉNOMS...

MOI, C'EST FATOU! "FATOU ELLE FAIT TOUT", COMME ME TAQUINENT LES COPINES...

MOI, GRAZIELLA! ÇA VEUT DIRE FAVEUR OU CÂLIN, EN LATIN!

ALORS, MON SALAUD! TU MONTES UN PLAN NÉNETTES SANS PRÉVENIR TON VIEUX POTE WAGNER?

HÉ, HRM... SALUT, DIEGO!

HO, TAM! TU CONNAIS PAS MES P'TITS FRÈRES? LES TRIPLETTES DE TERRORVILLE QU'ON LES APPELLE!

245

JE N'EN REVIENS PAS! MON PREMIER CINÉMA SEULE AVEC DIEGO!...

21

UNE PETITE SALLE DE BANLIEUE POUR CINÉPHILES... UN VIEUX FILM MUET EN NOIR ET BLANC... CETTE FOIS, PERSONNE NE GÂCHERA MA SOIRÉE CINÉ AVEC...

DIEGÔÔÔ!

NOSFERATU MURNAU

CINÉ FIL

HEU... BUENAS NOCHES, JOY.

TOI AUSSI, T'AIMES TROP L'EXPRESSIONNISME ALLEMAND?

JE DONNE MA 17E HÉMORROÏDE À COUPER QUE CE GAILLARD-LÀ NE VIENT PAS POUR LE FILM!

ASSIEDS-TOI PLUTÔT ICI, TAMARA! CE FAUTEUIL NE M'A PAS L'AIR DES PLUS SOLIDES!

GRRRR!

RRZZZ

JE SUIS UNE VRAIE TROUILLARDE! ÇA NE T'EMBÊTE PAS SI JE ME BLOTTIS CONTRE TOI QUAND ÇA DEVIENT TROP EFFRAYANT?

HEU...

LÀ, JE TOUCHE LE FOND! QUE POURRAIT-IL M'ARRIVER DE PIRE?

RRRZFLU

RRPOLBLRR

YERK

?

BOUF

G

MINCE! ELLE A ÉTÉ PLUS RAPIDE QUE MOI!...

MES... TU M'ÉCRABOUILLES LES...

MAL!

TRÈS!

246

JE LE SAVAIS! VOULEZ-VOUS BIEN CESSER D'IMPORTUNER CETTE INNOCENTE JEUNE FILLE!? COCHON!

OBSÉDÉ!

PERVERS!

JEUNE!

J'ÉTAIS SUR SES GENOUX ET IL NE M'A PAS REPOUSSÉE! SE POURRAIT-IL QUE...?

TAMARA N'EST PAS ENCORE LEVÉE?

...DÉJÀ PARTIE AU LYCÉE!

BIGZOUILLE! ELLE DOIT ÊTRE TROP AMOUREUSE!

CASA NOVA

BONJOUR, DIEGOOO!

?

DIEGÔÔÔ!

DIEEEGO!

COUCOU, DIEGO!

PAIN BEN

GRRR! SALES COPIEUSES!

BON COMME LE PAIN

TIENS! TAMARA? TOI AUSSI, TU AS L'HABITUDE DE NAGER QUELQUES LONGUEURS AVANT LES COURS?

EH BIEN... C'EST-A-DIRE QU'HEUUU...

JE NE SAIS PAS SI JE TE L'AI DIT, MAIS TA COIFFURE EST SUPER!

PANOS

BON COMME LE PAIN

247

PRENEZ VOTRE MANUEL, AUJOURD'HUI NOUS ALLONS ÉTUDIER LÀ...

GRRR! SALES COPIEUSES!

TOI, T'ES PRIÉ DE GARDER TES DISTANCES!

AGLAGLA! QU'EST-CE QU'IL FICHE, BON SANG!?

!

TOI, ICI!?

TU AS AUSSI L'HABITUDE DE NAGER CHAQUE MATIN 4 OU 5 KILOMÈTRES AVANT LES COURS?

4 OU 5 KILOMÈTRES? CARAÏ! NON! UNE DIZAINE DE LONGUEURS, TOUT AU PLUS!

J'AI FINI MON ENTRAÎNEMENT, VAS-Y QUE JE TE MAT... HEU QUE J'ANALYSE TA TECHNIQUE!...

MIAM-MIOUM!

PFFF! DOUZE LONGUEURS ET JE SUIS VANNÉ! J'AI ENCORE BEAUCOUP À APPRENDRE DE TOI!

MAIS... QUAND TU VEUX, DIEGO!

ON SORT? ON AURA JUSTE LE TEMPS DE SE PRENDRE UN P'TIT DÉJ' AU BISTROT D'EN FACE!

SORTIR? HEU...

IL NE FAUT SURTOUT PAS QU'IL VOIE MES BOURRELETS!

DÉSOLÉ, PETITE NATURE. JE DOIS ENCORE FAIRE MES TROIS KILOMÈTRES DE DOS CRAWLÉ!

VAYA! ÇA NE RIGOLE PAS, AVEC TOI!

248

ALORS, ADIOS, GUAPA!

ET MEEERDE!

UN AUTRE MAILLOT ENCORE PLUS AMINCISSANT!? IMPOSSIBLE, C'EST UN COMPRIM©!

Comprim
MA SILHOUETTE EN PRIME!

24

70!

CETTE FOIS, C'EST DIT! OBJECTIF 70 KILOS D'ICI L'ÉTÉ!

MAIS TAMARA! TU N'ARRIVERAS JAMAIS À PERDRE 70 KILOS EN QUELQUES MOIS À PEINE!

ET J'AI INTÉRÊT À M'Y METTRE TOUT DE SUITE! CE MATIN, JE PESAIS 82 KILOS ET 995 GRAMMES!

83, QUOI...

82, 995! ÇA FAIT TOUJOURS 5 GRAMMES DE MOINS À PERDRE!

"POUR QUE LA VACHE DONNE MOINS DE BEURRE, PRIVE-LA DE PÂTURE!"

YOLI, J'AI BESOIN DE TOI!

SOEURETTE, TOUJOURS PRÊTE!

FINI, LES GAUFRES, LES BONBONS, LES BARRES CHOCOLATÉES ET AUTRES PAQUETS DE CHIPS!

MÊME CEUX AU PAPRIKA?

HORS DE MA VUE, LES LIMONADES, LES CRÈMES GLACÉES, LES CHARCUTERIES, LES...

249

MGNNNN! MPFGNN!

SI, SI, JE T'ASSURE, TAMARA! MA MÉTHODE EST BÔÔÔCOUP PLUS EFFICACE!

BURP!

GRAS!

MPFGNNN! GNN!

MUF! MUF!

GLOUP! MIAM!

CHOMP!

"POURQUOI SE PRIVER DE PÂTURE QUAND IL SUFFIT D'EN ÉLOIGNER LA VACHE?..."

GRAS!

250

HEU... PEUT-ÊTRE NE DEVRIEZ-VOUS PAS RESTER DEVANT CETTE FENÊTRE !...

NON MAIS TU AS VU CE MORCEAU DE REINE, TAMARA!?

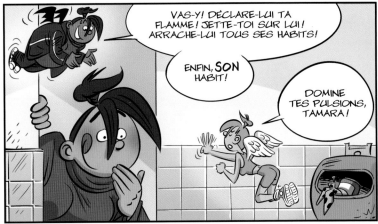

VAS-Y! DÉCLARE-LUI TA FLAMME! JETTE-TOI SUR LUI! ARRACHE-LUI TOUS SES HABITS!

ENFIN, SON HABIT!

DOMINE TES PULSIONS, TAMARA!

PASSE TON BAC D'ABORD!

TON BAC ET PUIS TES ÉTUDES UNIVERSITAIRES, TES 5 DOCTORATS, TES THÈSES...

IL SERA TOUJOURS TEMPS DE FAIRE DES FOLIES DE TON CORPS APRÈS TA PENSION!

NON MAIS ÉCOUTEZ-MOI CETTE SAINTE-NITOUCHE DE L'IMMACULÉE ABSTINENCE! ET L'AMOUR DANS TOUT ÇA? LA PASSION? LE SEXE!

PEUH! C'EST TRÈS SURFAIT, LE SEXE!

BON! J'AI COMPRIS!

FLAP FLAP FLAP

OÙ... OÙ VA-T-ELLE?

...SI! SI! JE VOUS ASSURE, ELLE N'ARRÊTE PAS DE PARLER DE VOUS...

HIN HIN

GLUPS!

LUI! MAIS...

ON VOUS A DÉJÀ DIT QUE VOUS AVIEZ DE BELLES CORNES ET UNE JOLIE PETITE QUEUE FOURCHUE?!

SI GUAPA, SI!

...ET CETTE DÉLICIEUSE ODEUR DE SOUFFRE QUE VOUS DÉGAGEZ... HMMMM!

NOUS AVONS LE CHAMP LIBRE! À L'ASSAUT!

QUE VOUS CROYEZ! LIBERTINE!

FLAP FLAP FLAP

251

POUR DÉVOYER DIEGO, IL FAUDRA D'ABORD ME PASSER SUR LE CORPS!

VOS DÉSIRS SONT DES ORDRES!

OOOH OUI! PLUME-MOI TOUTE!

OH, TOI! TOI!...

HI, HI, HI.

ET BIEN SÛR, QUI C'EST QUI RESTE SUR LE CARREAU?

MOI!

27

PFFF! BOARF! MWEP...

SI ON JOUAIT À COLIN-MAILLARD !?

OUAIIIS! C'EST DIEGO QUI S'Y COLLE!

COOL!

TU DOIS ATTRAPER QUELQU'UN ET LE RECONNAÎTRE RIEN QU'AU TOUCHER!

?

GLOUSS GLOUSS GLOUSS

PFF! C'EST CON, COMME JEU!

JOY? NON! ZAK!

GULPS

À TON TOUR!

POURQUOI NE PAS JOUER À 1, 2, 3 PIANO, TANT QUE VOUS Y ÊTES? BANDE D'IMMATURES, VA!

LAISSE, JE ME SACRIFIE!

BON APPÉTIT, MES PETITES MAINS! AU MENU: ORANGES, POIRES OU MELONS?

SLURP! MIAM!

POUÊT POUÊT

OH NOOON! CE VENTRE RAPLAPLA CES BOURRELETS TOUT PARTOUT...

À COUP SÛR, C'EST TAMARA!

PELOTE PELOTE

PFFF! BOARF! MWEP...

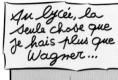
Au lycée, la seule chose que je hais plus que Wagner...

HÉ, TAM'! QU'EST-CE QUE T'ATTENDS POUR TE METTRE EN TENUE QU'ON PUISSE JOUIR DU SPECTACLE DE TON CORPS D'AMAZONE!

ARF, ARF!

...C'est la Gym!

AUJOURD'HUI, JE NE PEUX PAS... JE SUIS INDISPOSÉE!

VRAIMENT? IL FAUT ABSOLUMENT QUE J'APPELLE MA GYNÉCOLOGUE!

VOTRE GYNÉCO... POUR QUOI FAIRE?!

POUR LUI RAPPORTER LE CAS EXTRAORDINAIRE D'UNE JEUNE FILLE QUI A SES RÈGLES **8 FOIS PAR MOIS!**

EN TENUE! ET FISSA!

VESTI

SI C'ÉTAIT POUR QUE "TON" DIEGO NE VOIE PAS TES COURBES ALÉATOIRES, C'EST RATÉ!

CHEUDEUP, MISS BEURETTE! OU J'ENVOIE À TON PÈRE UNE PHOTO DE SA FILLE EN "TENUE DE GYM"!

MADEMOISELLE TRÉMOLO ÉTAIT À CE POINT IMPATIENTE DE DONNER À SON CORPS L'EXERCICE QU'IL MÉRITE QUE JE L'INVITE À COMMENCER CETTE SESSION D'EXAMEN!

PAS LA CORDE! MON DIEU, JE VOUS EN SUPPLIE, PAS LA CORDE!

253 A

HÉ, TAMARA, T'ES CENSÉE GRIMPER, PAS DESCENDRE AU SOUS-SOL!

QUE QUELQU'UN VIENNE L'AIDER AVANT QUE J'AILLE CHERCHER UNE FOURCHE!

C'EST- GNNN-SÛR, DIEU - HMF- N'EXISTE PAAAS!

?!

NE TE CRISPE PAS! RESPIRE CALMEMENT!

D... DIEGO?

MOI AUSSI AVANT, J'ÉTAIS NUL À CE JEU-LÀ!

ACCROCHE-TOI AU GROS NOEUD, LÀ!

JALOUSE JALOUSE

JE,...JE N'EN PEUX PLUUUS!

ANIMO! CHAQUE CENTIMÈTRE QUE TU FRANCHIS, C'EST UN RIRE IMBÉCILE QUE TU LEUR FAIS RENTRER DANS LA GORGE!

JE...! INUTILE! JE...

GN!

MPFF GN GN

RAARGN GN

GN

C'EST BON, TAMARA!

?

?

?

INUTILE POUR AUTANT D'ALLER ABÎMER LE PLAFOND!

PFFFF

253B

BRAVO, GUAPA! TU ES LA MEILLEURE!

BIZ!

JE NE CROIS PAS ME TROMPER EN DISANT QUE CET EXPLOIT VOUS VAUT VOTRE PREMIER DIX EN GYMNASTIQUE!

ÇA NE VAUT PAS. DIEGO L'A POUSSÉE!

OUI, MAIS QU'EST-CE QU'IL POUSSE BIEN!

Depuis, Croyez le ou non, Je n'ai plus raté un seul Cours de Gym!

MAIS!? ... MA CORDE!

SOUVENIR!

30

UN CHAGRIN D'AMOUR... SON PREMIER! TU DEVRAIS LUI PARLER UN PEU!

LUI PARLER?! MAIS JE LUI AI ENCORE PARLÉ CINQ LONGUES MINUTES L'ÉTÉ DERNIER...

SI ELLE A BESOIN DE LA VOIX RASSURANTE DE SON PÈRE, QU'ELLE ÉCOUTE MON DERNIER ENREGISTREMENT... "CHANTS APHONIQUES" DE SERGEÏ STOKENSTRUMFSKI...

POIGNANT!

TU ES VRAIMENT INCURABLE! JE TE PARLE DE TA FILLE QUI EST AU PLUS MAL ET TOI, TU RAMÈNES TOUT À TOI! ÉGOCENTRIQUE!

ÉGOCENTRIQUE? PARCE QUE PARTAGER MON ART DEVANT UNE SALLE QUI SE LÈVE POUR M'OVATIONNER, C'EST ÉGOCENTRIQUE, PEUT-ÊTRE?!

BON! PASSE-LA MOI!

OOOH, PAPA! DIEGO EST SI BEAU, SI INTELLIGENT SI... DIEGO, QUOI! ET MOI, JE NE SUIS QU'UNE GROSSE BOUSE DE VACHE MÊME PAS DIGNE QU'IL ME PIÉTINE!

TU AS MILLE FOIS RAISON, MA CHÉRIE!

FUIS L'AMOUR COMME LA PESTE! C'EST DANS LE MALHEUR QUE LES GRANDS GÉNIES ONT ENGENDRÉ LEURS PLUS BEAUX CHEFS-D'OEUVRE!

TIENS! PRENDS "ADOLPH ET SARAH," PAR EXEMPLE, LE SUBLIME OPÉRA DE SERGEÏ STOCKENSTRUMFSKI QUI CONTE L'AMOUR IMPOSSIBLE ENTRE UN DIRIGEANT POLITIQUE ALLEMAND ET UNE BEAUTÉ JUIVE!

POIGNANT!

VAUTRE-TOI DANS TON CHAGRIN! FAIS DE LA SOLITUDE TON UNIQUE COMPAGNE! ABREUVE-TOI DE TES LARMES! NOURRIS-TOI DE TA DOULEUR!

254

QUE TA VIE SOIT UNE LONGUE ET TRAGIQUE OEUVRE LYRIQUE!

À NOUS DEUX, DIEGO!

MÊME S'IL M'EN COÛTE, JE DOIS RECONNAÎTRE QUE SON PÈRE A SU TROUVER LES MOTS POUR LUI REMONTER LE MORAL!

255

PASSE-MOI LE SHAMPOING LIGHT!

DIS, TAMARA... SI JAMAIS TU ARRIVAIS MALGRÉ TOUT À SORTIR AVEC TON DIEGO... EST-CE QUE MOI... ENFIN... EST-CE QUE TU M'AIMERAIS ENCORE!?

MAIS BIEN SÛR QUE JE T'AIMERAIS ENCORE!

QU'EST-CE QUE JE DEVIENDRAIS SANS MA PETITE VOLEUSE DE CHIPS AU PAPRIKA PRÉFÉRÉE!...

SPROUTCH

JE POURRAIS ENCORE DORMIR DANS TA CHAMBRE, ALORS?!...

?

HEUUU, JE VOIS PAS LE RAPPORT...

BEN, OUI... SI TU SORS AVEC DIEGO TU VOUDRAS TA... TON TINTIN MITÉ...

IN-TI-MI-TÉ!

OUI! POUR FAIRE DES CHOSES MIAM-MIOUM TOUT PLEIN AVEC LUI!

L'EMBRASSER PENDANT DES HEURES... LUI FAIRE DES POUTOUS TOUT PARTOUT!

256

TE SERRER TRÈS FORT CONTRE LUI!

...TOUTE NUE!

DON'T DISTURB

PROPRIÉTÉ PRIVÉE

ON NE PASSE PAS

CHAMBRE DE TAMARA

COMPLET

J'AURAIS MIEUX FAIT DE LA FERMER!

QUE TU LE VEUILLES OU NON... TOI ET MOI, NOUS SOMMES CONDAMNÉS À DEVENIR AMIS!

POURQUOI TU VEUX T'ACHETER DES PRÉSERVATIFS?! C'EST TOUT JUSTE SI TON DIEGO SAIT QUE TU EXISTES...

K. POT

MEGA MAGA RAYON
YOUPLALA!

SACHE, MOUSTIQUE, QUE SELON LES STATISTIQUES, C'EST PRÉCISÉMENT À MON ÂGE QUE LES FILLES ONT LEUR PREMIÈRE EXPÉRIENCE SEXUELLE!

QU'ILS DISENT! L'AMOUR, C'EST PAS UN CON-COURS NON PLUS...

ET PUIS D'ABORD, ÇA NE MARCHE PAS, CES TRUCS! ILS SONT BÔÔÔCOUP TROP GRANDS! J'AI ESSAYÉ SUR MON AMOUREUX...

... TU SAIS, CELUI QUI EST AU C.P.

T'AS VU CE CHOIX?! C'EST ENCORE PIRE QU'AU RAYON CHIPS!

BIGZOUILLE! IL Y EN A MÊME EN FORME DE LAPIN!

BUNNY SEX

COMMENT JE PEUX SAVOIR CEUX QUI LUI PLAIRONT, MOI?...

FLUOS? GOÛT CHOCOLAT? STRIÉS?

SENSATIONS PROLONGÉES...

"SAVEUR CITRON" DEPUIS QUAND ÇA SE MANGE, LES PRÉSERVATIFS?!

257

AH ÇA, ÇA NE RATERA PAS! IL SUFFIT QUE TU CHOISISSES CEUX EN FORME DE GIRAFE, POUR QUE TON DIEGO TE DISE QU'IL NE SUPPORTE QUE CEUX EN FORME DE SERPENT!

ET ENCORE, EN CE MOMENT, CÔTÉ SEXE, ELLE EST PLUTÔT DANS UNE PÉRIODE CALME!

MEGA MAG

TU AS VU COMME DIEGO S'HABILLE MERVEILLEUSEMENT BIEN?!

TU AS VU COMME DIEGO PREND NOTE MERVEILLEUSEMENT BIEN?!

TU AS VU COMME DIEGO DISSÈQUE MERVEILLEUSEMENT BIEN?!

TU AS VU COMME DIEGO JOUE MERVEILLEUSEMENT BIEN AU PING-PONG?!

PING!

PONG!

TU AS VU COMME DIEGO...

ON A COMPRIS!

DIEGO RIT MERVEILLEUSEMENT BIEN! DIEGO RESPIRE MERVEILLEUSEMENT BIEN! DIEGO DORT MERVEILLEUSEMENT BIEN! MAIS EST-CE QU'IL EMBRASSE MERVEILLEUSEMENT BIEN, AU MOINS!?

EM... EMBRASSER?! SUR LA BOUCHE, TU VEUX DIRE? HEU... JE NE SAIS PAS... JE N'AI PAS ENCORE ESSAYÉ!

BON!

TU PERMETS? C'EST POUR UNE ENQUÊTE...

?

258

TU AS VU COMME DIEGO EMBRASSE MERVEILLEUSEMENT BIEN?

MAINTENANT, ON VA VOIR S'IL PRODIGUE AUSSI MERVEILLEUSEMENT BIEN LES PREMIERS SECOURS!

? ?

259

TES PARENTS SONT TOUJOURS AU MAROC, AUPRÈS DE TA GRAND-MÈRE MOURANTE?...

COMME TU VOIS!

ET MON NIGAUD DE PÈRE CROIT QUE JE DORS CHEZ TAMARA, LA "VERTUEUSE"...

GWA, DAMARA?

ELLE NE PIGUE, HIPS, PAS LES MECS DE SES AMIES, DAMARA!

ELLE... HIC! AURAIT BIEN DU MAL, D'AILLEURS!

T,T,T,T,T! CE N'EST PAS EN TE METTANT DANS UN ÉTAT PAREIL QUE TU VAS EMBALLER UN MEC, MA PAUVRE TAM'...

GUAND JE VEUX GUE JEM HIPS! BALLE UN MEC!

ET JE LE BROUVE! HEB! DOI! LE BEAU BEDIT CUL, LÀ!

ROVSMORGLSMUTCH!

À LA BONNE HEURE! ÇA ME FAIT PLAISIR QUE TU PROFITES ENFIN DE MA PETITE FÊTE!

260

SI, SI... AVEC WAGNER! IL LES LUI FAUT DONC TOUS!

JE... JE LA TRAÎNERAI EN JUSTICE POUR HARCÈLEMENT SEXUEL!

MAINTENANT, JE SAIS CE QUE ÇA FAIT, D'ÊTRE "PEOPLE"!

37

BON D'ACCORD, J'ÉTAIS SAOULE COMME TOUTE LA POLOGNE ET J'AI ROULÉ UNE PELLE À WAGNER...

ON VA PAS EN FAIRE LES GROS TITRES DES NEWS DU SOIR NON PLUS!...

IL Y AVAIT-QUOI?- 7 À 8 TÉMOINS, TOUT AU PLUS?

HEUU... ANAÏS A TOUT FILMÉ AVEC SON TÉLÉPHONE ET A TOUT MIS SUR YOUTUBE!...

T...TOUT?

TOUT! LA PELLE À WAGNER...

...PUIS QUAND TU AS VOMI SUR DIEGO QUI TE FAISAIT PRENDRE L'AIR...

JE ... J'AI FAIT ÇA, MOI?

AVANT DE TE LANCER DANS UN STRIP-TEASE HALLUCINANT SUR UN MORCEAU DE JUSTIN TIMBERLAKE!

... ENSUITE, TU T'ES ENFERMÉE DANS LES TOILETTES AVEC LA RÉSERVE DE BIÈRE EN HURLANT QUE TU N'EN SORTIRAIS QUE LES PIEDS DEVANT...

JUSQU'AU RETOUR PRÉMATURÉ DE MES PARENTS DU MAROC!

TRASH DE CHEZ TRASH!

261

JE BLAGUAIS!

POUR LE RETOUR DE MES PARENTS, DU MOINS... SINON TU PENSES BIEN QUE JE SERAI CLOÎTRÉE DANS MA CHAMBRE POUR MILLE ANS!

POC

2654 VISITEURS EN 24 HEURES !?

GASP! CETTE 🔣🔣🔣 D'ANAÏS N'A DÉCIDÉMENT RIEN RATÉ DE MA DESCENTE AUX ENFERS!

JE LA TUERAI!

OH! MON DIEU! C'ÉTAIT DONC VRAI! J'AI VOMI SUR DIEGO!

COUCOU, DIEGO! HEU... C'EST POUR REMPLACER LE T-SHIRT QUE J'AI FICHU EN L'AIR EN TE VOMISSANT DESSUS! TU AS DÛ ME MAUDIRE!?

PENSES-TU! J'EN AI VU D'AUTRES!

LA SEULE CHOSE QUE JE REGRETTE, C'EST QUE JE LAVAIS MON T-SHIRT DANS LA SALLE DE BAIN ET, DU COUP J'AI LOUPÉ TON FAMEUX STRIP-TEASE!

OUF! ENFIN UNE BONNE NOUVELLE DANS CET OCÉAN D'ADVERSITÉ!

HA, HA! MA TÊTE QUAND JE T'AI VUE DÉBOULER À MOITIÉ NUE DANS LA SALLE DE BAIN AVEC DES CANETTES DE BIÈRE PLEIN LES BRAS!

HA-HA!

HEU... À PROPOS, TAMARA! POUR CE QUI S'EST PASSÉ ENSUITE... TU NE M'EN VEUX PAS TROP, J'ESPÈRE?... MOI AUSSI J'AVAIS UN PEU BU ET...

PENSES-TU! J'EN AI VU D'AUTRES!

HOU LA!

MERCI! TU M'ÔTES UN FAMEUX POIDS DE LA CONSCIENCE! ADIOS, GUAPA!

A... ADIOS!

262

QUE S'EST-IL PASSÉ DANS CETTE SALLE DE BAIN !?

FASSE QUE CETTE PROVIDENTIELLE ANAÏS AIT TOUT FILMÉ PAR LE TROU DE LA SERRURE... FASSE QUE CETTE PROVIDENTIELLE ANAÏS AIT TOUT FILMÉ PAR LE TROU DE LA SERRURE!... FASSE QUE...

J'inviterai tous mes copains de classe! Sauf Wagner, évidemment... Je le hais!

"BUFFET DIVINATOIRE"? ÇA VEUT DIRE QU'ON DOIT DEVINER CE QU'ON VA BOUFFER?

ÇA COMMENCE À HUIT HEURES!

DÎNATOIRE, IMBÉCILE!

...Peut-être même que j'inviterai Diego...

SI J'EN AI LE COURAGE...

J'avertirai les voisins...

UNE BÊTE!? DANS L'IMMEUBLE!...

LAISSE, MAMAN! NE VOUS AVISEZ PAS DE METTRE VOTRE, HM, MUSIQUE TROP FORT!

SINON, J'APPELLE LA POLICE!

maman et chico me laisseront l'appart'...

TU ME DIRAS SI MON TIRAMISU A EU DU SUCCÈS!?

J'AI LAISSÉ LE NUMÉRO DE L'HÔTEL À CÔTÉ DU TÉLÉPHONE, SI JAMAIS...

ON VA AU PARC KID-PADDLE! ON VA AU PARC KID-PADDLE!

C'EST ÇA! C'EST ÇA! AMUSEZ-VOUS BIEN!

"...et ce sera..."

LA MÉGA TEUF DU SIÈCLE!

WELCO

263A

LES PREMIERS INVITÉS NE DEVRAIENT PLUS TARDER À ARRIV...

TRILILILI TRILILI

ALLO! TAMARA? C'EST JELILAH! JE NE PEUX PAS VENIR À TA FÊTE... MES PARENTS SONT RENTRÉS PLUS TÔT DU MAROC... ET MON PATERNEL S'EST DOUTÉ QUE JE NE VENAIS PAS CHEZ TOI POUR RÉVISER MES MATHS...

IL A UN DON, CE N'EST PAS POSSIBLE AUTREMENT! BREF, IL M'INTERDIT DE VENIR...

QU'EST-CE QU'ILS FICHENT?

MAIS QU'EST-CE QU'ILS FICHENT, BON SANG!?

DÉSOLÉ! LA FÊTE EST ANNULÉE! TAMARA NOUS A DEMANDÉ DE VOUS PRÉVENIR...

OOH!

C'EST SA MÈRE... LA MÉNINGITE "W"! TERRRIBLEMENT CONTAGIEUX!

LUI TÉLÉPHONER? SURTOUT PAS! ELLE EST AU CHEVET DE SA MAMAN...

ON CRAINT LE PIRE!

C'EST ÇA, LAISSEZ-MOI VOS CADEAUX... JE LES LUI REMETTRAI.

C'EST UN PEU SALAUD, CE QU'ON FAIT À TAMARA, NON?

ELLE N'AVAIT QU'À NOUS INVITER! AU LIEU DE NOUS TRAITER COMME DES PARIAS!

BEN, ELLE M'A INVITÉ, MOI!...

ATTENDS! TU N'AS PAS VU LE MEILLEUR!

263B

LA CAMÉRA DE MON PATERNEL! AVEC ÇA, ON NE RATERA PAS UNE LARME D'HIPPOPOTAMARA!

ENCORE UNE VIDÉO QUI AURA SON PETIT SUCCÈS SUR YOUTUBE!

NIQUÉE, LA GROSSE DONDON !

LA DONDON A DE LA VISITE!

VOILÀ! VOILÀ!

DING DONG
DING DONG

ENFIN!

JE SUIS VENUE VOUS FÉLICITER, VOUS ET VOS AMIS!

N... NOUS FÉLICITER?!

DEMANDE SI ELLE A CAPTURÉ LA BÊTE!

OUI! DES JEUNES QUI SAVENT S'AMUSER SANS FAIRE DE BRUIT, C'EST UNE DENRÉE RARE DE NOS JOURS!...

OME

¡LO SIENTO! JE PEUX ENTRER?

TOC TOC

¡HOLA GUAPA! C'ÉTAIT OUVERT... PERO? OÙ SONT LES AUTRES? LA FIESTA EST TERMINÉE?

DIEGO!?

QU'EST-CE QU'IL FOUT LÀ, CELUI-LÀ!?

HMM! ÇA LUI VA TRÈS BIEN, CE PANTALON MOULANT!

MAIS... JE NE T'AI PAS INVITÉ!...

APRÈS CE QUE J'AI FAIT L'AUTRE SOIR DANS LA SALLE DE BAIN... JE COMPRENDS PARFAITEMENT!

263C

LE MOMENT EST VENU DE JOUER MON NEIL ARMSTRONG...

NEIL ARMSTRONG?

LE PREMIER HOMME SUR LA LUNE... "UN PETIT PAS POUR MOI"...

... UN GRAND PAS POUR NOUS DEUX!

GLUPS

BONSOIR, MA CHÉRIE! JE ME TROMPE, OU TU AS ENCORE GROSSI?...

?

PAPA!? ? TA MÈRE ET SON ANIMAL EXOTIQUE NE SONT PAS LÀ?

JE DEVAIS CHANTER À L'OPÉRA CE SOIR LES "LIEDER POUR MON PETIT CHIEN POUPI ÉCRASÉ PAR UN MÉCHANT CAMION", UNE OEUVRE DE JEUNESSE DE SERGUEÏ STOCKENSTRUMFSKY - POIGNANT- MAIS...

HO! ÇA ALORS! UNE FÊTE SURPRISE EN MON HONNEUR?! JE SUIS TOUCHÉ, VRAIMENT!

COMMENT DIABLE AS-TU APPRIS QUE MON RÉCITAL A ÉTÉ ANNULÉ À CAUSE DE LA GRÈVE DES INTERMITTENTS DU SPECTACLE?...

ON VA PASSER UNE CHOUETTE SOIRÉE À NOUS DEUX! JE TE CHANTERAI DU STOCKEN-STRUMFSKY, TU ME...

C'EST QUE, PAPA ... JE NE SUIS PAS SEULE...

JE TE PRÉSENTE DIEGO

DIEGO, MON PÈRE!

¡ENCANTADO, SEÑOR! TAMARA M'A BEAUCOUP PARLÉ DE VOUS!

"DIEGO" AS-TU DIT?

CELA ME FAIT PENSER QUE JE DOIS RÉPÉTER LES "LIEDER POUR LES 387 ORPHELINS DE GUERNICA" DE SERGUEÏ STOCKENSTRUMFSKY QUE J'ENREGISTRE MARDI À SYDNEY...

POIGNANT.

263D

HEU... À PROPOS, FIFILLE...

... OUBLIE CE QUE JE T'AI DIT L'AUTRE JOUR AU TÉLÉPHONE...

LE BONHEUR AUSSI, ENGENDRE DES OEUVRES MAGNIFIQUES!

PHILIPPE-ANDRÉ, MON VIEUX, TU VIENS DE RÉUSSIR LA PLUS BELLE SORTIE DE SCÈNE DE TA CARRIÈRE!...

ALORS, NEIL ARMSTRONG, ET CE VOYAGE SUR LA LUNE QUE VOUS M'AVIEZ PROMIS...

JE T'AIME, TAMARA. JE T'AIME DEPUIS LE PREMIER JOUR QUAND JE T'AI VUE EN CLASSE!

J'AIME TA MÈCHE DE CHEVEUX! ON DIRAIT UN FEU D'ARTIFICE! J'AIME TON SOURIRE, TES YEUX QUAND ILS ME REGARDENT... ET PUIS... JE PEUX T'AVOUER UN SECRET?

J'AIME TES RONDEURS!

HAAA NON! JE VEUX ÊTRE AIMÉE POUR CE QUE JE SUIS! PAS POUR MON PHYSIQUE!

?!

263E

JE BLAGUAIS, IDIOT!

COMME LE DIT TOUJOURS MA MAMAN... CHEZ MOI, IL Y A PLUS À CARESSER!

263F

ET CE FUT... LA MÉGATEUF DU SIÈCLE!

ZIDROU
BOSSE DARASSE

COULEURS BENOÎT BEKAERT

...ET MERCI À CLARA BOURGIN!

LE MONDE, HEU... FASCINANT DES ADOS EXPLIQUÉ AUX PARENTS.

AUJOURD'HUI:

LE BLOG.